Six Sizzling Markets

How to Profit from Investing in Brazil, Russia, India, China, South Korea, and Mexico

PRAN TIKU

John Wiley & Sons, Inc.

Published by John Wiley & Sons, Inc., Hoboken, New Jersey.
Published simultaneously in Canada.

For general information on our other products and services or for technical support, please contact our Customer Care Department within the United States at (800) 762-2974, outside the United States at (317) 572-3993, or fax (317) 572-4002.

Wiley publishes in a variety of print and electronic formats and by print-on-demand. Some material included with standard print versions of this book may not be included in e-books or in print-on-demand. If this book refers to media such as a CD or DVD that is not included in the version you purchased, you may download this material at http://booksupport.wiley.com. For more information about Wiley products, visit www.wiley.com.

Library of Congress Cataloging-in-Publication Data:

Tiku, Pran, 1940–
Six sizzling markets : how to profit from investing in Brazil, Russia, India, China, South Korea, and Mexico / Pran Tiku.
p. cm.
Includes bibliographical references and index.
ISBN 978-0-470-17888-1 (cloth)
1. Investments, Foreign. I. Title.
HG4538.T55 2008
332.67'3–dc22

2007050506

10 9 8 7 6 5 4 3 2 1

Contents

Preface vii

Acknowledgments ix

Introduction 1

CHAPTER 1 Why Invest in These Six Sizzling Markets? 13

CHAPTER 2 Passion and Paradox: The History of Brazil 25

CHAPTER 3 The *Real* World: Brazil from 1994 to Today 33

CHAPTER 4 A Land of Opportunity: Investing in Brazil 41

CHAPTER 5 Catching up with the West: The History of Russia 57

CHAPTER 6 Blind Turns and Growing Pains: Russia from 1998 to Today 69

CHAPTER 7 Resources to Rubles in a New World Economy: Investing in Russia 79

CHAPTER 8 A State of Mind: The History of India 95

CHAPTER 9 Shadows to Sunshine: India from 1991 to Today 107

CHAPTER 10 Power in Numbers: Investing in India 111

CHAPTER 11 Tradition, Truth, and Transformation: The History of China 149

CHAPTER 12 Calculated Conduct: China from 1978 to Today 159

CHAPTER 13 Manufacturing a Future: Investing in China 169

CHAPTER 14 A Peninsula of Perseverance: The History of Korea 195

CHAPTER 15 A Blessing in Disguise: Korea from 1993 to Today 205

CHAPTER 16 High Profits in a Tricky Neighborhood: Investing in Korea 211

CHAPTER 17 Revolution and Exclusion: A History of Mexico 229

CHAPTER 18 Democracy and a Free Economy: Mexico from 1994 to Today 243

CHAPTER 19 The Second Mexican Independence: Investing in Mexico 249

CHAPTER 20 Tips for Investing in the Six Sizzling Markets 263

APPENDIX A Country Profiles 269

APPENDIX B World Economic Forum's Global Competitiveness Index for the Six Sizzling Markets 283

APPENDIX C Governance Indicators 287

APPENDIX D American Depository Receipts (ADRs) 291

APPENDIX E Mutual Fund Profiles by Country 327

APPENDIX F BRIC Fund Profiles 337

APPENDIX G Just Ask the Experts 341

Bibliography 351

Glossary 357

Index 367

Preface

Today's world is bound together as never before. Countries are connected not only by the visible means of trucks and trains and ships and planes, but also by invisible electronic pathways. There are an impressive number of trade and commercial agreements between nations that are unprecedented and historic and range from bilateral to global and create compacts between nations that provide a needed framework for the global economy. More and more countries have come to realize that opening their economies to the rest of the world is a likely gateway to future prosperity. In the global economy of today, a design change of a cell phone initiated in Seoul, Korea, may affect jobs for workers at Motorola in Austin or Chicago. And the fact that General Motors cars are more popular in China than in the United States may determine the fate of the largest car company in the world. The comparative advantage of nations is on display as a part of this global order. The addition, elimination, and shifting of jobs as countries compete can have a dramatic impact on individuals, families, and, in some cases, entire towns.

The new order is resulting in the forming of alliances at a rate never before seen. The emergence of the European Union, after centuries of bloodletting, as a unified political and economic force is a vivid example of such an arrangement. But other such unions are no less visible, such as the North American Free Trade Agreement (NAFTA) connecting the economic superpower United States with its neighbors Canada and Mexico. There are many such arrangements either in the works or already functioning in regions such as Latin America and South America as well as Southeast Asia, South Asia, and the Pacific.

As the world grapples with issues such as global warming, safeguarding the environment, and reducing poverty, there is more political and economic pressure to cooperate. The shrinking of the world is likely to continue as nations recognize the truth—that a world composed of a few economic superpowers is not very likely and that many of the colossal problems the world will face will have solutions only when nations engage. This book takes this theme and looks at the world for the next two to five decades and examines the opportunities that may become available to investors. It is our opinion that the six countries of Brazil, Russia, India, China, Korea, and Mexico, which are currently thought of as emerging countries, are likely to play a prominent part in the future world order, along with the United States, Japan, Europe, and Canada.

The ascendance of these six countries in the next decade or so is likely to provide investment opportunities that were not available to investors of U.S. stocks or European stocks a century ago. The book has been organized into six country sections to give readers more than a casual look into the historical as well as political background of the country, and then explain both the current and future economic potential as well as investment opportunities.

For those investors ready to take the next step, the appendices provide some additional tools to identify investment opportunities, from exchange-traded funds and other mutual funds to American Depositary Receipts (ADRs) listed on the U.S. exchange.

Acknowledgments

I would like to thank the many individuals, friends, and family whose contributions to this project have been extremely valuable. Your resolve and generosity are deeply appreciated and were instrumental in the making of this book.

Thanks to Elayne Sheridan (investments), Carolyn Wood (Brazil, Mexico), Andrew Vitvisky (Russia), Seung-Min Yoo (Korea), and Michael Brown (China, Russia, Korea) for their wonderful contributions and hard work.

My special thanks to my friend Richard Fey, econometrician and professor, who took time away from his teaching and research to offer valuable ideas on the book as a whole and particularly his insight into China, emanating from his travels and earlier research, which proved to be extremely useful.

My special thanks to Alexis Lefort, who handled the editorial duties of the project with remarkable composure. Thanks also to Kathryn Liebowitz, who copyedited and transcribed notes with wonderful zeal and great patience.

I would also like to thank my agent, Kenneth Lizotte, for handling the painstaking details of the early work and his encouragement while the project was in its beginning stages. I would also like to thank Erin McFee for her initial research when the book was just a germ of an idea.

My thanks to Deborah Englander (editor), Kelly O'Connor (development editor) for their valuable ideas, patience to guide me through the process, and painstaking detail during the editing process.

Great appreciation to my colleagues at Peak Financial Management—Kerry Luria, Justin Miller, Luisa Pandolfi, Alla Trachtenberg, and Neel Tiku—who not only stepped in when requested, but also worked extra hard during extended absences from the office in order to complete this book.

I would like to thank my entire family, especially my wife, Raj, and my three children, Seema, Neel, and Gita, whose vacations I ruined and events I missed due to obligations and preoccupations with this book. I am grateful to my sisters, Shana Mattoo and Arti Kaul, and my extended family throughout the United States and India, who were always there during the toughest of times. It could only be possible with their undying strength and love.

Lastly and most importantly, I thank my extraordinary parents Trilok Nath and Kanta Tiku. Their guidance and love are dearly missed. Without their knowledge and insight, this book would not have come to fruition. I am saddened that in their passing they could not see the book in print, but I am at peace in that I am able to continue their legacy with its completion.

Introduction

The world is on the threshold of a change, a change that is remarkable and silent, revolutionary and yet shrouded in mystery. There are no roaring throngs in the streets, but nonetheless this change will alter nations and affect millions of people around the world. It is a change that will be felt from the cornfields of the American Midwest to the crowded streets of Seoul, from the sunny beaches in the south of France to the frozen Siberian tundra. It is a change that will shift the center of gravity from the financial capitals of New York, London, and Tokyo to places such as Beijing, Mumbai, and São Paolo.

So, what is this change? It is a shift in the balance of power that will displace the cozy relationships among the current advanced nations and help create entirely new economic powers out of countries currently on the fringe or near fringe. The major beneficiaries of such a shift are likely to be what we refer to as the "six sizzling markets" or "BRIC+2" countries. The term *BRIC* (referring to Brazil, Russia, India, and China) was coined by the investment firm Goldman Sachs in an original study in 2003. The authors predicted that within several decades, these four countries would come into political and economic prominence as the eventual home to a large portion of the world's population and wealth. We argue that there is sufficient evidence to include Mexico and South Korea, both countries that are poised on the brink of a new economic order. Mexico and Korea will be strategic players in the global trade game, in large part due to the geographical and political significance in relation to the United States.

Brazil, Russia, India, China, Korea, and Mexico are poised to dominate the world economy. These six countries will become a great source of opportunity for their own populations as well as pivotal players in the global economy for generations to come. Investors have already warmed to the idea of international investing, as evidenced by the billions of dollars flowing into foreign markets annually. *Six Sizzling Markets* provides a basis for investing in the BRIC+2 markets by giving a brief historical background and then describing the current political and economic backdrop in each country. This book will guide potential investors into a world of heretofore unknown investment opportunities.

Investment opportunities in developing markets are neither well known nor well understood by most investors. Many people look at developing and emerging markets with a great deal of suspicion. After all, the returns of these markets have proven to be far from stable. These markets have generated high double-digit and even triple-digit gains in the past, creating excitement among investors, to be followed by subpar or negative returns for years. Our goal is to explore the remarkable opportunities that exist in the six selected countries. Understanding these countries and their markets will help readers take advantage of unparalleled investment opportunities for coming decades. With such opportunities, of course, also come difficulties and challenges. It is our aim to help the investor balance the risk inherent in investing in developing nations by providing effective strategies that will help mitigate risk.

Eight Tenets of Change

We have identified eight major forces causing this dramatic shift in the world's economic and political balance of power. These forces, which we call "tenets of change," are the prime movers of a phenomenon that we believe will help revolutionize the current world order and help investors reap substantial financial profits.

We believe that these eight tenets of change will disproportionately favor some aspect of these countries' markets and will likely create extraordinarily profitable opportunities for investors. Thus, in order to understand how you can profit from investing in one of these six sizzling markets, I will first define and explain these "tenets of change" so that you may have a better understanding of why they will play a critical role in the growth opportunities presented by these BRIC+2 countries.

Tenet One: Demographics

Large numbers of young people yearning to improve their lot in life is a timeless story, from the time of early industrialization to the postwar Baby Boomers. The difference today is the shift in locale. Not unlike the British, Portuguese, and Spanish colonists of the past, countries with burgeoning young populations are poised to take a big slice out of the world's resources, and in the process create exceptional opportunities not only for their own populations but for people around the globe.

The world has never witnessed such an explosion of concentrated populations. There are over 2.3 billion people currently living in China and India, which accounts for a full 43 percent of the world's population. This population explosion in developing and emerging countries is happening as the populations of current advanced nations such as the United States, Europe, and Japan are graying.

Is the East going to become the new West? Is the southern hemisphere going to become the new north? Will the world become unipolar, a nondirectional entity where the colossal Asian nations of China and India will rule alongside select southern nations such as Brazil and Mexico? The populations of these newly emerging countries are young, hungry, and enthusiastic. Half of the population of India, for example, is under age 25. This is a far cry from the United States, where the median age is 36, the highest it has ever been. Russia is an aging nation as well, while Korea and China's populations are younger. Mexico and Brazil are almost as young as India, with median ages of 25 and 28, respectively.

Tenet Two: Economic Perfomance

It goes without saying that the economic performance of a country is a tenet that substantially impacts a country; however, the way in which investors should measure a country's economic performance has often been unclear. As such, in this book, we consider economic performance to be primarily measured by four different factors: the growth of the middle class, the gross domestic product (GDP), the shift from agriculture, and urbanization.

A large and stable middle class is one of the characteristics of a developed nation with an advanced economy. A growing middle class is good news for investors for another reason—it signifies politically and socially stable societies and better standards of living.

The developing nations' population growth, combined with rising levels of disposable income, is likely to create the largest middle class in the history of the world. For example, India's middle class already accounts for nearly a quarter of its billion-plus population, while the McKinsey Global Institute estimates that by the year 2025, Chinese middle-class households will be the largest consumer market in the world (www.mckinsey.com/mgi/reports/pdfs/china_consumer/MGI_china_consumer_chapter_2.pdf).

Moreover, it is projected that within the next 10 years, as Brazil, Russia, India, and China become developed nations, these four countries will create a middle class equal to 800 million consumers. This number is greater than the entire population of the United States, Western Europe, and Japan today combined. This new influx of disposable income will create an increase in demand for consumer goods that will benefit all producing nations in the world. These future consumers will drive the growth not only in their own economies, but will also be the engine that propels growth in the current advanced nations. It is estimated that spending power in emerging markets will jump from \$4 trillion in 2007 to \$10 trillion by 2025. Therefore, a major consequence of this growing middle class is the push toward urbanization coupled with a shift away from low productivity agriculture to jobs in service and consumer industries.

Tenet Three: Technology

Emerging markets are undergoing a transition from slow technology growth and limited connectivity to hypergrowth. In many places, developing nations are leapfrogging technology to surpass developed countries. These technological leaps—such as the bypassing of ground lines to move directly into fiber optics and cellular technology—have accelerated the growth rates of the affected sector and carved out a niche of low-cost solutions without sacrificing sophistication. Asia, for example, has twice the number of cell phone subscribers as the Americas combined. Brazil represents the largest information technology market in Latin America, where mobile phone penetration surged ahead of fixed lines in 2003 and continues to grow dynamically.

Technological growth is influencing life on every continent. By now, it's not news that China is a manufacturing capital or that India is the world's call center and software hub. It is estimated that by 2008, there will be a demand for 1.1 million information technology (IT) engineers and technical support personnel in India and demand for another million international customer service workers. International demand for Indian IT workers for positions in other countries is projected to increase increase by 20 percent. What's not as well known is that companies such as General Electric, Microsoft, and Intel are opening innovation centers in India and China to focus on cutting-edge research. These and dozens of other companies from the United States, Japan, and Europe hope to leverage the opportunities afforded by these centers. World-class engineers and scientists, who not only excel in their fields, but do so at a fraction of the cost of developed nations, are performing this research. The result so far has been that these companies, locked in feverish competition for innovation, have produced hundreds of patents and received an extra edge in the quest to become a major global player.

Tenet Four: Open Trade

Although many emerging nations—most notably China, India, and Russia—have been slow in opening trade and borders, they are in varying stages of openness and transparency. The writing is on the wall: Emerging nations are realizing that in order to participate in the global market they must truly open their markets.

China's entry onto the world stage, punctuated by its eagerness to be an attractive member of the World Trade Organization (WTO) and its hosting of the Olympics in 2008, is pushing the country to open its borders, creating unheard-of opportunities for world players, and to serve its billion-strong consumer market. In India, the preferences, quotas, and tariffs prior to 1990 made it a virtually closed system with low efficiency, low productivity, and poor living standards. The new changes in India allow foreign entities at least 51 percent ownership in most sectors and up to 100 percent ownership in special urgently needed sectors.

In the WTO, Brazil has emerged as a leader of the G20 Group of Developing Countries, which includes India, China, and Mexico. They are primarily concerned with agriculture and leveling the playing field between developed and developing economies by negotiating for the removal of farming subsidies in the United States and the European Union. Brazil has formed a powerful coalition for advancing the interests of trade liberalization and development objectives by joining forces with other developing nations.

Mexico's trade policies are among the most open in the world, with free trade agreements with the United States, Canada, the European Union, and many other countries. It has abandoned price controls and encouraged competition through regulatory reform and export-led growth.

These changes have created a new dynamic for a worldwide exchange of goods and services that will result in lucrative opportunities for both the exporters and importers. But what ultimately will matter is that these economies allow free and fair competition from outsiders and move beyond the protected enclaves of domestic companies despite extreme pressure to maintain such protection. In China and India, the state-owned enterprises are entrenched both as a political force and an economic power. However, the expectation is that it is a new day and open trade and its rewards will be seen as expansionary and the benefits universal.

Tenet Five: Infrastructure Development

The developing economies of today are on the threshold of an explosion into a new world of superhighways and soaring skyscrapers, of mega power plants and super-size oil refineries. The boom in infrastructure development is breathtaking. It is estimated that at any time over half of the construction cranes in the world are located in China. The "golden quadrilateral" highway connecting the four corners of India is an example of the mammoth projects that are catching world attention. In Brazil, President Lula hoped to jump-start the country's economy by heavily investing in building airports, roads, railways, and seaports. The phenomenal opportunities afforded by this growth in infrastructure are greatly benefiting companies from advanced nations. Coincidentally, this comes at a time when such growth is slowing to a trickle in their own domestic economies.

The building boom sweeping these developing countries reflects industrialization and the continuing urbanization of populations desperate for shelter, roads, vehicles, power, running water, and sewage treatment. This is resulting in jobs, growth, and profits for both these consuming nations and suppliers. Shanghai already resembles New York City, and other developing cities far and wide are likely to follow.

Tenet Six: Transparency and Rule of Law

It is difficult to suggest that the emerging countries are currently meeting the high standards usual among developed nations for transparency and rule of law. The level of transparency—the degree to which government meetings and decisions, corporate budgets, and financial statements are open to public scrutiny—is a signal of fairness and openness, as there is less opportunity for authorities and executives to abuse the system in their own interest. Transparency varies from country to country, yet all are aware that the biggest confidence booster for foreign governments and investors is a country's ability to be transparent and have an established rule of law, along with an impartial judicial system to enforce laws and contracts.

One measure of perceived transparency is the Transparency International Corruption Perceptions Index. In 2006, Mexico, China, and Brazil each scored 3.3 on this index, on a scale of 1 (least transparent) to 10 (most transparent), indicating significant room for improvement. In contrast, South Korea scored 5.1 and Hong Kong scored 8.3, reflecting the relative maturity of their legal and financial disclosure rules.

Tenet Seven: Education and Training

Investments in education add significantly to a country's ability to generate growth in the future by strengthening its competitive workforce. Government spending on education for children and young adults includes salaries for teachers and money for supplies such as books and equipment, as well as capital spending on new schools. Funding for college and graduate education is often tied to industries that are identified by the government as having strategic value to the country, such as health care or technology.

China and India generate millions of college graduates annually who are entering the workforce with greater opportunities in the job market. This rise in intellectual capital will contribute to the movement toward higher wages and successive increases in disposable income. In 2005, for example, China produced some 3.1 million college graduates, nearly three times that of the United States. Moreover, China's engineering graduates that year numbered more than 600,000, compared to about 70,000 American engineering graduates. These figures demonstrate a keen sense of urgency in many of these developing countries that growth of intellectual capital is the gateway to riches by expanding productivity and innovation.

Tenet Eight: Sound Financial Systems and Policies

The chances that a country's economic growth prospects will be realized greatly increase if the government sets policies that promote orderly financial markets and manages its finances to control inflation and keep debt under control. Adequate regulation of the banking systems, including minimum capital requirements and standards regarding investments and underwriting activity, fosters greater confidence in banks as repositories. When citizens trust banks and keep their savings in bank deposits, these institutions can in turn lend those funds to businesses that need capital to grow.

Controlling inflation is equally important, since high inflation rates erode purchasing power and create a disincentive to saving. In the 1980s and 1990s, for example, Brazil's economy was crippled by periods of hyperinflation, resulting from poor fiscal policies as the government printed currency to fund spending. From 1980 to 1997, the cost of goods in local currency increased by one *trillion*. The annual inflation rate in 1990 alone was 30,377 percent. Real gross domestic product (GDP) growth (GDP adjusted for inflation) stagnated as a result, barely keeping pace with population growth.

These eight tenets are the basis for the extraordinary development occurring around the world today. This development is creating exciting investment opportunities in select countries for those willing to take the plunge. Investing in developing nations is not without risks, but the potential payoffs are huge. Below, we give you an introduction to these countries.

Six Sizzling Nations that Will Rock Your World

The six sizzling countries—Brazil, Russia, India, China, Korea, and Mexico—covered in this book all provide different investment opportunities, while at the same time presenting different financial challenges. There is plenty of hype and rumor surrounding these countries and plenty of reasons to be cautious, since information about international investments may not always be clear and transparent.

This book lays out a detailed and balanced case for investing in each country's market and helps separate fact from fiction. Here is a quick introduction to each country.

Brazil

Brazil is a country with enormous potential. With the largest economy in the Americas after the United States, Brazil also has a large population and abundant natural resources. Market indicators suggest that Brazil has outgrown its history of boom-and-bust cycles and that more rapid growth can be expected in the near future.

In recent years, the largest increases in government spending have consistently gone to welfare, housing, and social services. This demonstrates a deep commitment to improving the population's standard of living. Independent of government reforms, Brazil is benefiting from an unprecedented growth in foreign direct investment (FDI), as well as a trade boom fueled by strong demand from China. The country has experienced a steady increase in GDP growth over the past five years and appears to have inflation under control. From 1989 to 1994, average inflation was 1,378 percent per year, while inflation from 1995 to 2005 averaged only 9 percent per year.

Brazil is likely to become the star of Latin American economics due to the recent political stability and increasing attention to development.

Russia

Russia reemerged in 1998 as a strategically important global player. Its oil and natural gas supplies have become a vital source for western Europe and a significant factor for China and the United States. Important structural improvements have taken place since 1998. A flat tax has been introduced to simplify collection, reduce delinquency, and boost revenues. Official and corporate transparency has improved, although corruption and bureaucratic ineptness remain concerns for international companies seeking market entry. In an effort to upgrade financial and corporate governance, the government introduced a best practices initiative sponsored by the International Monetary Fund.

The more disciplined political and regulatory environment has, in fact, spurred economic revival. Russian GDP growth is over 6 percent per year. Inflation, which averaged over 340 percent per year from 1989 to 1994, is at a more stable 19 percent today. The expanding consumer market has expanded business opportunities, with local firms often forming manufacturing alliances with multinationals. A growing number of Russian businesses have launched initial public offerings (IPOs) in foreign securities markets.

Russia will find its place in the global markets, given its natural resources and strategic political position. Although the country's internal politics and legal system still raise some concerns among foreign investors, its enormous size, resources, and strategic position could combine to make Russia an economic powerhouse.

India

India first saw its potential to become a world player on midnight of April 15, 1947. Its own tricolored flag was hoisted to replace the Union Jack, and the morning dawned on a country full of promise and vigor. The country embarked on a course that was partially influenced by the Soviet Union.

India had a closed economy, but continued with open politics, sustained political stability, and a free press.

Today, India is well on its way to achieving its lofty goal of breaking free from the shackles of poverty. The government has embarked on a series of reforms and, with these, there is huge promise to deliver a higher standard of living for the country's billion-plus population—the young and restless who are willing to compete with the world. The meager economic growth rate was dubbed the "Hindu rate of growth" because it rarely exceeded 3 percent per year and resulted in a large percentage of the population's living in abject poverty. Now growth is reaching 8 percent per year, and India's future rivals that of its gargantuan neighbor to the north—China.

China

Discipline. Honor. Control. Obligation to ancestors. These are the prevailing attributes of this ancient culture. China is a paradox and defies description. This country, which was almost exclusively agrarian less than a generation ago, has become the nation that has become a destination for world capital and provides the world everything from clothes to color televisions, from sofas to software. Growth rates have been spectacular: From 1960 to 1970, the average growth rate per year was 3.6 percent. From 1980 on, GDP growth has averaged over 9 percent per year.

As nation creditor-in-chief to the United States, China will be partnered in a political and economic duet with the West indefinitely. What is the fate of its billion-plus population? If China plays its cards right, it can create a role for itself that may rival world powers of the past. Today's China is eager and feels its day has come. The stars seemed aligned for the nation to become a behemoth and a colossus among the nations.

Korea

Korea, the most developed of the nations covered in this book, is regarded as part of the East Asian miracle. In the second half of the twentieth century, Korea experienced one of the fastest rates of growth ever, sometimes referred to as "the miracle on the Han River." Korea has enjoyed growth rates of more than 8 percent per year for an astonishing 30 years.

At the beginning of this century, the government wisely predicted that the Internet would be of huge importance in the global economy and invested heavily in the IT industry, with astounding results thus far. Korea is the prime beneficiary of trade with China, and is of strategic geopolitical importance to both China and the United States. Korea, a thriving democracy, enjoys the support of Western powers, and is also of importance to Asia as a whole. All of these factors ensure this small nation will be a notable player in future global expansion.

Mexico

The image of Mexico as a poor country with frequent financial crises is outdated. The dynamic twenty-first-century Mexico has an expanding middle class, favorable trade policies, and a stable inflation rate, which has averaged 6.8 percent in the past five years.

The North American Free Trade Agreement (NAFTA), enacted in 1994, put an end to all restrictions on trade and investment flows between the United States, Canada, and Mexico, creating the largest free trade area in the world. Bilateral trade between the United States and Mexico has more than tripled since the implementation of NAFTA: from $81.5 billion in 1993 to $290.5 billion in 2005. To put this in perspective, Mexico and the United States do over $33 million worth of business together every hour of every day of the year (www.export.gov/articles/Mexico_MoM.asp).

With its strategic geopolitical location, Mexico is not only the third largest trading partner of the United States, but it is also the gateway to the emerging economies in Latin America. While the Mexican government has some critical challenges ahead, significant opportunities exist in Mexico, as this developing market is poised to become an important strategic player in the global economy.

The Time Has Come to Make a Profit

The six sizzling markets outlined above are in the nexus of a pivotal change, which could last for decades. In this book, I expose investors to the role that each of these counties plays on the world economic scene and discuss the hidden investment opportunities available within each of these countries so that you can reap substantial financial profits.

Organized by country sections, this book has been formatted to provide readers with vital information on each emerging market that goes well beyond the bottom line. In addition to the statistics, charts, and figures that investors have come to expect, the book includes a detailed synopsis of each nation's political as well as economic background, giving potential investors an enhanced historical perspective on each of the six sizzling or BRIC+2 nations.

With a frame of reference established, the book then delves into the specific investment areas, ranking each country in accordance with the eight tenets of change. As will be demonstrated, the tenets have been ranked as "favorable," "neutral," or "unfavorable" for investors, based on their current status and future trends that are likely to continue. Favorable conditions often highlight a major aspect of growth in each country, such as Korea's technology capacity or India's booming population. Neutral and unfavorable rankings, such as Russia's shrinking population and India's below-standard infrastructure, demonstrate the obstacles facing the nation itself as well as the individual investor. The country sections conclude with a detailed look at some of each nation's more lucrative industries, as well as specific companies within such industries that have the potential to provide significant profits. Finally, the appendices provide practical tools for both beginning and expert investors.

Thus, in covering everything from colonialism to consumer demand, this book will equip the investor with the knowledge required to navigate the often hazy world of foreign investments so that you may be able to profit from investing in Brazil, Russia, India, China, South Korea, and Mexico.

CHAPTER 1

Why Invest in These Six Sizzling Markets?

The history of international investing begins in ancient times. Two thousand years ago, wealthy individuals funded the growth of merchant trade along a harrowing 5,000-mile route from the Sea of Japan to China, the Middle East, South Africa, and Europe. The Silk Road, as it came to be called, laid the foundations of the modern world and helped shape the emerging economies of China, Egypt, Mesopotamia, Persia, India, and Rome. A few centuries later, investors began funding agricultural settlements known as "transplantations" to grow crops in remote lands. In 1100 AD, Europeans established sugar plantations in the eastern Mediterranean, and by the fifteenth century the practice had hopscotched across the Caribbean islands, finally reaching North America with investments in the settlement in Jamestown, Virginia. The first joint-stock company, the East India Company, was a forerunner of modern trading companies. Formed in 1600, the East India Company captured profits by exporting raw materials, such as cotton from India and finished textiles from Manchester, England. The lure of such investments in the so-called "dark continents" of North America and Asia, which could at that time have been classified as developing markets, was obvious. It was the lure of windfall profits, excitement, and speculation.

Today, the instant communications of fiber-optic technologies have brought investment opportunities in developing markets to the doorsteps of investors throughout the world. While there are similar elements of excitement, sophistication, and speculation surrounding such investments, the information gap has considerably narrowed, and the windfall opportunities are intertwined much less with speculation and more with education and information.

The risks inherent in investing in developing markets arise from a variety of sources. Even though information about the developing markets is getting better, investors continue to face a combination of challenges, such as lack of in-depth information or transparency, inadequate regulation, and lack of adherence to rule of law. These issues get compounded by imperfect accounting standards as well as unstable currencies that may be a result of high inflation or recession. In addition, the government's role in these markets can be either constructive or detrimental to business, as some policies may result in monopolistic or oligarchic business practices that thwart free and fair competition.

As evidenced above, the litany of risks can be long and troublesome. So why would investments in developing and emerging countries be appealing? One belief built throughout this book is that investors who make the effort to arm themselves with information and knowledge about the unique characteristics of developing countries will benefit from improved performance. Thus, the purpose of *Six Sizzling Markets* is to provide readers with a basic knowledge of the political and economic history and the investment opportunities within each of these emerging markets.

Why Invest in the Six Sizzling Nations?

The six sizzling nations are commonly referred to as the BRIC+2 countries. These nations—Brazil, Russia, India, China, Mexico, and Korea—belong to a category of investments known as developing markets. A developing market is generally smaller, less liquid, and riskier than the more advanced markets in western Europe and the United States. The political and regulatory environments in developing markets are considered more volatile than in developed markets, and typically offer fewer protections to investors. In addition, currency exchange rate fluctuations can influence investment returns.

In the United States, some 80 million people try to make money over time by investing in stocks.[1] A somewhat smaller group invests in stocks of companies in developed foreign markets, such as the United Kingdom, France, and Germany; and an even smaller number invest in stocks of companies based in developing markets. Lately, many investors have warmed to the idea of investing in developing markets in order to take advantage of the growth opportunities afforded by them despite some of the risks posed by such investments. These investors are seeking the highest potential price appreciation from their investments and want to take advantage of diversification benefits offered by such investments. As such, we will cover both concepts in the six selected countries throughout the course of this book.

With all of these added risks of investing in a developing market, why might an investor choose to put money into these stock markets? Developing

[1]The number of individuals owning equities in the United States stood at 84.3 million in January 2002, according to the Investment Company Institute (www.ici.org/shareholders/dec/02_news_equity_ownership.html).

markets have the potential to offer higher returns over time than their more established counterparts, making them attractive despite the higher risks. And, when combined in a portfolio with other types of investments, they potentially reduce portfolio risk by smoothing out some of the variability in returns over time.

The six sizzling BRIC+2 countries in particular are notable for their strong growth prospects. The picture of each country that this book provides will help the individual investor or professional investment adviser identify potential opportunities for long-term portfolio growth. Instead of quick snapshots, these country portraits offer enduring value, as the landscape for future prospects is painted from each country's unique historical and cultural context.

The Search for Potential Return

If the purpose of investing in developing markets is to gain exposure to higher potential returns, one might wonder what signals of future value to look for in choosing stocks. Investors can be fickle in the pursuit of higher returns, sometimes driving markets to dizzying peaks and then abandoning them in valleys of despair. For example, during the great "tulipmania" of the Netherlands in the early 1600s, the price of a single tulip bulb rose to 10 times the typical person's annual income. More recent examples of the effects of excess optimism include the run-up in Atomic Age stocks in the 1950s and the dot-com bubble of the 1990s. In retrospect, these examples are viewed as investment fads—a time when prices become unhooked from fundamental factors, such as a company's earnings or its liquidation value.

While fads are short term and speculative (it's unlikely a tulip bulb will again be worth the price of a castle), investment style refers to classes of stocks that cycle in and out of favor with some regularity, much like clothing styles. For example, "value" stocks typically outperform "growth" stocks for stretches of three to five years, before growth stocks again take the lead. Similarly, small-capitalization stocks have historically tended to outperform larger companies when the economy is just beginning to recover from a recession, and large-capitalization stocks tend to be more in favor during periods of stable or rising economic growth. As with a speculative run-up, an investment that is thought to be in style outperforms in part because there are more investors who are willing to pay a higher price to own it. In contrast to fads, however, style investing is more closely tied to fundamental factors. A fast-growing economy, for example, might benefit a technology-based company such as Microsoft or IBM. However, in a weaker economy, companies geared toward consumer staples such as Procter & Gamble are likely to have stable earnings.

Developing markets as a group tend to go in and out of style with investors. These cycles can reflect weakness or strength in the domestic market, changes in perceptions about market risks, and the global economic picture. Following a downturn in 2000, investing in developing markets came back into style. Data from the Institute of International Finance Inc. show money moving into the stock markets of developing economies jumped 43 percent in 2005 to $56 billion, and set a new record of $70 billion in 2006. Global mutual funds—that is, U.S.-based funds that invest globally—held, on average, just 43 percent of assets in the United States in 2006, compared with 49 percent in 2005 and 63 percent in 2002 (according to Morningstar, Inc.). During this period, global funds' average allocation to investments in Asia skyrocketed, rising from roughly 12 percent in 2002 to 23 percent in 2006.

Meanwhile, developing-market stocks overall gained an average of 35 percent a year from 2002 through 2006, compared to an average annual total return on U.S. equities of 11 percent (according to S&P 1500 index). Individual developing markets are often among the world's top performers. For example, in 2006, Korea gained 46.3 percent, and Brazil 45.3 percent, while the U.S. market rose 15.3 percent.

In the short term, fads and styles can make it more difficult to choose the best investments—the companies that have the best prospects for achieving real growth in value over time. Our premise is that, in the long term, the return from a particular stock investment reflects the company's ability to manage its capital wisely in order to generate profits. Thus, a well-run company is likely to outperform its peers over a period of many years. And, given a favorable economic environment and the right line of business, over time it is likely to do well.[2]

Although there are more than 60 countries that have national stock markets, only about 25 are considered well-established developing countries.[3] Yet, many of these countries are too small to offer significant opportunities

[2]Over a short period of a few years, stock prices can be affected by many transient factors. Perhaps real estate prices are rising rapidly, and investors sell stocks to buy houses. Although the price of the company's stock has dropped (its market value), the company's real value (the value of the future cash flow that it will generate) is unchanged. Once the boom in real estate ends, money is likely to flow back into the stock market, and the stock price will rise. The likelihood of short-term fluctuations in stock values is why stock investments should be reserved for money that one will not need to spend in the near term.

[3]The Morgan Stanley Capital International (MSCI) Emerging Market Index includes the countries of Argentina, Brazil, Chile, China, Colombia, Czech Republic, Egypt, Hungary, India, Indonesia, Israel, Jordan, Korea, Malaysia, Mexico, Morocco, Pakistan, Peru, Philippines, Poland, Russia, South Africa, Taiwan, Thailand, and Turkey.

to investors. Of these, we believe the BRIC+2 countries are particularly attractive. Success factors that will likely drive these economies and the companies within them are:

- Unprecedented economic growth
- Sound national financial systems
- Inflows in investment capital
- Investments in education

Unprecedented Economic Growth

The United States is today the world's richest economy, with gross domestic product (GDP) of around $12.5 trillion. While the U.S. economy is the largest, it is not the fastest growing. U.S. GDP typically expands by 2 percent to 3 percent a year. China is a comet by comparison, with GDP typically growing by 8 percent to 10 percent a year. China is today much smaller—with GDP of $2.2 trillion—and the remaining BRIC+2 countries are minuscule by comparison, with GDPs ranging from $760 billion to $800 billion. Research by the investment firm Goldman Sachs suggests that by 2040 the GDPs of the four BRIC economies could exceed the GDPs of the United States, Japan, Germany, France, the United Kingdom, and Italy combined. To achieve this result, the economies of the BRIC countries will have to grow at a much faster rate than these developed countries.

Key factors that will support this growth include huge reserves of natural resources (Brazil, Mexico, and Russia) for export markets, and a large and well-qualified workforce (particularly in India and China) with relatively low wage levels. Korea's economy will also grow, as its more advanced industries will benefit from increased trade and services with China.

Economists also expect growth in domestic consumer demand within the individual six sizzling BRIC+2 countries, stimulated by increases in income across broad categories of their populations. When a country's national income is spread out among its citizens rather than concentrated among a smaller subset of the population, the result is sustained domestic demand for goods and services, which can support additional GDP growth.

Modern Shanghai's per-capita GDP is about $14,000, while that of China nationally is only $1,700, as much of rural China is low income. However, as labor costs rise in China's more developed cities, industry is beginning to migrate to smaller inland cities and rural areas. This is expected to lead to higher per-capita GDP nationally, helping to fuel growth in domestic demand.

Demographic changes can also contribute to stronger economic growth. China is the world's largest country, with a population of around 1.3 billion, followed by India with 1.1 billion. Brazil and Russia are also in the top 10 based on population size with Mexico ranking 11th and Korea, a small country geographically, ranking 24th (www.census.gov/ipc/www/idbrank.html). The United States is the third most populous country, yet its population is less than one-fourth that of China. By 2020, China and India together are expected to have grown by 367 million people—more than the entire U.S. population. Countries with large populations have the potential to develop large domestic consumer markets, making them less dependent on exports.

The structure of a country's population is also important. India and Mexico have relatively young populations, while China and Russia are graying. The number of dependents per worker in India and Mexico is on a downward trend. Under the right circumstances, these countries can enjoy even higher economic growth as personal savings rates rise and provide capital to fund growing businesses.

Sound National Financial Systems

A strong financial system is built upon the pillars of well-managed government finances, a developed banking system, and the availability of capital to businesses to support expansion. Mexico, Brazil, and Russia have improved their government finances significantly since the 1990s, making them less susceptible to global economic cycles. Their current account balances—reflecting the net of payments for imports, exports, services, and interest to and from other countries—have improved substantially. Brazil and Mexico eliminated their current account deficits in 2006, while rising commodity prices have helped Russia accumulate a substantial surplus.

A strong private banking system is also a boon for business growth, as banks that have a healthy supply of customers' savings on deposit can in turn lend those funds to growing businesses to help fuel their expansion. The privatization of banks that has occurred in China and India is expected to be a strong impetus for growing liquidity in the financial systems of these countries. In addition, governments that gradually sell state-held assets into rising markets can realize substantial cash proceeds, boosting their financial reserves and providing funds to pay down government debt. In China, for example, privatization activities in 2005 generated $13.9 billion in government revenue.

Inflows in Investment Capital

Foreign direct investment (FDI) is money that is invested directly in tangible assets in a foreign country, for example, by building a manufacturing plant or setting up a new joint venture company with a local firm. These investments benefit local economies in multiple ways, such as by consuming local goods and services, providing jobs, generating tax and licensing revenues, and bringing advanced technology and management practices.

In general, the six sizzling BRIC+2 countries have made progress in allowing larger amounts of FDI. Limits on foreign investment, whether direct or indirect, restrict the percentage of ownership in a company that can be held by foreign investors. This limits the types of companies that foreign investors can own. In 1998, Korea passed legislation that greatly increased the number of business sectors open to foreign investment, simplified investment procedures, and established foreign investment zones. According to the *International Herald Tribune*, this has resulted in the soaring of foreign investment in Korean businesses, with foreigners owning 44 percent of Korean equities.

Investments in Education

Government spending on education promotes the development of an educated workforce, helping countries become better competitors in the world marketplace of the future. Labor economics studies assessing the effect of higher education on wages and labor productivity show a 3 percent to 6 percent gain in GDP in the long run for an additional year of education. Some recent studies also show that better efficiency in education spending can lead to similar effects on a country's GDP.

Many developing countries have relatively poor education infrastructure, with too few schools, books, and equipment for their young populations. Spending patterns show, however, that the six sizzling countries are increasing their education investments. Between 1995 and 2003, for example, spending on primary and secondary education in Mexico increased by 32 percent, amounting to about 6.3 percent of GDP (according to the Organization for Economic Cooperation and Development [OECD]).

Connecting Success Factors and Investment Returns

The strong economic growth potential of the six sizzling BRIC+2 countries has attracted the attention of some of the world's leading investment advisers, including Goldman Sachs and Lazard Asset Management. In 2004, HSBC Asset Management became the first major mutual fund company to launch a BRIC fund, and many more such funds have followed. As a result, investment in BRIC countries has surged, helping to propel market returns and creating, in essence, a self-fulfilling prophecy. The Standard & Poor's BRIC 40 index rose 360 percent from the beginning of 2002 to the end of 2006. Over the same time period, the U.S.-based S&P 500 index rose by 35 percent. In other words, a $1,000 investment mirroring the BRIC 40 index would have grown to approximately $3,600, while a $1,000 investment in an S&P 500 index fund would have grown to about $1,350.

Are such high returns for BRIC investments sustainable, or are they just a reflection of the current popularity of BRIC investments? What might investors expect from the four BRIC countries, plus Mexico and South Korea, over the next 10 or 20 years? We will explain how the economic success factors for each country bode well for long-term stock investors.

To assess the relative attractiveness of the BRIC+2 countries, we analyzed historic stock market returns across many different countries. The results show that economic factors such as GDP and labor force employment, combined with monetary factors such as a strong banking system and the availability of capital, are highly correlated with stock market returns.

Over time, an increase in annual GDP typically correlates with rising stock prices, which in turn translates to higher stock returns for investors. This is not unexpected. For example, the so-called Gordon formula says that stock returns equal the stock's dividends divided by the stock price (the dividend yield) plus the growth rate of stock prices. Assuming a "normal" market environment—one free of fads and shocks—the growth rate of prices should be about equal to the growth rate of GDP (according to "What Stock Market Returns to Expect for the Future?" by Peter Diamond). Thus, strong GDP growth can be considered a positive fundamental for stock returns.[4]

As noted previously, many economists believe that BRIC countries will enjoy significant growth in GDP in the coming decades. The engines of this growth—India and China—will drive increased demand for basic commodities including oil, natural gas, and minerals. Many of these needs can be supplied by resource-rich Brazil, Mexico, and Russia. India, for example, already imports two-thirds of its energy consumption, and that figure is likely to increase dramatically. Meanwhile, Russia has huge reserves of oil, natural gas, and coal that are being developed for export. Similarly, China's needs for raw materials as inputs to manufacturing are growing rapidly, resulting in massive imports of iron ore, manganese, nickel, platinum, uranium, sugar, and timber from countries such as Brazil.

GDP growth in developed markets such as the United States and western Europe tends to be relatively stable at 2 percent to 3 percent per year. Developing market GDP growth rates are typically much higher. China has averaged 9.7 percent growth per year for the last 30 years, while Korea topped 8 percent a year from 1960 to 1990 (www.macauhub.com.mo/en/news.php?ID=3319). Average GDP growth for most of the six sizzling BRIC+2 countries is forecast at above 4 percent annually through 2050. By

[4]A stock's total return is made up of dividends and price appreciation. The growth rate of prices refers only to the price appreciation; it does not include dividend returns.

TABLE 1.1 Estimated Change in Real GDP, 2005 to 2050

Country	2005 GDP ($millions)	Estimated annual GDP growth	2050 GDP	% change
United States	12,485,725	2.4%	36,300,434	290.7
Japan	4,571,314	1.2%	7,819,232	171.0
Germany	2,797,343	1.5%	5,466,604	195.4
China	2,224,811	6.3%	34,776,833	1,563.1
United Kingdom	2,201,473	1.9%	5,135,132	233.3
France	2,105,864	1.9%	4,912,116	233.3
Italy	1,766,160	1.5%	3,451,453	195.4
Canada	1,130,208	2.6%	3,587,481	317.4
Spain	1,126,565	2.3%	3,134,439	278.2
South Korea	793,070	3.3%	3,418,424	431.0
Brazil	792,683	5.4%	8,451,368	1,066.2
India	775,410	7.6%	20,945,156	2,701.2
Mexico	768,437	4.8%	6,336,741	824.6
Russia	766,180	4.6%	5,797,712	756.7
Australia	707,992	2.6%	2,247,292	317.4

comparison, economic growth in the United States is forecast at a modest 2.4 percent per year. This translates to a 1,500 percent increase in GDP for China versus a 290 percent increase in GDP for the United States. Hence, one might expect stock prices in the BRIC+2 countries to appreciate at a much faster rate over the next several decades than prices in countries with slower economic growth (see Table 1.1).

How much of the expected future growth in BRIC+2 countries is already factored into current stock prices? This is an important consideration—if future growth is already priced into the market, then investors could not expect "windfall" returns.

One way to address this question is to look at the relationship between market capitalization and GDP. Market capitalization measures the current value of the all of the stocks traded in a given country. Again referring to the Gordon rule, if stock prices generally rise as GDP increases, then market capitalization would also rise as GDP increases.

Actual market capitalization data may indicate that individual BRIC+2 markets are underdeveloped or undervalued. An underdeveloped market means that companies are not issuing public stock to raise capital, but are relying instead on other sources of funding such as debt or private equity. An undervalued market is one in which stock prices are lower than might be expected given companies' future earning prospects and cash flows. Market capitalization data can indicate that one or both of these factors is at play. China's economy, for example, expanded at an average of 7 percent to 10 percent annually from 1999 through 2006. While its stock market returns moved up and down during that period, the cumulative return was −0.2 percent, or essentially flat (according to the CITIC China 30 index cumulative return). Its market capitalization at the end of 2006 was just short of $600 billion, which was less than 30 percent of GDP. In contrast, the U.S. market capitalization was approximately $23 trillion at the end of 2006, about 175 percent of domestic GDP.

Another approach to assessing valuation is to look at price-to-earnings (PE) ratios. For example, Union Bank of Switzerland estimated in 2007 that BRICs were trading at about 11 times estimated earnings, compared to a multiple of 13 times earnings for the world market index and about 17 times earnings for the U.S.-focused S&P 500 index. This clearly demonstrates that BRIC stocks are undervalued.

Within the individual BRIC countries there are significant variations, with some markets and companies priced closer to actual values than others. Thus, investors will need to be selective in allocating their BRIC+2 investment dollars to specific countries and stocks.

Diversification Benefits of Developing Market Investing

Investments in BRIC+2 countries offer opportunities to diversify among companies that may be underrepresented in the U.S. economy. Some of the largest companies in Mexico and Russia, for example, are commodity companies that are without peers in the United States, such as Cemex and GazProm.

India, Brazil, and China also offer opportunities to participate in the potential growth of industry leaders. Brazil, for example, began industrializing in the 1930s, and today is home to some of the world's largest companies, in industries ranging from aerospace to soft drinks. Thus, investments in these developing markets may offer investors growth potential that is superior to many alternatives.

When combined with investments in U.S. stocks, holdings in companies based in developing markets can also help lower the overall variability in portfolio return. Developing markets tend not to move in lockstep with the United States, so when the U.S. stock market is declining, developing markets may be rising. In financial terms, this is known as *correlation*. It is always desirable that portfolios be made up of investments that do not correlate with each other in order to reduce the overall risk of the portfolio. Perfect correlation is indicated by a correlation coefficient of 1.00, indicating that markets move together in lockstep. On average, the correlation coefficient between the U.S. market and developing markets is about 0.60, indicating that there are significant opportunities to benefit from diversification.

Attractive Opportunities for Investors

How do the success factors outlined in the book for the six sizzling markets, the relative stock market values, and potential diversification benefits translate to actionable investment decisions? As will be outlined in *Six Sizzling Markets*, we believe that investing in the six BRIC+2 countries discussed represents an extraordinary opportunity for current and future investors, for both macroeconomic and country-specific reasons.

CHAPTER 2

Passion and Paradox

The History of Brazil

Brazil's land is American, its facade Iberian, and its soul African.
—Old Brazilian saying

European. African. Native American. Rich. Poor. Agricultural. Industrial. Traditional. Permissive. Brazil is a study in contrasts, a melding of the Old World and the New, but resembling no other country. Its coastal cities look toward Africa and Europe. Its people exhibit the features of many races mixed together. It is the largest Roman Catholic nation in the world, yet African religious rites continue to be practiced, even today.

The fifth largest country in the world, with a population of approximately 190 million, Brazil makes up one-third of the population of all of Latin America. Its land mass is 3.3 million square miles—slightly larger than the continental United States, and almost half of the continent of South America. Officially named the Federative Republic of Brazil (*Republica Federativa do Brasil*), the country has a strong federalist system comprised of 26 states and a federal district.

With the world's largest reserves of iron ore, as well as large deposits of bauxite, manganese, uranium, and precious gems, Brazil is exceptionally rich in natural resources. Centuries of coffee and sugar exports laid the foundation for Brazil's current position as the world's fourth leading exporter of agricultural products. Although late to industrialize, Brazil has made impressive strides in the past 60 years to become the 10th largest economy in the world, with strong aerospace, automotive, banking, and telecommunications industries.

Yet patterns established during Brazil's colonial history have continued to influence its economy and culture. In the seventeenth century, a small white elite controlled vast landholdings and dominated the economy and political system over a huge nonwhite majority. Four centuries later, the politics have changed and the economy has developed, but Brazil is a still a very rich country full of many poor people.

For example, the country's northeast contains the largest concentration of rural poverty in Latin America. According to a recent study by the World Bank, Brazil has the second most inequitable income distribution of any country in the world, after South Africa. It also has one of the most concentrated distributions of land, with an estimated 1 percent of the farmers controlling 46 percent of all available land in Brazil.

Colonization

In 1500, Portuguese explorer Pedro Alvarez Cabral left Lisbon on a voyage to the West Indies. Instead, he landed at Porto Seguro, in what is now the state of Bahia. The subsequent Portuguese claim to the territory that became Brazil initiated three centuries of colonial rule that was characterized by the exploitation of the area's natural resources, conflict with the indigenous population, and the importation of millions of African slaves.

A number of factors converged to make European colonization possible during this period, including:

- The development of technology, such as navigational tools, ships that could withstand the high seas, and artillery to defend themselves against native peoples.
- The desire to spread Christianity and "save souls" around the globe.
- The pursuit of wealth overseas as the capitalist system was emerging in Europe.
- Monarchs who wanted to expand their nation-states into larger empires.

Although far from smooth, the colonization of Brazil accomplished all of these European objectives, but the consequences of colonization have had a lasting impact on all levels of Brazilian society.

Specifically, the colonization of Brazil resulted in slavery and disease, and affected the nation's language and religion. It is estimated that the territory that comprises modern Brazil had a native population in the millions, divided among hundreds of tribes and language groups. Their ancestors had lived in this land for as long as 20,000 years. While there is no way to be sure of the exact size of the native population at that time, it almost certainly exceeded that of Portugal itself. Initially, the indigenous peoples were curious and hospitable toward the Portuguese. The arrival of the Europeans, however, signaled the introduction of numerous diseases, such as smallpox, measles, tuberculosis, and influenza. While the Portuguese tried to force the people into slavery, tens of thousands died as diseases were carried along trade routes. The Amerindians (the native people of Central and South America) had no biological defenses against these European diseases, and the results were disastrous.

The Amerindians who survived found a strong ally in the Catholic Church, specifically the Society of Jesus. The Jesuits arrived in Brazil in 1549 and immediately went to work converting the Amerindians to Christianity. Over many centuries, the Jesuits and the Catholic Church defended the rights of the native population against the colonists (who would exploit them for labor) and the Portuguese crown.

Today, most of the original Amerindian population has been either assimilated or exterminated, and the 2000 census reported that only 700,000 Brazilians identify themselves as indigenous. According to historian Marshall Eakin, "The voyage of Columbus initiated an irreversible exchange of plants, animals, diseases, and peoples that transformed the planet. The 'Columbian exchange' also unleashed a cultural and biological maelstrom that would enrich the Europeans and devastate Native Americans."

Slavery and Its Legacy

As the Portuguese embarked on a plan to export Brazil's natural resources, including brazilwood (the source of a red dye used in the textile industry in northern Europe), gold, and diamonds from the mining area of Minas Gerais, they needed a ready source of labor. Over a period of 300 years, from 1550 to 1850, approximately 3.5 million African slaves were brought to Brazil. By comparison, the United States imported about 750,000 African slaves during the same period.

Beginning in the mid-sixteenth century, slavery was an essential component for Brazil's transformation into a highly developed agrarian economy. By 1800, Brazil had the largest slave population in the world. By the end of the nineteenth century, coffee was the most important export product, accounting for 67 percent of Brazil's total export revenues between 1881 and 1890. Although sugar, cotton, rubber, tobacco, and cocoa were also important export products, coffee was the centerpiece of the economy. Slave labor was used to develop large sugarcane and coffee plantations.

In 1822, Brazil gained its independence from Portugal, and in 1889 became a republic. Pressure from English and American abolitionists put an end to the African slave trade in 1850, but slavery continued in Brazil until 1888, when Princess Isabel announced the "Golden Law," which finally ended slavery. After the slaves were freed, many of them worked as sharecroppers or farmers, and there was a massive flight to the cities. The country was faced with a serious rural labor shortage, particularly on the coffee plantations.

In Brazil, the legacy of slavery is complex and subtle. A shortage of white women, the subordination of the slaves, a large majority of blacks, and a less rigid culture produced a substantial *mulatto* population. The children of the Portuguese and Amerindians (called *caboclos*) added another level of complexity. Perhaps because Brazilian society as a whole was more mixed, segregation was never codified into law, as with the Jim Crow laws in the United States. Although racism and discrimination do still exist, Brazilians managed to form a racially mixed society. Currently, only 6 percent of the population self-identifies as black because to be considered black in Brazil means that you have no white ancestors and almost half of all Brazilians—an estimated 45 percent of the population—have African ancestors.

A Changing Society

From the last decades of the nineteenth century until 1930, massive immigration helped to reshape the socioeconomic landscape of Brazil. Along with the United States, Canada, and Argentina, Brazil received European and Asian immigrants eager to come to the Americas in search of a better life. At the height of immigration, from 1887 to 1914, 2.7 million foreigners came to Brazil, including large numbers from Germany, Italy, Portugal, and Spain, as well as smaller numbers from the Middle East and Japan. Today, Brazil has the largest population of Japanese in the world outside of Japan.

While some of the European immigrants went to southern Brazil to work as small farmers, the greatest percentage went to work on the coffee plantations in southeastern Brazil. By the turn of the twentieth century, the majority of citizens in São Paulo were immigrants and their children. These patterns of immigration have resulted in a predominantly white European south, a large group of Africans and people of mixed ancestry in the North.

The Vargas Years

In addition to immigration (and partly because of it), Brazilian society underwent a number of important political and economic changes in the first half of the twentieth century. In 1930, Getúlio Vargas seized power by revolution, ending the First Republic, a federation of semiautonomous states, and initiating a new model for industrial and urban development in Brazil. The revolution symbolized a significant shift in power, from the traditional oligarchs to the military, technocrats, young politicians, and eventually the industrialists. While the Brazilian revolution lasted only one month, it was part of the general upheaval that arose out of the world financial crisis of 1929.

Vargas is considered by many to be the most important political figure in twentieth-century Brazil. An extraordinarily adept politician, Vargas seemed to intuitively understand the Brazilian psyche. He held power continuously from 1930 to 1945, and again from 1950 to 1954. As a member of the ruling elite, Vargas recognized that the new urban groups and economic interests in Brazil had to be accommodated, but was careful not to offend the old powers. Because of the depression in world markets and excess coffee production, the central government intervened to provide support to the coffee economy, by buying and destroying large amounts of coffee, and thus the rest of the economy.

From 1930 to 1934, Vargas ruled as head of the provisional revolutionary government, called the Second Republic. In 1934, he was elected president by a constituent assembly. His regime became more repressive over time, and in 1937, with the help of the military, he led a coup and ruled for the next eight years as the dictator of a "New State" (*Estado Novo*). Although historians have compared Vargas to Franco of Spain, he has also been compared to Franklin D. Roosevelt. His promotion of a social welfare system included a minimum wage, maximum working hours, unionization, pensions, health and safety regulations, and unemployment compensation. Even though these reforms applied only to a small portion of the urban workforce, they were significant innovations.

The Beginnings of Industrialization

Vargas's greatest achievement was leading Brazil into a period of intense industrial development. Through economic nationalism and protectionism, Vargas promoted the growth of basic industries that would form the foundation of Brazil's future economic development. Helping to build the first integrated iron and steel complex in Latin America—Volta Redonda, near Rio de Janeiro—is just one example of Vargas's advancement of the industrial economy. Growth of the industrial sector was rapid: In 1920, agriculture represented 79 percent of gross domestic product (GDP), and industry was 21 percent; in 1940, agriculture had fallen to 57 percent, and industry had risen to 43 percent of GDP.

Vargas also spearheaded the creation of government-owned industries such as Petróleo Brasileiro SA (Petrobras), a Brazilian oil company headquartered in Rio de Janeiro. The company was founded in 1953, primarily due to efforts by President Vargas during his last term of office. In 1997, Petrobras ceased to be Brazil's oil monopoly, but today it remains a significant oil producer, with operations in 18 nations. While 55.7 percent of Petrobras common shares are owned by the Brazilian government, privately held shares are traded on BOVESPA, the Brazilian stock exchange located in São Paolo, as well as the New York Stock Exchange.

Vargas placed Brazil on the world stage in 1943 by joining the Allied forces and sending 25,000 troops to fight in World War II. As the only Latin

American country to send combat troops to the war effort, Brazil exhibited its growing role as a regional leader and international presence. Yet the troops faced a troubling contradiction: They were fighting for democracy abroad while living under a dictatorship at home. After the war, Brazilians demanded democratic elections, and Vargas resigned as president in 1945. He was democratically elected in 1950 for his final, and least successful, term as president.

The "Economic Miracle" of the 1960s and 1970s

After World War II, Brazil experienced two decades of democratic rule, highlighted by the presidency of Juscelino Kubitschek from 1956 to 1961. His economic policy, Program of Goals (*Programa de Metas*), defined 31 objectives spread over six areas: energy, transportation, foodstuffs, basic industry, education, and the construction of Brasilia, a new national capital city. Kubitschek's administration promoted state planning for infrastructure and supplying direct aid to industry, but also attracted foreign investment by offering incentives. One example is the creation of the nation's automotive industry, with firms such as Ford, Volkswagen, and General Motors coming to Brazil because of the favorable business climate and the market potential. By 1968, these three automakers produced 90 percent of all cars and trucks made in Brazil.

The Program of Goals produced impressive results. For example, between 1957 and 1961, Brazil's GDP grew at an annual rate of 7 percent, and a per-capita rate of almost 4 percent. In the 1950s, the GDP per-capita growth was nearly three times that of the rest of Latin America. In addition to industrial development, this period heralded the expansion of basic infrastructure, such as roads, the telephone system and other communication systems, and the construction industry.

Unfortunately, the positive effects of Kubitschek's leadership did not last. His successors, Jânio Quadro and João Goulart, lacked both support and political acumen, and in 1964 Goulart was ousted in a bloodless coup. More than 20 years of military rule followed. Brazil was one of many Latin American countries to succumb to military rule in the 1960s. Due to fear of the instability of civilian rule, as well as left-wing radical groups, many citizens at first welcomed the intervention of the military.

Ironically, the years of military repression coincided with enormous economic growth. During the so-called Brazilian miracle, the nation's growth rate was 11 percent per year, faster than any other country in the world. The right-wing military powers wanted to make Brazil a world power, and knew that wouldn't happen without a strong economy. By investing huge amounts of state money and attracting foreign investment, the military government built (among other things) the Trans-Amazon Highway, the world's largest hydroelectric dam, and a nuclear power program.

After a decade of the government's successfully crushing opposition and expanding the economy, General Ernesto Geisel, a moderate, came to power in 1973. He and his supporters began a process of opening (*abertura*), initiating reforms that gradually allowed limited political participation by civilians. But economic problems, caused by the first worldwide oil crisis in 1973–1974, signaled the end of the miracle. In the 1970s, Brazil was importing 80 percent of its oil, and the skyrocketing prices virtually crippled the economy.

Economic Crisis: Inflation and Recession

The government had borrowed heavily to finance economic growth, and by the early 1980s, the $3 billion of foreign debt of 1964 had turned into $100 billion. Although the economy continued to grow until 1982, the debt payments, combined with triple-digit inflation, created an economic crisis. In 1982, Brazil stopped payments on the principal of its foreign debt, and the economy sunk into recession.

After 20 years, the military regime was severely discredited by this severe economic downturn. In 1984, Brazilians took to the streets to demand immediate free elections. Although it would take another five years to accomplish this, the 1985 elections were a start. In an indirect election by an electoral college, the first civilian president, Tancredo Neves, was elected. Tragically, he died after only one month in office. His vice president, José Sarney, came to office, and faced two great challenges: the continuing transition to democratic government and the economic crisis. In 1985, inflation was close to 300 percent, the currency was quickly losing value, and foreign debt continued to mount.

In political terms, the transition from a military government to a democracy was remarkably successful. But in economic terms, the picture was mixed. Brazil had undergone a huge transformation since World War II. The country had developed an impressive industrial base, but the closed economy meant that these industries were not prepared to compete in world markets. A tradition of wasteful and irresponsible government spending was a drain on the economy.

Sarney took a drastic step. In February 1986, he introduced the Cruzado Plan, which called for the temporary freezing of prices and wages and the conversion of the currency into *cruzados* at a rate of 1,000 to 1. This attempt to stabilize the economy worked for several months, and Sarney's status grew to that of a national hero. Unfortunately, the government wanted to wait until after the November 1986 elections to "unfreeze" the economy, which proved too long. Once the freeze was over, inflation exploded once more. Sarney's day was over as quickly as it had begun.

Free Elections, Open Economy

In 1989, more than 80 million Brazilians participated in the first direct presidential election since 1960, and Fernando Collor de Mello was elected. Although Collor's presidency was ultimately a failure—he was impeached in 1992 on charges of widespread corruption—his one success was the implementation of a plan to gradually reduce the state's role in the Brazilian economy. The government started to sell off state-owned enterprises, dismantle protectionist trade policies, and open Brazil's economy to the rest of the world.

Brazilians' excitement over a return to democracy was genuine, but the economic situation was going from bad to worse: Government deficits and public debt were growing; inflation was out of control; and the constitution of 1988 included many provisions that the government simply couldn't afford. At the same time, about 35 percent of the population was living in poverty. In 1990, the Gini coefficient went above 0.6 for the first time since it was first measured in the 1960s.

Collor's vice president, Itamar Franco, served out the remaining two years of Collor's term, although he did little to remedy the inflation crisis. Then, in 1994, Franco appointed Fernando Henrique Cardoso, one of Brazil's most prominent intellectuals, as his finance minister. In an attempt to control runaway inflation and solve the debt crisis, Cardoso and his team of economists created the *Real* Plan (*Plano Real*).

CHAPTER 3

The *Real* World

Brazil from 1994 to today

Brazil is the country of the future—and always will be.

—Brazilian proverb

Is Brazil finally ready to become the country of the future? Since 1994, Brazil has continued its trajectory of tight fiscal control, privatization, and full participation in the global economy. The country's dramatically improved economic outlook has put it in a position to realize its enormous potential. There have been some bumps in the road, but the days of hyperinflation are over, democracy is firmly reestablished, and Brazil has taken a leadership role in promoting Latin American interests abroad. Two strong presidents, Fernando Henrique Cardoso and Luiz Inácio "Lula" da Silva, have steered Brazil through this critical time, providing political stability and strong fiscal policies.

President Cardoso's First Term: 1994–1998

Fernando Henrique Cardoso, a brilliant sociologist who had written widely on economic dependency and race relations, was inaugurated on January 1, 1995. A former Marxist who had been exiled by the military regime, Cardoso returned to Brazil and eventually began a political career as a progressive centrist. As a presidential candidate, he ran with the backing of traditional conservative politicians against the candidate of labor unions and the left, Lula. Lula, founder and leader of the Worker's Party, was running for the second time.

Cardoso's *Plano Real*

On July 1, 1994, prior to his inauguration, Cardoso's *Plano Real* was unveiled. This plan reformed the Brazilian currency, creating the *real*, and put into place measures to reduce inflation without artificial wage or price freezes. Inflation dropped from 45 percent to 50 percent per month in 1994 to 1 percent to 2 percent per month over the next two years. Between 1994 and 1997, inflation was the lowest it had been in decades. By 1998, inflation was almost zero. In addition, *Plano Real* balanced the budget and fixed the exchange rate, while the central bank raised interest rates, helping to drive inflation down from 2,500 percent in 1993 to 16 percent in 1996.

The success of *Plano Real* gave millions of Brazilians hope for the future and prospects of a better life. It also brought national attention to the man behind the plan. Cardoso's success made him a leading contender for the presidency in late 1994, which he won in the first round with 54 percent of the vote.

When Cardoso took office, he intended to revise the 1988 constitution, address fiscal imbalances, attract foreign investment, move away from economic nationalism, and reduce the enormous public sector. In addition, Cardoso was ready to lead Brazil into the market economy. He was against government-run monopolies in such industries as mining and energy, telecommunications, and natural gas—all of which were products of Vargas-era nationalism.

In 1995, Congress approved Cardoso's early proposals, but a second set of broader reforms—including tax reform, pensions, health care, and retirements—became mired in political infighting. At the same time, Brazil's economy benefited from the successful inauguration of the Southern Cone Common Market—a trade organization consisting of Latin American nations—which was established in March 1991 but was not fully effective until 1994.

Privatization

One of the most significant achievements of the Cardoso administration was privatization. Picking up where President Fernando Collor de Mello had left off in the early 1990s, Cardoso moved to privatize major state-owned utilities and businesses.

Beginning in 1995, Cardoso's privatization program brought billions of dollars of FDI into Brazil. The sale of Telebrás, a state-owned monopoly telephone company and Cardoso's crown jewel signaled that Brazil was determined to stay on the free-market course that he had implemented. Companies from the United States, Spain, Portugal, Italy, and Canada bought pieces of Telebrás, which was sold in 12 components: 3 regular telecoms, 1 long-distance carrier, and 8 cellular companies.

The sale of Telebrás benefited consumers immediately: The cost of getting a phone line dropped from $1,200 to $66, and cell phones became readily available. But many in Brazil were concerned. The privatization of

Telebrás triggered violent protests from labor unions, whose members were afraid of losing their jobs. Telebrás had employed close to 90,000 people. While Cardoso believed that the privatization would create as many as 1.5 million new jobs, the labor unionists had no guarantees.

According to a 2003 study by the United Nations, the short-term impact of privatization on employment in Brazil was negative, because of efficiency gains introduced by new managers who were focused on profits. But the long-term impact on employment was positive. Using the telecommunications industry as an example, employment increased because of outsourcing and various activities such as the installation of new lines and the establishment of large call centers. It must be acknowledged, however, that workers phased out by the initial impact of privatization did suffer in the process. In a January 2000 interview in *Outlook Journal*, Cardoso stated, "[Privatization] is also very important in terms of democratization, in terms of access to consumption. Six years ago, there was tremendous debate over how to break the state monopolies. Now no one is discussing if it is possible or not to compete."

In an effort to counterbalance the dramatic effects of privatization, globalization, and trade liberalization, Cardoso's government made major advances in the area of education, health, and income transfers to the poorest Brazilians. Recognizing that poverty was so severe that market forces could not be relied on to alleviate it, the government raised taxes to provide more benefits to the poor, the elderly, and the disabled. Although poverty levels were reduced from 35 percent of the population to 28 percent during Cardoso's first term, inequality decreased only slightly.

Low Inflation, But More Economic Challenges

Ordinary Brazilians initially relieved by the inflation stabilization achieved by Cardoso's *Plano Real* had by mid-1997 started to react to continued economic stringency. In August, thousands of protesters took to the streets in several cities. The Worker's Party organized the protest, called "Brazil, Open Your Eyes." In São Paulo, crowds blocked traffic on Avenida Paulista, the heart of the city's commercial and business district. Among the protestors were landless peasants, factory workers, and government employees. Speakers, including Lula, reminded the crowds that the government had spent billions to bail out failed banks, but white- and blue-collar workers were being excluded from the government's vision of a prosperous new Brazil.

The Asian financial crisis hit at the end of October 1997, prompting capital flight at a level of $500 million a day. The central bank was forced to spend billions of dollars in foreign reserves to defend the currency. The government reacted by increasing interest rates to almost 50 percent, announcing a fiscal austerity program, and promising to push for constitutional reforms.

An important part of the austerity measures was cutting the federal budget in order to reduce government debt, a highly unpopular move. In January 1998, in the midst of a Senate committee vote to reduce social security benefits, angry protestors from a left-wing labor union smashed through a bulletproof door to the committee chambers, interrupting the vote. The president of the Senate, Antonio Carlos Magalhaes, Cardoso's ally, was overheard telling policemen to clear the demonstrators out even if it meant shooting them. Seven hours later, Congress passed the bill.

To some, these painful measures were necessary. Because of generous retirement laws and bloated bureaucracies, many of Brazil's 26 states were spending 70 percent to 90 percent of their revenues on salaries. To others, the belt tightening hurt the working and middle classes, while Brazil's rich, historically insulated from the stresses of inflation and job pressures, continued to get richer on their investments in the stock market.

1998 Presidential Election

Although the Brazilian constitution barred presidents from seeking a second term in office, Cardoso's administration managed to have the rule changed, and Cardoso embarked on a campaign to become Brazil's first democratically elected president to serve two consecutive terms. Again, his most serious opponent was Lula, who was running for the third time. Lula opposed Brazil's participation in the global economy; he wanted emergency measures taken by the government that included massive public works projects to provide jobs; and he advocated taxing foreign corporations to pay for job training programs for young Brazilians. Although Lula assembled a large and broad-based leftist coalition, he failed to gain the support of the lower class. Low inflation had given the poor a boost in spending power, and they voted for Cardoso.

On October 4, 1998, Cardoso was reelected with 51.9 percent of the votes. Lula received 33.2 percent. While some experts speculated that Cardoso's victory was based on the voters' gratitude for the success of *Plano Real* in 1994, the economic reality four years later was quite dire. At the time of the 1998 election, the country was on the brink of financial disaster, due in part to the pressures put on Brazil when the Russian economy collapsed in August. The budget deficit was close to 7 percent of gross domestic product (GDP), and investors again began to pull money out of Brazil. Cardoso knew that the government would have to act quickly or the *real* would perish.

In a move to reassure international investors, President Cardoso pledged to raise taxes and to push for congressional passage of social security and civil service reform. In exchange, the International Monetary Fund (IMF) coordinated a $42 billion loan that would help get Brazil back on track.

President Cardoso's Second Term: 1999–2002

As his second term began in January 1999, President Cardoso was convinced that drastic action was needed. The high interest rates keeping the *real* in place were dramatically increasing government debt and preventing economic growth. On January 13, the head of the central bank, Gustavo Franco, resigned. Franco had been one of the staunchest defenders of a strong *real*. His successor announced a lowering of the *real* against the dollar, effectively devaluing the currency by nearly 9 percent overnight. By mid-November, the *real* had been devalued by 37 percent, the economy had contracted, and unemployment had increased, fueling general discontent.

Cardoso's second term was marked by a major increase in volatility, making the economy more vulnerable to external shocks. Additional shortcomings of *Plano Real* became painfully apparent: The central bank's foreign reserves fell from $51 billion in 1997 to $35 billion in 1999, and the stock market index fell from 10,197 to 6,784 during the same time period. While the Cardoso government made major advances in terms of price stability, fiscal discipline, and the competitiveness of the economy, it failed to lead the country toward sustained growth. After robust GDP growth averaging 4 percent to 5 percent in the mid-1990s, the GDP fell to an average of 1.3 percent in Cardoso's second term, with the exception of 2000, when the economy grew 4.4 percent.

The economic uncertainties of his second term seriously challenged President Cardoso's credibility and popularity, which opened the door for the election of the opposition candidate, Lula, in 2002. Cardoso's legacy was mixed: He accomplished major structural reforms, liberalization, privatizations, and new social programs, but these were tempered by slow growth and an enormous government debt.

President Lula: Is He for the International Economy?

When preelection polls showed that Lula was the likely winner of the 2002 presidential election, foreign investors became nervous. Remembering his leftist rhetoric, some investors predicted that Brazil could follow Argentina in defaulting on its foreign debt, especially since Lula had defended that idea in previous presidential campaigns. Brazil's country risk went from 700 to 2,000 in just a few months.

On his fourth run for the presidency, Lula was elected in October 2002 by a comfortable margin in the second round of voting. A former shoeshine boy, metal lathe operator, and union leader, Lula was the first blue-collar president in Brazil's long history. His life story resonated with many of Brazil's poor. Of mixed race, Lula was born in 1945 in Pernambuco, a poor section in the northeastern party of the country. When he was five years old, Lula's family moved to São Paulo in search of a better life. With only an elementary school education, Lula went from factory worker to union leader to party leader to president—truly an inspiration in Brazil, a country that traditionally has had little social mobility.

Lula was also the first left-leaning president since Goulart, who was overthrown by the military in 1964. Brazilians and the rest of the world waited to see whether Lula would prove to be a statesman and global leader in the mold of Nelson Mandela of South Africa or a loose cannon like his friend, President Hugo Chavez of Venezuela.

Quelling the fears of many, Lula moved to the center politically, skillfully negotiating a broad coalition of parties in Congress. The real challenge Lula faced was how to keep the economy growing while simultaneously reducing poverty and inequality. He based his strategy on macroeconomic stability, strong export promotion, and wealth redistribution. During his first term, Lula implemented strict fiscal policies, overseeing economic stabilization, falling levels of inflation, and decreasing foreign debt. He managed to increase government savings, pay off the balance owed to the IMF, and steadily reduce interest rates. In addition, Lula revamped the pension system, increased the minimum wage, and helped millions of poor families through social welfare programs, including Zero Hunger (*Fome Zero*) and Family Grant (*Bolsa Familia*).

Lula Is Reelected: 2006

In October 2006, Lula won the presidential election in a landslide victory. Yet the question of whether Lula's strategies would allow Brazil to become a high-growth economy still remained among investors. Earlier in the year, McKinsey & Co. Brazil, a consulting firm, published a study suggesting that for Brazil to grow like China and India, it would have to overcome five main obstacles:

1. Reduce the size and importance of the informal sector.
2. Correct some macroeconomic deficiencies, such as high interest rates and high government debt-to-GDP ratio.
3. Reduce the "Brazil cost" or excessive bureaucracy involved in doing business.

4. Improve the quality of public services, like education, justice, and security.
5. Develop a new infrastructure.

If Lula keeps on this balanced course, he could succeed where Juan Perón, Fidel Castro, and Salvador Allende failed—that is, by bringing about genuine social reform without causing economic disaster, political upheaval, or both.

CHAPTER 4

A Land of Opportunity

Investing in Brazil

I want to continue with policies that reduce inequalities among people and among regions. Brazil is ready to grow over 5% per year.

—President Lula, November 2006

Brazil's economy is the largest in South America and is now becoming a force in world markets, thanks to rising exports and progressive trade and fiscal policies. Agriculture, mining, and manufacturing are significant parts of the economy. Its young, growing population and large consumer markets have attracted significant inflows of foreign investment in recent years. It boasts the world's fourth largest airline manufacturer and one of the largest beverage companies in the Western hemisphere. Yet in many ways, it is just beginning to transition from "frontier" country status to developing market, as if finally emerging from a forest canopy to a place in the sun.

Here is a look at this nation's prospects from the perspective of our eight tenets.

Demographics: *Neutral*

Though Brazil boasts one of the largest populations in the world, the composition of its populace leads it receive a neutral ranking. According to International Monetary Fund (IMF) gross domestic product (GDP) statistics, Brazil's estimated population of 195 million (2008) is the fifth largest in the world and one of the fastest growing. Figures 4.1 and 4.2 show that Brazil's rapid population growth is expected to continue through 2050, while China's population will stabilize and populations in Russia, Korea, and Mexico will decline.

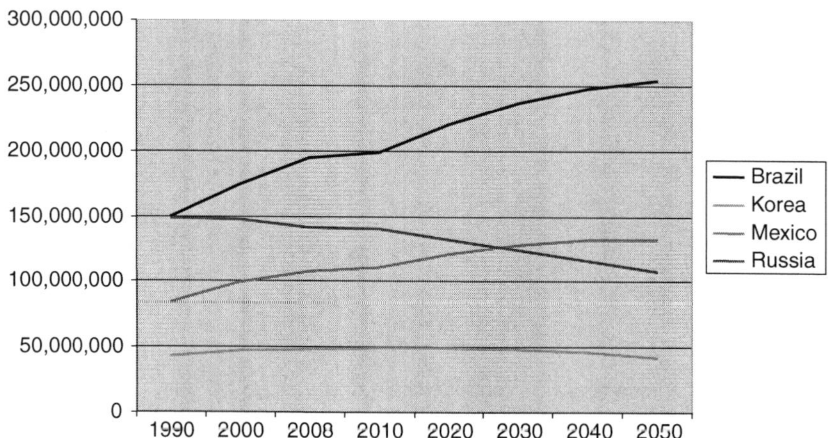

FIGURE 4.1 Population growth (based on UN projections).

Although Brazil's young population today represents more than 25 percent of the total, it is still well below the proportion of youth in India, where nearly 35 percent of the population is under age 15 (see Figure 4.3).

At the same time, the percentage of Brazil's population over age 60 is projected to be slightly higher than India's and Mexico's (see Figure 4.4). Thus, Brazil's population is already aging relative to these countries. Brazil's dependency ratio is forecast to begin rising in the near future as

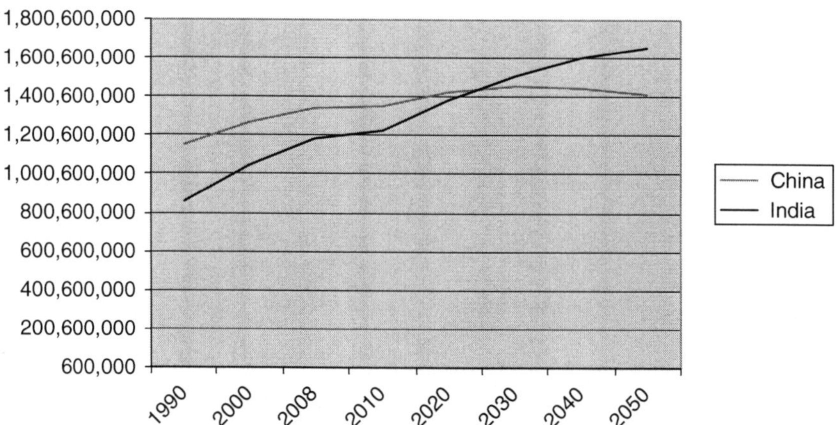

FIGURE 4.2 India and China population growth.

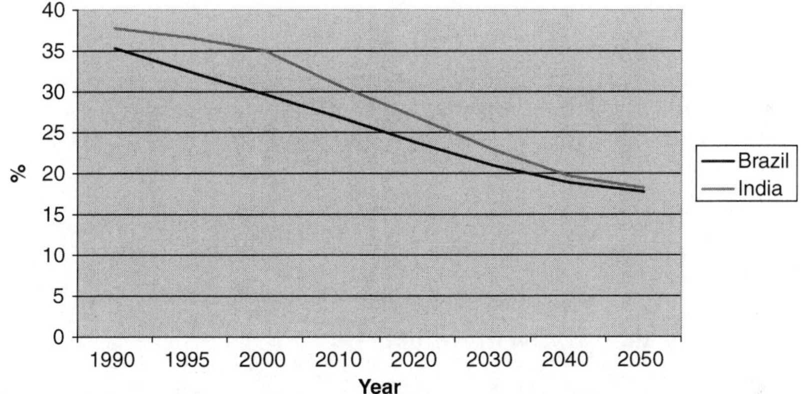

FIGURE 4.3 Children age 0–14 as percentage of total population (based on UN projections).

more workers reach retirement age, while India should enjoy a declining dependency ratio through 2030 at least, and Mexico through 2020.

Although Brazil's population is forecasted to grow rapidly, it is not expected to enjoy the "demographic dividend" that can occur with declines in the number of dependent children per worker. In contrast, both India and Mexico are positioned to realize higher per-capita incomes and declining dependency ratios.

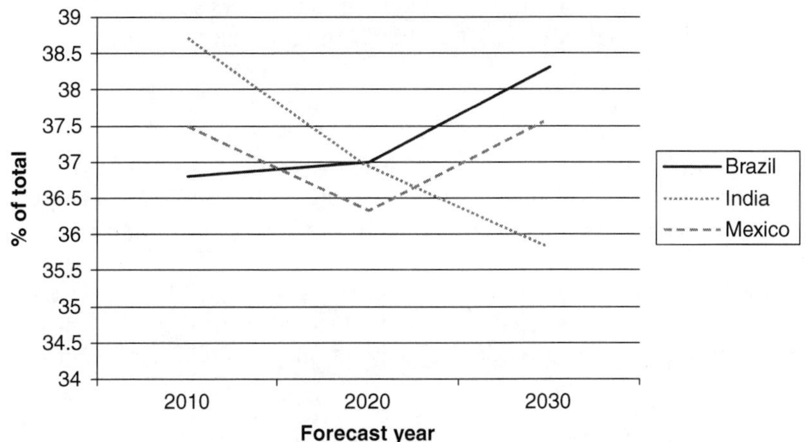

FIGURE 4.4 Combined percentage of population age 1–14 and over 60.

Source: Data from United Nations

These factors combined could possibly lead to accelerated growth in personal savings, which in turn could fuel faster business expansion and a stronger economy. The growth of Brazil's population is a double-edged sword; that is, the improvements it expects to gain from this increase can offset the stress placed on the economy from such an explosion in its population.

Economic Performance: *Neutral*

Expanding Middle Class and GDP Growth

Brazil's large population is primarily employed in low-wage, labor-intensive jobs such as agriculture, retail sales, and construction. Total GDP is around $800 million, about the same as South Korea. Per-capita GDP is roughly $425 per person today, or about $8,600 on a purchasing power parity basis (2006 estimate). While per-capita GDP has grown at about 1.5 percent per year in absolute terms, during the past several decades it has declined relative to Korea, Russia, India, and other emerging-market countries that have posted GDP gains of 6 to 9 percent or more each year. In comparison, Brazil's economy registers as anemic, with real growth rates often falling below 3 percent.[1] As Figure 4.5 shows, India's per-capita GDP (PPP) is about to surpass that of Brazil, although a decade ago Brazil's was nearly twice that of India's.

Most experts point to poor labor productivity as the main culprit behind Brazil's slow GDP growth. About 20 percent of the population is employed in low-wage agricultural jobs, an industry that represents just 8 percent of the economy. Brazil also has an enormous informal economy comprised of workers who do not hold regular jobs with benefits. Many individuals and companies operate in this gray economy to avoid taxes. Some studies conducted by McKinsey suggest that this segment accounts for 55 percent of total employment, and more than 80 percent of new job growth. World Bank data show that this segment of the labor force represents 40 percent of Brazil's GDP, compared with about 10 percent for the United States and less than 15 percent for China.

These factors also contribute to Brazil's standing as having one of the world's least equitable income distributions. United Nations data show that the wealthiest 10 percent of the population controls 48 percent of the

[1]In 2007 the Brazilian Statistical Institute (IGBE) released revised GDP data for 1995 to 2006, incorporating changes in the methodology used to collect data and calculate the statistics. As a result, real GDP growth was revised from an average of 2.5 percent from 2002 to 2006 to 3.25 percent.

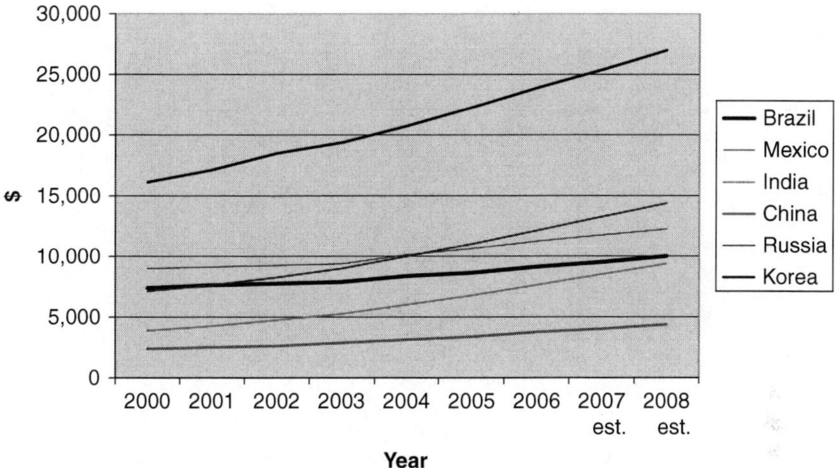

FIGURE 4.5 Growth in PPP per-capita GDP.

Source: Data from IMF World Economic Outlook Database, 2007

nation's wealth, and the poorest 20 percent only 2.5 percent. More than 30 percent of the population lives in poverty, and one in five survives on less than $2 a day. This concentration of wealth is in sharp contrast to the goal of developing an economy driven by strong domestic consumption. Some observers, however, suggest that the concentration of wealth in a minority of the population is a necessary phase in the development of an economy, and that income will begin to become more broadly dispersed as per-capita GDP rises.

What are the prospects for faster economic growth in Brazil? Some indicators are negative. For example, Brazil's macroeconomy ranked 114th in the World Economic Forum's (WEF's) Global Competitiveness Index in 2007, down from 91 in 2005. The WEF attributes this decline to high government debt levels and inflexibility in reallocating government spending. However, the WEF report notes that greater spending on areas that would result in faster gains in labor productivity, such as education, could help boost growth rates.

On the positive side, in 2007 the IMF revised its earlier forecasts by increasing its near-term projections for GDP growth in Brazil by about half a percentage point.

By all measures, real economic growth began to accelerate in 2002, and Brazil is enjoying its longest growth cycle in 25 years. Some of this is due to stronger prices for Brazil's commodity exports and stronger demand from China and other emerging economies for iron ore and steel, which account

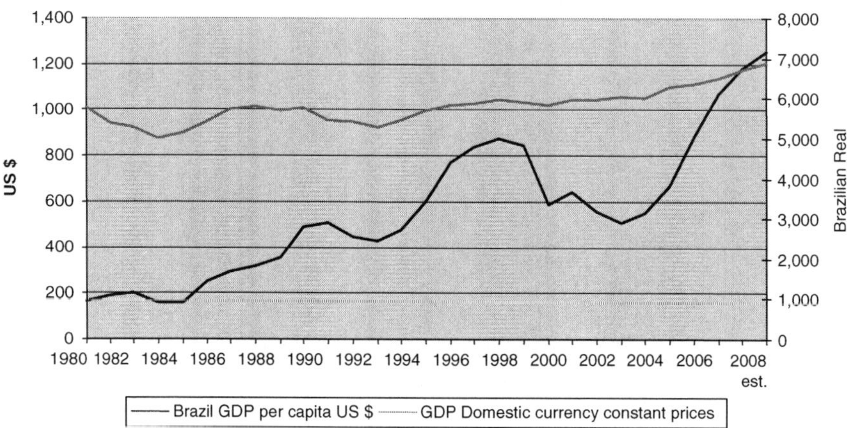

FIGURE 4.6 Brazil's real GDP, 1980 to 2008.

Source: Data from IMF World Economic Outlook Database, 2007

for 15 percent of Brazilian exports. According to the *Financial Times,* the export share of Brazil's GDP jumped from 12 percent to 17 percent from 2002 to 2006 (see Figure 4.6).

Technology: *Favorable*

Brazil's technology factors are very positive for economic development. The WEF ranks Brazil 53rd among all countries in its Networked Readiness index. The index assesses countries' capacity to take advantage of Internet-based information technology and communication (ITC), which reflects the nation's regulatory climate, ITC infrastructure, business and consumer acceptance of these new technologies, and actual usage.

One reason why Brazil is considered to have a favorable technology ranking is that its urban population increasingly relies on cellular phones and the Internet. Brazil's high urban concentration makes it less costly for telecommunication providers to deliver mobile telephone and broadband Internet services across the country. With about 85 percent of the population concentrated in urban areas, Brazil boasts more than 100 million cell phone users, a penetration rate of 50 percent based on total population. According to International Telecommunications Union data, about 40 million Brazilians have Internet access, representing about 21 percent of the population. These relatively high penetration rates are possible partly because most Brazilians live in metropolitan areas. Were the country's population spread more evenly across its vast forests and mountain ranges, telecommunication and Internet transmission capabilities would be much more costly to provide, and penetration rates would undoubtedly be lower.

Open Trade: *Favorable*

Brazil's open trade is also considered favorable for economic development. Brazil's trade policies could be considered liberal compared with some of its neighboring countries. Such open policies are attractive for investors of the six sizzling BRIC+2 nations, where openness to trade is a common source of frustration. According to IMF data, Brazil's average export tariffs were only slightly ahead of China and nearly one-third less than Mexico in 2006. While both imports and exports are rising, export growth is outpacing imports, resulting in a trade surplus of more than $45 billion in 2006, up from a surplus of about $25 billion in 2003.

The country's major exports include metals used in airplanes and other transport applications, such as aluminum, titanium and magnesium alloys, metals, oils and fuels, soybeans, and grains. Growing demand for basic materials in other fast-growing emerging countries is a positive sign for Brazil. Its exports of heavy manufacturing inputs such as iron ore could grow rapidly for years to come.

Agricultural products are a significant part of the country's exports and are central to the Brazilian economy, which is responsible for 20 percent of Brazil's labor force. In recent years, prices have risen for corn and sugarcane commodities as they are being increasingly used as biofuel and feedstock in foreign markets, consequently driving higher export revenues (see Table 4.1).

TABLE 4.1 Brazil Major Exports (2006)

Products	Value ($billion)
Transport material	20,444
Metallurgic material	14,676
Oil and fuel	13,005
Ores	9,755
Soybeans and products	9,311
Chemicals	9,112
Meats	8,510
Sugar and ethanol	7,771
Machines and equipment	7,692
Electrical equipment	5,807
Paper and pulp	4,006
Footwear and leather	3,989

Source: Brazil's Trade Profile, Consulate General of Brazil, www.brazilsydney.org/Ingles/tradeProfile.html

In other respects, Brazil is less open than its neighbors. For example, the World Bank ranks Brazil as one of the most difficult countries in the world in which to start a business, at about 152 days, compared to roughly 60 days in Mexico and 40 days in China. It typically takes 15 months to obtain licenses needed to build a warehouse in Brazil, compared to about two months in the United States.

Although investment in Brazil is impeded by such obstacles, the fact remains that the nation is comparatively more open to foreign trade than most BRIC+2 nations. Thus, its foreign trade appears to be a profitable investment opportunity.

Infrastructure Development: *Neutral*

Infrastructure in Brazil is uneven and has been given a neutral ranking. Brazil claims one of the world's largest aerospace companies and admirable cell phone penetration rates, yet its interior regions are virtually trackless. In the WEF's infrastructure quality ratings, Brazil ranked 8 out of the 12 Latin American countries in 2006. A major hurdle is the dismal quality of the country's roadways and ports, which ranked 12th (last place) and 10th (close to last place), respectively, on the WEF scale.

Offsetting these factors are adequate supplies of electricity, high-quality air transportation, and the underdeveloped miles of navigable rivers that could help speed transportation of fresh agricultural products from interior regions to urban and international markets. Roughly 56 percent of Brazilians enjoy advanced telecommunications systems supported by four large mobile phone operators.

Company Profile: Embraer

Embraer, or *Empresa Brasileira de Aeronáutica SA,* is a Brazilian aircraft manufacturer. Although the company was officially founded in 1969, its history began in the 1940s, when the Brazilian government initiated plans for an aeronautics industry. The industry was officially established in 1954 with the founding of the IPD, *Instituto de Pesquisas e Desenvolvimento*, or Research and Development Institute (currently the IAE, *Instituto de Aeronáutica e Espaco*, or Aeronautics and Space Institute).

Embraer produces military, commercial, and corporate aircraft. Among all aircraft manufacturers, it currently has the third largest yearly delivery of commercial aircraft, behind Boeing and Airbus, and, with almost 24,000 employees, the fourth largest workforce, after

Boeing, Airbus, and Bombardier. The company's headquarters, main production facilities, and engineering and design offices are in São José dos Campos, in the state of São Paulo. Embraer also has commercial sites in the United States, France, Singapore, and China. As of June 30, 2007, Embraer had a firm order backlog of $15.6 billion.

During the 1970s and 1980s, Brazil's Ministry of Aeronautics contributed significantly to the growth of Embraer, and the company produced a variety of military and commercial aircraft for both domestic use and export. But by the late 1980s, the government had reduced its investment in the aerospace industry due to external factors (i.e., the end of the Cold War) and a changing political climate in Brazil, especially under the new constitution of 1988. By the early 1990s, Embraer was in a financial crisis.

On December 7, 1994, Embraer was privatized, and Mauricio Botelho was named the new president. Before privatization, the Brazilian government controlled 51 percent of Embraer, with the remaining interest owned by private investors. After privatization, three Brazilian investment groups (Previ and Sistel pension funds and Bozano Group) each held 20 percent of voting capital. Another 20 percent was acquired in 1999 by a European consortium as part of a strategic initiative to develop advanced military aircraft. The remainder was publicly traded, but the Brazilian government retained a 1 percent share, which allowed it to veto certain deals regarding technology transfer or military aircraft sales to foreign countries.

In July 1999, Embraer introduced plans for a new family of aircraft, the E-Jet series. In 2002, the first model took its inaugural flight. Seeing an opportunity to compete in the regional air markets, Embraer spent an estimated $1 billion to develop the E-Jets. Their smaller size allows carriers to service markets that were previously unattractive because airlines couldn't fill all of the seats in a large jet. JetBlue, for example, bought a fleet of E-Jets to create daily routes from New York and Boston to Austin, Texas; West Palm Beach, Florida; and the Bahamas. "We thought it was worth the risk given the hundreds of new routes we are going to be able to serve," said David Neeleman, CEO of JetBlue.

In March 2006, Embraer underwent a capital restructuring. Currently, the largest stockholders are the Bozano Group (11.1 percent); Previ (16.4 percent); Sistel (7.4 percent); BNDES, the Brazilian Development Bank (6.3 percent); and the Brazilian government (0.3 percent). The remaining shares are traded on Bovespa and the New York Stock Exchange.

(*continued*)

In April 2007, Frederico Fleury Curado, a long-time Embraer executive, succeeded Mauricio Botelho as the company's president and CEO, but Botelho remained chairman of the board of directors. Today, Embraer's jet category includes the Lineage 1000, the Phenom 100 and Phenom 300, and the Embraer Legacy 600. Defense production is also quite strong, with customers including Brazil, Greece, Mexico, and India.

From its beginnings as a project of the Brazilian government, Embraer has grown over the past four decades to become one of the world's premier private aeronautics companies.

Source: Antoine van Agtmael, *The Emerging Markets Century: How a New Breed of World-Class Companies Is Overtaking the World*. New York: Free Press, 2007.

Transparency and Rule of Law: *Unfavorable*

While Brazil's financial and economic prospects have gradually improved in recent years, its scores in the area of openness and rule of law have declined and are considered unfavorable. Transparency International is an independent organization that surveys business executives worldwide about their perceptions on the level of transparency in legal and business transactions and the enforceability of laws and contracts. In its 2007 Corruption Perceptions index, Brazil ranked 73rd among all countries, representing a cumulative drop from a ranking of 42nd over the last seven years and from 63rd in just the last two years.

The WEF's assessments, meanwhile, show an inefficient legal system as a major factor that could contribute to poor rule of law scores and in turn low levels of capital investment in Brazil. In addition, allegations of corrupt political practices in the highest levels of the country's administration have become routine, and many Brazilians view bribery as a normal course of business, thus leading to this unfavorable ranking.

If businesses' contracts cannot be enforced cost-effectively, people will be less willing to invest in ventures that could put their intellectual property and other types of assets at risk. Investors should keep the condition of a state's legal system in mind when considering any investment.

Education and Training: *Unfavorable*

Education and training in Brazil have done little to contribute to the nation's recent economic growth, and, as such, it has been given an unfavorable ranking. Although Brazil has a fairly high level of literacy, with more than 85 percent of the population able to read and write, formal education at the primary and secondary levels is failing to produce students capable of competing in math and science with students from other regions of the world. Moreover, low levels of public funding for college-level programs makes it more difficult for poorer students to attend institutions of higher education. United Nations data show that Brazil ranks 75 out of 125 countries based on the number of students enrolled in post–high school–level programs.

President Lula's administration has tried to perpetuate educational gains made by former President Cardoso by investing in new poverty relief programs that include a component for primary education, such as the *Bolsa Familia* Program, which helps provide a minimum income for 8 million families. Continued efforts may help slow the widening gap between Brazilian students and those in countries that have historically made more substantial investments in education, including India and Korea.

Stronger economic growth would mean higher tax revenues for Brazil's government and more money to spend on education. This likelihood of increased tax revenue should please investors, many of whom remain apprehensive about the nation's poorly funded infrastructure.

Sound Financial Systems and Policies: *Favorable*

Brazil has made enormous strides in improving its financial position in the past decade, and has received a favorable ranking. The country's currency reserves have more than doubled since 2000, providing the government with a cushion to help absorb cyclical changes in the global economy. According to the *McKinsey Quarterly* of May 2007, a floating exchange rate, lower inflation rates, and tight fiscal policy are yielding good results, with budget surpluses now at about 4.5 percent of GDP.

On the negative side, Brazil has very high levels of public debt, close to 72 percent of GDP. A large chunk of public spending is allocated to particular projects or categories that limit the government's ability to spend on investment that could help spur faster economic growth. In 2006, the government was able to shift some of its debt to domestic bonds issued in local currency.

Interest rates are also quite high, ranging in the 17 percent to 19 percent range during much of the past seven years, with occasional spikes above 20 percent. These rates have helped keep inflation low—now at about 3 percent per year—but also make it costly for companies to borrow to fund business start-ups or expansion. This in turn limits the economy's growth engine, as small and mid-sized businesses typically create most of the new jobs.

The fiscal responsibility displayed by the Brazilian government will continue to attract investors, who in previous years had shown signs of wavering confidence.

Brazil's Growth Industries

Now that you are aware of the rankings of the various tenets in Brazil as well as their implications on what you, as an investor, can do to profit from them, it is important to know the different industries that are available for you to invest in. The accompanying table shows that the investable universe for foreign investors in Brazil is dominated by:

- Basic materials companies
- Energy companies
- Financials

These three economic sectors account for about 70 percent of the market capitalization of the Morgan Stanley Capital International (MSCI) Brazil Index, a replicable benchmark that is representative of the components of Brazil's economy (see Table 4.2).

In the remainder of the chapter, we will highlight the most viable investment opportunities available to the individual investor.

Materials

The materials segment includes companies that manufacture building materials, chemicals, packaging, or forest products, and metals and mining firms.

TABLE 4.2 MSCI Brazil Index Sector Weights (as of August 31, 2007)

Economic sector (Global Industry Classification System)	Float adjusted shares (% of investable index)
Materials	31.50
Energy	22.22
Financials	16.10
Consumer staples	7.10
Utilities	6.95
Industrials	4.80
Telecommunication services	4.70
Consumer discretionary	3.26
Information technology	0.75
Health care	0.30

Some possible industries in this sector are companies in Brazil's forest products and metal and mining companies.

FOREST PRODUCTS Brazil's forest products industry boasts annual revenues of $30 billion, or about 4.5 percent of GDP. An estimated 500,000 workers are employed in this industry, processing wood pulp that is used for making paper, manufacturing furniture, and creating processed timber products such as door frames and other manufactured goods. The World Bank estimates that Brazil's exports of forest products have the potential to expand by 5 percent to 10 percent a year.

Exports of furniture have grown by 10 percent annually for the past few years, and prices can be 10 percent to 20 percent lower than competitors, virtually ensuring strong growth opportunity in the future.

Currently, Brazil accounts for only about 2 percent of the world's forest products trade. This market share is expected to increase as competitors' growth potential declines. While some harvesting of native forests is still taking place, Brazil is also experimenting with sustainable harvesting methods. ArborGen, based in Campinas, São Paulo, began planting genetically modified trees in 2006 and sought a second license in 2007. Through initiatives such as these, the industry hopes to increase production and export revenues without jeopardizing the health of the Brazilian Amazon forest.

President Lula signed new legislation in 2007 creating incentives to individual states for practicing forest conservation. These contracts would allow winning bidders to log trees under a sustainable development plan.

METALS AND MINING Brazil is one of the top three producers in the world of iron ore, bauxite, zinc, and nickel. Its production of iron ore already accounts for 34 percent of the world total. Brazil's share of world production in each of these metals will likely grow as multinationals look for opportunities to tie up with domestic firms. A partnership between Companhia Vale do Rio Doce (CVRD), the largest metals and mining company in the Americas and one of the largest in the global metals and mining industry, and German manufacturer ThyssenKrupp Steel is an example of such a tie-up. Under the ThyssenKrupp joint venture, the companies will build a new plant in Rio de Janeiro with a capacity of 5 million tons of steel per year beginning in 2009.

Energy

In the past decade, Brazil has transformed itself from a major oil importer to a potential net exporter of crude oil by 2010. The country's crude oil reserves are the second largest in South America after Venezuela, totaling approximately 11.7 billion barrels of proven reserves.

Brazil is also one of the fastest-growing oil producers in the world. The state-owned oil firm Petrobras, which trades on the Brazilian security markets and as an American Depositary Receipt (ADR) in the United States, aims to become one of the world's top five oil producers by 2020. The company's strategic plan calls for it to expand its operations vertically and horizontally to become an integrated company across the industry. The company will identify target markets for oil, oil products, petrochemicals, gas and energy, biofuels, and distribution.

Biodiesel Opportunity

Brasil Ecodiesel Indústria e Comércio de Biocombustíveis e Óleos Vegetais S.A. is Brazil's leading biodiesel production company. Commercialization of biodiesel in Brazil is accomplished through public auctions, through which Brasil Ecodiesel has supplied 488,000 m^3 of biodiesel, or more than one-half the total supply.

In order to expand and consolidate its position of leadership in the market, Brasil Ecodiesel is investing in new production units to augment the three plants currently in operation in Crateús, Iraquara, and Floriano.

Financials

Brazil's financial services sector is considered underdeveloped by international standards. Equity markets account for only about 60 percent of GDP, a low level suggesting that many more firms could potentially access equity markets as a source of capital. Bank deposits are also low relative to GDP, at 32 percent in Brazil compared with 64 percent in Chile and 66 percent in India. Thus, banks and investment firms can play a bigger role in helping the country's domestic businesses tap into much-needed financing. On the consumer side, Brazil's large population is a ready market for financial services offered by investment firms, banks, and credit card companies.

Foreign firms can enter Brazil's market directly to compete for business and retail customers or by partnering with a domestic institution. In 2006, for example, UBS, a German bank, acquired Banco Pactual to reinforce its investment banking and trading capabilities in Brazil's fast-paced markets. In announcing the deal, UBS chief executive Peter Wuffli told reporters, "Brazil has one of the world's fastest growing financial markets."

Investing in Brazil is not without its risks, as the nation's turbulent history has illustrated. Yet in spite of its dilemmas, the economy continues to grow. As the government further promotes more efficient trade policies with foreign nations and a higher standard of living for its residents, the economy of Brazil remains on pace to become a global economic power. As this transformation process continues, investors can expect the number of lucrative opportunities to multiply.

CHAPTER 5

Catching up with the West

The History of Russia

The secret of politics? Make a good treaty with Russia.
—Otto von Bismarck

Even before Winston Churchill described it as a "riddle wrapped in a mystery inside an enigma" the inner workings of the Russian state had long confounded the outside world. A nation that had endured violence, upheaval, and instability, Russia also experienced great triumphs and progress as a global power throughout its modern history. From the Bolshevik Revolution to the collapse of communism, the perceptions of Churchill, and indeed much of the outside world, had been defined by suspicion, apprehension, and uncertainty. This mind-set on the part of the West, in particular, fueled the conflicts and rivalries that would come to define Russian history over the course of generations.

Even today, almost two decades after the fall of the Soviet Union, Russia continues to be hampered by misperception. As the country embarks on the path toward a free-market system, possessing vast territory, population, and resources, its authoritarian legacies often obscure its impressive and unique transition. While the Russian economy grows at historic rates, the modern world is once again scurrying to solve the riddle—a baffling endeavor without an adequate point of reference. To understand Russia's standing and role in the world economy, both now and for decades to come, is to appreciate the scope and significance of a national history like no other.

Prerevolutionary Russia

The eighteenth and nineteenth centuries in Russia were marked by industrial policies aimed at stimulating growth, military victories and defeats against European powers, and an impressive flowering of the arts and sciences, all presided over by an authoritarian monarchy under growing challenge to its rule.

Czar Peter the Great (1692–1725) was the first Russian monarch to introduce policies for modernizing the country's defense industry to meet Western threats. He promoted mining and the production of metals, importing technology and mobilizing labor as well as capital. To integrate Russia with the modern world, Peter the Great imposed European culture and learning onto a recalcitrant population. He invited European engineers, architects, and craftsmen to lead his modernization projects, while Russians were dispatched to Europe for education and training. His geopolitical goals focused on access to the Baltic Sea, which in 1700 led to the Northern War with Sweden, from which Russia emerged victorious.

During this time, St. Petersburg became an important port city through which Russia gained access to European maritime trade. Economic modernization was based on the exports of metals, ores, and grains. The proceeds of these exported goods were used to import manufactured goods. By the turn of the nineteenth century, Russia was a major world producer of iron ore and munitions, achieving gross domestic product (GDP) growth of 6 percent to 8 percent per year. In keeping with the country's history of authoritarian rule, the czarist state was the primary agent and source of economic development and investment.

Russia Falls Behind

Despite its economic progress, Russia failed to keep pace with the explosive growth of the European powers. In England, France, and Germany, exponential advances in technology, industrial production, and trade far outstripped those of Russia, while a military buildup expanded colonial empires. For all of its progress, the Russian economy of the nineteenth and early twentieth centuries remained 80 percent agricultural, unable to generate capital surpluses on par with Europe. Nonetheless, Russia enjoyed competitive advantage because of its vast territories and accompanying natural resources.

Russia's limited development was brought to light by military defeats by England and France in the Crimean War of 1854 to 1856, and in the Russo-Japanese War in 1905. These defeats exposed the inferiority of Russia's military technology and civil infrastructure. Shaken by the setbacks, the monarchy sought to recover its authority through political reforms, some far-reaching, but many merely symbolic.

One such political reform was Czar Alexander II's (1855–1881) action of abolishing serfdom, a practice that had disappeared in western Europe after the Middle Ages. Serfdom, which had been blamed for low productivity in Russia, indentured peasants for life to the master of the land on which they labored. In addition, Alexander II invested in rail and communications and created a functioning banking system. The czar's government reforms were aborted by his assassination and the radicalized intelligentsia, which opposed the autocracy. Alexander III reacted to his father's assassination by strengthening internal security agencies. His successor, Nicholas II (1894–1917) alternately promulgated and abolished constitutions, allowing parliamentary elections only to have the assemblies disbanded. After strikes and demonstrations in 1905, some infamously put down by force, Nicholas II became increasingly isolated in the face of growing opposition.

World War I, Revolution, and the Rise of the USSR

In the late nineteenth century, under the rule of Nicholas II, Russia concluded mutual defense pacts with France and England, forming the Entente alliance. Germany and Austria-Hungary, in turn, formed a similar defensive alignment called the Central Powers. Political unrest in Serbia, a Slavic principality of the Austro-Hungarian Empire, provided the spark for the outbreak of World War I in August 1914, pitting the Entente against the Central Powers. The war turned into a critical test of Russia's economic and military competitiveness.

After initial victories against Austria, Russia suffered a succession of defeats against Germany on the Eastern Front. Despite superiority in manpower, Russia's weakness in military tactics, logistics, and industrial capacity proved no match for the modern German war machine. High inflation and food shortages, along with the 1.5 million war casualties led to dissension among the military and government as well as uprisings of troops and factory workers. German control of the Baltic and Black Seas severed Russia from suppliers and foreign markets. In the face of military setbacks and growing unrest, Nicholas II stepped down as czar in July 1917.

The collapse of the monarchy created an abrupt vacuum of power and authority, one not adequately filled by a provisional government based on the parliamentary majority of the Constitutional Democrat and Social Revolutionary parties. The government's efforts to restore economic order and rally the war effort were ineffective, creating an opportunity for the minority Bolshevik party, with the support of military factions, to stage a *coup d'état* in October 1917.

The Bolsheviks Consolidate Power

The Bolsheviks advocated the overthrow of the monarchy and the creation of a communist regime. Their popular support was narrow compared with other Russian parties and the large socialist movements of western Europe.

Nonetheless, by decisive and ruthless tactics, the Bolsheviks managed to establish a totalitarian government, which they maintained by a campaign of terror.

The leader of the Bolsheviks, Vladimir Lenin, was an intellectual with a relentless drive for power, who became the architect of the communist state. He was tactically astute, molding the Bolshevik party into a disciplined group that successfully seized control at the critical hour. To achieve power, Lenin summarily crushed all opposition. In Europe, he had become a disciple of Karl Marx, the German philosopher whose influential tract *Das Kapital* (1876) denounced capitalism as inequitable, exploitative of the working class, and a source of the disintegration of society and economy. Marx proposed a new order based on his communist principles, of which Lenin became Russia's standard-bearer.

In 1918, the new Bolshevik government concluded a peace treaty with the Central Powers, ceding much Russian territory. After the war, these areas were reclaimed from a defeated Germany, but the new regime became involved in a civil war against monarchist leaders of the Russian military. Former imperial territories inhabited by the Ukrainians, Georgians, and Uzbeks declared themselves independent republics. The Bolsheviks, however, taking advantage of defections from the czarist officer corps, created the Red Army, a successful fighting force that had defeated the monarchists and subdued breakaway territories by 1921. In 1923, the new rulers formed the Union of Soviet Socialist Republics (USSR), a multinational federation of former imperial regions, of which Russia was the largest republic.

The Bolshevik's austerity program, implemented from 1917 to 1921, left the country with severe shortages of food and consumer goods. To alleviate the crisis, the new rulers introduced the short-lived New Economic Policy (NEP) in 1922, which allowed agriculture and small enterprise to remain private. The resulting economic relief led to a period of stability in which the arts and culture, dormant during the war, experienced a revival.

Stalin: Collectivization and the Great Terror

Following the death of Lenin in 1924, Joseph Stalin assumed leadership of the Bolshevik party. Stalin had been imprisoned by the czarist state and later joined the Bolsheviks, where he proved his organizational genius by a rapid rise to power. He built up a cadre of loyalists and ruthlessly outmaneuvered rivals, many of whom were imprisoned, exiled, or assassinated as he created a cult of a personality around his leadership image. He consolidated dictatorial control through the secret police, which reached deep into Soviet society. His regime saw the most extensive control of the economy by the state in Russia's history. In pursuit of industrial and military parity with the

West, the communist government took ownership of all manufacturing and financial assets and regulated all commercial transactions.

The "well-to-do" peasants of this era, called *kulaks,* whose existence was irreconcilable with communist dogma, naturally became the targets of ruthless persecution. The government expropriated their land and crops in the mass collectivization of 1933 to 1938, causing millions to perish from famine and forced resettlement. Accompanying this state violence was a wide political crackdown on suspected opponents of the regime. Thousands of army officers, professionals, and artists were imprisoned, tried by mock tribunals, executed or exiled to the gulag, a vast network of forced labor camps in Siberia.

World War II

By the mid-1930s, most Western nations, including the United States, had diplomatically recognized the USSR. In an attempt to protect the country's western flank, in 1939 Stalin entered into a nonaggression pact with Nazi Germany, by then a resurgent military power. In November 1939, the Soviet Union invaded neighboring Finland, resulting in a quasi-colonial status of the latter. In an action condemned but not actively opposed by Western nations, the USSR occupied the sovereign Baltic states of Estonia, Latvia, and Lithuania in June 1940.

Hostilities commenced when German armies invaded the western border of the USSR in June 1941 and drove the Red Army, in full retreat, deep into Soviet territory. As Germany advanced into Ukraine and Belorussia, Stalin ordered that the industrial plants be relocated eastward so that they would not fall into German hands. Soviet casualties from combat and privation reached staggering proportions. The Germans laid siege to Leningrad (today St. Petersburg), the former capital of 2.5 million inhabitants, where nearly a third perished from starvation during World War II.

The German offensive was halted at several major encounters. In December 1941, they were prevented from taking Moscow, the capital of 4 million, by special Red Army winter-trained divisions. At Stalingrad (now Volgograd) on the river Volga in October 1942, Soviet forces held the city after months of deadly street combat, blocking the path to the oil-rich southern provinces coveted by the invaders. In July 1943 at Kursk, in the black-earth plain of central Russia, the largest tank battle in history turned the tide against the Germans. The Red Army's tactics took advantage of the overextended German lines over vast territory, the severe Russian winters, and the Soviet superiority in manpower. The German retreat opened the way for the Soviet occupation of Poland, Czechoslovakia, Hungary, Romania, Bulgaria, and the eastern provinces of Germany, including the eastern part of Berlin.

World War II had brought the USSR to the brink of occupation and collapse. However, in contrast to its defeat in World War I, the Soviets had managed to repel invaders and occupy new foreign territory, emerging from the war as a major military power.

The Cold War

The conquests of foreign territories ushered in a time of unprecedented international power and influence for the USSR, based on its military superiority and assertive foreign policy. The rise of both the United States and the USSR to superpower status after World War II initiated a bipolar geopolitical system of competition. Soviet expansionist policies in Central Europe, the Middle East, and Africa were countered by the formation of the North Atlantic Treaty Organization (NATO), a mutual protection alliance of western Europe and the United States.

The Cold War was a period of East-West competition, tension, and conflict short of full-scale war, characterized by mutual perceptions of hostile intention between military-political alliances or blocs. There were real wars, sometimes called "proxy wars" because they were fought by Soviet allies rather than the USSR itself, along with competition for influence in the Third World and a superpower arms race.

After Stalin's death in 1953, he was replaced as Communist party leader by Nikita Khrushchev. Introducing modest reforms, the new leader denounced the brutal legacy of Stalin and relaxed censorship of the arts and media. Though less harsh than his predecessor, he became infamous for public demonstrations of bravado, including a public debate with then–Vice President Richard Nixon in the model kitchen of an American exhibit at a trade fair in Moscow in 1958. Khrushchev embarked on risky foreign policy ventures, including the Cuban Missile Crisis in 1963. He was deposed by political opponents in 1964 and replaced by party hardliner Leonid Brezhnev.

Brezhnev and his supporters steered a status quo economic course and sought *detente*, a mutual relaxation of geopolitical and military tension with the United States. When Brezhnev died in 1982, the party leadership appointed Yuri Andropov, for many years chief of the KGB secret police. Andropov voiced concerns about economic problems and promoted limited reforms. He died of illness after barely two years in office.

Economic Crisis, 1980 to 1990

The goal of the Soviet leadership during the Cold War was to surpass the West in economic growth, demonstrating the superiority of the communist system. However, the Soviet economy had gone through cycles of growth and stagnation.

The Soviet economy started showing signs of weakness in the early 1980s, a trend that continued to the end of the decade. GDP growth dropped from an average of 2.5 percent per year from 1970 to 1980, to 1.8 percent from 1980 to 1985, and barely over 1 percent from 1986 to 1990. The decline has been attributed to a range of factors, including:

- The Soviet system that discouraged individual initiative and a strong work ethic.
- The depletion of readily available natural resources.
- A lack of consumer goods due to disproportionately large spending on defense and military buildup.

In addition to these and other detriments, the central bank had not been effective in controlling the money supply, and the state central planning system caused productivity to remain flat. Low levels of technological and entrepreneurial innovation reflected the lack of incentives for these activities. Although not fully brought to light until the late 1980s, high levels of bureaucratic corruption served as disincentives to efficient production, draining the economy. The central state planning agency, GOSPLAN, lacked a workable economic model of the Soviet economy, relying rather on authoritarian directives and control.

The Gorbachev Reforms

The ascent of Mikhail Gorbachev to the leadership of the Communist party of the Soviet Union marked the beginnings of a dramatic transition not anticipated in the West. Gorbachev represented a generation of leaders who, disillusioned with the existing regime and alarmed by the country's decline, advocated political and economic reform. Following the deaths of three elderly party leaders in rapid succession from 1982 to 1985, the Central Committee elected the relatively youthful Gorbachev as party general secretary in March 1985. By this time, Gorbachev's outlook had been influenced by foreign travel and by a cadre of intellectuals and political leaders who were arguing for fundamental change.

Beginning in 1985, Mikhail Gorbachev's program of economic, political, and social restructuring became the unintended catalyst for dismantling what had taken nearly three-quarters of a century to erect: the Marxist-Leninist-Stalinist totalitarian state. Seeing regeneration of the Soviet economy as their primary objective, Gorbachev and his allies on the Politburo for the first time in decades permitted economic shortfalls to be mentioned in official pronouncements.

Gorbachev initiated a number of reforms, the most important of which was the policy triad of *Perestroika* (economic restructuring), *Glasnost* (political liberalization and freedom of expression), and *Novoye mneniya* (new thinking in foreign policy).

The *Glasnost* reforms allowed new voices to enter public discourse apart from official party dissenters. The new policy was severely tested during the 1986 Chernobyl nuclear disaster, when officials did not disclose the extent of the accident for two weeks. Nonetheless, Gorbachev promoted a spirit of spiritual and intellectual cultural openness in an effort to increase public support and participation in *Perestroika*. However, the resulting exposure of problems, including poor housing, food shortages, and alcoholism, undermined the authority of the communist state. Political openness allowed the Soviet constituent republics to elect regional assemblies and assert increasingly nationalist agendas. Estonia, Latvia, and Lithuania called for independence from Moscow's rule, while nationalist movements took hold in Ukraine, Georgia, and Azerbaijan. *Glasnost* also allowed increased contact with the Western world, as restrictions on travel were relaxed and business and cultural contacts were increased. The policies increasingly threatened the authority of the government and party, leading to a backlash among conservative elements by 1991.

Overall, the reforms had virtually no effect on the sluggish economy of the late 1980s, a period when the government was increasingly losing control. Subsidies to unprofitable enterprises increased, and consumer price subsidies continued. Tax revenues declined, while relaxation of central controls led to a breakdown in supply-chain relationships. Rather than improving efficiency, the reforms resulted in production bottlenecks. In 1991, the Soviet economy moved from stagnation to decline, with the GDP dropping 17 percent during that year. Inflation rose between 1990 and 1991, with retail prices increasing by 140 percent.

Attempted Coup and Dissolution of the USSR

By 1991, Gorbachev's reforms had led to separatist movements in the constituent republics, which he sought to neutralize through a new Union agreement scheduled to be signed on August 20, 1991. Conservatives in the military, KGB, and the government, whose power would have been undermined, attempted a *coup d'état*. A Committee for the State of Emergency placed the vacationing Gorbachev under house arrest, dispatched troops to key positions around Moscow, shut down independent media, and banned noncommunist organizations. The troops, who were ethnic Russians, hesitated to fire on their countrymen or arrest Boris Yeltsin, by then the president of the quasi-independent Russia. Yeltsin took a stand against the plotters. In front the White House, the Moscow building of the Russian government, Yeltsin mounted a tank to rally opponents of the coup under the eye of worldwide TV.

By August 21, the coup had collapsed, but by the time Gorbachev returned to Moscow power was in the hands of Yeltsin, whose Russian government during the coming months forced the Soviet ministries out of office. Independence initiatives in the republics accelerated, and on December 8, 1991, the presidents of Russia, Ukraine, and Belarus met in Belarus to declare that the Soviet Union had ceased to exist, creating in its place a loose grouping known as the Commonwealth of Independent States (CIS). The CIS protocol was ratified in December 1991 in Kazakhstan by the other 11 former Soviet republics, except the three Baltic states and Georgia. On December 25, Gorbachev resigned as Soviet president and by the end of 1991 all Soviet institutions ceased to exist. The Russian Federation assumed the USSR's seat on the UN Security Council, all Soviet embassies became Russian, and armed forces on Soviet territory pledged their allegiance to the Russian state. The Soviet experiment, begun in 1917, had come to an end, with the Russian Federation becoming the main successor state to the now-defunct USSR.

Early Yeltsin Reforms

In June 1991, Boris Yeltsin became the first popularly elected leader in Russian history, guiding the country through a stormy decade of political and economic changes until his resignation at the end of 2000. Yeltsin had risen through the Communist party ranks of the Sverdlovsk region, becoming first secretary of the party committee in 1976. In March 1989, having climbed the ranks, he won a seat in elections to the USSR Congress of People's Deputies (the new Soviet Parliament) on a platform of anti-Soviet Russian nationalism. A year later, on May 29, 1990, the Parliament elected Yeltsin president of the Russian Republic. In the same year, he resigned from the Communist party. As president of independent Russia, Yeltsin launched the formidable project of transforming the economy and political system.

During his first year in office, President Yeltsin launched a conversion of the largest state-controlled economy in the world to a market-oriented system. For this task, he relied on the advice of both liberal Russian economists and experts from Western countries. The latter promoted a program based on the neo-liberal "Washington Consensus" of the International Monetary Fund (IMF), the World Bank, and the U.S. Treasury. The main objectives of the reforms were curbing inflation and incentivizing efficient, market-oriented production. These policies, which came to be popularly known as "shock therapy" because of their severe effects, were liberalization, stabilization, and privatization.

Privatization began in January 1992 by liberalizing small enterprises, including retail, household services, construction, and elements of transportation and housing. Small enterprises were sold through auctions and the process, despite obstacles from racketeering and crime.

Large-scale privatization of state-owned enterprises presented the larger challenge, as the government sought to make the process equitable and transparent. The mass privatization program was launched in 1992, granting each citizen 10,000 rubles of vouchers redeemable in cash or exchangeable against shares in enterprises transformed to joint-stock companies. Employees could acquire company shares at a discount at public auctions. By June 1994, approximately 70 percent of enterprises had been sold off by this process. Western economists have argued that the privatization allowed shares of enterprises to be held by insiders, who managed to accumulate the stock. This process included manipulation of the large mass of voucher holders who poorly understood the value of the shares.

As such, the Russian privatization was widely criticized as a "theft of the state"—that is, a transfer of assets back to the same managers or their proxies who had run the enterprises under the Soviets. The said "managers" were in many cases the "oligarchs," politically connected newcomers who accumulated vast assets. Anatoly Chubais observed ruefully about the new owners, "They steal and steal and steal, and no one can stop them." As genuine owners, he hoped, they would in the future manage the privatized companies with new responsibility and prudence.

Constitutional Crisis of 1993

In 1992, Yeltsin's policy of radical privatization was largely opposed by the Congress of People's Deputies, a conservative parliament that had been elected in 1990 under Soviet rule. The legislators also proposed amnesty for the leaders of the 1991 coup and required the government to submit quarterly budget reports for approval. The president's attempt to dissolve parliament in 1993 was opposed by the Constitutional Court. Parliament, in turn, voted to depose Yeltsin and appoint Vice President Alexander Rutskoy in his place. A confrontation emerged as members of Parliament staged a sit-in. Yeltsin ordered army units to storm the building and arrest the dissident parliamentarians.

A new constitution was approved by referendum in December 1993, based on a strong presidency, a legislature with reduced authority, and a reconstituted Constitutional Court. New parliamentary elections were held in February 1994 and the country did its best to move on.

Continuing Economic Problems

Russia's economic struggle was precipitated by a series of ill-conceived policies. Yeltsin's first prime minister was the 35-year-old economist Yegor

Gaidar, who proceeded to lift government price controls, which induced rapid inflation. The latter was accelerated by the central bank, which printed money to finance government debt. The government pursued macroeconomic stabilization to curb this trend, initiating austere monetary and fiscal policies. Prices and interest rates were allowed to rise, government expenditures on industry and social programs were cut back, and taxes were increased to raise revenue. State enterprises, and indeed entire sectors of industry, found themselves in financial crisis as state orders for production were cut and financing options curtailed.

The new policies faced serious obstacles. Although the Russian population had high levels of literacy and education, the work ethic was underdeveloped due to decades of disincentives. In addition, management skills, including risk and reward–centered behavior, were not cultivated under the Soviet economy. Defense producers, which represented 15 percent of the Soviet GDP, were unable to retool production or find new markets to adjust to post–Cold War reality. Regions devoted to defense production were severely affected, with their unemployment rising sharply. Under the Soviets, the social services systems had been maintained by large enterprises. Faced with a drastic decline in the economy, the social services system rapidly lost support, which the government was unable to replace.

The first stage of insider privatization resulted in market distortions that kept unemployment rates low and wages high, in keeping with past Soviet practice. Efficiency of production suffered, with costs of inputs often exceeding the market value of products. Russian enterprises were unprepared to function in a market environment. In order to raise cash, companies either liquidated their assets or engaged in bartering to settle their obligations.

The formation of Russian capital markets was hampered by a succession of problems. A rapid decline in the standard of living since 1991, corresponding with the start of Yeltsin's tenure, prompted Russia's industrial workers to stage massive demonstrations. (Oddly enough, upon winning the election, Yeltsin promised to "lay his head on the rails" if Russia's standard of living were to fall any lower.) In one instance, hundreds of workers, many of whom hadn't been paid in months, blocked the railroad lines in Russia's coal-mining regions in an effort to pressure the government into paying wages. Industrial workers were not alone in their displeasure, as teachers, students, and more educated workers began to echo the same sentiments. By that time, Yeltsin too had become aware that the economy was going nowhere fast.

In addition, hyperinflation had practically wiped out savings held by depository institutions. Financial scams and pyramid schemes extracted large amounts of cash from an unsuspecting public. The government financed its deficit through high-interest short-term bonds, and defaults on the bonds drained the financial system. The economic and financial crises resulted in capital flight at the rate of $2 to $3 billion per month in the early 1990s. No less serious was the emigration of many qualified specialists in science, medicine, and education, creating a brain drain on the country's human capital.

Election of 1996

The Russian economy of 1995 had dropped by 45 percent since 1980. Thirty-five percent of the population was living below the poverty line. Wage arrears in state enterprises and government were mounting. Energy and metallurgy exports, potential sources of revenue and foreign exchange, were down due to low world oil prices and diminished production. The war with breakaway Muslim region Chechnya, which cost Russia dearly in lives and resources, had reached an impasse and become an embarrassment. Discontent with reforms was widespread.

Parliamentary elections of 1995 brought in a communist majority. At the same time, Yeltsin's popularity reached a low point, with presidential elections scheduled for 1996. His main opponent, Communist party leader Gennady Zyuganov, was favored to win the election.

Early in 1996, a coalition was formed between reformist political leaders and oligarchs who had much to lose in the event of a Yeltsin loss. They made a pact to orchestrate his reelection by funding the campaign, muzzling the media, and bringing in Western political consultants. Media coverage of Zyuganov was curtailed through political pressure.

The June elections ended in a run-off between Zyuganov and Yeltsin. Yeltsin prevailed with support of the third-place finisher, General Alexander Lebed, who had been promised a high government post.

The election has been described as the reinvention of an unpopular president by supporters who applied power, wealth, and influence to stack the odds against the opponents. To secure support, Yeltsin had made questionable government concessions and deals with private interests, but many believed that blocking communists from returning justified the compromises.

By the mid-1990s, rates of poverty and social inequality rose sharply, while public health indicators declined. The population fell by 750,000 between 1990 and 1998. Prices increased sharply. While the supply of consumer goods grew by comparison with the Soviet era, the impoverishment of the populace made them unable to participate in the market economy. Discontent with the reforms was growing from year to year.

CHAPTER 6

Blind Turns and Growing Pains

Russia from 1998 to Today

Close scrutiny will show that most "crisis situations" are opportunities to either advance, or stay where you are.

—Maxwell Maltz

In the aftermath of the 1998 Russian financial crisis, Grigori Yavlinski, then leader of an opposition party, remarked, "In Russia, only an idiot would make predictions." Yavlinski's cynicism was not hard to come by at that juncture. The months preceding the economic meltdown had witnessed scores of well-educated and highly influential "idiots" proudly touting what they perceived to be the start of a prosperous fiscal year. Mikhail Delyagin, a top economic adviser before the crisis unfolded, had characterized the Russian economy as "gathering its strength for the upward pull." Anatoly Chubais, business tycoon, politician, and expert economist, went as far as to say, "It seems to me that nothing can stop Russia from a long, steep, powerful upward trajectory of growth, constantly gaining in strength." Even the World Bank's politically neutral economists were predicting a 6 percent rate of growth for Russia in 1998.

By August of that year, however, the Russian economy was in ruins, along with the predictions of said "idiots." Many of the state's largest commercial banks had been forced to shut down, either by scandal or bankruptcy, and the ruble had nearly fallen off the globe. The working class, who had gone months without a paycheck, was staging loud, mass protests, often unsure of who would be on the receiving end of their messages. The country was acquainting itself with its third prime minister in less than two years. If Russia were indeed gaining strength, no one wanted to be around for the upward pull.

Though a few idiots may have failed to predict the Russian economic collapse in 1998, even fewer would have forecasted its remarkable recovery.

By 2006, less than eight years removed from economic upheaval under a shaky political system, Russia had become the world's ninth largest economy, with a gross domestic product (GDP) growth rate at just over 6.5 percent, making it the fastest growing nation in the G8. With a stable political system not witnessed in years past and an unmatched abundance of natural resources, predicting the "upward pull" of the Russian economy was no longer an undertaking for idiots.

Domestic Disturbance

Economic chaos and political disorder are virtually inseparable—one invariably follows the other in some form. Russia in the late 1990s would prove to be no exception. As discussed in Chapter 5, the economic collapse in August 1998 was preceded by a hectic period of internal Russian politics, marked by rotating governments, political polarization, and widespread dissatisfaction with Yeltsin's leadership.

As early as January 1998, it was apparent that Russia was lagging in several key economic areas. Capital investment had already shrunk nearly 7 percent, as had real income. Total profits in the industrial sector, which had already begun to plummet in early 1997, fell by 15 percent in the first month of 1998. Losses in the industrial sector increased by 140 percent. Foreign debt had topped $6 billion and domestic debt totaled 530 billion rubles—a situation that had forced the government to restructure or "denominate" the ruble in 1997, whereby the last three digits of all bank notes were removed. With a drastically reduced working budget, Russia struggled to pay its own workforce, to say nothing of foreign creditors.

Yeltsin Cleans House

On March 23, 1998, with economic chaos ensuing (and more on the horizon), Yeltsin forced his entire cabinet to resign—a decision that would permanently tarnish his legacy. Among the victims were high-profile figures such as interior Minister Anatoly Kulikov and Anatoly Chubais, who were settling into their roles as the *de facto* economic liaisons to the West. Perhaps most shocking of all was the dismissal of Prime Minister Viktor Chernomyrdin, who had been considered a strong presidential candidate to replace Yeltsin in the 2000 elections. It was a political move as hasty as it was unexpected, as the Russian leader gave no immediate reason for the cabinet's dismissal. The consensus among analysts suggested that Yeltsin's sweeping dismissals were born not of pragmatism, but of emotion and ego. Yeltsin's bold move sent shockwaves through the corridors of power in Russia. Any remaining confidence in a political system already embroiled in chaos evaporated overnight.

In place of Chernomyrdin, Yeltsin assigned the duties of acting prime minister to a 35-year-old businessman named Sergei Kiriyenko, who had served as Russia's minister for fuel and energy. Kiriyenko was viewed as little more than a lackey, handpicked by Yeltsin, and this perception was not confined to the Russian border—Western investors had begun to take notice of the situation. In the months following the ousting of "the big three"—that is, Kulikov, Anatoly Chubais, and Prime Minister Chernomyrdin—it was estimated that as much as $15 billion was removed from the Russian market.

A Vote of No Confidence

According to author Roy Medvedev, in his book *Post-Soviet Russia*, which chronicled the Russian financial disaster, this loss of confidence was nowhere more apparent than with the "oligarchs." Between 1991 and 1996, large government assets were transferred into private control, a process sometimes referred to as *grabification,* as major new companies were created through government influence and concessions. The oligarchs, therefore, a small, select group of beneficiaries, accumulated great wealth in a short span of years. These included owners of energy and metallurgy firms, new commercial banks, distributors of high-demand imported goods, and media moguls.

Although the communist bureaucrats who controlled assets during the Soviet era had been discredited and dispossessed, a new cadre of operators emerged, who used the fluid political situation to their advantage. The newcomers were supported behind the scenes by the officials seeking to prosper in the new environment. The prominent oligarchs included Vladimir Potanin, head of Onexim Bank; Boris Berezovsky, a foreign auto importer and media magnate; and Piotr Aven, Alpha Bank president. Mikhail Khodorkovsky came to head the giant Yukos Oil Company, becoming the richest man in Russia by 2003, with a net worth of $15 billion before eventually being the target of a massive government crackdown on corruption.

At a time when the general population was experiencing hardship, huge fortunes accumulated overnight by questionable means fueled resentment against the new regime. Assets had again concentrated in the hands of a minority through political influence rather than merit or competition. The newly rich used their leverage on the financially faltering state by extending loans in exchange for concessions. The wealth and power of some oligarchs fed their political ambitions and posed a threat to the political elites that controlled the state. Set to endorse Chernomyrdin in the 2000 election, the oligarchs were suddenly on to Plan B in learning of his dismissal. Controlling absurd amounts of wealth, such parties were in desperate need of a stable political environment.

Russia's banking system, which had been dominated by oligarchs since the mid-1990s, was steadily deteriorating as economists spoke in hushed tones of a denominated ruble. Toko Bank, for instance, which had been the first Russian bank to obtain a hard currency license, was forced into a receivership as its profits sunk. Though interest rates were raised as a salvage tactic, Toko Bank and other financial institutions were unable to stop the bleeding as the cost of credit rose. Toko Bank had gone from a top 20 bank, attracting capital from around the world, to bankruptcy in a span of less than three years.

With an unpopular leader governing in isolation, an artificially propped-up currency, and a polarized and unpaid population, the political environment in Russia had made it ripe for the economic crisis that was to follow.

Fuel to the Fire

The Asian financial crisis, which began in Thailand in July 1997 and culminated with stock market crashes in the Asian Tiger nations, set off a series of unfortunate events for the Russian economy. Though leading economists had optimistically predicted that Russia would remain unscathed by the neighboring chaos, the crisis eventually spread to Russia. Among other things, the crash of the Asian markets had resulted in a serious reduction in demand for and price of raw materials such as oil. Relying almost entirely on materials such as petroleum, natural gas, timber, and metals for their exports, Russia, which had already been sensitive to price fluctuations of raw materials on the world market, soon realized that its revenues were about to take a near-fatal hit.

Prior to the Asian financial crisis, oil prices had hovered around $20 per barrel. By January 1998, that figure had fallen to $11 per barrel. For Russia, whose costs of production ranged between $13 and $15 per barrel at the time, this meant that oil would no longer provide a major source of revenue. In fact, it would now *cost* Russia to produce oil. This reality was difficult to accept for a nation that exported over 100 million tons of oil every year. The government and oligarchs had grown accustomed to revenues from this industry, which was now the most serious drain on the economy. According to the State Duma's budget report, the Russian Treasury lost $1.5 billion between January and March of 1998 as a direct result of the falling oil prices.

Despite the drop in commodity prices, Russia had no choice but to continue exporting oil. Already feeling the pressure from the coal-mining strikes, Yeltsin could not simply shut down oil production, an industry that employed thousands of workers, without committing political suicide. Furthermore, nearly the entire Baltic region was dependent on Russia for energy. Yeltsin and his economic advisers believed that losing these clients would be far more detrimental in the long run than operating at a loss. Unable to profit and unwilling to cease production, the Russian economy was in a state of perpetual paralysis and at the mercy of the global market.

Funny Money

A Ponzi scheme, similar to a pyramid scheme, is an operation whereby investors are paid high rates of return with funds from new investors. With no actual income being produced, it is inevitable that when new investors can no longer be drawn in, the Ponzi scheme will collapse. Such operations are generally conducted on a small scale and in secrecy, yet this is essentially what had been transpiring in Russia since 1993. The issuance of GKO bonds—short-term government bonds— proved to be the Russian economy's undoing when, in 1998, the Russian government defaulted on these loans, to the tune of hundreds of millions of dollars.

How could this have happened? In 1993, when the bonds were introduced, Russia was in the midst of a governmental crisis. Attempting to inject the economy with new capital in order to finance immediate needs and a growing bureaucracy, the Russian government may have felt that conventional methods were out of the question. With a narrow-minded focus on the short term, it is plausible that the government was so desperate for capital that it resorted to the scheme, knowing full well that a collapse was inevitable. With the constant shifting of governments, those who orchestrated this policy may have figured that they would be long gone by the time it imploded. They were right.

The GKO bonds began to display signs of weakness by 1995. As the income of new capital from the bonds gradually lessened, so did the government's ability to pay back the loans. To compensate, Russian officials extended the bonds first to foreign citizens, whereas they had previously been issued only domestically to corporations, then to the greater Russian population. Not surprisingly, foreign investors, lured in by the promise of enormous returns, began purchasing the bonds in great numbers in 1996. By 1998, foreign investors accounted for one-quarter of all the GKO bonds. George Soros, the prominent financial speculator, had purchased nearly $2 billion worth of these bonds through his Quantum Investment Fund. By May 1998, Russia's central bank, in reaction to the soaring GKO yields, actually raised the interest rate to 150 percent, though it would prove to be too little, too late.

Intervention

One final attempt at staving off the impending economic crisis came in the form of an International Monetary Fund (IMF) financial assistance package.

Yeltsin, who was vacationing at the time, appointed Chubais, the man he had fired in March, as his personal representative to the IMF. Seeking a relief package, Chubais was successful in getting the IMF to assist Russia's short-term budgetary needs, though the funds may have been used for other purposes. In May 1998, in an incident that drew worldwide attention, almost $5 billion in IMF relief funds were stolen, presumably by top-ranking government officials. Yet the aid of the IMF and other outside lenders only delayed the inevitable. By mid-June, Russia requested another $10 billion in aid from the IMF, who was rightfully apprehensive about another round of loans. In early July, Russia received $22.6 billion from various international lenders, in addition to a $1.5 billion structural adjustment loan from the World Bank. During that same time frame, as bailout funds steadily poured in, Russian banks began spending huge sums of foreign currency to maintain a six-to-one exchange rate on the ruble, since Yeltsin had promised no devaluation. By August, the country's reserves were virtually empty. Panic ensued.

Rubles for Sale!

The economic crisis of 1998 began with Russia's commercial banks, most of which were centered in Moscow. After selling most of their government securities for rubles, hundreds of banks began converting their assets into foreign currency. On August 11, Russian banks purchased over $100 million worth of foreign currency. Only two days later, demand for the dollar had increased 20 times over, causing the central bank, which had become paralyzed by the frenzy, to impose limits on the purchase of foreign currency. Stock prices had fallen to a two-year low, and whispers of ruble devaluation were becoming more and more audible as Russians scrambled to obtain dollars and foreign currency.

Meanwhile, Yeltsin returned to Moscow on August 16 and called for an emergency summer session of Parliament. Though he gave the Kiriyenko administration a vote of confidence, it was clear that the government was in the midst of a full-blown crisis. One day later, the Russian government, along with the central bank, introduced what they called a "new floating exchange rate." The doublespeak did little to calm investors, who realized that the Yeltsin government had simply devalued the ruble. Other conditions of the so-called anticrisis legislation included a 90-day moratorium on most hard currency transactions, meaning that Russian banks could not accept new credits or pay off existing debts until November 1998. In addition to allowing investors to convert their GKO bonds (which wouldn't be paid back anyway) into equally worthless government securities, the government called for another provision: prohibiting nonresidents from investing short term.

It had been Yeltsin's insistence that the Russian government would not devalue the ruble that, ironically, led to its downfall. During the first month and a half of the crisis, the central bank had spent almost $3.8 billion in an effort to maintain the ruble's exchange rate and could no longer afford to throw away valuable foreign currency for the free-falling ruble. On August 19, the rate of rubles to dollars was 7 to 1. The first week in September, that rate rose to nearly 20 to 1 by official accounts, with widespread rumors of a 40-to-1 ratio. Many pursued the purchase of dollars and other forms of currency on the black market despite restrictions on such transactions.

Revolving Governments

On August 23, 1998, Yeltsin would again shake up the Russian political environment, this time dismissing the Kiriyenko government and nominating Chernomyrdin as prime minister. It has been viewed as one of Yeltsin's more ironic decisions, not only because Kiriyenko had little to do with the collapse, but because the Chernomyrdin government had been the primary reason for the situation. The Duma swiftly rejected Yeltsin's nomination, and by September of that year both Yeltsin and the Duma had compromised on Yevgenly Primakov.

Yevgeny Primakov would last less than a year as prime minister before Yeltsin dismissed him in May 1999. Amid threats of impeachment, citing that not enough steps had been taken to heal the economy, Yeltsin named Sergei Stepashin as prime minister. Many analysts contend that Primakov had been let go due to his views on corruption. As prime minister, Primakov had initiated a campaign targeting corruption, and as such practices involved some of Russia's more prominent, influential families, it has been suggested that he was removed by the criminal elements of the Russian state.

Yeltsin's dismissal of Sergei Stepashin, just three months after that of Primakov, brought Vladimir Putin to the center of Russian politics. Having served as director of the Federal Security Service (the successor to the infamous KGB), Putin was little known outside the Kremlin and seemed like a weak successor to Yeltsin, who had hinted at a forthcoming retirement.

Putin Takes Charge

As second in command by law, Putin became acting president and wasted little time in pushing through several major changes. After being inaugurated on May 7, Putin restructured the Russian political landscape into 85 districts of equal representation. Though supposedly equal, Putin signed a law allowing him to remove the leadership of any districts at his whim, eliciting cries of authoritarianism among critics. Putin would come to be known as a politician not afraid of change. He even gave his approval to change the words of the Russian national anthem.

Putin's role in Russian politics coincided with a resurgence of the crisis in Chechnya. Shortly after assuming the duties of prime minister, Putin sent troops to back into Chechnya in the aftermath of several bomb explosions that had been blamed on Chechen extremists. His tough stance and "law and order" rhetoric solidified his popularity among the Russian people, who would elect him to the presidency by a landslide margin one year later.

Putin's rise to power would not have been sustained without the healing of the economy. The Russian economy rebounded in dramatic fashion following the crisis of 1998, as the result of a sudden and sharp rise in world oil prices by the year 2000. The years following the crisis saw overall improvements in Russia's foreign relations, despite well-publicized clashes in Chechnya. Reaching an arms agreement with the United States in 2002, and signing energy pacts with Iran and China, Russia was no longer exporting oil at a loss. In 2005, Russia signed a deal with Germany to build a gas pipeline under the Baltic Sea between the two nations—an unthinkable agreement just years prior. The Stabilization Fund of the Russian Federation, signed on January 1, 2004, introduced precautionary measures should oil ever drop below $27 per barrel. The policy, supported by Putin, has been instrumental in balancing the Russian budget and shows signs of discipline and patience in the economy. A country on the verge of bankruptcy in 1998 now wields a multibillion-dollar surplus, and the ruble, which had returned from the brink of complete annihilation, even became a convertible currency in July 2006.

Since 1998, Russia's GDP growth has averaged 6 percent, more than the combined averages of all the G8 nations, according to the World Bank. In that same time, private industry has flourished with government encouragement. Oil revenues have been managed more effectively, and a simplified income tax system has been introduced. Foreign debt, which had accounted for almost 50 percent of Russia's GDP at the start of Putin's first term, was reduced to 30 percent by 2005. The $3.3 billion in IMF loans was actually repaid ahead of schedule. Foreign exchange reserves, which had been nearly exhausted in 1998, amounted to $225 billion in 2005. Millions of dollars of foreign capital began to work its way back into the economy as well.

Yet numbers themselves fail to convey this remarkable transformation, as statistics often change well before perception. The Russian response to the collapse of 1998 may go down in history as one of the finest examples of crisis management. A disaster that was predicted to last decades was overcome in a matter of months.

In the twenty-first century, the country continues to baffle the Western mind as it again proves its resilience, rebounding from the collapse of communism to emerge with a period of impressive growth beginning in

1999. The country survived defeats in part by drawing upon vast territorial and natural resources to even the odds against more advanced adversaries. In the twenty-first century, Russia's role as a leading world producer of oil and gas once again makes it a force to be reckoned with. Western capital markets and producers have taken note, investing $28.4 billion in FDI and $1.2 billion in portfolio investment in Russia in 2006. Nonetheless, Russia continues to confound Western observers with an apparent paradox: economic resilience accompanied by a retreat from the recently established democratic government.

CHAPTER 7

Resources to Rubles in a New World Economy

Investing in Russia

The Russian economy returned from the brink of financial collapse in 1998 to become one of the strongest economies among the six sizzling BRIC+2 nations, growing by almost 37 percent during that eight-year span. Easily the world's largest country in terms of landmass, almost twice the size of the United States, Russia also has the ninth highest population total, at just over 140 million people, making it a force in the world labor market. With an unmatched supply of natural resources, Russia has relied heavily on its energy sectors for economic growth, exporting oil, wood, metals, and other raw materials to almost every corner of the globe.

Still in the process of transforming from a centrally planned economy to a more free-market system, Russia faces some of the same problems of other emerging economies, but also some that are very unique. A declining population, political uncertainty, and overreliance on certain sectors for growth have made some experts skeptical about Russia's future. Nevertheless, its economy continues to expand, and it remains the world's largest holder of natural resources. Russia is predicted by the World Bank to sustain a 4.6 percent gross domestic product (GDP) rate of growth through 2050—a feat that few would have predicted in 1998.

Demographics: *Unfavorable*

A nation's demographic makeup can have a major influence on its economic success. Though Russia bodes well with regard to several of these conditions, as will be demonstrated, its overall decline in population, among other factors, have made it unfavorable when compared to other emerging economies. By 2020, the Russian population is expected to decrease by almost 7 percent, or about 10 million people. Though this is rather uncommon for the BRIC+2 nations—China and India, for instance, are expected to grow by a combined 31 percent over that same time frame—it is a familiar trend in Europe and other developed countries.

As of 2007, death rates stood at 16 per 1,000 people, while birth rates were just under 11 per 1,000 people. Russian officials are cognizant of this demographic crisis, yet no actual policy has been put forth to deal with the growing concern. Russia, which is the first country in the modern world to deal with a natural decline in population, will have to tackle this problem without any precedent to follow.

Aside from military concerns, the demographic problems in Russia will mostly affect its workforce. With over 73 million people in the labor pool, Russia has only modest unemployment rates but suffers from significant underemployment, as workers are often forced to take second jobs. Unemployment, which totaled 6.6 percent in 2006, is prevalent among both women and young adults. Between 1989 and 2002, the percentage of those under the working age shrank from 25 percent to 19 percent, indicating how rapidly the population is aging.

As a result of this seemingly unfavorable population decrease, Russia's dependency ratio will increase as the population ages. Unlike China and India, where the number of inhabitants under the age of 15 is extremely large, Russia's population is almost entirely between 15 and 65. Its dependency ratio has declined over the last decade, but the trend is expected to reverse by 2010 and continue its upward pattern until at least 2025 when the nation will consist of more elderly residents in need of financial assistance (see Table 7.1).

With this trend, investors can expect Russia's demographics to increasingly hinder such factors as consumption and purchasing power in the coming years, since a larger percentage of the population will no longer be of working age and thus have less disposable income.

TABLE 7.1 **World Bank Dependency Ratios (%)**

	2000	2005	2010	2015	2020	2025
Mexico	64.26	57.22	50.81	48.13	47.38	48.18
India	62.49	58.26	54.06	50.18	47.35	46.21
Brazil	51.38	47.52	45.85	45.64	46.19	47.06
China	47.97	42.78	40.31	40.20	43.87	46.57
South Korea	39.36	39.44	38.56	37.06	39.39	46.30
Russia	43.6	40.88	37.09	38.95	42.48	47.91

Source: World Bank, 2005 data

Economic Performance: *Favorable*

Like other emerging economies, Russia's recent success can be attributed to a wide range of internal factors, such as the strength and trends of its middle class, its GDP growth, agricultural policies, and the rapid process of urbanization. Russia is ideally situated to capitalize on each of these factors and, as such, has received a favorable ranking.

GROWTH OF THE MIDDLE CLASS The ability of a nation's middle class to stimulate growth through its demands for modern goods is directly related to almost every emerging nation, and Russia proves to be no exception. Of Russia's massive population, almost 20 percent is categorized as middle class. Though small compared to industrialized countries, Russia's middle class accounts for nearly 30 percent of total GDP and, in some cases, 60 percent of GDP in the urban areas. The middle class is exceptionally entrepreneurial, investing profits into their own businesses, creating new jobs, purchasing more luxury items, and in turn fueling the nation's growth independent of government directives. Part of this mind-set stems from a general distrust of both the government and the country banking system. The Russian middle class is also relatively new, since wages were determined by the state under the Soviets. A large portion of the sector, therefore, consists of young to middle-aged professionals residing in urban areas, who have a strong proclivity for consumer goods, such as foreign cars and computers. It came as no surprise that in 2006, disposable income grew by just over 10 percent, resulting in a considerable boost in the nation's private consumption, as the demand for consumer goods skyrocketed. Since 1999, household consumption has risen 10 percent per year, surpassing exports as the leading factor of demand growth.

Though Russia's middle class is relatively small, it should be noted that the percentage of the population living below the international standard of poverty ($2 a day) stands at almost 8 percent, a low figure compared to the other BRIC+2 countries. Overall, the growth of Russia's middle class is encouraging. Real incomes have expanded by 12 percent per year, as poverty steadily declines. Just two years after the financial crisis, Russia had accumulated a budget surplus, which has been linked to the increase in domestic consumption. If expectations for the Russian economy are achieved, the middle class will likely continue to expand, which should further drive domestic consumption and GDP growth.

GDP GROWTH In 2006, Russia concluded its eighth straight of year of positive GDP growth, a remarkable accomplishment given the state of the economy in 1998. The Russian economy weathered the crisis by implementing economic reforms that encompassed taxes, banking, labor and land laws, as the government tightened its fiscal policy. Although GDP growth is primarily attributed to oil and natural gas, Russia's private sector, including wholesale, retail, banking, insurance, transportation, and communications, has grown over 10 percent in the last eight years. As the Russian economy attempts to diversify—the government is still overwhelmingly reliant on oil for revenues—it will test several methods, such as special economic zones and state-run investment funds, to try to lure uneasy investors back to the region. Economists have predicted a 7 percent rate of growth for Russia in 2007, which, if met, would make the nation the fastest growing among the G8 countries. Since 1998, Russia's GDP has jumped 37 percent, an astonishing figure given the circumstances.

SHIFT FROM AGRICULTURE The transition from a centrally planned economy to a market system affected nearly every sector of the Russian economy, particularly that of agriculture, where state farms, which had previously relied on large government subsidies, suffered through almost 10 years of declining production.

The Soviet agriculture system consisted of two main types: state farms, or *sovkhoz*, and collective farms, or *kolkhoz*. In both previous systems, farms operated by mandates from Moscow, where the government issued both quotas and prices. After the Soviet Union's collapse, more than 50 million Russians were handed deeds to their lands, and due partly to a resistance to this change, production decreased each year from 1990 to 1998. Rebounding in 2001, in part because of land code reforms, the Russian agriculture sector is expected to continue its modest increases in production, even as the sector decreases in size.

As of 2006, Russian agriculture accounted for only 5 percent of total GDP, a miniscule figure when compared to industry (22 percent) and the service sector (60 percent). Further hindering agricultural expansion is the fact that Russia, although vast in territory, has neither the land nor the climate suitable for a thriving farm system, with only 7 percent of Russia's land suitable for farming. Agricultural products rank near the bottom of Russia's exports and domestic farms account for roughly 14 percent of grain production. Rural unemployment remains high, and living standards in the farm regions are noticeably poor. Yet despite an obvious shift from agriculture to manufacturing and services, the Russian government has increased its "credits" to farms every year since 2002. This, in addition to an easing of the tax burden for both private and state-owned farms and resurgence of domestic investment in this sector, should contribute to its expected growth over the next 10 years.

URBANIZATION As mentioned earlier, Russia's population is overwhelmingly urban in composition, with almost 80 percent of the population residing in a metropolitan area. In 1970, by contrast, that figure totaled 70 percent. The nation's main cities, Moscow and St. Petersburg, account for nearly 10 percent of its total population, with 10.4 million and 4.7 million citizens, respectively. The number of people living in rural villages has slowly decreased since the early 1960s, as migration to Russia's cities increased with the demands of industrialization.

Technology: *Favorable*

The launching of Sputnik and the nuclear arms race with the United States are common reminders of the Soviet Union, one of history's most technologically sophisticated empires. Present-day Russia continues to be one of the world's innovators in technology for a variety of reasons.

Trailing only India and China as the world's leading exporter of software products, Russia's information technology (IT) sector has grown tremendously over the past seven years, averaging between 30 percent and 40 percent rates of growth per year. System and network integration, which accounts for almost 30 percent of its total market revenues, has been the staple of its technology sector.

Moreover, offshore programming, one of Russia's more lucrative service industries, has boomed in recent years. In 2005, revenues from offshore programming exceeded $1 billion. Utilizing Russia's highly educated workforce, corporations such as Motorola, Intel, Boeing, and Nortel established research and development centers inside the nation, with significant encouragement from the government. Russian programming products increased by 80 percent from 2005 to 2006, exceeding the $1.8 billion mark. With the world market of such products expected to rise to almost $100 billion by 2010, Russia is in an ideal position to further capitalize on its IT exports.

Russia's middle class has spurred domestic demand for these technological innovations, reaching 100 percent mobile penetration in 2006, as more than 140 million mobile connections were recorded, quadrupling over the span of three years. Such enthusiasm on the part of Russia's domestic market, along with the government's innovative strategy of fostering competition among providers, bodes well for the future of Russia's technological expansion. Several government officials have stated that Russia has the potential to become the world leader in mobile communications.

The Russian government will need to play a pivotal role in meeting these technological expectations, and so far it has. The construction of 10 IT "technoparks" by the end of 2010 will help increase growth in the sector, as the government continues to think outside the box. Investing from $80 to $100 million in each of the four parks and issuing various tax breaks and incentives, officials believe that Russia can further develop its niche in the IT world.

Open Trade: *Neutral*

A nation's openness to trade greatly affects its ability to expand. Trade policies that restrict and impede commerce between neighbors is typical of emerging nations. Russia's openness to the world market has increased substantially in the postcrisis years, yet there still remain several obstacles to trade, such as its fragile legal system and impractical tariffs on foreign imports; therefore, Russia has received a neutral ranking in this regard.

First, Russia's legal system is obscure, subjective, and usually serves to protect state interests. The lack of protection afforded to shareholders and property owners has been a common source of anxiety for foreign investors as well. Third, high tariff rates and discriminatory licensing and approval procedures, aside from being a problem for investors, have been major sticking points in the government's prolonged World Trade Organization (WTO) negotiations.

The U.S. government is one of many governments frequently criticizing Russia's trade practices, claiming the restrictions are excessive and protectionist, particularly in agriculture, manufacturing, and automobiles. Since 1995, tariffs and other import restrictions have ranged between 5 percent and 30 percent, and despite the modest efforts of the Russian government to reverse that trend, it remains a problem. In 2003, for instance, the government increased the customs duties on cars to 25 percent, preventing many foreign automakers from competing in its markets.

Similar protections for its aircraft industry overshadow restrictions on smaller-scale goods, such as alcohol, beef and poultry, televisions, and sugar. Though the government has relied less on tariffs and import taxes for revenue in recent years, its tendencies from the Soviet era have proven difficult to break. Despite these barriers, Russia remains a major player in the world market, and investors have taken notice. FDI, which had suffered mightily during the crisis in 1998, hit the $14 billion mark in 2005, and reached an estimated $30 billion in 2006.

Though improvements have been made in this realm, investors should remain cautious about Russia's restrictive, and often one-sided, trade policies, as such practices inherently exclude free-market competition.

Infrastructure Development: *Neutral*

Russia's infrastructure, though steadily improving, is still considered inadequate to address the demands of a developing economy, yet it equals or exceeds that of the other six sizzling BRIC+2 nations by comparison. Russian infrastructure had been deteriorating for decades, even prior to the fall of the Soviet Union, and with the transition from communism, the government had been slow to respond.

Given Russia's vast territory and the fact that the population is overwhelmingly urban, large parts of the nation lack access to modern transportation. Almost 90 percent of Russia's economic routes, such as railroads and highways, run through Moscow. Relying almost entirely on railways for the transport of goods and materials, Russia's roads are ill equipped to accommodate a developed trucking industry. The rail system ranks among the largest and most expansive in the world, with over 90,000 miles of tracks, but roughly half of that distance is designated for passenger service. Of Russia's 600,000 miles of highway, huge portions remain unpaved and receive inadequate maintenance.

Russia's waterways and airports, however, help offset the negative aspects of Russian infrastructure. With over 1,600 airports, 50 of which can accommodate international flights, Russia has greatly improved on the foundation established by the Soviet Union. Russia's waterways, which span almost 65,000 miles, serve as an efficient conduit for Russian goods in cities such as Kaliningrad, Kazan, Moscow, and St. Petersburg. The nation's merchant marine fleet has almost 800 oceangoing ships.

Russian success in developing its infrastructure has been attributed to a surge in capital investment, especially from the government. In September 2007, the Russian government promised to invest $1 trillion in the nation's infrastructure by the year 2020. Much of that investment will be allocated toward the oil industry and projects such as the 2,500-mile-long Druzhba pipeline, which connects Russia to central Europe, will likely increase in the coming years.

Though Russia's infrastructure is aging and insufficient, investors can expect sectors such as construction to boom in the coming years as the government prioritizes the developments with massive amounts of public and private funding.

Environment

Like most developing economies, Russia is plagued by a host of environmental problems and consequently receives an investment ranking of unfavorable. Years of Soviet mismanagement and irresponsibility contributed to Russia's current state. While some categories of pollution dropped as the economy contracted in the 1990s, major threats remain, and experts believe that real progress in combating these environmental hazards is years away. Among the more serious concerns is that of water pollution, as less than half of Russia's population has access to safe drinking water. Industrial sources, municipal waste, and nuclear waste combine to worsen this situation. A leading spokesman for Russia's Environmental Protection Committee stated that the cost for Russia to comply with international drinking water standards could exceed $200 billion.

Much like China, Russia's air quality is exceptionally poor, with the air in more than 200 cities exceeding international pollution limits. This situation is likely to worsen with the proliferation of automobiles and expanded highways, as added emissions negate the improvements in industrial air pollution. As Russia has become more of a consumer market, so too has it witnessed a disturbing rise in the amount of solid waste. Local municipalities, though improving, have neither the management skills nor suitable infrastructure for the disposal of such waste. Finally, problems with nuclear and chemical waste, exacerbated by the well-publicized incidents of Chernobyl and the Kursk disaster, will remain a pressing concern for both Russia and the international community.

Transparency and Rule of Law: *Unfavorable*

Steady investment cannot be sustained without a strong legal structure that is capable of enforcing a nation's laws and regulations. If the rights of shareholders are not upheld, investments will rapidly deteriorate, as they did for Russia in 1998. As such, Russia has an unfavorable ranking of transparency and rule of law.

While the Russian government has enacted several reforms, its legal apparatus remains a source of apprehension among investors, as Russia lags behind all the other six sizzling BRIC+2 nations in this regard. Contract enforcement, specifically, has been a major obstacle to investment. Because Russia's court system is in the process of transformation, it is inherently weak and unable to compel parties one way or another. Without a strong legal foundation, agreements between investors and the business community are reliant almost exclusively on personal relationships. Corporate governance, or lack thereof, highlights another shortfall of the Russian legal system. Security of ownership, where a privatization deal can be rescinded up to 10 years after it is signed, has discouraged many investors from long-term commitments.

Financial regulations also play a part in Russia's investment climate. Though its banking sector has largely recovered from the crisis, major reforms and restructuring have been slow to take shape, as bureaucratic obstacles remain. State-run banks still dominate the sector, and the Russian government has shown few signs of altering this policy.

In spite of these and other issues of transparency and law, the situation in Russia is improving. A 2002 survey by the Economist Intelligence Unit (EIU) of 75 multinational corporations operating inside Russia found that:

- 82 percent of respondents felt that the economic situation in Russia was improving.
- 66 percent believed that the tax system showed signs of progress.

TABLE 7.2 World Bank Governance Indicators*

Country	Political stability	Government effectiveness	Regulatory quality	Control of corruption	Rule of law	Average
Brazil	43.3	52.1	54.1	47.1	41.4	47.6
China	33.2	55.5	46.3	37.9	45.2	43.6
India	22.1	54.0	48.3	52.9	57.1	46.9
South Korea	60.1	82.9	70.7	64.6	72.9	70.2
Mexico	32.7	60.7	63.4	46.6	40.5	48.8
Russia	23.6	37.9	33.7	24.3	19.0	27.7

*Percentile rank: 0–100. Percentile rank scores indicate the percentage of countries that rank below the selected country.

- More than half categorized Russia as a favorable investment opportunity.
- More than 80 percent reported making profits.
- More than 70 percent reported hiring new personnel.

The prevention of more capital flight, as well as the acquisition of new foreign investments, will be determined by the government's eagerness to adopt reforms in the realm of law and transparency. If its postcrisis behavior is any indication, there is reason to believe that Russia will make serious attempts to comply with international norms as it attempts to gain membership into the WTO (see Table 7.2).

Education and Training: *Favorable*

The Russian educational system ranks among the finest in the world, as evidenced by the nation's 100 percent literacy rate. Thus, it is no surprise that it has an investment ranking of favorable.

In the Soviet tradition, subjects such as math, science, and engineering continue to be the major focus of Russia's students, who flood the labor market with expertise in a variety of areas. With over 700 institutions of higher education, Russia has more academic graduates than any other European nation. As a percentage, Russia ranks ahead of the United States in terms of middle-aged residents with an advanced degree.

Though well educated, Russia's workforce still suffers from unemployment, as the application of such knowledge is complicated by the transition to a supply-and-demand market economy. Russian graduates often find their expertise is not appropriately utilized. For example, as of 2004, 1.3 million Russians held degrees in computer science engineering and related fields, and only 70,000 were employed in the IT sector. For the most part however, that trend is changing, as Russia's IT industry has grown beyond expectations in recent years. Tech-savvy graduates, who during the Soviet years would have been assigned to military duties, are now utilizing their skills in the private sector, fueling Russia's growth in software engineering and services. *Brain drain,* a term coined to describe the emigration of scientists, doctors, and other educated professionals from Russia in the late 1980s, is no longer a major concern.

The expertise of Russia's educated workforce have made the nation a hotbed for technological investments, and this trend is expected to continue well into the coming years, as the nation will remain a source of some of the world's brightest, most innovative minds.

Sound Financial Systems and Policies: *Unfavorable*

Russian fiscal and monetary policy of the precrisis years bears little resemblance to the Russia of today. An economy paralyzed in 1998, Russia has had a growing surplus since 2001, as much of the revenues generated from a rise in world oil prices were saved. The new tax laws of that year implemented a 13 percent flat tax for both individuals and corporations, simplifying the tax collection process across all sectors. Even so, the Russian government still faces domestic pressure to curb spending, while inflation and sudden exchange rate appreciation continues to be a major concern.

The fiscal policy of Russia, though far from perfect, still managed to attract over $30 billion in FDI in 2006. Though much of this investment growth is derived from Russia's recent consumer and retail surge, a large percentage has been attributed to its financial services and telecommunications sector.

Russia's Growth Industries

By now it is clear to the individual investor that emerging markets opportunities, though abundant, are often difficult to access. Russia is no exception and presents a greater difficulty, as its economy is one of the newest emerging markets with a very short history. According to Oleg Biryulyov of JP Morgan's Russian Fund, there are currently about 100 tradable Russian stocks of any meaningful size out of almost 2,000 companies. There is a substantial lack of equity culture, typical of the Russian population, who has shied away from owning shares in domestic companies. For U.S. investors, opportunities continue to reside in a handful of Russian country funds, emerging-market funds, or American Depositary Receipts (ADRs; see Appendix D).

Capitalizing on Russia's impressive rates of growth requires an examination of its industry outside that of oil and natural gas. Though fossil

TABLE 7.3 MSCI RUSSIA Index Sector Weights (as of September 12, 2007)*

Economic sector (Global Industry Classification System)	Float-adjusted shares (% of investable index market capitalization)
Consumer	16
Financials	14
Natural Resources	12
Utilities	13
Cellular Telecom	9

*Industry sectors are classified according to the Global Industry Classification System (GICS) developed jointly by Standard & Poor's and Morgan Stanley Capital International (MSCI). The GICS consists of 10 economic sectors covering 24 industry groups, further segmented into industries and sub industries. The MSCI country indexes sector weights represent 85 percent of the investable market capitalization of each economic sector of the country's economy. The index is rebalanced several times a year to ensure the index sector weights continue to reflect the underlying economy.

fuels continue to generate significant revenue for the Russian government, investors have found sectors such as consumer goods, financial services, telecommunications, and others to be extremely profitable. Only 5 percent of Russia's oil industry is tradable, as the government keeps the lucrative sector under its own control. The industry does not even rank in Russia's top five according to the Morgan Stanley Capital International (MSCI) index (see Table 7.3). Thus, the market capitalization is extremely dispersed, especially for a developing economy.

In the case of Russia, therefore, we have departed slightly from using the MSCI country index in order to better focus on the Russian economy's more dominant industries. Instead, we have opted to highlight the DAX Global Russia Index (see Table 7.4), which is comprised of companies with market capitalization greater than $150 million that have an average trading volume of at least $1 million over six months.

In the remainder of the chapter, we will highlight the most viable investment opportunities available to the individual investor.

TABLE 7.4 DAX Russia Index Sector Weights (as of September 31, 2007)

Economic sector	Float-adjusted shares (% of investable index market capitalization)
Natural Gas and Oil	39
Telecommunications	18
Electrics	11
Financials	8
Others	5

Natural Gas

The success of the Russian economy has depended largely on the world's growing demand for energy, as oil and natural gas constitute its main source of revenue. Russia is the world's leader in natural gas production and its third leading producer of oil, and is likely to remain or advance in that regard in the coming years.

Natural gas in Russia is dominated by a few select companies, the most notable of which is Gazprom. Inherited from the Soviet Union, Gazprom essentially holds a monopoly on the natural gas sector, yet despite its dominance of the market, the company will likely require a significant amount of infrastructure upgrade, as much of its structure is aging and inefficient. Nevertheless, natural gas remains the primary source of Russia's energy consumption, accounting for over 50 percent of total use in 2004. With almost two quadrillion cubic feet of proven natural gas reserves, this domestic reliance is expected to continue well into the coming decades.

Gazprom

Founded in 1989, Gazprom has become largest natural gas company on the globe, holding almost 20 percent of the world's total natural gas reserves and exporting to over 30 countries, primarily the European Union and eastern Europe. Despite its huge share of the market—the company controls 90 percent of Russia's domestic market—Gazprom continues to be among Russia's more progressive companies, as it spends a considerable amount of its capital in geological exploration and other prospects.

Though a majority of the company is controlled by the Russian government, Gazprom now offers foreign investors the opportunity to purchase shares. In 2005, the price of the company's share rose nearly threefold, and foreign investors were eager to get in on the purchase. Dubbed the "big bang" of the Russian economy, Gazprom going public was seen as a long-awaited move for outside investors, and one that would attract thousands of investors from across the world. In the first three days that the companies stock was traded publicly, its price increased 24 percent, with the amount of trades expanding as well. Energy disputes with Ukraine, an uneasy political environment, and other problems on the periphery have done little to deter investors from purchasing Gazprom stock. In all likelihood, the company will remain one of Russia's more attractive investment opportunities.

Source: www.gazprom.com

Foreign demand for natural gas is also likely to persist, as Russia will continue to export natural gas to all parts of Europe. An intense examination of the country's reserves is also expected to turn up new, more convenient sources of natural gas, as almost three quarters of its current production comes from the Siberian fields in the western part of the nation, which, given Russia's harsh terrain, are often difficult to access. Yet as the nation's overall infrastructure improves, so too will the productivity of Russia's natural gas production, making the sector highly sought after from an investment perspective.

Oil

Russia is the world's leading exporter of oil outside the Organization of Petroleum Exporting Countries (OPEC) nations. Russia's oil sector has undergone a significant process of privatization over the last decade and a half. Russia's oil industry was segmented into almost fifteen separate companies as part of the massive economic reforms of the mid-1990s. Despite having some of the same problems as other Russian economic spheres (poor infrastructure and issues of law and transparency), Russian oil continues to be the economy's most lucrative sector. With oil reserve estimates exceeding 60 billion barrels, Russia compensates for its shortcomings with vast supplies. In 2006, over 70 percent of Russia's crude oil production went to supply outside nations, primarily through pipelines such as the Druzhba pipeline, which alone was responsible for over 12 million barrels per day of exports. The pipeline extends to central and eastern Europe.

Prominent Oil and Gas Companies

- LukOil
- Rosneft Oil
- Gazprom Neft
- Unified Energy Systems

Cellular Telecommunications

Russia's cellular telecommunications industry has grown tremendously over the last eight years, due to the surge in consumer spending. Among the industry leaders is VimpelCom, one of Russia's most well-known and profitable telecommunications companies. With over 47 million subscribers inside Russia, the telecom giant recorded $1.7 billion in operating revenues in the second quarter of the 2007 fiscal year. Introducing Russia to its first dual-band cellular network while presently developing more wireless telecommunications services, VimpelCom reaches about 139 million people, or 95 percent of the total population, in almost 80 regions of the country. Foreign investors have become quite familiar with VimpelCom, as it was the first company in Russia to list its shares on the New York Stock Exchange.

Financials

Russia's financial sector is modest in size when compared to developed economies, yet it accounts for a large percentage of foreign investment. U.S. investors, for instance, exported nearly $30 billion to Russia's financial services sector in 2005. As this sector becomes increasingly open to the outside world, it is also likely to diversify. Financial companies such as Sberbank presently account for an overwhelming percentage of the market.

External shocks, rather than voluntary reform, have been attributed to changes in Russia's financial sector over the last seven years, as financial crises in both Asia and Russia prompted the government to reform its pension laws, among other things. Even as Russia rebounds from its financial crisis and wages increase, the average Russian remains skeptical about putting funds into banks. The high rates of consumption in Russia coincide with extremely low rates of savings, with around only 2 percent of Russian households investing in a private mutual fund. This trend, however, is expected to reverse. As Russia's financial institutions benefit from legal and political stability, they will be likely to gain the trust of a middle class with an abundance of wealth to invest.

Sberbank

Sberbank, also known as the Savings Bank of the Russian Federation, is easily Russia's largest financial institution, with over 20,000 branches across the country. Sberbank has about 30 percent of the market share and based on that, we can estimate that the entire Russian banking sector has a market capitalization of about $240 billion. Sberbank has about 60 percent market share in mortgages and is likely to keep its position in this segment. The bank will benefit from higher consumption, more diversified products, and more lending and banking activity. Though the Central Bank of Russia holds almost 60 percent of its total assets, foreign investors have found Sberbank to be a major source of profit. With the rise of the Russian consumer, Sberbank has extended its lending to over one million corporate entities and almost 250,000 residents. Aside from capitalizing on Russia's newfound consumer climate, Sberbank has benefitted from the nation's bold plans for infrastructure development as well as its energy-producing capabilities. Financing projects ranging from the construction of power stations to chemical facilities, Sberbank's status as the nation's top financial lender is unquestioned.

Source: www.sbrf.ru/eng (Sberbank)

Prominent Financial Service Company

- Open Investments

Consumer

Despite a growing income disparity, overall purchasing power in Russia is booming, with plenty of room for further growth. In 2004, disposable income grew by almost 20 percent, and a sharp rise in the purchase of consumer goods and services soon followed. Currently, Russia's per-capita GDP is about $7,000, or 10 times that of China and India, allowing it to compete with larger economies despite its relatively smaller population.

As mentioned earlier, Russia's expanding middle class has fueled increases in consumption every year since 2000. Russia's main cities (primarily Moscow and St. Petersburg), have become national centers of culture and lifestyle, where malls selling luxury goods are frequented by thousands of shoppers every day. Roughly 20 percent of Russia's consumers fall into the high-consumption category. This consumer demographic has a strong affinity for branded goods and often purchases in excess everything from clothing and electronics to cosmetics, food, and beverages, as well as foreign cars and various retail goods. Foreign companies such as Nestle, Coca-Cola, and others were quick to provide Russia's emerging middle class with outlets for spending their increased wages.

Prominent Local Consumer Companies

- Wimm-Bill-Dann
- SUN Interbrew
- Pyaterochka
- Metro AG
- Eldorado
- Ikea
- Sportmaster

Mining and Metals

Russia has long been a world leader in mineral production. Accounting today for almost 20 percent of the world's nickel and cobalt production, 40 percent of palladium, 15 percent of platinum, and around 8 percent of coal and iron, Russia continues this trend, strengthening its standing in the international market for natural resources. Devoting a significant amount of capital to prospecting and upgrades, the Russian mining sector continues to search for more productive methods of mineral extraction and exportation. With a large percentage of its natural resources east of the Ural mountain range, and therefore difficult to access, the future success of Russia's mining sector will depend largely on its ability to improve its infrastructure.

Though private investors make up a significant share of ownership, Russia's mining and metals industry remains under the direction of the government's Ministry of Natural Resources, which charges a 6 percent gross royalty tax on all mining companies.

Norilsk Nickel

Norilsk Nickel is the largest producer of nickel, copper, cobalt, platinum, and palladium in Russia. Estimated to produce about 75 percent of Russia's copper and more than 90 percent of its nickel output, Norilsk Nickel holds roughly a 45 percent share of the world's nickel market. Involved in exploration, prospecting, extraction, and other similar practices, Norilsk Nickel is devoted to remaining a key player in the world market for natural resources. In 2006, the company increased its revenues from roughly $7 billion to over $11 billion, with net profits rising from 32 percent to 43 percent.

Source: www.nornik.ru/en (Norilsk Nickel)

Though Russia faces its fair share of problems as it shifts from a centrally planned economy, such as its aging population and murky trade policies, its prospects for overcoming these obstacles remain sound, as evidenced by the country's educated workforce and abundance of natural resources. As it continues to recover from its economic collapse in 1998, Russia figures to remain a major player in the high-stakes market for oil, natural gas, and other fuels. Not to be ignored by investors, however, is Russia's likely ascent to become of one the world's forerunners of technology, entering the company of nations such as China, India, and the United States in that regard. And it is consumerism, not communism, which is Russia's most powerful ideology. As the standard of living in the former Soviet Union remarkably improves, so will the demand for goods and services. In short, investors would be wise to remember that Russian oil and gas are not the only Russian industries capable of prosperity.

CHAPTER 8

A State of Mind

The History of India

India is held by strong but invisible threads ... about her there is an elusive quality of a legend of long ago; some enchantment seems to have held her mind. She is myth and an idea, a dream and a vision and yet very real and pervasive.

—Jawaharlal Nehru, India's first prime minister

India is a nation, a state, a republic, a culture, and an experiment. It is a dream embodied by its ancient creators as a repository of values, traditions, mysticism, philosophy, and religious thought. The modern world of science, technology, and economic progress confronts and conforms with the ancient and spiritual culture of this great land. The metaphysical realm and the material growth of this burgeoning country collide, but then compromise in an ongoing drama played out millions of times a day. This is the story of modern India.

This ancient land, dating by some accounts over five millennia, has held global sway at different times but until very recently has been mostly ignored. The country, now home to a billion people, is an unorthodox amalgam of civilizations, religions, and languages. This land of unimaginable diversity is suddenly being pushed onto the world stage with alacrity and an aplomb not seen since the Portuguese Vasco de Gama landed on the western coast of Cochin in 1492 and opened India to the west.

Origins of New Civilization

India's origins, like many early civilizations, are shrouded in mystery, are hard to decipher, and continue to be the focus of vigorous debate. The ruins of Mohenjo-Daro and Harrapa (both now in Pakistan) are some of the early archeological finds and were only discovered in 1920s. The early "Indus Valley civilization" has drawn comparisons to Egypt and Mesopotamia and was later named the Harrapan civilization. These ruins show the remnants of structures made mostly of brick, which was both sun baked and kiln fired. Carbon dating suggests the dates of these ruins to be between 3000 and 1700 BC. The native and indigenous people inhabiting these lands are said to be Dravidians. The biggest and the longest-lasting civilization in India, however, by most accounts was the result of mass migration (or aggression). This civilization, known as the Aryan civilization, is believed to have descended from central Asia between 1500 and 1300 BC. This civilization is credited with the ancient literature and philosophy, language, and religion. The epic books of Mahabharata and Vedas, written in the ancient language of Sanskrit, form the philosophical basis of this civilization. Vedic Philosophy, as these scriptures are popularly called, spans all the spheres of life from daily living to diplomacy and from statecraft to the rules of war making. These ancient scriptures have also formed the building blocks of the most permanent of India's religions—Hinduism. Based on these ancient texts, as early as 900 to 500 BC, the Aryan civilization had developed tools of agriculture and begun to grow crops such as rice wheat and barley.

Rise of New Religions: Early Invaders

Hinduism, a legacy of the Aryan civilization, is more a way of life than a religion. However, a new prominent religion originated after the Siddhartha Gautama "Buddha" in the eastern part of India in 400 to 300 BC, who set on a quest to inquire about the mystery of human condition. It is believed that he attained enlightenment under a tree after a prolonged meditation in "Buddha Gaya" (present-day Bihar state) when he was 35. Thus, Buddhism, one of the most prolific religions, was born. There were other religions such as Jainism, which was inspired by Mahavihara and included strict adherence to nonviolence and avoidance of harming any living beings, including insects.

These religions and sects became absorbed by the broader Hinduism, which acted as a big tent for competing philosophies.

However, soon the invasions into the "land of Arya" started looking for adventure as well as treasure. Invasions to India by foreigners were treacherous. This land is naturally protected in the northwest by the Hindu Kush mountains in what is today's Afghanistan, in the north by Himalayan peaks, and in the northeast by Tibet and China. In the south, the Indian landscape forms a peninsula, which is surrounded by the waters of the

Arabian Sea in the west and the Bay of Bengal to the east. These were the natural barriers presented to foreign invaders who, through folklore, had dreamed about an entry into this land of plenty with golden temples and jewels of Deccan Plateau.

Alexander the Great—Prize Unattained

One of the earliest adventures to this land was by Alexander the Great, a Macedonian. Alexander's great adventure was not the invasion itself but the challenge of getting there. Alexander reached India through Anatolia (modern Turkey) in 334–333 BC, after his successful adventures in Syria, Palestine, Egypt, and Libya. He was 25 years old and had already amassed the largest empire to date and was looking for the next big prize: India. He pushed south through Arachosia (Afghanistan), crossing the Hindu Kush through Uzbekistan, and by 327 BC was close to Kabul. He had a ready force of 50,000 battle-hardened soldiers with him ready to cross India's northwest frontier. He ran into a great resistance near Taxila by King Porus. A death struggle ensued. Alexander's cavalry and overwhelming force carried the day against Porus's chariots and elephants. Porus's valiant fight against Alexander the Great, which he survived, continues to be a footnote of Indian bravado even to this day. Alexander's sojourn to India, however, was short and unprecedented. He had suffered through India's harsh mountains and deep skepticism of his army bordering on mutiny, and he withdrew and headed back to his conquered lands. During his return, he suffered a punctured chest. He died of hepatoma within two years after his return from his long adventure, his dream of returning to India unfulfilled forever.

Ashoka: The King Who Refused to Fight

Ashoka, a king who ruled between 268 and 233 BC, was the third king in the proud dynasty of Maurayas. As with most kings, he saw his primary duty to protect, consolidate, and expand his empire. He embarked on a campaign to conquer Kalinga (today's Orissa) around 260 BC. The battle was particularly brutal, as close to 100,000 people were slain and an additional 150,000 were deported or perished. This incident would have hardly deserved a mention in the history of the period except for the most breathtaking turn of events, which makes Ashoka and Kalinga stand out as a major event in Indian history. On conquering Kalinga, King Ashoka felt disgusted and dramatically remorseful of his actions in causing death and destruction and stated: "When an independent country is conquered, the slaughter, death, and deportation of people is extremely grievous."

Ashoka became a convert to Buddhism and forswore violence and dispatched missionaries around the world to spread the message of non-violence and peace. The inscriptions of Ashoka are the monuments in many corners of India, and pillars or *stupas* have become an important part of Indian heritage.

Muslim Invasions

The Muslim invasion on Indian territory mostly from the northwest started soon after prophet Muhammad died in 632 AD. His followers were imbued with zeal to spread the word of the prophet and outran states such as the Byzantine empire in Syria and Egypt, the Sassanid empire in Iraq and Iran, and North Africa, Spain, and Afghanistan and central Asia. The Muslim invasions of the day were the largest conquests to date and stretched from Arabia to Indus. By the year 700, China and India shared their borders with Muslim neighbors, who were as hungry to spread the word of the prophet Mohammad as they were eager for plunder and treasures.

To get to the territories of India presented a vast challenge; however, once there, Indians were easy prey. India was divided into small kingdoms ruled by monarchs who suffered from greed and insane jealousy. The Muslim invaders had fighting armies, which would dwarf any of the local fighting forces. There was the Arab conquest of Sind (modern Pakistan) in the eighth century. The Muslim invaders were aware that India's economy was one of the most sophisticated, with advanced knowledge of science, mathematics, and languages and a deep adherence to religion. There also was a large treasure of gold and silver, which in many cases adorned the Hindu temples. Therefore, an attack on Hindu temples served a twin purpose: providing the precious bounty of gold and silver statues as well as destruction of the temples, which fulfilled their desire to rid the world of idolatry as practiced in Hindu temples—anathema to the tenets of Islam. Once in power, they also imposed *Jizya,* a religious tax on nonbelievers of Islam and those who were unwilling to convert to the Islamic faith.

In a curious turn of events, even Genghis Khan, a Mongol, crossed into India in 1222, which also created a large influx of Muslim refugees from Genghis Khan's invading army from India's neighbors to the North.

Mughals—Invaders Who Built a Dynasty

Of all the Muslim rulers who ruled India, the ones who have left a lasting legacy are the Mughals. They dominated the life of the country for over two centuries. The first Mughal invader to come by way of Persia and Afghanistan was Babur. In order to succeed, he had to fight the current ruler, Sikandar Lodhi, around 1505. Babur's campaign, in which he was aided by his son Himayun, lasted about a quarter of a century. Babur laid the foundation for an empire that has left an indelible mark on Indian culture, history, art, language, and, above all, architecture. He died at age 90, having assured for himself and his dynasty a place no foreign invader other than the British have been able to duplicate.

King Akbar, the third king in Mughal dynasty, not only consolidated and extended the empire, but also was a philosopher king who wanted to bridge the two religions of Hinduism and Islam into a new religious philosophy called *Din Ilahi* or "Voices of God." Later, the great Mughal, Shah Jahan, who ruled from 1627 to 1658, built the architectural masterpiece, Taj Mahal, in honor of his beloved wife, Mumtaz Mahal. His fate, however, takes a turn for the worse when his son, Aurangzeb, later imprisons him in an Agra fort. Shah Jahan dies in 1666, while confined to his prison cell and in painful view of the Taj Mahal across the Jamuna River.

Aurangzeb was one of the last Mughals to rule. He was ruthless, and with cunning zeal liquidated his brothers and expanded his empire. But he was also an extremely pious Muslim—he banned music and dance and was determined to create an Islamic footprint wherever he went.

British Company Creates an Empire

Foreign business interests were quite active in India from the early days after the Portuguese landing on the coast of Calcutta in 1492. The Portuguese ruled the tiny enclave of Goa on the western coast until 1961, long after India was free from British domination. The French retained the tiny possession of Pondicherry on the eastern coast. However, it was the British who were particularly determined to get access to India in order to extend their empire. It was with this backdrop that a company called the East India Company received a charter in 1600 and petitioned the Mughal emperor to receive an imperial directive called *Farman,* which would guarantee a favorable access to the company as a trading partner.

The East India Company's trading consisted of exports of cotton textiles, silk, molasses, saltpeter, and indigo, and was quite profitable to its English stockholders. The Company was primarily stationed in the port city of Calcutta. The East India Company carried with it contingents of soldiers. There were serious conflicts along the way; one of the most serious conflicts was at Plassey in 1757 against the local ruler, which also resulted in many British casualties, including the famous "Black Hole" (of Calcutta) where many British occupants of a building suffocated to death. The East India

Company's operations in Calcutta, Bombay, and Madras were run as virtual governments, in which the president or "governor" exercised full control, including judicial powers. The Company's power and fortune expanded to other parts of India; by 1790, they were controlling parts of the south, and by 1800, they had wrested control of new provinces including Delhi, which became a mainstay of Pax Britannica. The British expansion continued into the northern territories of Punjab and Sind and Afghanistan by the middle of the nineteenth century. The battles with the local forces were sometimes long and tedious, particularly against the bravery of local armies such as the Punjabis, Rajputs, and Marathas—the elite martial races who struggled but suffered defeat after defeat. The combination of superior arms and discipline served the British well. There were, however, stirrings of dissatisfaction in the air.

First Mutiny

The year 1857 is called by many Indians the first war of independence. This was the first serious collective challenge to English might. The local soldiers or *sepoys* objected because they suspected that the cartridges provided to them by the English were coated with either pig or beef talon. For Hindus, beef is forbidden, and for Muslims, pork is forbidden. The incident set off a mutiny, which spread far and wide for a while, but finally petered out by September 1857.

There was one important change, however: In 1858, Queen Victoria specifically took control of the colony and disclaimed any "desire to impose our conviction on any of our subjects" and ordered British officials to abstain from interfering with Indian beliefs or rituals "on the pain of our highest displeasure." The East India Company continued to retain its business interests. The British crown was represented by a viceroy, who was empowered with great authority to act on the queen's behalf.

A Nation Awakens

By 1880, there was restlessness among citizens, and by December 1885, the first Indian National Congress was convened. This was not a movement but more of a forum to express grievances. Soon, the agenda was expanded to demand curtailing of imports in order to improve local economy. The *Swedeshi* (meaning "our own") movement began to catch fire, particularly against British textiles. The export of raw jute and yarn and silk to England and import of finished goods from England to India meant work for factories in England at the expense of local jobs. The masses joined in from a call by their leaders in the Congress party to protest and shun the use of foreign imports, particularly of textiles. The spinning wheel became a major symbol for such a movement to encourage people to spin from raw yarn and wear clothes devoid of any foreign labor. The next step in the movement was demand for self-rule, and in 1906, Congress passed a resolution demanding *swaraj* or "self-rule."

Gandhi Appears

Mohandas Karamchand Gandhi, a British-trained barrister, was working in South Africa and had gotten involved in protecting the rights of minorities there. He now was making his way to India and soon plunged headlong into the Indian struggle. After a brief delay, he launched *satyagraha* or civil disobedience in 1919—something he had briefly tried first in South Africa. This was a unique test and had never been tried before. It meant that protesters would resort to breaking the law but do so without using any violence. The results were mixed. The English resorted to jailing all the major leaders, including Gandhi, Nehru, and Patel and a host of others. During this time, there was a massacre in Amritsar by General Dwyer when he ordered fire on civilians who were assembled for a peaceful protest, and over 1,200 people, including women and children, were killed.

Protests grew in intensity, and so did the reaction by the English. Gandhi became the guiding light of the movement with its unique and untested nonviolent struggle. His Salt March in 1930–1931, to protest the salt tax by breaking the law and making sea salt, was a masterstroke, along with his numerous hunger strikes, that proved tactically difficult for the English.

The Congress party gained strength as a national movement; new leaders such as Jawaharlal Nehru provided the inspiration for the people. By 1920, Gandhi and Nehru and the Congress party were unified in asking for *swaraj*. The English responded, and there were elections in provinces.

Divide and Rule Works

There were wrinkles appearing in the national agenda, however, and with a clever divide-and-rule policy the English took advantage of any disagreement between communities, particularly between Hindus and Muslims. A major stumbling block was the lack of unified goals between the Congress party and the predominant Muslim party, known as the Muslim League, which was headed by Mohamed Ali Jinnah, another British-trained lawyer. The Muslim League remained steadfast in wanting to divide the Muslim majority areas into a separate country called Pakistan. Congress steadfastly opposed the plan to break the country into two parts.

The freedom movement, however, was gaining ground. By 1942, Congress had moved its agenda from "self-rule" to "Quit India." There was no looking back. World War II was raging. Indian Congress leaders supported the British war efforts but insisted on achieving full freedom.

In February 1947, British Prime Minister Earl Attlee declared that the British rule would end by June 1948. However, it became clear that there was likely to be no compromise between the Muslim League's demand of the partition of the country and the Congress party's desire to keep the country a single unit. But partition of the country into Muslim majority Pakistan (which also included East Pakistan—now Bangladesh) and India was a *fait accompli*. In March 1947, Lord Louis Mountbatten was appointed the last viceroy to oversee the conclusion of two centuries of British domination over the subcontinent. The die was cast.

On August 14, 1947, a new nation of Pakistan under Mohammad Ali Jinnah raised its white flag with green crescent in its new capital of Karachi. This move toward independence was overseen by Lord Mountbatten. On August 15, 1947, he flew to New Delhi, the capital of Independent India, to see Jawaharlal Nehru lower the Union Jack and replace it with the tricolor flag of India. A new nation was thus born.

The Mixed Blessing of Independence

After more than three centuries of subjugation, India achieved independence from Great Britain in 1947. On the eve of independence, freedom fighter and newly elected Prime Minister Jawaharlal Nehru spoke at the historic Red Fort in New Delhi. Moved by the historical significance of the moment, he declared:

> *At the stroke of midnight hour, when the world sleeps, India will awake to life and freedom. A moment comes, which comes but rarely in history, when we step out from the old to the new, when an age ends and when the soul of a nation long suppressed finds utterance. It is fitting that at this solemn moment we take the pledge of dedication to the service of India and her people and to the still larger cause of humanity.*

Following independence, the people of this massive nation dreamed of serving as a model of freedom and democratic values around the world and bringing a future of hope and a better life to its own citizens. But these dreams remained largely unfulfilled as the international political and economic storm winds of the latter part of the twentieth century did not favor this massive South Asian nation.

Jawaharlal Nehru

Nehru became a champion of India, particularly after the tragic assassination in 1948 of Mahatma Gandhi, who was gunned down by a radical, primarily for his religious tolerance. Nehru inherited a country paradoxically imbued with a spirit of achievement shackled by poverty. The country was free to innovate but enslaved by tradition, its caste system, and a lack of modern education, particularly for women. It was Nehru's vision of a secular, free, and dynamic democratic republic—so demonstrative of his lauded foresight—that would be his framework for achieving national greatness. In order to reach this vision, one of Nehru's early goals was to create an extensive network of educational institutions to inform and liberate the young.

Another of Nehru's goals was to establish international relationships with the world's superpowers—the West and the Soviet Union. In establishing these diplomatic relations, Nehru and his Congress party engaged in projects that benefited the indigenous populations of India. For example, they collaborated with the West as well as the Soviet Union to build massive steel plants and use the vast natural resources of iron ore and coal.

Simultaneously, the government embarked on the massive dam-building projects of Bhakra Nangal in the northern state of Punjab. This project would serve the multifaceted purpose of mitigating the scourge of the annual floods due to monsoons, creating the largest source of hydroelectric power in the country, and channeling the water to the fields of Punjab. This initiative made an already fertile region even more abundant in grain, and became a staple source of trade for the nation.

The Real Awakening—Tiger or Elephant?

From the point of its independence, the Indian economy was a curious mixture of state control, protective private enterprise, and labor union domination. To a large extent, it drew its inspiration from the socialist model.

The socialist movement presented itself as the salvation of the masses, providing the burgeoning population opportunities beyond their meager existence. From steel mills to coal mines, power to the then-luxurious telephone service, and roads to railways, the entire infrastructure development process was handed to state-owned enterprises. Even heavy industry, automobile manufacture, and later-stage finance dealings were in the hands of the faceless and nameless: the unelected bureaucrats. The protection of these nascent industries was the operative rationale of the regime. The goal was to provide jobs and benefits to the masses and to prevent the exploitation of the poor. As is often the case with utopian philosophies that fall victim to temptation, all of this had somewhat predictable results and unintended consequences. Corruption became rampant in the licensing and quota system, with the intended subsidies never making it to the hands that were truly in need. The exports, though encouraged, never materialized, largely due to shortages in domestic supply and inefficient production.

For 44 years after India's independence, the economy and the country as a whole sank to new depths. The bureaucrats who controlled the state enterprises became the powerful elite, not unlike the old colonial powers. Even in a working democracy, all of the economic decisions of consequence were left in the hands of civil servants who ran their fiefdoms from their protected enclaves—with the nod and wink of elected officials.

This political structure has greatly affected India's economy. According to an article in *Time* magazine, 104 of the 237 public-sector companies had losses amounting to 40 billion rupees, or over $1 billion, from 1992 to 1993. India's utilities public sector lost $2.2 billion (70 billion rupees) in the preceding 12 months.

India produced steel at $650 per ton when the world market was at $500 per ton, even though it had enough raw materials to shadow the production of South Korea, which operated with the handicap of importing its coal and iron ore.

The Indian rulers of the day suffered from an "East India Company complex." The British company had taken hold of small businesses in Calcutta 200 years prior, and its home nation went on to rule Indian people until their independence. Protectionist inclinations were ingrained in the subconscious mind-set of the rulers, who then fell prey to their own slogan of self-reliance instead of seeking an active role in globalization. They then sold the country on such rationales.

To them, their neighbor to the north, the colossal superpower of the Soviet Union with its centralized economy, was doing well (or so the story went). To initiate the capitalist model of the United States was pure heresy—particularly where America was bent on power alliances—and had no sympathizers in the Congress party, who viewed them with distrust. The American alliance with sworn enemy Pakistan, whose dictatorships enjoyed a cozy relationship with Washington, D.C., further supported their domestically driven policies. The three wars with Pakistan, and one failed engagement with China, only aggravated the issue. There was little room for compromise, and a prevailing atmosphere of apprehension toward foreign overtures.

The labor unions, with their vested interest of protected jobs and benefits, used their political muscle to control the politicians. They engaged in strikes, both violent and nonviolent, each time a politician raised his voice in order to curtail the wasteful, inefficient state enterprises.

At any sign of opening the economy, there were fierce howls of protest from those powerful elite with their fortunes tied to perpetuating the noncompetitive environment, and even larger shortages. It would take months, years, sometimes longer for an honest businessman to get a license to open a new enterprise. Not surprisingly, the process was particularly difficult if the proposed venture were competing with a government enterprise.

The Drama of the Unmaking

History drove India inevitably to have a deep and intense suspicion of foreigners, trade, and capitalism. These negative feelings greatly affected their economic structure, as politicians feared a backlash if they suggested anything that changed the status quo. As a result, things initially remained the same—a large part of India's population was still deeply entrenched in low-productivity agriculture and lived in villages under subsistence conditions. The country continued to suffer from very low literacy rates. The government was wedded to the socialist economic system and was therefore unable (or unwilling) to unshackle the masses from this poverty.

Real economic growth in the first three decades following independence was a mere 3.5 percent per year, dubbed the "Hindu rate of growth" because it was both disappointing and widely accepted with resignation—disappointing because India was falling steadily behind other Asian transition economies and widely accepted because India's socialist regime was strongly influenced by its history, choosing a policy of dogged self-sufficiency and isolation from the outside world.

In the late 1980s, according to India's Bureau of Industrial Costs and Prices, the rate of return on capital in state-owned enterprises averaged barely 1.5 percent, with many cases of negative returns. Absent foreign competition, the costs of these inefficiencies were simply passed through in the form of either higher prices or higher taxes. This problem was exacerbated by India's policy of not allowing firms to fail. At the end of 1987, there were 160,000 firms that were currently operating at a loss and whose liabilities exceeded their assets.

To make matters worse, severe political difficulties, including Hindu militancy and Hindu-Muslim riots, disrupted transport and production, reducing economic growth and dramatically shrinking government revenue. These events produced a rapid and severe deterioration in the economy. India's foreign exchange reserves fell by half between September and December 1990, with barely enough to cover 20 days of the imports by year-end. Inflation reached an unprecedented rate of 12 percent. Faced with mounting deficits, the government borrowed more while inflation continued to rise, the trade deficit widened, and both domestic and foreign debt increased substantially.

Time for Economic Reform

Economic reforms introduced in the 1980s focused on import liberalization, especially of capital goods and intermediate inputs, and the extension of tax incentives for exports. However, the impenetrable labyrinth of import controls, known as the *license raj*, remained largely untouched. In 1988, of the imports that actually got through the system controls, only 16 percent were in the category of open general license, that is, unrestricted. In the late 1980s, India's exports increased by an average of 12.8 percent per year—modest growth when compared to Thailand, at 27.8 percent. In addition, India had the highest average tariff rates of any Asian nation at 141.2 percent. Fueled by these limited reforms, India's average annual rate of growth increased to 5.5 percent. This growth was attained at the expense of much larger government budget deficits and extensive foreign borrowing and was seen by economists as unsustainable. Interest on past borrowing became the largest and most rapidly growing item of government spending, reaching 30 percent in 1991.

With these economic reforms under way, India was quietly emerging as a major player in the global economy. But it was not until the government surrendered their mistrust of capitalism and political change that they were able to "open everything up" and emerge as a prosperous nation.

CHAPTER 9

Shadows to Sunshine

India from 1991 to Today

Long years ago we made a tryst with destiny, and now the time comes when we shall redeem our pledge, not wholly or in full measure, but very substantially.

—Jawaharlal Nehru, India's first prime minister

After the independence, the imprint of self-reliance from Nehru and Gandhi became a core consideration for economic policy measures. Although it was only grudgingly that the country finally opened its doors in the late 1980s to the developed nations, India eventually embraced modernization. While the Indian economy continued to be dominated by state enterprises, the country was a step closer to participating in the global economy. Growth was still slow under the state modernization, but this economic climate forced the masses of India to be creative and imaginative in order to maneuver through shortages of raw materials and equipment. Thus, a nation of innovators was born.

Overcoming the Obstacles

India remained outside the consciousness of the world powers, which were engaged in Cold War politics where India's role as a "nonaligned" nation was looked on by Western powers with suspicion. The only time the world's attention fell on India was when the border disputes with its neighbor Pakistan expanded into full-scale wars and threatened to escalate into something larger. The danger of these two countries engaging in nuclear war created a nightmare scenario for the world at large.

In early 1991, an article in *The Economist* stated, "The hopes of 1947 have been betrayed. India, despite all its advantages and a generous supply of aid from the capitalist West ... has achieved less than virtually any comparable Third World country. The cost in human terms has been staggering. . . . India . . . is an economic miracle waiting to happen."

There was a new government in place in 1991 headed by Narasimha Rao, who was chosen as an afterthought as a successor to the young and dynamic Rajiv Gandhi, son of Indira Gandhi and grandson of Jawaharlal Nehru. Gandhi, the last of the dynasty of Nehru/Gandhi, had been killed while campaigning in southern India by a Tamil extremist outfitted with a suicide bomb, for Gandhi's efforts in mediating the Sri Lankan peace.

Prime Minister Rao, along with his cabinet ministers Manmohan Singh, the new finance minister, and P. Chidambaram, the commerce minister, were at their wits' end. They badly needed the foreign funds to pay for imports—particularly for imported oil, as oil prices had recently surged through the roof. The lender of last resort was the International Monetary Fund (IMF), which was ready to deal but came armed with conditions. The IMF's conditions were neither easy nor palatable, but it was the only deal on the table. Among other conditions for borrowing from the IMF, India would be forced to privatize state-owned enterprises, institute budget restraints, and open its domestic markets to international markets.

And then there was the ultimate slap in the face: The IMF required collateral in the form of gold reserves. For an Indian, gold is the last refuge. For generations, Indian brides have received gold jewelry as part of the dowry from their parents to cushion any financial mishap and to provide the security of the shining hard metal better than any paper currency could. But the government was pushed to the wall and was forced to swallow this bitter medicine. The leaders shared the predicament with the opposition parties, so as to create consensus for what was to be a hard economic road full of sacrifice.

The government, after implementing the IMF's conditions, still had to take further steps. First came two bouts of devaluation of the rupee, which was overvalued and priced on the black market at least 25 percent above the official price. This curtailed imports and created opportunities for domestic exporters to be more competitive, easing somewhat the balance of payments problem.

"Let's Open Everything"

During a cabinet meeting, Prime Minister Rao is said to have stated, "Let's open everything," which was a prelude to what was to come in the weeks and months following the IMF strictures.

The package of reforms introduced by the Rao government included:

- The abolition of industrial licensing and narrowing the scope of public-sector monopolies to a much smaller number of industries.
- Liberalization of inward foreign direct and portfolio investment.

- Trade liberalization that included the elimination of import licensing and progressive reduction of nontariff barriers to imports.
- Wide-ranging reforms in the banking system and capital markets followed by reforms in insurance later.
- Liberalization of investment and trade in important services such as telecommunications.

The results were spectacular. The budget deficit reduced dramatically. Foreign exchange reserves rose from $1 billion to $20 billion in 20 years. Foreign direct investment (FDI) flowed in, inflation dropped, exports rose, and growth rates for the first time exceeded over 5 percent per year.

In addition, there was a sharp acceleration of all underlying measures of growth. For example, the annual average rate of growth in gross domestic product (GDP) per worker increased from 0.7 percent in the 1970s to 3.3 percent in the 1990s, while growth in total factor productivity, a measure of industrial efficiency, increased from –0.5 percent in the 1970s to 1.6 percent in the 1990s. In contrast to the growth of the 1980s, which was fueled by an unsustainable buildup of external debt and trade deficits that culminated in the crisis of 1991, the growth in the 1990s was accompanied by such external stability that India was largely untouched by the East Asian crisis.

Clearly, the reforms of the 1990s transformed the Indian economy. A new era had started.

New Businesses Thrive

There are many dramatic stories of early entrepreneurial successes in India post-1991 that were spurred by Rao's economic reforms. Jet Air is one of the best examples. Prior to these initiatives, domestic air travel was monopolized by the state-sponsored Indian Airlines. There simply was no competition, despite large demand. Airline employees considered this a personal fiefdom and considered travelers unwelcome intrusions. The corruption, delays, and lack of accountability were operational standards. Then, the government allowed an entrepreneurial airline to operate in domestic air space. The start-up Jet Air was a major hit. People loved its courteous service, better food (a major attraction for Indian travelers), and clean planes. In the process, Indian Airlines was forced to compete in the open market and significantly improve its service. The sunshine of competition was ushered in, and it appeared that the government's willingness to experiment with opening up the domestic market was an enormous success.

Changes also began to appear on the business horizon in the years following 1991, when the government gave the green light to opening the economy to foreign investors. Multinationals saw this as an opportunity to tap into India's billion-plus consumers. Manufacturing collaborations between Japanese/European companies and Indian companies became the new business mantra. From Mitsubishi to Mercedes and from Honda to Hyundai, foreign companies set up shop with local companies, exchanging know-how, creating jobs, and bringing efficiency.

Although business was flourishing in India, the government had to balance the emerging entrepreneurial interests against those entrenched groups, such as labor unions and monopolies, which benefited from protectionism. The tension between the past and present was palpable and constant. The intelligentsia, expanding middle class, newly arrived business interests, and consumer groups wanted the freedom to innovate and compete. But the protectionists were ready to defend their power enclaves against this new opening, using their political muscle. The government moved forward with its open-door policy slowly and cautiously, and there was steady and dramatic progress. Prosperity was beginning to affect larger and larger segments of society, and the public could see, smell, and taste the fruit of open competition and lack of scarcity.

The economy improved by all measures. The balance of trade improved while foreign reserves grew. Foreign investments doubled each year, from $150 million in 1991 to $3 billion by 1997. Both rates of unemployment and inflation decreased, while per-capita income increased. According to the IMF and International Financial Statistics, other improvements include the following:

- Real GDP per capita has grown at 4.7 percent annually since 1993, while inflation averaged only 5.6 percent annually.
- Foreign exchange reserves recovered to $19 billion in 1994 and reached $37 billion in 2000. In 2006, they reached $170 billion.
- Foreign capital inflows more than tripled from 1991 to 1996.
- FDI in India rose from a paltry $74 million in 1991 to $3.6 billion by 1997.

A poll taken before the opening in 1991 showed that less than 40 percent of the population was satisfied with the direction of the economy, while a poll taken shortly after 1999 showed that 70 percent of the population was content.

The fact remains that India has a long history of open commerce and free trade. The bazaars, shops, and mills are thriving places where capitalism, profit, and the principles of supply and demand are in full vogue.

CHAPTER 10

Power in Numbers

Investing in India

At the beginning of the Industrial Revolution in 1770, India contributed about 20 percent to the world economy. Such was the case with another great economy of the time—China. After about two centuries of tumultuous history, both countries bypassed the Industrial Revolution, and both countries achieved the dubious distinction of recording about 3 percent of world output.

In the case of India, colonization by the British for almost two centuries, misplaced priorities after independence, and a closed economic system resulted in a stagnant economy barely averaging 3 percent growth. Meanwhile, India's population more than doubled during the first 50 years of self-governance. The result was entrenched poverty and neglect that persisted until recently. This all changed with a new beginning in the late 1980s, and an even more dramatic transformation of the country's economy continued through the 1990s. Today, India promises to have one of the fastest-growing economies in the next half century. It has achieved an auspicious, if short, history of strong growth, with the emergence of world-class companies in many cutting-edge industries. Indeed, today's India is beginning to be hyphenated with the other power from the late 1700s—China.

Here is a look at India today and its prospects for tomorrow in relation to the eight tenets of our investment model.

Demographics: *Favorable*

India's large population, in conjunction with a large number of working-age adults, is a major factor that makes the demographics favorable. India, located in Southeast Asia, is the world's second most populous country, home to 1.1 billion people, which is about 3 times the population of the United States and more than 10 times that of Mexico. According to the

Euromonitor International Report of 2006, it is also one of the world's youngest countries—over half of its population is under the age of 25, while those over age 65 account for less than 6 percent of the total population. Combined, these two variables portend an unstoppable forward motion in coming decades. By 2015, India's population is expected to grow by approximately 250 million people. This increase equals more than the current population of the world's fourth largest country, Indonesia, and is not far behind the population of the United States. In the same period, China's population will grow by less than 10 percent, and the gap between China and India will shrink by 60 percent to about 80 million people. By 2025, India will claim the lead as the most populous country in the world.

Many research studies show that a country's population growth or decline is not in itself strongly linked to investment returns. However, population growth is tied to other factors in the economy that do influence a country's competitive position in world markets. The structure of the population—the relative percentage in each age group—is a critical factor. A high percentage of young people translates to a higher dependency ratio (more dependent children per worker), while a higher proportion of working-age individuals increases savings, which in turn helps finance more investment and boosts output. The dependency ratio, defined as the population of those under 20 and over 65, as a proportion of the total population for India in 2005 was 47 percent and expected to go down to 43 percent by 2010 (according to the Euromonitor International report, *The Market of Consumer Lifestyles in India,* June 2006).

Economists have coined the phrase "demographic dividend" to refer to the increase in economic growth that can occur as a country's birth rate begins to decline, pushing down the dependency ratio. These per-capita income boosts are not automatic, however, but rely on the government's ability to enact wise economic policies affecting the labor markets and education. The International Monetary Fund (IMF) cites "relatively open and competitive markets, substantial investments in basic education, fiscal discipline, and a relatively deep financial sector" as keys that have helped East Asian countries such as China benefit from the demographic dividend in the past.

While India currently lags behind China in the demographic boom, it is already experiencing declining fertility rates as its national income is increasing. Meanwhile, its working-age population is expected to grow by 140 million in the next 10 years, a number equal to the entire working population of the United States, up from 58 percent in 2000 to a peak of 64 percent in 2035. Researchers at the Australian National University suggest that while China's demographic dividend is past, India's could continue for another two decades at least. Hence, India's growing population can be a strongly positive force provided the nation succeeds in nurturing and educating its youth and achieves a broad distribution of wealth and resources. India's enormous potential, if properly cultivated, can transform into a supercharged engine of growth and innovation.

Economic Performance: *Favorable*

India's favorable ranking for economic performance is based on analysis of its expanding middle class, robust gross domestic product (GDP) growth, and greater productivity. These factors are likely to result in further growth in the coming decades.

Growth of the Middle Class

An expanding middle class promises an abundance of consumers with disposable income, helping to sustain domestic growth and reduce reliance on export markets. It can create a "virtuous circle" by generating demand for goods, which in turn means job growth and new investment. By many estimates, the 25 percent to 30 percent of India's population that is today deemed middle class on the basis of purchasing power represents 250 to 300 million people, about equal to the entire population of the United States. These consumers are moving rapidly up the consumption scale, buying homes and furnishings, purchasing autos instead of scooters, and enjoying meals at McDonald's (which offers a special spiced-up version of mutton burger and cold coffee). The prospect of a fast-growing consumer market is attracting investment from multinational firms such as Wal-Mart, which is tying up joint ventures with local retailers.

According to the National Council for Applied Economic Research (NCAER), there are about 30 million households considered middle class, which drive the current growth. Another 75 million households, amounting to about 430 million people, can be considered "aspiring class," poised to embark on a wave of consumption. The trend of growth in the consumer class, a decade in the making, has strong reasons to propel it forward (see Figures 10.1, 10.2, and 10.3).

Indicators of the size of a nation's middle class include per-capita income (GDP divided by population) and the ratio of richest to poorest individuals, reflecting whether wealth is concentrated among a small subset of the population or is distributed more equitably.

GDP Growth

Growth in India's middle class depends on higher rates of GDP growth and engaging more of the population in productive employment. India's

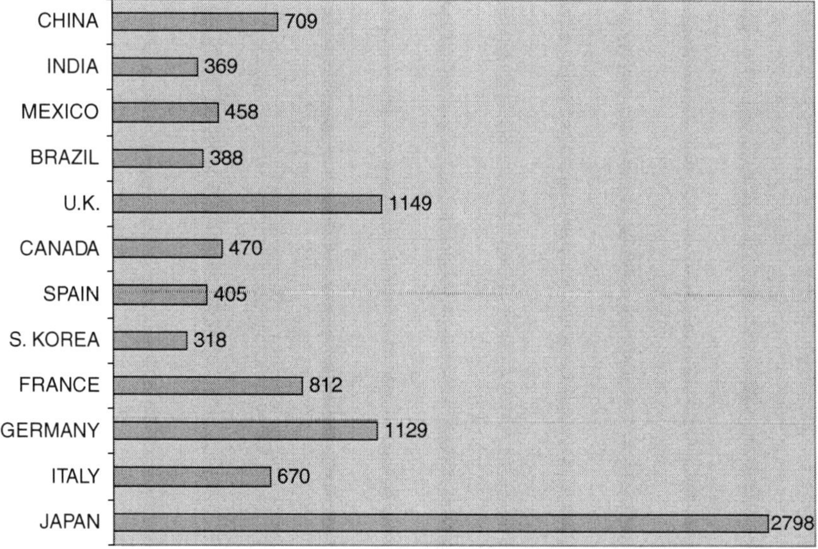

FIGURE 10.1 Top world consumer markets in 2005 (excluding U.S.).
Source: McKinsey Global Institute, www.mckinseyreport.com

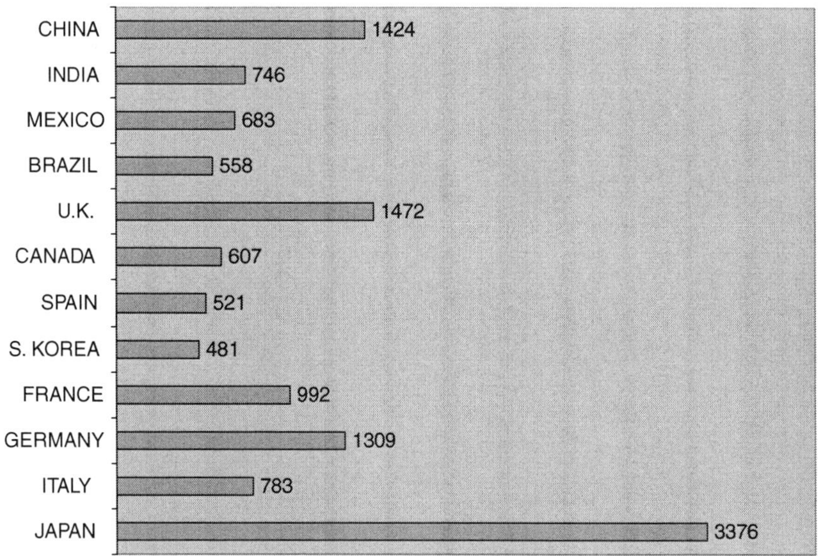

FIGURE 10.2 Top world consumer markets in 2015 (excluding U.S.).
Source: McKinsey Global Institute, www.mckinseyreport.com

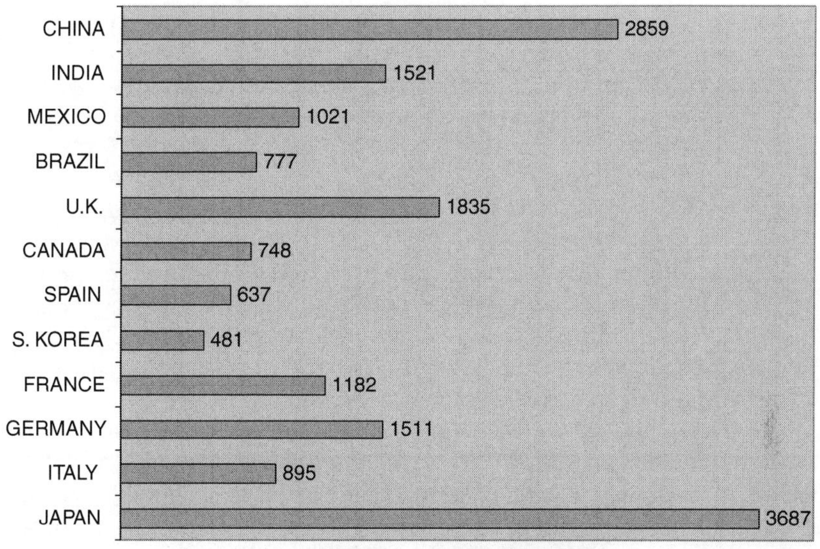

FIGURE 10.3 Top world consumer markets in 2025 (excluding U.S.).
Source: McKinsey Global Institute, www.mckinseyreport.com

prospects are excellent on both fronts. Its real GDP growth reached above 9 percent in 2006 and is forecast at 7.8 percent for 2008. India's five-year plan, begun in April 2007, aims for an annual after-inflation growth rate of 9 percent to 10 percent over the 2007 through 2012 period, and some experts suggest real growth could reach 12 percent per year. Longer term, growth is forecast to average 7.6 percent per year through 2050, making India one of the world's fastest-growing economies. With annual GDP growth expected to stay above 7 percent for the next several decades, per-capita income of at least $1,660 per person is likely by 2020.

India's growth will remain about 5 percent throughout the period to 2050. India has the potential to raise the U.S. dollar GDP by 2050 to 35 times the current level.

Shift from Agriculture

The lack of jobs in agriculture, along with low wages, has created a noticeable shift in employment to other industries such as construction, services, and manufacturing. India's per-capita income has increased as a result of structural reforms begun in the 1990s. The number of people living in poverty declined from 36 percent in 1993–1994 to 26 percent in 1999–2000.

Today, the IMF estimates that India's real (after inflation) per-capita income will double every 13 years. India ranked twelfth in GDP at $775 billion in 2006, slightly behind Russia, which translates to a per-capita income of about $698 per person. So even though India's ratio of poor to wealthy is quite low, at about 4.8, an estimated 800 million people, or 70 percent of the population, still live on less than $2 a day. This is due in part to the relatively high percentage of the population involved in agricultural production, estimated at 60 percent, and is the primary reason the World Economic Forum ranks India's macroeconomy as one of the weakest of the 6 countries in our portfolio, with a rank of 88, compared with 6 for China and 13 for Korea. To date, India's large labor force has been a victim of weak growth in manufacturing exports, at only 8 percent of GDP in 2004, compared with 27 percent for Mexico and 30 percent for China.

In India, there is a massive shift under way from agriculture to manufacturing and services. According to a January 2007 study by Goldman Sachs, labor is four times more productive in industry and six times more productive in services than in agriculture. This change could enhance the population's vertical shift to higher prosperity, increasing the ranks of the middle class.

Reform efforts are under way to improve prospects for India's rural poor. India's 11th Five-Year Plan (2007–2012) calls for doubling the percentage of national income attributed to the agricultural sector, from 2 percent to 4 percent, and doubling the country's per-capita income by 2017.

Urbanization

India, like other emerging nations, is going through a major shift in populations from rural to urban areas. In 1991, India had 23 cities with populations of one million or more. Today, that number has risen to 35. An estimated 140 million people will migrate to urban areas by 2020, and a staggering 700 million by 2050. India's current urbanization rate of 29 percent is low compared to 81 percent for South Korea, 67 percent for Malaysia, and 43 percent for China, suggesting significant opportunities for acceleration of growth.

This shift of urbanization will result in increased opportunities for sectors such as consumer services, manufacturing, and construction.

Technology Expansion: *Favorable*

Technology in India is expanding at a breakneck pace, with over 300 million people currently assumed to be in the middle class, taking advantage of some of the latest gadgets. This, along with higher growth and productivity is likely to create a strong climate for technology utilizations. As such, India has received a favorable ranking.

Technology Penetration

The penetration of consumer technology in India is still quite low, but is increasing rapidly as the "digital divide" of affordability begins to diminish. The number of new subscribers to cell phones has reached 30 million per year, exceeding the growth rate in China. Soon, there will be computers for the masses, and access to the Internet will increase dramatically. Along with this spread of technology will come higher productivity and greater efficiency in business, education, and government services. India is also making its mark in skilled manufacture. Railways, shipping, and the Indian passport offices are among those that have recently digitized their operations.

Cell Phone Use

Use of cell phones has lept forward from fewer than 3.5 million in 2000 to 66 million users in 2005. Between 2003 and 2004, there were 2 million users added each month, and in 2005 that number skyrocketed to 3 million per month. Forecasters predict 191 million users in 2010, and 215 million in 2015.

Source: World Bank (Euromonitor)

"The game here really isn't about saving costs, but to speed innovation," says Oliver Bow, managing director of Guillermo Willie. The center opened in 2000, and engineers here had filed for 95 patents in the United States by late 2003. "India always had brilliant educated people," says Paul Saffo of the Institute for the Future in Menlo Park, California. "Now Indians are taking the lead in colonizing cyberspace" (Pete Engardio, *Chindia*. New York: McGraw-Hill, 2006, p. 46).

Old engine maker Cummins is using its new research and development (R&D) center in Pune, India, to develop sophisticated computer models needed to design upgrades and prototypes electronically, says International vice president Steven M. Chapman. "We will be able to introduce five or six engines a year instead of two on the same $250 million R&D budget—without a single U.S. layoff" (Engardio, 2006, p. 54).

Outsourcing

It is estimated that India currently has about a third of the world's software engineers. This skilled export has produced billions in income for the country; as long as the differential in wages continues, the trend is likely to persist.

According to "The Rise of India," an article in *BusinessWeek* (December 8, 2003), India has a "deep source of low-cost, high-IQ English-speaking brainpower [which] may soon have a more far-reaching impact on the U.S. than China." The article explains that India excels in services, and since services represent more than 60 percent of the U.S. economy and employ two-thirds of its workers, India is in a leading position to capture a large market share of the economy. India's knowledge workers are making their way up the value chain to penetrate global markets using their marketing management skills and creativity.

Indian companies gained credibility from their work onsite in the United States during the late 1990s. In early 2000, the dot-com bubble burst. The subsequent recession put technology budgets under constraint. Indian technology companies came to the rescue: They had already established themselves as problem solvers, and now they were not only offering their services to perform routine maintenance, but were also able to perform more sophisticated tasks. And they were willing to do it cheaply.

The cost of fiber-optic communication had decreased, and it was easy for American corporations to set up satellite communication and offload the work to India. A place like Bangalore became a quasi–Silicon Valley by default. Nestled in the southwest part of India, Bangalore's temperate climate, technological and science institutes of repute, and millions of English-speaking technically trained workers became a Mecca for high-technology companies from around the world. The work could be done there during the day, transmitted in the evening, and received in the United States in the morning, thereby gaining the critical time advantage of a 24-hour time clock.

Infosys—From Bangalore to the World

When Infosys, a new software development venture took its first savvy steps into the world in 1981, the founders, seven software professionals, knew their company's future relied on gaining an intrepid international presence. While CEO N.R. Narayana Murthy stayed in India to generate local business, the others made frequent forays to the United States to offer onsite programming to corporate clients, among them Reebok International, Ltd. The company won its first big client, Data Basics of the United States, in its third year.

Enter Kurt Salmon Associates (KSA), a management consulting firm in Atlanta. In 1987, the two companies formed a partnership: KSA sourced jobs; Infosys provided the technical expertise from India.

Meanwhile, India had liberalized its economic policies, and its business climate had grown more hospitable to foreign investment. This gave Infosys the springboard it needed. In the next few years, the company posted revenues of RS 100 million and ventured into information technology (IT) consulting, business processing outsourcing, and packaged software solutions. It took advantage of India's booming economy and lenient land lease policies to build its company headquarters in Bangalore. This sparked policy reform. Turning its geographic distance to its advantage, Infosys focused on offering offshore services to its American clients. It terminated with KSA in 1996, opened a marketing office in the United States, won a huge contract with Reebok of France, and soon acquired clients like GE, Nestle, and Holiday Inn. With faster turnaround time—while the United States slept, India worked—and greater flexibility in use of its resources, the company could earn more working on home turf and charge less.

On the cusp of the millennium, Infosys launched its American Depositary Receipt (ADR) listing on the Nasdaq. At the same time, Infosys started to build offices around the world. In 2006, on its 25th anniversary, Infosys became the first Indian company to ring the Nasdaq opening bell. Infosys's forays into the global market had paid off.

Sources: Harvard Business School, Infosys

Medical tourism is evolving as another area where India's combination of a highly skilled, technology-enabled workforce and low costs is carving out market share. Where previously the United States was the international mecca for sophisticated medical treatment, today patients from the United States, Canada, and Europe are traveling to India's medical centers for surgeries such as joint replacements and heart valve repair. This is likely to continue to be a growing business as both governments and private companies in advanced countries continue to look for ways to cut health care costs for their aging populations.

Medical Tourism

The Confederation of Indian Industry (CII) estimates that India has the potential to attract one million tourists annually, bringing as much as $5 billion. In 2004, the estimate was 150,000. CII's goal is to develop India into a world destination for yoga, ayurveda, and allopathic and holistic medicines.

The growth of medical professionals between 2000 and 2005 shows that there are 548,000 more doctors or an increase of 13.43 percent, and 670,000 more nurses, or an increase of 12.54 percent.

Source: Euromonitor International, "The Market of Consumer Lifestyles in India," Report, June 2006

India's low labor costs and highly educated workforce have made it a leader in the area of developing custom software applications for Western companies. Indian companies are now moving beyond their traditional enclave of software to business process outsourcing, chain-link management, inventory control, and a wide range of high-level business consulting at competitive prices. Tata Consulting, for example, has extended its services to sophisticated logistics and supply-chain management, and along with Wipro and Infosys are leading companies in the development and business process outsourcing fields around the globe. A. T. Kearney Inc. predicts 500,000 financial services jobs will go offshore by 2008.

Andy Grove, former CEO of Intel, suggested in a software conference in October 2003, "From a technical and productivity standpoint, the engineer sitting 6,000 miles away might as well be in the next cubicle on the local area network" (Engardio, 2006, p. 47.)

Wipro Is a Tech Company with a Mission

Wipro has taken a page out of Toyota's workbook by taking the tricky problem of transferring the Toyota principles of manufacturing into servicing business. "What we do is apply people technology and processes to solve a business problem," says T. K. Kurian, the head of Wipro's 13,600-person business process outsourcing unit. Day and night, thousands of Wipro employees line up at long rows of tables in an assembly line; signs hanging over each aisle describe what process is being handled there—accounts receivable, travel, entertainment, and so on. Team leaders set goals at the beginning of each shift and tasklike Toyota factory electronic displays mounted on the walls will shift from green to red if things bog down.

Just as Toyota had to struggle to attain the efficiency, high quality, and low costs to take market share, Indian companies are doing the same.

According to Jeffrey K. Liker, a business professor and author of *The Toyota Way*, "If Indians get this right, in addition to their low labor rates, they can become a deadly competition."

Source: Pete Engardio, *Chindia*. New York: McGraw Hill, 2006, p. 94

Biotech Innovation

India is becoming a technological innovator in some industries, such as drug development and biotech research. These efforts, although nascent, could transform India's drug and biotech firms into a competitive position in the world markets. Dr. Reddy's Laboratory, a large pharmaceutical firm, is on the verge of a major push into producing vast quantities of high-quality, low-cost generic drugs not only for the billion-strong domestic population but potentially for underserved markets in Africa and less developed parts of Asia.

More generally, India has taken a leading role in providing clinical trials for global drug companies. Its large population serves as an immense resource for conducting the exhaustive and fast-track clinical trials for new drugs required by biotech and multinational drug companies, and at lower costs than in their domestic markets. Already, India possesses the largest number of Food and Drug Administration (FDA)-approved pharmaceutical labs outside the United States.

Information Technology

Other innovations show India utilizing technology to develop educational, financial, and navigational tools that have the potential to catch on worldwide. On the education front, Tata Consultancy Services (TCS) has developed a software program to teach India's 200 million illiterates to read in their own language. Words float across the computer screen while a narrator repeats the sounds. In a test, TCS engineers found that in 10 weeks adults learned enough to sign their names and slowly read a newspaper.

In the financial realm, ICICI Bank has developed a product that bundles micro loans to provide double-digit returns to investors, while helping small entrepreneurs and farmers, particularly women, create jobs and other career opportunities for themselves. Bangalore's HCL designed a navigation system for Airbus A340 and A320 Jetliners in just 18 months.

Nine hundred engineers of Texas Instruments' Bangalore chip-design operation have 225 patents, and Bangalore's Intel campus is leading worldwide research on 32-bit microprocessors for servers and wireless chips. "These are corporate crown jewels," says Intel's India president Ketan Sawpal (Engardio, 2006, p. 50).

Sequoia Capital's Michael Moritz, who nurtured Google, Flextronics, and Agile Software, states, "We can barely imagine investing in a company without at least asking what their plans are for India." He adds, "India has seeped into the marrow of the valley" (Engardio, 2006). India has over 1,500 research laboratories. Between 2002 and 2003, they filed over 1,700 patents with the U.S. Patent Office, and over 15,000 patents in India (Aaron Chaze, *India: An Investor's Guide to the Next Economic Superpower*. Singapore: John Wiley & Sons, 2006).

Slum Computer

NIIT is a computer training company and a pioneer in working with various states in providing computer education in schools, particularly in rural areas.

In an experiment, Sugan Mitra, NIIT's head of research, placed a computer in a Delhi slum. He fixed it into a boundary wall along with a touch pad—but without a keyboard. He also hung a hidden camera on a tree to monitor what happened. Within a week, he found that the illiterate slum children had begun surfing the Net, and in three months created a thousand folders among them. The most avid users were six- to twelve-year-olds who had taught themselves to draw on the computer and browse the Web.

Disney.com was the most popular site because of the games. The children also liked the Microsoft paint site. They had never had access to paper and paint, and now they could paint without paper. And once they discovered MP3 digital music files, they began to download Hindi film music and played it all day long.

Dr. Mitra found that some ninth-graders were able to teach themselves physics concepts directly from the Internet without the aid of a teacher. The slum experiment also teaches that up to a point the English language is not a barrier. Dr. Mitra's slum computer had a Hindi interface that gave kids links to hook up with web sites on their own.

These computer experts compare learning computer literacy to learning how to ride a bike—both are intuitive and difficult to explain.

Source: Das Gurcharan, *India Unbound*. New York: Random House, 2002, p. 339.

Indians are aware of the limited time and advantage in fierce competition from the likes of China, Brazil, and eastern Europe—all pushing hard to share in the technology and outsourcing boom. Indians want to flourish and not just exist. That shows up time and again in conversations both inside and outside the country with Indians ranging from average to extraordinary.

Open Trade: *Neutral*

India has historically been one of the most restrictive countries in terms of open trade, seeking to protect its domestic markets. Thus, reforms aimed at placing India in the mainstream of the world's competitive markets will require more massive adjustments compared with those of its neighbors. Consequently, it receives a neutral ranking. China, for example, reduced its average tariff by 72 percent from 43 percent in 1992 to12 percent in 2002. During the same period, India reduced its average tariff by 75 percent, but because its starting tariffs were an astounding 128 percent, the net result was a reduction to 32 percent. Its tariffs still rank among the highest in the world and more than twice that of China.

Nevertheless, since 1991, India has increasingly embraced an open trade policy, and many critical economic sectors, such as infrastructure and labor-intensive manufacturing, are opening up to partnerships with private industry. India's economy may not yet look like that of Australia and Canada, but it is inching its way toward broader and deeper accessibility. Indeed, India's trade with the European Union (EU) represents nearly 20 percent of the country's exports. In 2007, the EU began negotiating the terms of a free trade agreement with India that could lead to significantly more trade in the near future.

India's global trade, valued at more than $430 billion, is rising at 8 percent a year due to continued strong worldwide demand for the country's high-technology services and labor-intensive manufacturing. Reforms that have helped narrow the gap between India's trade policies and those of other developing nations, such as China, are helping India secure better trade relations with Western countries. Trade within the Asian region is also growing because of strong economic growth in China and the continuing development of the region's other emerging economies.

Rural reforms include expanded financial services as banks and investment firms build service capacity in rural areas. Citibank, Bank of America, HSBC, and Deutsche Bank are some of the large multinationals opening rural branches or buying stakes in India's domestic banks. Citibank alone has invested nearly $1 billion in the last two years to expand its operations in India's markets.

Indian Foreign Direct Investment

Indian foreign direct investment (FDI) totals are quite low because of past restrictions. The European Union is India's largest source of FDI, but India has only 1.3 percent of the EU's worldwide direct investments. But the liberalization of India's markets is paving the way for larger FDI inflows from other regions in addition to the EU. The FDI confidence index (an annual survey conducted by the consulting firm A. T. Kearney) showed India as the second most popular destination for FDI. India's attractiveness factors include the upswing of sentiment toward investments by foreign companies, the establishment of fast-track approvals that reduce the need to interact with Indian bureaucracy, increases in FDI caps, and the availability of favorable financing terms. These are signs of openness that are likely to encourage foreign firms to increase their expansion in India and profit from the investment opportunities made available to them. Total FDI inflows to India have grown from $100 million in the early 1990s to more than $5 billion today.

The current policy allows FDI up to 100 percent in many sectors, including power, mass transit, airports, oil and gas exports, drugs and pharmaceuticals, mining, construction, houses, and infrastructure. According to the Economic Intelligence Unit, firms in the export processing or special economic zones can also be 100 percent foreign owned.

Privatization

India has embarked on a plan to privatize its large stakes in public enterprises, from steel to energy to banking. The pace of such privatization ebbs and flows based on the political climate and election season. There are still entrenched interests resistant to changing the status quo. These range from leftist elements to labor unions that see privatization as a diminution of control and a source of lost jobs and benefits. However, the government's continuing need for capital to spend on poverty-eradication projects and to develop infrastructure will likely result in the reduction of its ownership, causing higher efficiency, more open competition, and greater opportunity for increased FDI.

Privatization of these state-owned enterprises has been received with great enthusiasm by domestic and foreign investors. The pace of such privatization is likely to increase in the future, creating even more opportunities for investors.

Infrastructure Development: *Unfavorable*

Infrastructure plays an important role in economic growth and activity. Basic utilities, sanitation, ports, urban and freight transport, and rural roads add to the efficiency and profitability of production as well as quality-of-life factors that influence a nation's economic success. Indian authorities have come to recognize that without proper infrastructure development, the economy will suffer. Despite serious attempts to improve in this category, this will continue to be a challenge, given the massive amount of resources needed to complete the task at hand. Therefore, India receives an unfavorable ranking.

Studies of the importance of infrastructure investments on economic growth are mixed, ranging from no effect to rates of return in excess of 100 percent per year. In India, significant investments will be required to provide essential components such as electricity, sewers, and transport routes. If the country invests too little, economic growth will suffer. Yet too high a percentage of GDP can mean neglecting other important levers of growth such as education and financial stability, with the same result. In this situation, a developing country can try to manage this balance and find the "sweet spot" by attracting private capital to infrastructure investments, such as entering into public-private partnerships (PPPs). These financing structures have been used extensively in the telecommunications and energy sectors in central and eastern Asia, and are being embraced by India's state and national governments. For example, the telecom sector is treated as infrastructure and enjoys applicable benefits such as tax holidays and project-import duties based on concession.

A significant caveat on India's growth potential is its dependence on imports of energy supplies. The lack of internal energy resources is likely to keep the growth in check, particularly if energy prices continue to rise. Energy generation and distribution, oil refining, and various infrastructure projects are priority areas for new investments. Today, India imports about 70 percent of its oil and derives 30 percent from internal reserves; the reverse was true in 1980. Finance Minister P. Chidambaram estimates that high oil prices shave at least 1 percent from GDP growth. Greater energy efficiency and new investments in nuclear power are seen as possible ways to ease the energy crunch. Currently, India consumes about 1.5 barrels of oil per $1,000 increase in GDP—triple that of Italy, France, and Germany and about twice the U.S. ratio.

The 2005–2006 Economic Survey of India estimated that power shortages of 12 percent at peak levels and 8 percent at nonpeak levels alone resulted in an estimated $68 billion in lost GDP. However, there is more than a glimmer of light on the horizon. According to a report by the World Bank, the number of private participation projects in infrastructure amounted to $22 million in 1990, and in 2005 participation had increased to $8 billion, amounting to a total of about $50 billion in the last decade.

The Asia Development Bank cites programs such as the National Horticulture Mission, which is upgrading irrigation infrastructure, expanding the rural roads network, and strengthening agricultural storage and marketing infrastructure. A $27 billion National Urban Renewal Mission, affecting 63 cities, will provide better housing, water, and sanitation—and, ultimately, better delivery of other basic services such as health, education, and social security. The future plans are that by 2009, all of the country's 600,000 villages are scheduled to have a telephone line and clean drinking water, with broadband connection to follow by 2012.

At the same time, India's government is taking new steps to spur investment in industry, through the establishment of SEZs (special economic zones). These industrial enclaves will increase the proportion of land used for industry (currently only about 0.1 percent) and boost the nation's exports. More than 350 SEZs have been approved. When operational, they will generate an estimated 4 million jobs, many in industries that employ relatively unskilled workers. Sponsored by large, well-known companies such as Nokia and Hyderabad Gems, the SEZs enjoy benefits such as fast approval and tax holidays, while providing jobs and (in many cases) essential services to employees.

India, like China in the previous decade, has enormous opportunity to capitalize on growth by increasing infrastructure development with resulting opportunities for real estate construction, engineering, and many other sectors. The government and the private sector is keen to remove obstacles in order to sustain future growth.

Transparency and Rule of Law: *Neutral*

Investors' confidence in a particular country is greatly enhanced when a consistent legal and regulatory framework is in place, supported by adequate enforcement and judiciary capabilities. *Transparency* refers to the accuracy and availability of information about corporate and government affairs. Corruption, which thrives on secrecy, is less likely in a highly transparent environment.

A country's investment environment is more transparent when there are regulations in place requiring open and full disclosure of financial and corporate governance matters, and independent verification of financial records. Adequately staffed enforcement bodies that have the authority to audit organizations for compliance—and to bring sanctions or legal action against those who do not comply—must also support the application of these laws and regulations. Finally, the judicial system must be fair and free of corruption.

India's judiciary is fiercely independent and relatively free of political oversight. As such, it receives a ranking of neutral. It has at times raised eyebrows and ruffled feathers by handing out verdicts against the government or powerful elite. Examples of such decisions range from ordering the government to retrofit government and public transport so as to protect public health in Delhi and demolish unauthorized structures despite huge demonstrations from entrenched forces. At the same time, according to some sources, bribes are not uncommon in the day-to-day operation of the judiciary. Transparency International, an independent European nonprofit, reports in its 32-country Global Corruption Report in 2007 that 77 percent of India's citizens described the judicial system as corrupt, and that 36 percent reported paying bribes. The country's judiciary also has an enormous backlog of cases.

Nevertheless, India is improving its ranking in Transparency International's Corruption Perception Index, jumping to number 76 in 2006 from 92 in 2005, with a score of 3.3. This places it on a par with Brazil (number 70), China (71), and Mexico (77). By comparison, the United States ranked 23 with a score of 7.3, South Korea ranked 43 with a score of 5.1, and Russia ranked 127 with a score of 2.5, about the same as in 2005. The World Bank's indexes show similar improvement, with India's rank in regulatory quality rising from the 40th percentile in 2004 to nearly the 50th at the end of 2006, and its rank in corruption control reaching above 50 percent for the first time (see Table 10.1).

TABLE 10.1 Law and Order Governance Indicator

	Year	Percentile rank 0–100	Governance score −2.5 - +2.5	Trend FNUF	Trend UND
Voice and accountability	2006	58.2	+.35	N	N
	2002	59.1	+.40		
	1998	58.2	+.34		
Political stability	2006	22.1	−.84	UF	UP
	2002	17.8	−1.01		
	1998	21.2	−.83		
Government effectiveness	2006	54.0	−.04	UF	UP
	2002	55.5	−.11		
	1998	53.1	−.16		
Regulatory quality	2006	48.3	−.05	UF	UP
	2002	41.5	−.35		
	1998	34.6	−.28		
Rule of law	2006	57.1	+.17	N	UP
	2002	53.3	−.02		
	1998	58.1	+.15		
Control of corruption	2006	52.9	−.21	UF	UP
	2002	42.2	−.41		
	1998	47.6	−.27		

(F=favorable, N=neutral, UF=unfavorable)
Source: World Bank Governance Indicator Country Snap Shot—2007; http.//info.worldbank.org/governance/wg2 2007

India is a thriving democracy—the largest on the planet, with maximum participation of any country in the elective franchise. This fact is dramatic when one considers that all its neighbors from south to north are either state controlled or ruled by military juntas or dictators. Yet it has retained an open, thriving democracy since gaining its freedom from Britain.

The assessment of transparency and rule of law is boosting investor confidence in FDI and the development of joint ventures and business relationships.

Education and Training: *Favorable*

Despite India's enormous rural population and lack of infrastructure, the country boasts a highly educated workforce that makes it a formidable presence in the world market for skilled labor. While India lags in secondary education levels on a percentage basis from its more developed peers such as China, the country on an absolute basis has among the largest numbers of science, technology, and engineering graduates in the world. India produces over 400,000 graduate engineers, second only to China's 490,000. It boasts more than 6,000 PhDs a year; only China and Japan produce a larger number. The graduates of Indian colleges and science and technical schools are fully fluent in English, enabling them to collaborate efficiently with U.S. corporate customers. Thanks to minuscule telecommunication costs, this competitive workforce is able to work at a fraction of the cost of similarly skilled workers in developed countries.

India has determined that its edge in the twenty-first century will likely be based on skills, education, training, low wages, and an army of knowledge workers who can easily compete on the economic field.

The World Economic Forum ranked India's global competitiveness 43rd overall on the strength of its capacity for innovation and process management and the skills of its scientists and engineers. These factors are strong enough to offset India's still low levels of per-capita income, lack of widespread technology, and low literacy levels—about 40 percent of India's population cannot read or write.

Sound Financial Systems and Policies: *Favorable*

India's financial standing has improved substantially since 2000 because of recent growth in exports and greater productivity, and due to this it has been ranked as favorable. The national government's budget deficits have declined as the GDP has increased, falling to 6 percent of GDP in 2007, compared with more than 10 percent of GDP in 2002. The current account deficit is being used to finance infrastructure investments that are essential to generate sustained domestic demand. As a result, outstanding public debt remains high at approximately 80 percent of GDP. Efforts to ensure sound fiscal policies are maintained include the Fiscal Responsibility and Budget Management Act, which sets targets for the national government's deficits, the adoption of a value-added tax (VAT) structure, and the Twelfth Finance Commission, which encourages states to adopt fiscal responsibility legislation.

Monetary Policy

The Reserve Bank of India (RBI—the central bank) has endeavored to balance large government borrowing with the industry's need for credit, while keeping inflation under control. RBI has generally been successful without creating undue upward pressure on interest rates. RBI uses bank rates, reverse repo rate, and cash-reserve ratio (CRR) to calibrate short-term movements in interest rates and liquidity. RBI has focused on reducing interest rates and cutting rates frequently since 1998. However, it will not hesitate to tighten liquidity to control volatility in foreign exchange rates and discourage speculation, and it remains vigilant on inflation.

Exchange Rates in Currency

The rupee is expected to float, and there is likely to be no change in India's managed process policy by the RBI. The government could move toward full convertibility of currency from the current status of convertibility onto the current accounts in the next two to three years. According to a Goldman Sachs study, currencies appreciate as productivity in the country increases to the level of purchasing power parity. The three catalysts for currency appreciation are growth in employment, growth in capital stock, and growth in technical productivity. By these standards, Wilson, Purushothaman forecasts that the rupee is likely to advance further.

Inflation

Annual average inflation rates as measured by the wholesale price index was 4.5 percent in 2005–2006 fiscal year, compared to 6.4 percent for 2004–2005. The economy had real GDP growth of 8.4 percent in 2005–2006, which was higher than the real GDP growth of 7.5 percent in the previous year. The efforts by the RBI to control its monetary policy through interest rate adjustments by most experts have been quite successful, since inflationary pressure can generally result from increase in foreign exchange reserves caused by export growth. The RBI has expressed its intention to continue to monitor inflation.

India's debt markets are not as well developed relative to some of its neighbors, making it more difficult for firms to obtain financing for expansion and growth. Indian firms rely more extensively on equity capital provided by private investors rather than debt or government finance, with the result that corporate managers emphasize profits and performance.

Fiscal Control

In recent years, India's deficits have been a result of extra spending on social programs, infrastructure, and defense. Although India's current account deficit remains an area of concern, these deficits have been trending down for the last several years. In fiscal year 2005–2006, the deficit amounted to 4.1 percent of GDP, and the government is hoping to reduce that to 3.8 percent in 2006–2007. The government passed a revised Fiscal Responsibility and Budget Management Act to eliminate the deficit by fiscal year 2009.

External Debt

India's external debt has been going up marginally, but the debt service continues to be a smaller portion of the economy. This again is a positive sign for the economy if the present trends hold. External debt in India presently accounts for 21 percent of GDP, with a debt-service ratio around 16 percent of total exports—a reasonable figure when compared to that of Mexico (25 percent) and Russia (13 percent).

Securities Markets

India has 23 stock exchanges, the most important of which are the National Stock Exchange (NSE), the Bombay Stock Exchange (BSE). NSE and BSE are among the top five markets in the world, by number of trades.

The NSE is an electronic order–driven market linked by satellite to 240 towns and cities in India. The Securities and Exchange Board of India (SEBI) is the controlling authority of all the securities markets with very strict oversight, and it has all the regulatory framework expected of a modern securities system. India is one of the few countries where stock futures have been a big success. Stock futures are traded in 119 large-cap stocks as well as on indexes.

India's Growth Industries

Publicly traded Indian companies potentially available to foreign investors are restricted in number and represent a small fraction of what is available to local investors or to foreigners who register as institutional money managers. Therefore, the universe of investing is limited to those listed on foreign exchanges, such as the New York Stock Exchange (NYSE) as ADRs, or global ADR (GDRs) in other countries. In that regard, India is not very different from many emerging countries, since it is concerned about inflow of "hot money" and a quick exit of such money if there is a financial or political shock.

India has liberalized its rules dramatically by allowing an "easier" registration process for foreign financial services companies and thereby allowing foreign investors to participate in the securities market. Since many of these businesses are global, they are also interested in raising capital overseas, or in providing the prestige of listings in New York, London, Singapore, or Luxembourg. Many of these companies are listed on exchanges and are available for investment.

A broad overview of the Indian stock market is represented by various Indexes such as the BSE 100 Index (Bombay Stock Exchange). However, the MSCI India Index is a benchmark made up of about 160 publicly traded Indian companies (see Table 10.2).

An investor purchasing shares of an exchange-traded fund (ETF) such as the iShares MSCI India fund (managed by Barclay's Global Investors and traded on the Singapore Exchange) would come close to replicating India's entire investable universe cost effectively. Another option is to buy shares of mutual funds (see Appendix E). Managers of these actively managed mutual funds may apply their own valuation standards and judgments in selecting stocks for their portfolios, such as PE ratios and profitability, projected growth rates, and so on. They may also selectively overweight or underweight certain sectors, reflecting the portfolio manager's view of the market opportunities and prices.

TABLE 10.2 MSCI India Index Sector Weights (as of July 31, 2007)

Economic sector (Global Industry Classification System)	Float-adjusted shares (% of investable index market capitalization)
Financials	25
Energy	18
Information Technology	17
Industrials	11
Materials	7
Consumer Discretionary	5
Consumer Staples	5
Telecommunication Services	5
Health Care	4
Utilities	3

Another option for investors is to choose to weight your investments in India more toward certain industry sectors by purchasing individual company stocks whenever available to build a portfolio or to complement an ETF or mutual fund holding. In making such selections, it is wise to consider both future growth prospects and the current market value of companies in the target industries. Companies with very high price-to-earnings or price-to-book ratios for their industry may already have priced in much of the growth potential for that particular industry.

In the remainder of the chapter, we will discuss these and other investment opportunities available to a foreign investor.

Financials

Financial services companies in India represent enormous potential as per-capita incomes increase. Many domestic banks and brokerage firms are small by international standards, limiting the size of deals that they can manage. Well-capitalized domestic banks, and the entry of Western banks, are helping to finance India's growing businesses (many of which are still substantially state owned) as they expand the services offered to urban populations and expand into rural areas. *The Economist* forecasts annual growth in business loans by India's banks will average 21 percent through 2009, and a sharp acceleration in the rate of consumer loan growth for vehicles, mortgages, and credit cards. Banks such as HDFC, ICICI Bank, and State Bank of India are favorites of many portfolios. They are taking advantage of the boom mortgage and consumer loans such as auto loans.

China vs. India: A Comparison of Equity Markets

A *BusinessWeek* analysis of financial data from Standard & Poor's Compustat shows Indian corporations are more competitive than Chinese firms. Of 340 publicly listed companies from 1999 through 2003, with a few exceptions Indian firms have outperformed Chinese firms in both return on equity (ROE) and Return on invested capital (ROIC).

India is a well-functioning market economy and focuses on profits and performance. China's government has big stakes in most publicly listed companies, so managers are mindful of government agendas such as employment, says Joydeep Mukherjee, a director in the sovereign rating group at Standard & Poor's.

It is quite difficult to get capital in India, says Marcus Rosagen, regional head of equity research for Citigroup in Hong Kong.

In India, firms raise a large share of capital in equity markets, so private investors play a key role in allocating capital and place emphasis on return of capital. In China, given its enormous saving rate and large sum of FDI, the cost of financing is quite low, which fuels excess capacity and reduces hurdles to starting a new business. The Chinese are also concentrated in low-margin manufacturing as opposed to high-end services, which is the forte of the bulk of Indian firms.

Source: Pete Engardio, *Chindia*. New York: McGraw-Hill, 2006, pp. 122–123

Energy/Utilities/Power

India has enormous and growing needs for petroleum and natural gas. Its planning agencies estimate that over the next 20 years imports of oil and gas will rise to 90 percent of yearly consumption.

Energy generation and distribution, oil refining, and various infrastructure projects are priority areas for new investments. According to India's planning commission, India needs to triple its power generation over the next two decades. Beyond that, it needs more oil and natural gas to keep up with its growth.

Currently, India imports over 70 percent of its oil largely from the Middle East, or about 4 percent of its GDP. Bombay's Strategic Foresight Group predicts that by 2030 India could import 90 percent of its oil and gas. That's why India is scouring the world for energy supplies from Africa to Latin America, and Kazakhstan to remote parts of Siberia.

The leading energy company ONGC (Oil and Natural Gas Commission) and its subsidiaries are scouring the world to acquire oil fields and rights to exploration in future. There is no doubt that India will embark on diplomatic forays around the globe and compete strongly with other nations such as China and even the United States in some of the remotest places in Africa, Russia, and Southeast Asia, to secure energy supplies. However, according to China National Petroleum Corporation (CNPC), China spends about $40 billion to India's $3.5 billion on energy investments per year (2003).

For India, like China, future energy supplies will determine the path of growth and the welfare of its large population.

Meanwhile, demand for natural gas, which stood at 0.6 trillion cubic feet (tcf) in 1995 had reached 0.9 tcf by 2002 and is expected to touch 1.2 tcf by 2010 and 1.6 tcf by 2015. Domestic sources of supply met over 90 percent of demand as late as 2003. However, despite the increased reserves discovered by recent exploration, the country will need to import up to one-third of its projected consumption needs by 2015.

In the gas market, the Gas Authority of India Limited (GAIL) has started to invest heavily in equity stakes in liquefied natural gas (LNG) plants in Oman and Iran, and is building port facilities and pipelines at home to handle large imports. GAIL is also pursuing plans for direct pipelines from neighboring Bangladesh, Burma, Iran, and even Pakistan.

In recent years, India's Oil and Natural Gas Corporation has bought equity stakes in oil fields in Iraq, Sudan, Libya, Angola, Burma, Sakhalin in Russia, Vietnam, Iran, and Syria.

Other Indian public-sector undertakings have become involved—not only in acquiring exploration and exploitation rights, but also in establishing sales outlets for Indian petroleum products and in offering a variety of technical services.

Prominent Local Energy Companies

- GAIL (India) Limited Energy Oil & Gas Operations
- Oil & Natural Gas Corporation
- Reliance Energy
- NTPC

Prominent Local Utility

- CESC Ltd.

Information Technology

Information technology industries include business process outsourcing, computing services, software design and development, hardware, and semiconductors. This sector represents about 17 percent of the total market. India's past technology exports have concentrated on development and labor-intensive business processing services. Today, India's strong ranking in innovation (ranked 26 in the WEF competitive index) portends a growing market share in software design and innovative technology offerings. Deutsche Bank Research, for example, forecasts that software exports from Indian companies will continue to grow by around 50 percent annually, in part because of India's steady supply of well-trained, English-speaking staff at salaries that are a fraction of their Western counterparts.

Millennium Bug!

The "Millennium Bug" phenomenon may prove to be the single event that altered the landscape of the Indian technology industry, particularly software. Beginning in late 1998, there was widespread concern over computers crashing at the beginning of the new millennium. This proved to be a great gift to Indian software businesses. India had thousands of trained software engineers looking for opportunities. The American high-tech market was booming. American software engineers were irked by the drudgery of having to fix and recode the computer systems so that the change in millennium would not prove disastrous. There was fear of banking systems failing, air traffic control being incapacitated, and widespread blackouts. American corporations discovered that not only could these Indian software engineers fix the bug, they could do so at a fraction of the cost. Given the urgency and time constraints, this was fortuitous. An army of Indian engineers was hired and sent overseas to American companies to fix the systems. They fulfilled their assignments in a timely manner, long before the dreaded midnight hour, and saved companies a bundle in the process. The millennium came and went with no notable mishaps. Indian engineers had performed well, and American companies were delighted with the results.

India's National Association of Software and Service Companies (NASSCOM) is a leading trade association for India's IT industry that provides a wealth of information on industry trends. NASSCOM data shows that all of the country's IT industries are expanding. Total revenue from the IT segment jumped from 1.2 percent of GDP in 1998 to about 5.4 percent in 2007, and now stands at $48 billion. Business process outsourcing (BPO) services are expanding at above 25 percent a year, and include complex processes involving rule-based decision making and knowledge-based research services in addition to traditional data entry processing. Domestic demand for IT services, software and hardware is also picking up, rising 21 percent in 2007 to $16 billion. Total software and services (excluding hardware) revenues are growing at more than 30 percent a year, while hardware sales are expanding by more than 17 percent annually. Kiran Karnik, president of NASSCOM, predicts that new IT innovation services, including process innovation, product innovation, and business model innovation, could add an additional revenue stream worth $50 billion by 2012.

Increases in direct investments from non-Indian multinational corporations (MNCs) will also propel growth in Indian IT (see Table 10.3). In 2007, MNCs announced that a record $10 billion is planned in new investment over the next few years, according to NASSCOM.

Prominent Local IT Companies

- Tata Consultancy Services
- Infosys Technologies
- Wipro Technologies

TABLE 10.3 Key Highlights of Indian IT Sector Performance

USD billion	FY2004	FY2005	FY2006	FY2007	FY2008E
IT Services	**10.4**	**13.5**	**17.8**	**23.5**	**31.0**
Exports	7.3	10.0	13.3	18.0	23.1
Domestic	3.1	3.5	4.5	5.5	7.9
BPO	**3.4**	**5.2**	**7.2**	**9.5**	**12.5**
Exports	3.1	4.6	6.3	8.4	10.9
Domestic	0.3	0.6	0.9	1.1	1.6
Engineering Services and R&D, Software Products	**2.9**	**3.8**	**5.3**	**6.5**	**8.5**
Exports	2.5	3.1	4.0	4.9	6.3
Domestic	0.4	0.7	1.3	1.6	2.2
Total Software and Services Revenues	**16.7**	**22.5**	**30.3**	**39.5**	**52.0**
Of which, exports are	**12.9**	**17.7**	**23.6**	**31.3**	**40.3**
Hardware	**5.0**	**5.6**	**7.1**	**8.5**	**12.0**
Exports	n.a.	0.5	0.6	0.5	0.5
Domestic	n.a.	5.1	6.5	8.0	11.5
Total IT Industry (including Hardware)	**21.6**	**28.2**	**37.4**	**48.0**	**64.0**

Source: Nasscom

- HCL Technologies
- Cognizant
- Satyam Computer Services
- Tech Mahindra
- Patni Computer Systems

Industrials

The industrial sector encompasses a large number of industries, ranging from heavy construction and engineering to electric power generation equipment, shipping, and aerospace. Many of these have enormous growth potential as public and private organizations invest in roads, airports, ports, schools, electric capacity, and other infrastructure improvements. The International Development Finance Corporation (IDFC), set up in 1997, offers loans and private equity funds to help finance many infrastructure projects and companies in related industries.

Industrials are the indication that the country is on a major path to prominence in the coming decades. India, although slow to achieve the industrial transformation of the last century, is now on a warpath to achieve quantum gains. The industrial sector is gaining ground from manufacture of agricultural machinery to wind turbine, and from earth-moving equipment to indigenous manufacture of aircraft parts.

Prominent Local Machinery Companies

- Larsen & Turbo
- Bharat Heavy Electricals
- Crompton Greaves
- Reliance Industries
- Ashok Leyland
- Bharat Forge

Infrastructure Development Finance Corporation

India's creaking infrastructure is a daily nightmare for millions who are weighed down by the toll it takes on their lives. However, Indians are becoming keenly aware of it. A private/public partnership is on the way for a long overdue fix.

When the company called IDFC (Infrastructure Development Finance Corporation) went public, its shares nearly doubled on its first day of trading due to the expectation and hope surrounding its mission. "Investors realize the huge investment potential in Indian infrastructure," declared Partha Bardhan, the New Delhi–based executive director of the consulting firm KPMG.

IDFC will lend money to developers of roads, ports, airports, energy, and telecom projects. Its biggest and most versatile public/private enterprise so far is the massive $38 billion project to rehabilitate India's roads. Companies will build highways with government assistance and then operate them for profit by charging tolls. Competition for the contract is stiff. About a fifth of the planned 30,000-mile road network is now finished, with the remainder scheduled for completion by 2012. There is a major underground metro for Delhi, with ambitious expansion into surrounding suburbs to relieve the chokehold on the roads in the capital city.

The public/private partnership is scheduled to improve airports in Delhi, Mumbai, Hyderabad, and Bangalore, with both global and local contractors making a major push to finish the projects.

Source: Pete Engardio, *Chindia*. New York: McGraw-Hill, 2006, p. 219.

Transportation

The transportation infrastructure subindustry includes airports, owners of railways and toll roads, and seaports. One project is a $38 billion investment in a 30,000-mile network of toll roads and highways, scheduled for completion by 2012. Others include airports in Delhi, Mumbai, Hyderabad, and Bangalore. PPPs are also active in this subindustry. The Kalyani Group of Companies and SAB International, for example, have formed Nandi Infrastructure Corridor Enterprises (NICE) to develop the Bangalore-Mysore Infrastructure Corridor. The new tollway will drop the commute between Bangalore and Mysore from 4 hours to 90 minutes.

Passenger airlines, another transportation subindustry, are expected to benefit from India's growing travel and tourism business. As a result of deregulation, the number of domestic airlines is increasing rapidly, serving both business travel demand and tourism. U.S. aerospace manufacturer Boeing forecasts domestic travelers on Indian airlines will rise from 60 million in 2006 to 100 million by 2010.

Prominent Local Transportation Companies

- Container Corporation
- Sical Logistics Limited Air India
- Air Sahara
- Jet Airways
- Kingfisher Airlines

Construction, Engineering, and Heavy Industry

Other segments of the industrials sector that focus on infrastructure are construction and engineering, electrical equipment, and industrial machinery. Quipo Infrastructure Equipment Limited, the country's largest equipment rental company, was able to raise RS1.5 billion in private equity funding through IDIC in 2007 to expand its services and provide equipment for heavy construction, oil, and gas infrastructure development.

Prominent Local Companies

- Jaiprakash Construction
- Hindustan Construction
- Nagarjuna Construction Co. Ltd.
- Housing Development and Infrastructure Ltd.
- Bharat Heavy Electricals Limited (BHEL)
- Larsen & Toubro
- Bharat Electronics

Basic Materials

The basic materials sector includes companies that manufacture chemicals, construction materials, glass, paper, wood products, metals, and steel. It also includes mining. India has vast reserves of metals including iron ore, coal, and bauxite (used in aluminum production) and some precious metals. Packaging and containers is another significant subindustry. Given India's massive construction projects, building materials such as cement are in great demand. Ironically, lack of roads can be a major impediment to their timely delivery.

Some Prominent Local Companies

- Associated Cement
- Ultratech India Limited

Chemicals

India's chemical industry accounts for about 7 percent of GDP and just 2 percent of the global market. At current growth rates, it is forecast to grow to $60 billion by 2010, about 8 percent of GDP; however, some observers estimate revenues as high as $100 billion in 2010 assuming greater investment in higher-margin fine chemicals and specialty chemicals. A recent report by U.S.-based consulting firm McKinsey & Company suggests that India's technological capabilities in chemistry, engineering, and effective process management could make it one of the developing world's top two exporters (along with China) of specialty chemicals. Ciba Specialty Chemicals (India) Limited, for example, has established a Research and Technology Centre in Mumbai. The Indian fertilizer industry has emerged as the fourth largest producer of fertilizers in the world after China, the United States, and Russia.

Price pressures are forcing companies toward offshoring. Given India's capability in chemistry, engineering, and cost reduction, the country has the potential to become one of the developing world's top two exporters (along with China) of specialty chemicals and to increase exports as much $15 billion by 2015.

Prominent Local Companies

- ION Exchange
- Jubilant Organosys

Consumer Discretionary

The consumer discretionary sector includes industries that may be more sensitive to economic cycles. These include automobiles, household furnishings and appliances, clothing retailers, recreation equipment, entertainment, and the travel and hospitality segments. India's growing consumer demand for goods and services bodes well for this sector, as do trends in the travel, hospitality, and entertainment industries.

AUTOMOBILES India's car market has emerged as one of the fastest growing in the world. The number of cars sold domestically is projected to double by 2010, and domestic production is skyrocketing as foreign makers are setting up their own production plants in India. The government's 10-year plan aims to create a $145 billion auto industry by 2016.

According to McKinsey, the auto sector's drive to lower costs will push outsourcing. The auto sector could be worth $375 billion by 2015, up from $65 billion in 2002. McKinsey thinks India could capture $25 billion of this amount. Out of 400 Indian suppliers, 80 percent have the ISO 9000 certificate—the international standard for quality management.

Toyota in India

In 2001, Toyota was the first automaker to see India as a source of components; after concluding that the advantages outweighed any near-term shortcomings, the company invested almost $200 million in six joint ventures to help local suppliers develop scale in their manufacturing operations. Toyota also focused on localizing the content of Qualis and Corolla models. Local content now accounts for 74 percent and 55 percent of the cost of Qualis and Corolla, respectively. Through economy of scale in manufacturing, Toyota then turned India into a regional sourcing hub.

Among the ranks of foreign companies pouring money into India's auto sector is DaimlerChrysler, which has more than 20 joint ventures with Indian suppliers to produce cars at the company's factory near Mumbai. Meanwhile, Fiat and Tata Motors Ltd. are making cars, engines, and transmissions; Germany's MAN has joined with Force Motors; and Swedish manufacturer Volvo has partnered with Jaico Automobiles. The country's largest passenger car manufacturing plant, with capacity as high as 800,000 cars a year, is a $900 million facility being built in Chennai by French manufacturer Renault, its Japanese subsidiary Nissan, and India's Mahindra & Mahindra. Production is slated to begin in mid-2009.

Most of India's auto production at present is destined for local markets, which is set to experience a boom known as "motorization" as per-capita income approaches $1,000. This boom is expected to support massive increases in production, fueled by some $8 billion in new manufacturing capacity scheduled to be built in the next three to four years. By 2015, India's domestic auto market is forecast to be one of the top 10 markets for vehicle sales, with sales of four-wheel vehicles rising to 4.2 million, up from 1.1 million in 2006.

The People's Car–NANO

In 2001, Tata Group—the largest conglomerate of diverse business in India that had for years been making sturdy trucks—decided to embark on the business of making passenger cars. The result was the first indigenously made car, known in India as Indica. Tata used its low-cost engineering skills to work to produce the car that has been a big seller.

The Tata Indica retails for about $6,600 and is exported to Europe. Tata's decision to use cheap but skilled labor instead of robots, as used by the Japanese, shaved about $1 billion in costs, and India can break even at only 8,000 vehicles, about 30 percent less volume than global auto companies need to generate profit.

However, the dream of CEO Ratan Tata is to produce a car in India that will sell for $2,200—a "people's car." He says, "I wanted to change the rules of the game." He adds, "I wanted to change the way business is done."

At $2,500, Tata's "people's car" compact is designed to appeal to 5 million Indians who currently own motorbikes and cannot afford a standard economy car.

Tata's "people's car," shown in January of 2008, will use a combination of steel and composite plastic for its body, put together with industrial adhesive along with nuts and bolts. But Tata will attempt to do something radical by replacing the traditional model of supplying the car from the factory through established dealer networks. It is his plan to make all basic components of the car in Tata plants, and then to send the car off the assembly line much like a bicycle in a knocked-down kit form.

These will be shipped across the country to Tata-trained franchises. The mechanics will keep kits in their garages and assemble the cars on demand for customers and then service them as needed. "It will give an opportunity to young capable people to create an enterprise," says Tata. But the move will also save an estimated 20 percent of the automaker's production costs. Kumar Bhattacharyya, director of Warwick Manufacturing Group at the University of Warwick in Britain, says, "Tata's plan makes the car a commodity."

Source: Pete Engardio, *Chindia*. New York: McGraw-Hill, 2006, p. 90.

Exports of passenger vehicles are also set to rise, forecast at 500,000 vehicles by 2010, up from about 170,000 passenger cars in 2006. Already, India's component manufacturers are becoming important players in components and aftermarket parts. India's auto component exports grew at an annual rate of 25 percent in five years to 2003 and are now worth $1 billion of the U.S. market. LG is making handsets in India to take advantage of the local market. Others include Mahindra & Mahindra, a market leader in general utility vehicles that formed a global network of custom parts factories to serve Western carmakers, and Bharat Forge, an exporter of chassis and engine components.

Some Prominent Local Companies

- Mahindra & Mahindra
- Maruti Udyog, Ltd.
- Bajaj Auto
- Tata Motors

TRAVEL AND HOSPITALITY India's tourism hotel and aviation industries are booming as record numbers of business and leisure visitors descend on the country's major cities. The 20,000 hotels that comprise organized businesses in India, accounting for about 500,000 hotel rooms, are expected to see higher room rates of 10 percent or more over the next five years, according to a study by Crisil Research. Other studies show that metropolitan four-star hotels are seeing increases in room rates of 15 percent to 30 percent a year in the near term as demand for premium lodging outstrips supplies.

Prominent Local Companies

- Indian Hotels Company Ltd. (IHCL)
- Hotel Leelaventure, owners of the Leela group of hotels
- Hotel developers like ITC, EIH, Bharat Hotels, Viceroy, DLF, Unitech, and Royal Palms
- Air India
- India Airlines
- Jet Airways
- Kingfisher Airlines

RETAILING India's huge consumer population goes hand in hand with opportunities in retailing. Retail businesses account for 10 percent of GDP, 8 percent of the employment, and more than $300 billion in annual revenue. The Indian retail industry has a market size of about $312 billion, with organized retailing comprising only 2.8 percent—estimated at around $8.7 billion—of the total retailing market. The vast majority of this business is made up of small, independent shops run by nearly 15 million store owners.

Chain stores claim less than $10 billion of total revenue today, but that figure is forecast to grow to $30 to $70 billion by 2010.

India has kept the retail sector largely closed to outsiders to safeguard the livelihood of small store owners and allows only 51 percent of foreign investment in single-brand retail with prior government permission.

The retailing industry seems poised for significant growth in the coming years, owing to the presence of a vast market, growing consumer awareness about product quality and services, higher disposable income of consumers, and the desire to try out new products. According to the Global Retail Development Index of 2005 conducted by A. T. Kearney, India was ranked first among the 30 "most attractive" retailing destinations across the globe.

Organized retail will form 10 percent of total retailing by 2010. From 2006 to 2010, the organized sector will grow at the compound annual growth rate (CAGR) of around 49.53 percent per annum. Cultural and regional differences in India are the biggest challenges confronting retailers. This factor deters the retailers in India from adopting a single retail format.

Today, India is on the cusp of modern retailing, having emerged from early stages. The growing preference of the affluent and upper middle classes for shopping malls and upscale stores for convenience and choice has been the driving factor behind this transformation. From supermarkets such as Big Bazaar or Foodworld, which are large self-service stores selling a variety of products at discounted prices to malls and department stores such as Crossroads, Lifestyle, and Westside, Indian consumers are fast catching up with their global counterparts.

As per a survey by Euromonitor International on the retail industry in India (March 2004), there were only 14 companies that ran department stores in the country and two with hypermarkets. While the number of businesses operating supermarkets was higher (385 in 2003), most of these had only one outlet.

Prominent Local Retail Companies

- Arvind Mills Ltd.
- Pantaloon Retail India Ltd.
- Trent Ltd.
- Bata India Ltd
- Videocon Appliances Ltd.
- Godrej Agrovet Ltd.

ENTERTAINMENT (TV/MOVIES) Bollywood is the largest producer of commercial movies in the world, easily surpassing Hollywood. Mass television is the new medium, however, with hundreds of channels available to visitors. The growth path for the entertainment industry is likely to be both impressive and competitive.

Most Prominent Local Company

- ZeeTele Films

CONSUMER STAPLES These are companies whose business is less sensitive to the economic cycles, including manufacturers and distributors of food, beverages, and tobacco, and producers of nondurable household goods and personal products. These companies benefit from rapidly growing populations with rising spending money.

India has also become one of the fastest-growing markets for cosmetics and toiletries, and marketers are recognizing the tremendous potential in this budding market. Despite having among the lowest levels of per-capita spending on personal care products, the market is evolving into one of the most promising worldwide, particularly with regard to skin care.

Prominent Local Companies

- ITC
- Nestle India
- Colgate Palmolive India
- Hindustan Lever

Telecommunications Services

One of the fastest-growing sectors in the country, telecommunications has been zooming up the growth curve at a feverish pace in the past few years. The year 2007 saw India achieve the distinction of having the world's lowest call rates (2 to 3 U.S. cents), the fastest growth in the number of subscribers (15.31 million in four months), the fastest sale of a million mobile phones (one week), the world's cheapest mobile handset ($17.20), and the world's most affordable color phone ($27.42).

The phenomenal subscriber growth has now topped 60 million new subscribers a year. Mobile phone sales, currently worth $15.6 billion a year, are growing by 15 percent to 20 percent annually, and some experts predict the country's production of handsets will grow 25 percent a year to reach 95 million in 2011. Service providers are projected to more than double by 2010, rising to $33 billion from $13 billion in 2006. Bharti Televentures and Reliance are among the large mobile operators. Bharti Televentures has 12 million subscribers and 22 percent market share. The company contracted with Western network providers to support services, allowing it to focus on signing up new customers and managing customer accounts.

The recent deregulation of the telecommunications industry is attracting a huge influx of foreign investment. British firm Vodafone invested $2 billion in 2007, amounting to about 20 percent of its total global expenditure. Infrastructure and equipment providers are also entering the Indian market.

Essar Telecom Tower and Infrastructure, GTL Infrastructure, and Quipo built 18,000 new towers in 2007 alone. Meanwhile, U.S.-based Cisco is investing $1 billion in the Indian market, including a factory in Chennai to manufacture phones configured for the Internet.

India offers an unprecedented opportunity for telecom service operators, infrastructure vendors, manufacturers, and associated services companies. Not to be left behind, Indian cellular operators have lined up investments of about $20 billion over the next two years to bring over 80 percent of the population under mobile coverage. The planned investment for the next couple of years is 50 percent higher than what has been invested in the last 12 years.

Prominent Local Telecommunications Companies

- Bharti Televentures
- Reliance Communications
- Tata Communications

Bharti Televentures

Bharti Televentures is one of the largest mobile operators in India. It has 12 million subscribers and 22 percent market share. In 2005, it earned $330 million on sales of $1.8 billion. CEO Sunil Mital boasts, "Bharti charges 2 cents per minute on its cellular services and retains 1 cent from each call." How does the company do it? Bharti realized that the Western model of building and manufacturing a hugely expensive cellular network while providing cheap reliable service was impossible. So the company tried something radical. It signed a $725 million three-year contract with cellular network providers Ericsson, Nokia, and Siemens. This allowed Bharti to fix its costs by "outsourcing" and instead to turn its attention to marketing and customer service. One year after that, Bharti added six million subscribers, one quarter of the annual subscriber growth, and by far the fastest growth sign-up rate in India. According to Erik Oldmark, who runs the marketing strategy for Ericsson, "It is a big transformation and it is becoming a global model."

Health Care

Health care services in India are experiencing double-digit growth rates, and are expected to reach $50 to $60 billion within a few years, accounting for an estimated 6 percent to 7 percent of GDP. A growing supply of skilled doctors, nurses, and technicians will help bring health care to India's rural populations. Growth in private health insurance and government incentives to encourage private investments in care facilities will also help make medical care affordable for a large portion of the population. Currently, only about 40 million Indians have health insurance; this number is expected to rise to 160 million by 2010.

Medical tourism is growing rapidly and is forecast to reach $2 billion by 2010, thanks to highly skilled, Western-trained surgeons and the rise of private-sector companies such as Apollo Hospitals, Escorts Group, and Fortis Healthcare. The United Kingdom's government health agency, National Health System, has designated India as a preferred destination for surgery. Costs related to advanced surgeries are just 10 percent the cost in the United States.

Industry sectors that will benefit from growing demand for health care services include hospitals, diagnostic centers, and medical device manufacturers.

PHARMACEUTICAL AND BIOTECHNOLOGY India's drug industry is growing at about 9 percent a year, enjoying low production and R&D costs and a supply of highly skilled scientists and technicians. Although the pharmaceutical industry is highly fragmented, with more than 250 competitors keeping margins low, the largest (Dr. Reddy) has a 7 percent market share. Producers of generic drugs and companies in the biotechnology industry may have unique growth opportunities.

Recently adopted patent laws offer some protection to Western firms that will outsource manufacturing or set up joint R&D ventures in coming years.

As a result of the expansion, the Indian pharmaceutical and health care market is undergoing rapid growth in its coverage, services, and spending in the public and private sectors. The health care market has opened a window of opportunities in the medical device field and has boosted clinical trials in India.

A highly organized sector, the Indian pharmaceutical industry is estimated to be worth $4.5 billion, growing at about 8 percent to 9 percent annually. It ranks very high in the Third World, in terms of technology, quality, and range of medicines manufactured. From simple headache pills to sophisticated antibiotics and complex cardiac compounds, almost every type of medicine is now made indigenously.

The leading 250 pharmaceutical companies control 70 percent of the market, with the market leader holding nearly 7 percent of the market share. It is an extremely fragmented market with severe price competition and government price control. The pharmaceutical industry in India meets around 70 percent of the country's demand for bulk drugs, drug intermediates, pharmaceutical formulations, chemicals, tablets, capsules, orals, and injectables.

Manufacturers are free to produce any drug duly approved by the Drug Control Authority. Technologically strong and totally self-reliant, the pharmaceutical industry in India has low costs of production, low R&D costs, and innovative scientific manpower. India is well placed to take advantage of this, according to a study that looked at 21 Indian firms.

India's importance in the pharmaceutical sector is growing as an important market and as a source of capabilities. In a survey of 179 global pharmaceutical executives conducted by Bain & Company and Knowledge@Wharton, 45 percent of respondents were from companies with headquarters in North America. The study showed that the global pharmaceutical executives believe India will figure prominently in their businesses five years from now; 38 percent thought doing business in India is extremely important today, and 62 percent expect it to be so five years from now.

India has amended its patent laws in line with World Trade Organization regulations to include all patent protections and not just the manufacturing process. This new law will allow global companies to set up R&D and take advantage of the low-cost scientific talent without fear of cheap copies being sold before patents expire. According to Ranjit Sahani, vice chairman of Novartis India, "India has emerged as a reliable source of quality medicine at affordable prices."

Prominent Local Health Care Companies

- Cipla
- Glenmark Pharmaceuticals
- Dr. Reddy's Laboratories
- Apollo Hospitals
- Nicholas Piramal India Ltd.
- Sun Pharmaceuticals Ltd.

Health Care Innovations

Eye Care

Arvind Eye Care Center is located in Madurai in southern India. Designed by an ophthalmologist, Dr. G. Venkataswamy, the center provides inexpensive cataract surgery for $50 to $300, compared to $2,000 in the United States, which includes locally made intraocular lenses inserted during the surgery.

(*continued*)

At Arvind's three hospitals, 300 doctors perform 50 surgeries a day. At any one time in the operating room, four doctors are working on patients side by side. Patients are sent home to their villages the next day, to be followed by paramedics for postoperative care. According to Burjor P. Banaji, a well-known ophthalmologist in Mumbai, the "assembly line" procedure does not hurt the outcome, and results are excellent. According to Arvind, the lenses are manufactured for $5, which is a major reduction from the $50 the hospital used to pay the American company Allergen for its lenses.

Source: Pete Engardio, *Chindia*. New York: McGraw-Hill, 2006, pg. 1570.

Jaipur Foot

In 1960, a Hindu temple sculptor named Ramchandra developed an artificial limb in the city of Jaipur in northern India. He observed that the commercially made and imported limbs were unable to function efficiently under Indian conditions and accommodate to postures such as squatting, cross-leg sitting, or immersion in water. Prosthetic feet manufactured in the United States, for example, cost $250 to $1,500—a huge sum for the average Indian. Ramchandra developed the "Jaipur foot" from rubberized material, which is more flexible, accommodates difficult Indian conditions as well as postures, and can be immersed in water by those working on farms. The cost is $30. It costs so little because of cheap yet flexible and sturdy materials, labor-intensive (low cost in India) production, and because its production uses less machinery. Now, the Jaipur foot is distributed by the charitable organization BMVSS (Bhagwan Mahaveer Viklang Sahayata Samiti) and exported around the developing world.

In 2002, BMVSS collaborated with India's Space Research Organization to improve the limb by using lightweight polyurethane normally used for making rocket propellant. This is likely to reduce the weight by half and cut the production costs by 10 percent to $27.

Source: Peter Engardio, Chindia. New York: McGraw-Hill, 2006, pg. 158.

CHAPTER 11

Tradition, Truth, and Transformation

The History of China

The Chinese use two brush strokes to write the word "crisis." One brush stroke stands for danger; the other for opportunity. In a crisis, be aware of the danger—but recognize the opportunity.

—Former President Richard Nixon

Upon returning from his historic trip to China in February 1972, United States President Richard Nixon—having just planted the seeds of diplomacy inside a communist nation during the Cold War—enlightened his "beloved" press with the insightful, yet paradoxical observation stated at the beginning of this chapter. Years later, fictional everyman Homer Simpson would condense this bit of Nixonian wisdom, coining the term *crisatunity*.

Though Nixon's words ironically foreshadowed his own downfall—America's 37th president would suffer many crises before his eventual resignation—they perhaps best summarize the modern history of China. A nation that has endured famine, war, poverty, and immense social upheaval, China has been no stranger to turmoil over the last 60 years. Evolving from a so-called "backward nation of peasants" into a political and economic giant, China has withstood crises that have crippled nations and relegated empires to the footnotes of textbooks. This ascent to prominence has not only redrawn the boundaries of modern history, it has redefined the global balance of power. With the world's second largest economy, mirrored by increasing political influence, present-day China bears little resemblance to a nation that only decades ago was subject to foreign occupation. A past marked by turbulence and uncertainty has been co-opted, replaced by a future epitomizing promise and prosperity. Crisatunity indeed.

A fixture on the front pages of newspapers around the world, China's actions are impossible to ignore. Pundits talk of the nation's economic prowess, politics, and problems on a daily basis, yet the nation itself—its history, culture, and particularly its *direction*—is still widely mischaracterized. Whether it is the nature of the Communist party, which continues to rule; its fragile relationship with Taiwan and the West; or that of pollution or human rights violations, China is commonly plagued by misperception. How can this be? How can the globe's most populous nation, with over one billion inhabitants and a history predating Jesus Christ by 4,000 years, be considered to have emerged only recently? How can a civilization that introduced the world to innovations such as the compass, paper, and gunpowder be perceived as having a "backward" past? Finally, why is a society with more than 50 minority groups, more than 50 separate languages, and 17 religions considered, even by some experts, to be homogeneous? Understanding where China is heading is impossible without first realizing where it has been.

Ancient History

The catchphrase "emerging nation" is often associated with China. Whether it is the nation's thriving economic sector or its entrance into organizations such as the World Trade Organization (WTO) and the United Nations, few can resist labeling Asia's largest country as "new." Though it is a nation undoubtedly in the midst of an epic transformation, the fact remains that China is one of the world's oldest civilizations, with historical records dating back nearly 5,000 years.

Seasons Change

The "spring and autumn" period, lasting from the latter half of the eighth century BC to the first half of the fifth century BC, witnessed a golden age of Chinese thinking, in effect laying the foundation for both competing ideologies and the rich philosophic tradition known today. The advancements of new religions, such as Confucianism and Taoism, were spreading rapidly, along with philosophies such as legalism and Mohism. Ideals such as upholding tradition, acquiring knowledge, and stressing trust and morality—ideals particularly applicable to Confucianism—continue to define the Chinese people nearly 3,000 years later. Also written during this period, and in contrast to the positive virtues inherent in Confucianism, was Sun Tzu's military strategy guide *The Art of War,* a text still widely referenced across a broad range of disciplines, highlighting the dark side of Chinese literature.

Conflict consumed the Chinese people until 200 BC, when the Zhou dynasty, which had ruled for almost 1,000 years, succumbed to the warlord known as Qin, who united China under his rule. Outlasting seven separate factions vying for control of the land, a distrustful Qin would consolidate power in extraordinary fashion. Under his guidance, the Great Wall of China, one of the greatest architectural achievements known to man, had been completed to the point where invaders from the north were no longer a pressing concern. Both units of measurement and language had been standardized, and anyone not adhering to these standards would be killed, as Qin gained further control. Though Qin's reign would not last long—his son Han succeeded him six years later—his legacy inspired future generations of Chinese leaders.

As the Han dynasty gave way to those of Tan, Song, and Yuan, China had become a global economic power. The famous Silk Road between China and Europe, which is still traveled today, reminds one that globalization had been a part of the Chinese economy long before modern technology. With superior shipbuilding skills, and having pioneered paper, printing, the compass, and gunpowder, China had trading partners spanning the globe. Though this expansionist mind-set had subsided briefly—the Mongolian rulers from 1279 to 1415 had no intent on scaling back further conquests—and returned in grand fashion with the onset of the Ming Dynasty rule.

Though up for debate, it has been suggested that China reached the Americas almost 70 years before Christopher Columbus, and sailed around the globe a century before Ferdinand Magellan, reinforcing the undisputed fact that China had exceptional naval capabilities.

The Qing dynasty (1760–1911) had taken over at a time of great prosperity. Chinese expansion had been resurrected, with developing economies in Europe providing an increase in demand for its exports of tea and silk, among other items. Through trade with European nations, it became painfully apparent to the Chinese that they had been left behind in the areas of science, technology, and military development. Imports, conversely, would prove to be the Qing dynasty's downfall, as British opium poured into the country. Powerless to cease the imports diplomatically, China declared war on Britain in 1840. In defeat, China realized just how far they had fallen behind the West. Signing the Nanking Treaty in 1842, China was forced to surrender Hong Kong in addition to a number of other one-sided provisions favoring the British. It was not until 1997 when Hong Kong was returned to the Chinese government, that the cloud of foreign occupation would be lifted entirely.

The defeat in the Opium Wars resulted in a new nationalist revolutionary movement that led China into the modern age. Disenchanted with the ruling elites and unwilling to accept foreign domination, the nationalists founded the Republic of China and promised improvements across all facets of life. After several short-term leaders, Sun Yat-sen assumed leadership and attempted to unify the country by proposing alliances with rival groups, such as the Chinese Communist party. After the death of Sun Yat-sen in 1925, power shifted into the hands of Chiang Kai-shek.

Coping with Victory (1949 to 1978)

The modern era of Chinese history is generally considered to have begun on October 1, 1949, when Mao Zedong, leader of the Chinese Communist party (CCP), proclaimed the birth of the People's Republic of China. As he stood before the masses at the gates of Tiananmen Square in the city of Beijing, Mao's words precluded more than 4,000 years of ancient dynasties, the rule of emperors, and imperial regimes. As Mao spoke of the communist victory over the nationalists and the dawning of a new era, it was as if all of that had suddenly been wiped away. China had become, in Mao's own words, a "blank slate." The ceremony was also a culmination, of sorts, of a more recent period characterized by violence and instability, as the Chinese Civil War (1927–1949) which had ravaged the countryside and claimed the lives of hundreds of thousands of troops, formally came to a close. Japan, which had occupied China during much of World War II, had fled the country in the aftermath of the atomic bombing of Hiroshima and Nagasaki. The CCP's domestic rival, the nationalistic Kuomintang (KMT), was also defeated and in near full retreat to the island of Taiwan. For the first time, Mao and the CCP suddenly found themselves in near complete control of the mainland—*near* being the operative word.

The CCP's victory in the Chinese Civil War carried with it great responsibility. A nation besieged by decades of war against enemies both foreign and domestic, China was also beleaguered by poverty and hyperinflation. The CCP was burdened with the unenviable task of rebuilding both the infrastructure and morale of a nation teetering between promise and complete demise. As new political institutions were created, the CCP's authority was consolidated and its popularity soared. Even those sympathetic to the old guard became optimistic in their expectations of the promise of peace from the new government. Though the specifics of the CCP's plan were somewhat vague in the immediate aftermath of victory, several distinct objectives were conveyed. In addition to formalizing its alliance with the Soviet Union, the CCP prioritized the restoration of the urban economy and, most importantly, a dramatic reform of the nation's land laws. With little time to waste, Mao and the CCP were forced to act promptly.

This Land Is Your Land

The arduous process of mass reforms began in the countryside. The rural population, consequently the CCP's base of political support, had become demoralized. Years of violence and the oppressive rule of the land-owning class had left the peasantry powerless and desperate. In the true sprit of socialism, Mao's government initiated a campaign called the Agrarian Reform Law in June 1950, which forced landlords to relinquish their farmlands to the tenant workers. Violent and widespread class conflict ensued, resulting in the virtual elimination of the land-owning class. The fortunate landlords had their property reapportioned and were assigned to "cultivating duties," while those less fortunate were simply executed. It has been estimated that some 800,000 landlords were killed during this period.

In all, it was a brutal campaign but one that accomplished a number of Mao's goals. First, the reform law solidified the CCP's popularity with the peasantry in the countryside. Second, by marginalizing or simply eliminating the land-owning class altogether, Mao effectively removed any potential sources of counterrevolution. Third, and perhaps most important, was that the land reforms were viewed as a means to increasing (and controlling) agricultural production—which Mao acknowledged as a precursor to true socialism. If China were to become a technically sophisticated modern socialist state, as was promised by Mao and the CCP, it would first need to greatly improve its agricultural output.

Though the land reforms of Mao's early years may have been perceived as unconventional through a Western lens, they were hardly original. Borrowing the model employed by its Cold War ally, the Soviet Union, China instituted a three-fold system of government, which divided power among the bureaucracy, the party (CCP), and the military (the People's Liberation Army). The reasoning behind such a structure was clear: Mao had little patience for the political process. The chairman did not want to influence agendas—he wanted to order them. This would require a centralized government as well as a rigid, planned economy, in which his policies would encounter few forms of resistance.

The New Urban Economy (Same as the Old)

With the drastic land reforms laws of the early 1950s already under way, the CCP shifted its efforts toward revitalizing the urban economy, a sector that posed a set of problems totally unique from its rural counterparts. The final years of KMT rule in China's cities were exceptionally disastrous. Currency had become essentially useless as post-war inflation skyrocketed. It has been estimated that the average cost of living rose 25 percent each week during the KMT's final six months of authority. Corruption became rampant, as well as opium addiction, prostitution, and petty crime. Much of the urban population starved as production reached a virtual standstill.

Naturally, then, China's cities were teeming with people who had no affinity for the outgoing government. For the most part, the industrialists, and indeed the urban society itself, proceeded largely unabated in the early years of Mao's rule. This, in turn, fueled the CCP's popularity in the cities. State-run enterprises of the old regime became instruments of the new ruling elite, as those who formerly controlled such institutions had, for the most part, already fled to Taiwan. Yet many lower-level bureaucrats remained, and so too did the routine procedures. Unlike in the rural areas, the Communist party was able to salvage some components of the existing apparatus to smooth a difficult transition.

The early stages of Mao's urban economy have historically been labeled as "national capitalistic" in nature, and in some sense this is true. Industries, including banks and other commercial organizations had, in fact, been nationalized without compensation. Though in most cases restricted, many sectors of the urban economy, including shopkeepers and craftsmen, retained capitalistic qualities. In some instances, merchants were actually encouraged to expand. In inheriting an urban nightmare, it was both practical and necessary for Mao's government to first rehabilitate the economy before it could be reformed. Because of this, the term "planned economy" is considered to be a more accurate characterization.

Upon seizing control of the mainland in 1949, the leadership of the CCP proclaimed their goal to be: "Three years of recovery, then ten years of development." Though often brutal and repressive, the Communist party restored order to China's cities, where crime rates fell as quickly as production rose. Conversely, the CCP facilitated a wildly popular "land to the tiller" movement in the rural areas, empowering thousands of workers who had grown accustomed to harsh working conditions and gross exploitation from the land-owning class. In short, the promise of three years of recovery was realized. A population still recovering from chaos suddenly had reason to believe that the new promises would come to fruition.

Eastern Ally, Western Adversary

The immediate success of Mao's regime may have proved to be impossible without the support of the Soviet Union. In 1949, China had "emerged" onto a political environment of bipolarity, with the Soviet Union and the United States engaged in a Cold War for global supremacy. The United States continued its support of the KMT government, and with anticommunist sentiments reaching a fevered pitch, as evidenced by the McCarthy episode, Mao had little choice but to side with the Soviets. Only weeks after his famous speech at Tiananmen Square, Mao traveled to Moscow, where he solicited the aid of Joseph Stalin. Though their alliance became gradually weaker from the outset, it was a relationship that paid early dividends for China. Granting financial aid, as well as dispatching economists and planners to the region, Russia became a mentor for China during its transition years. Technology and other valued forms of information were provided to

China, as was the assurance of military support in the event of an attack on its mainland. In return, China was required to give the Soviets access to strategic locations, including several of its ports and mines—much to Mao's dismay. Though paying a hefty price, Mao rationalized the Soviets to be the only entity powerful enough to address the needs of his nation.

The outbreak of the Korean War in late June 1950 furthered tensions between China and the United States. Perceiving North Korea's surprise attack against the South as a Soviet plot, the United States sent troops to the peninsula under the banner of containment—playing what was later called "the China card." In 1953, after enduring three years of direct combat against U.S. forces, as well as withstanding fierce rhetoric from American military leaders, China found itself greatly distanced from the United States. Even after the Korean War subsided, relations between the United States and China were far from cordial. Economic sanctions imposed by the United States forced the Chinese to rely on the Soviets to an even greater extent. Additionally, the United States further insulted the Chinese by formally recognizing Taiwan as China's only legitimate government. It would take almost 20 years, and some bold diplomacy from both sides, before the United States and China could even begin to fathom a formal relationship.

The Great Leap Nowhere

The central theme of the Great Leap Forward was this: Mao Zedong believed that China could "leap" over the arduous stages of modernization and become an industrialized society through an extraordinary series of mass movements. One such movement, which may sum up the entire "leap" altogether, was called the Great Sparrow Campaign. To increase grain exports, Mao called upon the masses to kill as many sparrows as humanly possible. Such tactics primarily included yelling and banging pots and pans together so as to scare the birds and prevent them from landing. After a few minutes, the birds would collapse from exhaustion. This act was mimicked nationwide, and soon the entire landscape was littered with dead birds. That same land would be plagued the very next year by the sparrow's favorite meal: the locust.

By 1958, China had made substantial economic and political strides. Boasting sizable rates of growth, China's economic strategy had produced an economy that was as stable as at any point in the nation's history. Having battled the powerful U.S. military to a "victorious" stalemate, China had been propelled to the world stage, wielding newfound political clout. Prestige and prosperity seemed to define the nation. The Great Leap Forward would ironically and emphatically eliminate that perception, as well as that reality. Preceding this hectic and brutal period was the first Five-Year Plan, a series of major reforms from 1953 to 1957. Though numerically pleasing—economic growth had risen, on average, to almost 9 percent per year during that span—the policies essentially reversed the decrees that had made Mao Zedong so popular in the first place.

The peasant farmers, for instance, who had flourished as *de facto* capitalists after the land reforms of the early 1950s, were suddenly stripped of their ownership rights, as government procurement agencies gradually seized control of the farmlands. Agricultural collectivization, as it was called, proved to be exceptionally disastrous, as large communes operated in a state of disarray. Lacking incentives, the agricultural production, though promising early on, soon plummeted, and the nation entered a period of famine that would claim the lives of nearly 25 million people. Labor was redirected away from crop management and aimed at increasing production in sectors such as iron, steel, and mining operations—"modern" sectors that Mao believed should take precedence over agriculture. From 1959 to 1962, China's agricultural production worsened in every major category. Adding insult to injury was a series of natural disasters, beginning with the flooding of the Yellow River in 1959. Ranking as one of the worst natural disasters in modern history, the flood directly killed as many as 3 million people. The regions untouched by the flood were hardly fortunate, having suffered a bitter drought.

Urban society was also beginning to unravel. The educational system, which had largely continued without interference following the communist victory, was drastically restructured in accordance with the Soviet model. Private universities fell under control of the state. Intellectuals were encouraged to let "one hundred flowers bloom" or, in other words, to openly criticize authority, only to incur the most severe of punishments when those opinions differed with Mao's agenda. Suppression (and suspicion) of the intellectuals would prove to be a recurring theme for Mao and a major source of tension for the Chinese people.

In terms of economic gains, the urban sector saw a dramatic rise in several key industries during the first Five Year Plan. Coal mining, along with cement, iron, steel, and electricity operations rapidly accelerated national production, yielding a 20 percent rate of growth between 1953 and 1958. Yet this five-year period of prosperity, in the end, served only to distract Mao and the CCP from China's rapidly transforming social structure. The Great Leap Forward, born of optimistic delusions, paranoia, and half-baked promises, would have ramifications lasting decades.

The Cultural Revolution

The Great Leap Forward was an abject failure and, despite being the brainchild of the nation's hero, was not without opposition. The Soviet Union joined many CCP leaders in openly deriding China's sudden economic and social deviations. The Soviets would, in fact, later remove from China pivotal sources of financial aid, worsening a situation that had been exacerbated by a prolonged period of inclement weather. This "perfect storm" of national disasters, both self-inflicted and otherwise, fomented a crisis mentality within Mao Zedong, who encored one historic mishap with an even greater one: the Cultural Revolution.

Toward the latter half of 1966, sensing that his political influence was fleeting, Mao set out to once again consolidate power through his preferred method of mass mobilization. Disillusioned with what he considered an increasingly corrupt government and a young population without the spirit of revolution, Mao initiated one of the most violent and bizarre episodes in modern history. The mass movement principle under which China had thrived, and indeed the principle which had brought Mao to power, was channeled instead for destructive purposes. Though its consequences were very tangible, scholars and historians can only speculate as to Mao's exact motives. Several allude to China's line of succession at the time, which had Liu Shaoqi assuming the role of party leader after Mao's death. Distrustful of Liu, and preferring Lin Biao, Mao had hoped to instill in the public a sense of outrage for party and government officials, like Shaoqi, who had "taken them down the capitalist road." Furthermore, Mao wanted to once again dramatically alter the nation's social makeup. Believing that income disparity had risen too high, Mao cut wages in the urban sector and moved health care resources away from the cities and into the countryside. The educational system was also to be revamped under his plan: Stressing ideology, loyalty, and practical knowledge over true scholarship, Mao forced universities to eliminate entrance exams, thereby eradicating academic standards.

Though the Cultural Revolution contained practical elements, at least in Mao's view, the underlying principle was undoubtedly that of suppression. Mao considered China's youth lacking the revolutionary character that had defined its modern history. So to instill this "virtue," Mao formed the Red Guards, who blindly carried out the bold orders of their leader. Consisting mostly of urban college and high school students, the Red Guards were routinely encouraged by Mao himself to "make revolution." This, in turn, manifested itself in the form of extreme, sadistic violence against huge portions of the populace. As Mao ordered China's army to stand down during this period, the Red Guard was free to wreak havoc in both the city and countryside. Books and ancient relics were burned, stolen, or destroyed. Intellectuals, pacifists, and revolutionaries of the prior generation were humiliated, beaten, or murdered as the Red Guard furthered its terrorist campaign.

But less than three years after the start of the Cultural Revolution, the Red Guards began to turn on each other. Now armed with automatic weapons, with numbers estimated at more than 30 million, the loosely knit conglomeration of youths began to fracture, absent any real ideology or bond. Arguments over who could more accurately recite the words of Mao Zedong often ended in bloodshed. In a span of only three years, more than 40 million people were killed by members of the Red Guard. Those fortunate enough to survive did so with painful memories.

In 1969, the Red Guard phase of the Cultural Revolution had drawn to a close. Unable to maintain cohesion, the spirit of the movement fizzled along with Mao's enthusiasm for the campaign. Yet power had shifted dramatically back into the hands of Mao Zedong, as was his plan. Sifting out dissent through mass violence, intimidation, and coercion, Mao, like most tyrants, had surrounded himself almost entirely by like-minded people. The power and prestige Mao had regained, however, did not signify any real improvement in the nation's outlook. Conditions had worsened, in fact. The masses had not become the "next generation" of revolutionaries Mao had envisioned—quite the opposite. What remained was a decidedly antipolitical populace. Moreover, the means of production were still firmly in the hands of party and government planners, who scurried to heal a dormant economy.

CHAPTER 12

Calculated Conduct

China from 1978 to Today

Besides the noble art of getting things done, there is the noble art of leaving things undone. The wisdom of life consists in the elimination of non-essentials.

Lin Yutang

In 1966, China looked more like Lewis Carroll's Wonderland than a functioning socialist state. The powerful dictator Mao Zedong, globally recognized for uniting a historically fractured nation, was tarnishing his greatest accomplishments by spearheading the Cultural Revolution. Likewise, the revolutionaries of a previous generation who had struggled alongside Mao for independence found themselves beaten, humiliated, and killed on the orders of their national icon. Meanwhile Deng Xiaoping, a mainstay of the Chinese Communist party (CCP), was imprisoned—bound to the harsh confines of the Xingjian County Tractor Factory in the rural Chinese province of Jiangxi. He had become a victim of a society he helped create. Up was down, black was white, and China was a nation through the looking glass.

Deng Xiaoping was stripped of his political power and arrested by the Red Guards in 1966 on the explicit orders of his long-time colleague Mao Zedong, who perceived Deng and other "capitalist roaders" of the CCP as a threat to his power, status, and, most of all, his legacy. Like so many other pragmatists of his time, Deng and his family became targets of Mao's Red Guards. His son, Deng Pufang, had become a paraplegic after the Red Guards threw him from a fourth-floor window—an incident all too common for the era. Laboring as what Mao called a "regular worker," the CCP's future leader was afforded much time to think about the future of his country in between shifts.

Deng Xiaoping: "An Acrobat with Nerves of Steel"

Deng Xiaoping began his career with the CCP in 1924, only three years after the party's inception. By the time of his arrest, no one, with perhaps the exception of Mao Zedong, had invested as much time and energy into China's fortunes than Deng Xiaoping. Yet neither personal grief nor physical confinement would ever weaken his resolve. And though Mao Zedong is generally credited with being the father of modern China, few could argue against Deng Xiaoping's being its savior. Instituting unprecedented economic reforms, Deng's ideas and foresight would emphatically catapult China from a state of crisis into the modern age.

One of the more eloquent statesmen of his era, Deng Xiaoping once remarked, "Keep a cool head and maintain a low profile. Never take the lead—but aim to do something big." Though he never held an official title as head of state, Deng Xiaoping assumed control of the CCP in 1978. Standing less than five feet tall, he kept as low a profile as could be expected from a national leader. With support from the more rational elements of the CCP, Deng was able to politically outmaneuver Hua Guofeng, Mao's handpicked successor. In all, it was a strange journey to the top of Chinese politics for Deng, who was jailed again by Mao in 1976 as the Cultural Revolution drew to a close. After being "rehabilitated" and released from prison, Deng, whose objections to the Cultural Revolution had made him extremely popular with the Chinese people, returned to politics, this time as leader of the CCP. With political support not born of fear, coercion, or intimidation, Deng would begin his rule as leader.

Having long called for China's modernization, Deng wasted little time in implementing a series of major reforms. Although China would indeed undergo a multitude of changes in the coming years, Deng insisted from the very beginning that several ideals of the past would be preserved. In a speech in March 1979, he declared four basic principles, or prerequisites for achieving China's ultimate goal of modernization:

- "We must keep to the socialist road."
- "We must uphold the dictatorship of the proletariat."
- "We must uphold the leadership of the Communist Party."
- "We must uphold Marxism-Leninism and Mao Zedong thought."

Having suffered through the final years of Maoist rule, Deng inherited a society that was eager to accept a more centrist approach, yet apprehensive about sudden departures from the status quo. The most significant reform was aimed at the economy. "Reform is China's second revolution," he once said, and as the rapid development of the Four Tigers (Taiwan, Hong Kong, Singapore, and South Korea) illustrated, it was a feasible process and one that was long overdue. Realizing that a planned economy was inherently weaker than a market-based system, and accepting that his popularity would rest almost entirely on improvements in the standard of living, Deng set in motion the wheels of reform, promising an "opening up" of China. Though his ideas stood in stark contrast to Mao Zedong, Deng's second revolution, like that of his predecessor's, would first occur in the countryside.

Cash Crops

Beginning with the agricultural sector, which had experienced both promise and failure under Mao's planned economy, Deng quickly decollectivized the communes, though he was careful to avoid such capitalistic terminology. Labeled the Household Production Responsibility System, this new policy called on farmers to fulfill government-issued quotas but also allowed them to sell their remaining goods on the open market or retain them for their own consumption. Though ownership of the farmlands technically remained collective, the restructuring process reduced the amount of workers assigned to each plot, providing them with a more vested interest in their labor.

The Household Production Responsibility System became a policy that fueled the opening up of rural markets. Competition between farmers for business resulted in higher-quality products, among other things. The pricing structure gradually began to reflect a functioning market system, and practices forbidden under Mao's government, such as the raising of livestock, soon returned. With the famine resulting from Mao's Great Leap Forward still fresh in the minds of the CCP, grain production was tagged as a top priority. Having not yet begun to import grains, China was forced to become self-sufficient in terms of food production. Accounting for 22 percent of the world's population at the time, such an endeavor was not to be taken lightly.

By 1985, all but 2 percent of China's farms had made the transition to the Household Production Responsibility System, and the benefits were clearly recognized. That same year, China ranked as the world's largest exporter of grains, exporting more than 400 million tons of products, including cotton, tobacco, and soybeans. In 1978, by contrast, total production figures stood at 300 million tons. The annual growth rate for agriculture during that six-year period hovered around 3.5 percent, roughly the same rate as under Mao's commune system, but with a significantly fewer amount of workers. This labor surplus could therefore be utilized elsewhere, mainly in China's industries.

"Let Some People Get Rich First"

Having transformed the countryside, Deng and the CCP shifted their efforts toward the industrial sector. While rural farmers were eager to accept more responsibility and reap the newfound rewards of a market system, their urban counterparts needed a bit more coaxing. Industrialization, which had been the central theme of Deng's economic reforms, would prove exceedingly difficult, particularly in China's state-run enterprises. Accounting for 70 percent of all industrial output in 1978, state-run enterprises were operating in more than 9,000 separate locations throughout China, making the enforcement of any mass reform exceptionally troublesome. Hesitant to relinquish control of these units, many leaders of the CCP maintained that the state should continue to dictate the direction of such institutions rather than allow outsiders any sort of control. The bureaucracy, in universal fashion, was reluctant to accept change. Party members who had developed vested interests in these enterprises would not let go of them without resistance.

Due to such factors, Deng realized that reform of the state's enterprises, like that of the modernization process itself, would have to be pursued under the doctrine of gradualism. Implementing what was called the Economic Responsibility System, the State Planning Commission announced that a test run of sorts would be undertaken, and that its effects would be observed and analyzed before mass reforms would be instituted. Components of such experiments primarily included granting certain enterprises the responsibility of managing profits, expenses, and other practices associated with free markets. It was a policy that came to symbolize Deng's approach. Never claiming to possess a master plan, Deng instead focused on problems as they arose, allowing for flexibility and adaptation in the reform process.

The transformation to a market economy that began in 1978 was accompanied by three brief outbursts of inflation. The enterprise reform of 1984–1985 allowed state-owned enterprises to deal directly with banks and resulted in excessive loan increases, causing the money supply to increase by 50 percent. Government intervention quickly returned the money supply to stable growth. However, additional reforms in the late 1980s expanded the financial freedom of enterprises and consumers. In 1988, the money supply again expanded by 48 percent, causing an annual inflation rate in excess of 30 percent. Here, the government intervened with administrative quotas on loan volumes by banks. However, that inflation, coupled with widespread corruption, undoubtedly contributed to the crisis at Tiananmen Square in 1989. Finally, after the government announced a policy of speeding up reform and further opening the economy to foreign investment in 1992, growth in demand again posed the threat of serious inflation in 1993. Once again, the government turned to administrative controls imposed on banks to limit lending, and there were no further episodes of inflation.

The Point of No Return

In October 1984, encouraged by the economic experimentation but sensing the need for permanent mass reforms, Deng's government boldly restructured the Chinese economy. At Deng's insistence, the Twelfth Central Committee of the CCP implemented an economic reform consisting of the following elements:

- The issuance of autonomy to state-run enterprises in regards to production, supply and demand, marketing, pricing, investment, and personnel decisions.
- The drastic reduction of centralized planning.
- The allowance of prices to be determined by the market, rather than economic planners.
- The creation of a banking system capable of managing taxes, interest rates, and fiscal policy.
- The promotion of efficiency and development of collective enterprises.
- The promotion of foreign trade, investment, and technological exchanges with foreign countries.

Perhaps the most significant tenet developed by the committee was that of foreign trade and investment. Deng had long advocated opening China's market to foreign capital, yet until 1978, China's economy had been virtually closed. The combined totals of exports and imports, for instance, accounted for only 7 percent of China's national income. In less than 10 years after the reform process started, that figure would skyrocket to nearly 25 percent.

Banking Trust

In parallel with the economic reforms beginning in 1978, China also began to reform its banking system. The People's Bank of China was changed to a central bank in 1983. Four large banks were established to handle the loans to state-owned enterprise (SOE) made at the direction of the government and to have some autonomy in making other loan decisions to market-oriented enterprise. In the 1980s, China created the Bank of Communications, a nationwide bank with no government-directed loans, no restrictions on the scope of its lending activities, and with authorization to conduct foreign exchange business.

More important, at no time in the reform era did the Chinese public lose confidence in their banks. Prior to reform, household savings were quite small, about 0.5 percent of gross domestic product (GDP), and cumulative household savings were perhaps 6 percent of the GDP in 1978, the beginning of reform. Since household savings are the principal source of bank deposits in market economies, China's extraordinary growth would have been severely curtailed for lack of financing if the public had lost confidence in its banks and placed its savings in shoeboxes in their closets, as was the case in Soviet-era Russia.

Such improvements in foreign investment can be linked to, among other factors, the implementation of joint ventures and special economic zones (SEZs). One particular SEZ, and one that perhaps encapsulates the overall process of opening up, was the Shenzhen SEZ. Located on the border of Hong Kong, which was then prospering under British control, Shenzhen underwent a rapid transformation from a rural fishing village into one of the nation's centers of commerce. In allowing foreign investors to set up factories and utilize a cheap labor force, China also attracted foreign capital by issuing tax breaks to various corporations. As a result of this policy, Shenzhen's urban sector grew from less than 3 square kilometers in 1979 to more than 50 square kilometers by 1987, making it China's fastest-growing city by a wide margin. Among the main targets for investors were construction and manufacturing, and it has been estimated that foreign investment had risen nearly 60 percent per year during Shenzhen's first five years.

"Black Cat, White Cat"

These and other innovations became the trademarks of Deng's "Socialism with Chinese characteristics." Though he was clearly implementing capitalistic practices, he was adamant in refuting claims that he had abandoned the Marxist ideals of the CCP. In many instances, Deng would often cite that it was Mao, not he, who had deviated from the main tenets of Marxism. "One of our shortcomings after the founding of the People's Republic was that we didn't pay enough attention to developing the productive forces," Deng once remarked. "Socialism means eliminating poverty. Pauperism is not socialism, still less communism." To become a true communist state, Deng insisted, entailed developing the nation's productive forces and accumulating an abundance of material wealth. It mattered little to Deng and the pragmatists of the CCP how the economy accomplished this task, just as long as it did. Or, in Deng's own words: "It doesn't matter if a cat is black or white, so long as it catches mice."

And catch mice it would. By the mid-1990s, more than half of China's state-run enterprises had adopted the Economic Responsibility System—the industrial equivalent of the rural Household Production Responsibility System. The tenets of the Twelfth Central Committee were gradually accepted in the industrial sector as sound policy, which the statistics began to reflect. With the opening up of markets, both domestic and international, state-run enterprises were averaging an annual rate of growth rate of 14.6 percent. Overall, China's gross national product (GNP) had risen from $140.9 billion in 1978 to $434.8 billion in 1991. Exports, which—aside from the Soviet Union—had been almost nonexistent when Deng came to power in 1978, rose an astounding 700 percent in that time frame. With strong commitments to staving off inflation, as well as several reforms of price control and the banking system, the world's most populous nation had also become its fastest-growing economy, averaging a 9.6 percent annual rate of growth. Though the economy's transformation was not yet complete, China had, for the most part, gone from a planned economy to a market-based economic system in less than a decade.

The Consequences of Success

Though Deng's second revolution of economic reform had, by and large, transpired without the economic and political upheaval so common to that time frame, its impact on a society so accustomed to mass movements and Maoist dogma should not be underestimated. In 1980, for instance, as the reforms commenced, Deng Xiaoping became the target of political assassination. In March of that year, he would survive an attempt on his life by a local guard and fervent Maoist outside the Jinan military complex. Shouting "Down the capitalist Deng Xiaoping," the guard fired several rounds, none of which hit the CCP leader, before being arrested. Though appearing to have acted of his own accord, many researchers believe the attack was orchestrated by remnants of the old guard—perhaps symbolizing how dangerous widespread change, and displaced elites, can be.

While Deng embraced economic development and change, the same cannot be said about the political realm. Political reform, or more accurately, his resistance to it, brought to light the dark side of Deng's rule. From his inception as leader, Deng insisted that China not deviate from the socialist road, and the population would soon learn firsthand how committed he was to this ideal. As the infamous incident at Tiananmen Square would illustrate, vast economic change and improvements in the overall standard of living are often accompanied by calls for democratization, and China proved to be no exception to this rule.

Tiananmen Square

In April 1989, as Deng and the CCP grappled with political reform, large numbers of students and labor rights activists gathered throughout China's cities to promote, among other things, democracy and the expansion of workers' rights. With economic success came economic disparity, as the benefits reaped in the agricultural sector were not duplicated in other areas. Unemployment and inflation, consequences of a market-based system, left hundreds of thousands of intellectuals and urban industrial workers feeling disenfranchised. Refusing to accept the status quo, they began to collectively voice their displeasure.

The most infamous of these protests occurred in Beijing's Tiananmen Square, where by May 4, 1989, the number of "pro-Western" demonstrators exceeded 100,000. The protests escalated, with hunger strikes, organized marches, and slogans such as "Down with Deng" reverberating throughout Beijing. Believing the demonstrators were undermining the economic reform efforts and having unsuccessfully tried to negotiate with the various groups, the Chinese government finally declared martial law on May 20. Impeded by swarms of protesters, however, the armored personnel carriers of the People's Liberation Army were not able to penetrate the city center until June 3, at which point the crackdown ensued. Death toll estimates from the incident vary greatly, depending on the source of the information. Estimates range from 300 students, according to several CCP leaders, to more than 7,000, according to North Atlantic Treaty Organization (NATO) intelligence. Whatever the figure, the violence at Tiananmen Square had become known worldwide, incurring multiple sanctions against China, even from several of its allies.

Though Tiananmen Square may have symbolized the social consequences of mass reform, its tangible affects on China's economic transformation were minuscule at best. The aftermath of the bloody incident did not signify the end of economic development—in fact, quite the opposite. China would continue to succeed in economic terms throughout the 1990s, aiding the healing process, not only with its own population, but with that of foreign nations as well.

"Seek Truth from Facts"

Deng's role in Chinese politics would deteriorate after the Tiananmen Square incident. He retired from politics in 1992, but his influence on the nation's affairs continued until his death in 1997. Like Mao Zedong, Deng's legacy depends largely on one's perspective. Having lost a significant amount of prestige following the Tiananmen Square massacre, Deng was nevertheless the primary actor in transforming China's backward economy. Had he retired from his leadership post in 1988, he would have likely been regarded as one of history's most accomplished leaders and an even greater reformer. Yet such an ending may not have befitted Deng—a man who believed in keeping a low profile. While portraits of Deng are not scattered across the landscape, as they are for Mao Zedong, he has undoubtedly left behind more lasting reminders of his rule. Having once said, "It is glorious to get rich," Deng Xiaoping's legacy is omnipresent: It can be seen with the construction of every new factory, with every product shipped overseas, and with every improvement in China's economic outlook.

The Post-Deng Years

China's economy continued to grow in the late 1990s, even as the Asian financial crisis of 1998 wreaked havoc across the region. Though its expansion had been somewhat curtailed due, in part, to the sudden decline of purchasing power of nations such Japan and South Korea, China's economy nevertheless managed to post growth rates hovering between 7 percent and 8 percent from 1997 to 1999. In 1994, by contrast, China's rate of growth totaled 13 percent. Though the 1990s would see sharp improvements in several categories, including standard of living, infrastructure, wages, poverty, and unemployment, it would not be without its dilemmas. State-run enterprises, for instance, proved to be a drain on the government, as economists scrambled to keep such nonefficient entities afloat. In the late 1990s and early 2000s, China would shut down a significant number of its state-run enterprises. Though the public sector continued managing the nation's utilities, heavy industries, and energy systems, the government's overall role in the Chinese economy had been drastically reduced. In its place, private industry in China began to flourish. This transformation process was widely realized in 2001, when China became a member of the World Trade Organization.

After moving to a market economy, the Chinese government was faced with the same issues that confront all market economies trying to achieve a balance between spending and production. For example, the production problems caused by the Asian financial crisis of 1997 caused substantial reductions in demand in many of China's export markets. Using modern Western-style economics, the Chinese government immediately announced a series of projects to stimulate domestic demand in order to achieve its target of 8 percent real GDP growth in 1998. These projects included much-needed investment in infrastructure, including railways; highways; land and water resource control, especially flood control; and environmental protection facilities. It has been estimated that a total of US$1.2 trillion was invested between 1988 and 2000—signifying that the Chinese economy was still very much capable of moving forward. The end result was that actual growth in real GDP in 1998 reached 7.8 percent at a time when many Asian countries were suffering negative GDP growth. Yet no numbers or statistics can put into words the remarkable transformation China had undergone during this period. This process promises to be the subject of analysis for many years to come, as China continues to grow at a historic pace.

CHAPTER 13

Manufacturing a Future

Investing in China

To get rich is glorious.

—Deng Xiaoping

In 1974, Deng Xiaoping visited the United States, addressed the UN General Assembly, and observed firsthand how far the Chinese economy had fallen behind the West. Appointed vice-premier under Zhou Enlai in 1952, Deng played a prominent role in the government until the Cultural Revolution in 1966, when he was denounced as a capitalist and purged. He was subsequently restored to all posts.

After his ascent to power in 1978, Deng Xiaoping discovered that China's income, productivity, and living standards had barely budged for almost a century and were paltry compared to those of advanced nations. Its gross domestic product (GDP) in 1978 was barely 3.5 percent of that in the United States. An economic revolutionary, Deng Xiaoping introduced a market-based economic system that transformed China from a stagnant, isolated economy into a high-growth economic powerhouse with global reach. According to Penn World Tables 6.2, today Chinese real GDP per capita is nearly 15 percent of the United States' and gaining steadily.

Demographics: *Favorable*

Demographics play an integral part of a nation's financial success, and due to the size and composition of its population, China has received a favorable ranking in this regard. Currently the world's most populous country, with a population of over 1.4 billion people, China is a key force in world growth. Its population is expected to grow by another 140 million in the next 10 years. Although a large population may not by itself be a *sine qua non* of growth, it is generally believed that the nature and mix of populations can be crucial to such growth.

One key measure of future growth lies in the dependency ratio, which is the ratio of dependent population (those under 15 and over 64) to the overall population. Currently, China's ratio is 0.4, meaning there are four dependents for every 10 workers. By comparison, in India, another comparable population, the ratio is 0.6, or 6 dependents for every 10 workers. According to the U.S. Bureau of the Census, because of China's long-standing one-child policy, however, the dependency ratio is likely to rise to about 0.5 (5 dependents to every 10 workers) by 2025, which will bring the country closer to India's at about 0.47 (4.7 dependents for every 10 workers). According to *The Economist*, Goldman Sachs believes that the rising dependency ratio in China will be offset by the increased productivity of an increasingly well-trained labor force. For the next two or three decades, China will continue to enjoy demographic advantages in the growing population of workers and consumers, and therefore continue to maintain its ascent to status as a major economic power.

Figure 13.1 shows how the one-child policy would eventually cause the growth of the working-age population in China to slow, as it already has in the high-income industrial West. This would seem to suggest that the

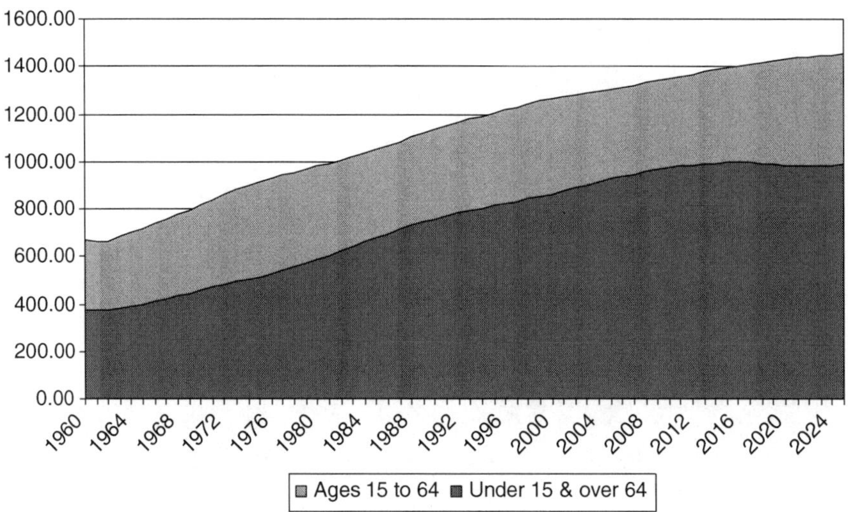

FIGURE 13.1 China's aging population.

Sources: World Bank: World Development Indicators; U.S. Bureau of the Census: International Database

Chinese growth rate would slow down by around 2015, were it not for the large rural population that will continue to fuel China's industrial growth at rates well above those in the high-income countries.

Currently, unemployment is only 3.3 percent, on a par with or better than most advanced economies. This is especially significant as China continues to absorb redundant workers from privatized state-owned enterprise.

Economic Performance: *Favorable*

China's "favorable" ranking with respect to economic performance was based on an analysis of the nation's growing middle class and the corresponding process of urbanization within its borders. Other important components of the category, including GDP growth and the country's shifts in agricultural policies and objectives, proved exceptional when compared to the other BRIC+2 nations.

Growth of the Middle Class

A burgeoning middle class is a strong driver of future growth as it signifies the ability of the people to move from the bare necessities to luxuries. The addition of new consumers is likely to propel the growth of China's economy. There are several factors that are likely to create a large class of new consumers.

China's unprecedented growth of over 10 percent a year in real terms for over three decades has made it an exporting machine extra with ballooning trade balance and current account surplus. This, however, has brought to the attention of Chinese policy makers their own dilemmas. Chief among these are pressures from trading nations such as United States to reduce trade imbalance by revaluing currency, as well as internal realization that the investment-led growth is likely to be unsustainable and is already creating overcapacity, reducing productivity, and potentially increasing inflationary pressures. Since the ultimate goal of growth in most societies is to provide the largest benefit to a maximum number of people, China seems to be making a serious attempt in that direction. If these policies succeed, the likely result will be perhaps the emergence of the largest middle class in the history of the world.

Today, China's economy bears little resemblance to the centrally planned economy of the past. The country allows broad discretion and competition within sectors. Foreign automakers such as GM, Honda, Volkswagen, and Hyundai, for example, thrive in the Chinese market along with cell phone providers Motorola, Nokia, and Samsung, who compete feverishly for the domestic market. The competition keeps prices low and encourages innovation.

On the one hand, the business relationship and the opening of China means U.S. multinationals like Procter & Gamble, GM, Motorola, Boeing, and hundreds of others big and small can pry open a huge market at precisely the time when their domestic markets are dismally weak. They are selling cell phones and shampoo, designer bags, new autos, tractors, and personal computers to a middle class that, within a decade, may be as large as the entire population of the United States.

Autos

By 2008, China's car capacity is likely to reach 8.7 million vehicles annually, double the number of expected buyers. According to Honda senior manager for China, Atsuyoshi Hyogo: "[Honda] will use China as one of [its] export production bases." According to Honda, from their tests, Honda Chinese version cars are superior to U.S. manufactured models.

Source: Pete Engardio, *Chindia*. New York: McGraw-Hill, 2006, pg. 183–184.

Most of these products have been marketed to affluent urbanites, skimming the cream from the top. However, new research from the McKinsey Global Institute finds that over the next 20 years, a huge new urban middle class will emerge with spending power that will redefine the Chinese market (see Table 13.1).

The initial surge will create 140 million households spending 3.6 trillion yuan. By 2025, the total middle class will have grown to 70 percent of urban households with consumption spending power of 14 trillion yuan after

TABLE 13.1 Share of Chinese Urban Households by Income

	Affluent >100,000 yuan	Upper middle class 40,000-100,000 yuan	Lower middle class 25,000-40,000 yuan	Poor <25,000 yuan	Households (millions)
2005	0.6%	9.4%	12.6%	77.3%	191
2015	6.0%	21.2%	49.7%	23.2%	280
2025	11.0%	59.4%	19.8%	9.7%	373

Source: McKinsey Global Institute

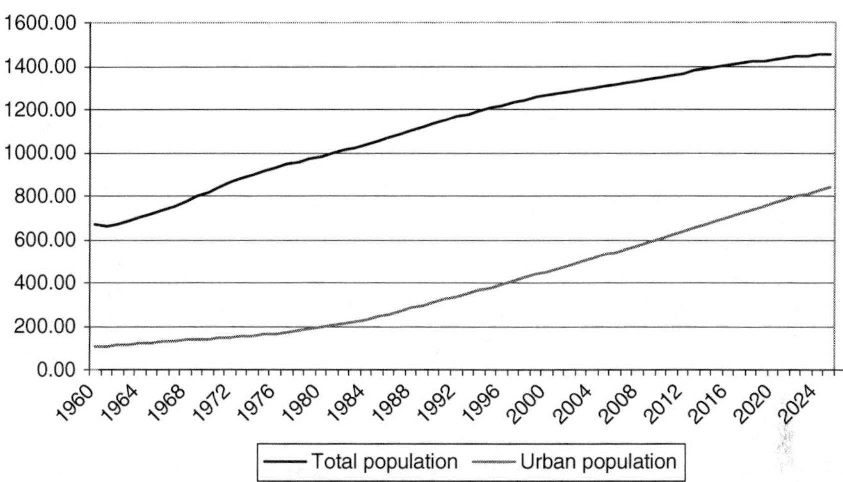

FIGURE 13.2 China population, 1960 to 2025 (millions).

Sources: World Bank: World Development Indicators; U.S. Bureau of the Census: International Database

taking account of China's high saving rate. Finally, because urban middle-class incomes will require a higher level of education than the older generation obtained, McKinsey estimates that the country's wealthiest consumers will be from 25 to 44 years old.

Shift from Agriculture

A major consequence of urbanization and industrialization is the shift away from low-productivity agriculture to jobs in industry and service sectors created by the new economy.

Note in Figure 13.2 that while the overall trend in population growth in China will be slowing, urban population growth, which accelerated with the beginning of reforms in 1980, will continue to grow significantly faster than the total population. Therefore, China is likely to be able to sustain economic growth rates above those typical of the advanced developed nations by taking advantage of this opportunity.

GDP Growth

China's growth over the past three decades has been a remarkable feat. China's GDP in 2005 was 12 times what it was in 1978 when Deng Xiaoping started his economic transformation. China is now the world's fourth largest economy and third largest trader.

China's GDP growth has been miraculous since its economic turnaround after 1978, and is likely to continue as domestic consumption increases and is balanced by strong exports. GDP growth has averaged an astounding 9.8 percent from 1980 to 2005. According to an estimate by Goldman Sachs, the per-capita GDP of China in 2005 of $1,753 is estimated to rise to $44,074 by 2050.

However, China's dependence on exports may be less important in the future as internal growth accelerates. Plans are already being initiated to stimulate the growth of domestic consumption.

The low-cost manufacturing of components has dramatically lowered the cost of goods domestically and made those goods competitive in world markets. It has also made many of their companies profitable—reducing inflation, creating a domestic consumer boom, and keeping the interest rates much lower than would be possible without this cost saving. As capital flows into China, creating modern factories, it has an ever-ready supply of more than 350,000 engineering and science graduates annually whose work is both cheap and skilled.

Urbanization

Currently, China's urban population is about 40 percent of its total population. However, this figure is likely to increase as with other countries likewise experiencing urban job growth due to industrialization. In Korea, for example, the urban population exceeds 80 percent of the total. Indeed, by 2025, it is estimated that China will have an urban population of 800 million. China's recent industrialization has already shifted about 273 million people to urban centers as it continues to make a concentrated effort to industrialize large parts of the country and diversify its industrial base.

Urbanization will continue, as millions leave rural areas and climb the economic ladder to create a new massive middle class. The lure that draws global companies:

- Consumers earn 100,000 yuan (about $12,500 per year) and command 500 billion yuan, nearly 10 percent of urban disposable income despite equaling less than 1 percent of the total population.
- Consumers buy globally branded luxury goods.
- Consumers are concentrated in big cities, easy to serve both for new companies and older, established companies.

Early movers such as Coca-Cola and Procter & Gamble have begun to target this segment of the population. But 77 percent of urban Chinese households live on less than $25,000 (3,000 renminbi [RMB]); that figure will drop to 10 percent by 2025, creating the largest consumer market in the world, spending some 20 trillion RMB. Urban households will on average save 20 percent of their disposable income every year.

In sum, the process of urbanization and the rise of China's middle class is still very much in its intermediate stage, meaning that there is plenty of room for further growth, as evidenced by its soaring GDP figures. As consumerism spreads throughout the country, a nation that relies heavily on exports will become increasingly linked with domestic consumer demands, in effect multiplying opportunities for investors.

Technology: *Favorable*

The advancements in China's technological capabilities over the past decade have been remarkable, and, as such, China has received a favorable ranking. Technology penetration is proceeding at a rapid pace along with the expansion of manufacturing and services. State-of-the-art machinery is being installed in ultra-modern manufacturing plants that attest to the fact that China is embracing technology and innovation with exuberance never before displayed in its history.

China turns out over 350,000 trained engineers annually, whose high skill level and low wage expectation is likely to maintain the momentum of technology utilization both for domestic and export purposes. Many large technology companies, including Microsoft, have located their advanced research centers in China.

There are 22 new silicon wafer plants planned for construction in China in the next three years, and there are 50 chemical plants, each involving at least $1 billion in investment, under construction. State-of-the-art high-tech machinery is being installed in manufacturing plants everywhere, debunking the theory that China is the home of low-grade, cheap labor and lower-level manufacturing.

Digital Electronics

As China emerges as a producer of sophisticated goods that require innovation, its presence is expanding on a global scale, creating a huge challenge for the American, Japanese, and European manufacturers of electronics, unless they, too, keep climbing the value chain. China is on their tail, just as it is catching up to and exceeding the furniture, textile, and shoe manufacturers of the world.

China is now the leading producer of digital electronics, from color televisions to cell phones, desktop computers, and DVD players. It has

350 million mobile users, is fast becoming the land of broadband, and plans to change to digital TV faster than the United States. China is rapidly becoming the testing ground for most consumer electronics worldwide. According to most experts, China will keep the cost of electronic goods competitive as its exports surge.

China has consistently ranked third or fourth, behind the United States and Russia and tied with France, in space vehicle launches. In addition, China ranks eighth in the world in patents granted to residents, following Russia (sixth) and Korea (fourth). Computer maker Lenovo has purchased IBM's ThinkPad and reworked its strategy of producing competitive yet low-cost products for the Chinese and overseas markets.

There is little to reason to doubt that China will improve its status as a technological power in the world economy. As these innovations are exported around the globe, they will also have a positive impact on the nation's standard of living. Trickling down into other aspects of the Chinese economy, technological advancements will contribute to the nation's growth for decades to come.

Open Trade: *Favorable*

A nation's openness to trade, or lack thereof, has a major influence on the overall success of its economy. China's stated objective to improve ties with foreign nations has been its underlying objective since the late 1970s, making the situation in China quite favorable today. Arguably the most significant aspect of China's economic reform in the 1980s, in fact, was its foreign trade policy. Using the most widely recognized measure of openness to trade, the sum of exports plus imports as a percentage of GDP, the following chart shows the dramatic trajectory of China's economy from isolation and self-sufficiency under Mao to globalization and export-led growth with a market economy (see Figure 13.3).

From the beginning of economic reform, the government's economic growth policy was focused on exports. Trade policy required strict control of imports such as essential consumer goods and new technology capital goods, combined with significant incentives to export to compensate for the financial outflow. To ensure that the foreign currency earned by exporting would be available for essential imports, the government imposed strict controls on the exchange rate and prohibited Chinese residents from owning or trading foreign currency without a special permit.

The price advantage offered by China in manufacturing has resulted in a trade surplus of over $31 billion annually from 1997 to 2004. In 2005, the surplus more than tripled to $124 billion and then to $209 billion in 2006, five to seven times previous averages. Facing pressures from

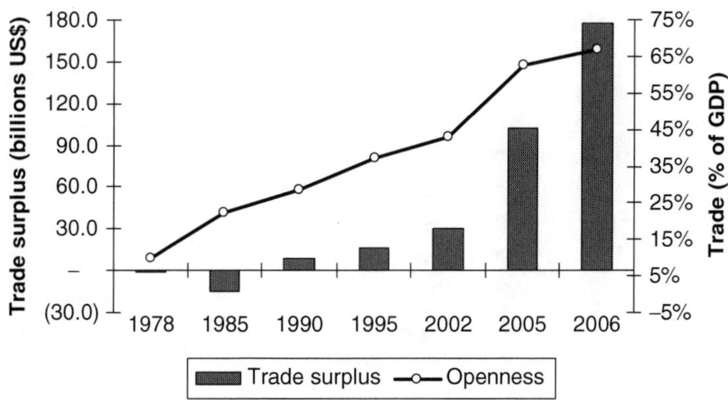

FIGURE 13.3 China's trade surplus and openness.

foreigners, particularly U.S. politicians and government, the Chinese have relented somewhat and begun to allow the fluctuation of its currency by about 3.2 percent in 2006 to about 5 percent in 2007. By most accounting, the Chinese currency is extremely undervalued and China's policy to continue to build export and discourage domestic consumption is unlikely to sustain over the long term. China currently has acquired over $1 trillion in foreign exchange reserves primarily in U.S. government bonds. These enormous reserves are a substantial buffer against crises or shocks that have been a regular feature of many emerging nations.

Although the CCP exercises a high degree of control over economic matters, few experts envision China's openness to trade to regress in the coming decades. As China continues to be a world leader in consumer exports, many expect the nation to remain committed toward improving its trade barriers.

Infrastructure Development: *Unfavorable*

Perhaps there is no national infrastructure properly suited for a population of well over 1.4 billion. China's infrastructure, as one might expect, has been overwhelmed by its conditions, and despite modest improvements, China has been given an unfavorable ranking.

The Chinese cities of Shanghai, Guangzhou, Beijing, Dalian, and Tianjin are the focus of super-size growth in modern architecture, ultra-modern manufacturing complexes, and leading-edge technologies. They have served as magnets for millions who relocated to these centers of worldwide trade and attention. They not only boast glass and concrete buildings that touch the heavens and state-of-the-art airports, but they are now surrounded by modern malls and fashion avenues along with petrochemical plants and shoe factories. The growth of China's infrastructure in the past two decades surpasses the boom in post–World War II construction in Japan and Korea. According to the World Bank, China has invested over $72 billion in private infrastructure over the past 15 years, more than $27 billion of which was allocated for electricity generation, and $25 billion for transportation. Currently, 99 percent of the population has access to electricity.

Nor is the boom likely to end anytime soon. New population centers with new mega cities are being planned more inland to draw the rural populations away from the coast to make more Chinese a part of the manufacturing and services workforce. Demand for infrastructure is likely to continue for decades. However, there is a major logjam in the country's railroads that have been starved of capital—perhaps due to lack of influence by railroads in government circles to direct appropriate funding on such projects. According to reports in 2004, 25 percent of those seeking to ship goods by rail were turned away. Still, China ranks third behind the United States and India in length of road networks.

Environment

Challenges for Chinese government and society are likely to be at the cost of environment. Despite massive investments since 1990 to reduce earth, air, and water pollution and some improvements, the unprecedented economic growth is overwhelming environmental protections. China now has the sixth worst air quality score, the fourth highest concentration of ozone, and an overall environmental performance index of 56.2 compared to 77.5 for Russia, 78.5 for the United States, and 85.6 for the United Kingdom.

China's dependence on coal, a plentiful natural resource, combined with expanding car ownership without modern emissions controls, has led to air pollution of 72 mcg per cubic meter compared to 23 mcg for the United States. Currently, China produces 2.73 tons of carbon dioxide from coal, nearly 30 percent of the world total. If present trends continue, by 2025, China will produce about 40 percent of the world's total carbon dioxide—or twice as much as the United States. Coal burning also produces a great deal of sulfur, and subsequently causing acid rain damage to affect 30 percent of China's land mass.

Energy

The energy demands of China's rapidly growing industrial sector have been the main source of air pollution emissions in China. China is both the second largest producer and the second largest consumer of energy after the

United States. Relatively poor in natural resources with the exception of coal, China uses more coal than the United States, European Union, and Japan combined. Every week to 10 days, another coal-fired electricity generating plant large enough to serve Dallas or San Diego opens somewhere in China. However, the availability of coal means that China has low energy dependence—net energy imports equal only 2 percent of energy use—and 79.4 percent of its electricity is produced by coal-fired plants.

Water Supplies

Rapid economic growth has also resulted in a significant increase in the demand for water resources in China. The situation has been further complicated by the fact that per-capita water resource availability is relatively high in southern China and relatively low in northern China, which is north of the Yangtze River. The core of the crisis, the Huai, Hai, and Huang river basins, supply nearly half the country's population, with demand projected to increase another 20 percent by the year 2030.

The problem stems from several sources. China's water was not priced in relation to scarcity, with the result that low-value water-intensive cereals dominated agriculture production. In industry, Chinese companies use 4 to 10 times more water than their counterparts in industrial countries. To address the crisis, the Chinese government has raised water prices and imposed regulatory measures to increase the efficiency of water use in agriculture and industry. On the supply side, the government engineered a massive south–north water transfer to divert more than 40 billion cubic meters of water—more than the total flow of the Colorado River—from the glacial runoff in Tibet to the Hai basin in the north.

While there is clearly a crisis in water supply and urban air quality, there is equally a significant commitment by the Chinese government to solve these problems. Currently, the Chinese government has committed about 1.3 percent of GDP to environmental protection investments. According to the World Bank, a conservative estimate of what will be needed in the future is closer to 3.5 percent of GDP.

China faces extraordinary problems with respect to its infrastructure, the condition of which has restricted, among other things, the efficiency of the economy. Investors should be mindful about a population that is increasingly urbanizing, as this transition will further test an already fragile system through demands for fuel and depletion of resources.

Transparency and Rule of Law: *Neutral*

The strength and integrity of a nation's legal system is directly related to its ability to grow. Though China continues to develop its legal institutions, they are considered insufficient by common standards, as illustrated by the World Bank's corruption index. However, when compared to other emerging nations, such as Russia, China's legal framework is considerably more advanced, resulting in its neutral ranking.

Rule of Law

Political issues occupy the minds of those who invest in emerging countries. The institutions are not always well established and political rights not always easy to enforce.

The World Bank's combined index of political stability for China is 33.2, compared to 57.5 for the United States and 23.3 for Russia. The World Bank's combined Index of Government Effectiveness for China is 55.5 compared to 92.9 for the United States and 37.9 for Russia.

Corruption Index

China ranks low in the control of corruption, with a World Bank Index of 37.9, compared with 89.13 for the United States and 24.3 for Russia.

Corruption and the lack of a sound legal system can be a major deterrent for investors who desire a government capable of enforcing its laws. However, as China aims to curb corruption and develop its institutions, it is important to consider the amount of growth the nation has achieved in spite of such conditions.

Education and Training: *Favorable*

Education and training have been the backbone of China's economic growth in recent years, and have received a favorable ranking for this reason. China has a literacy rate of over 90 percent, the highest of any emerging economy, and the country is making a serious effort to create a next generation of technically trained professionals from software engineers to scientists to health workers. There are first-rate engineers, managers, and highly trained personnel numbering in the millions, with millions more to follow who will fill the pipeline of skilled workers in a few generations.

This new force is likely to descend on the world scene armed with knowledge, skills, training, and low expectations for wages. China sees the millions of best-trained workers with brainpower as a part of its value-added export, in the future more important than its manufacturing power, which supports only less skilled labor. The World Economic Forum ranked India's labor force 49th, with an index rating of 4.35. China, by contrast, ranked 77th, at 3.68.

Investors should expect China to maintain its vast reserve of educated workers to compete in an increasingly specialized economy that demands such expertise. The sheer number of educated workers able to contribute to the economy will keep wages low, and productivity high, in a formula that has proven to be lucrative over the last several decades.

Sound Financial Systems and Policies: *Favorable*

China's remarkable ability to limit inflation and adhere to disciplined fiscal policy are two parts that contribute to its favorable ranking. The importance of a sound financial system has been demonstrated repeatedly in the financial crises of the past 25 years. In the United States during the 1980s, the savings-and-loan crisis resulted in a number of bank failures exceeding those of the Great Depression. Yet the banking system as a whole remained solvent and functioning, while the economy suffered only a brief recession and returned to strong economic growth in the 1990s. By contrast, the real estate investment crisis in Japan revealed structural weaknesses in the Japanese banking system, resulting in a number of bank failures and a deep recession lasting more than a decade. Similarly, when the real estate boom in Thailand went bust in 1997, its fragile banking system was overwhelmed and the resulting financial crisis quickly spread throughout Southeast Asia.

Sound banking systems such as those in Korea, supplemented by a bailout of temporary funds from the United States, helped the country weather the storm, and its economy quickly recovered its steady GDP growth. It is important to note that during the 1997 Southeast Asian crisis, China—a major trading partner of all the crisis-ridden countries—suffered no financial setbacks, and its economy continued to grow without interruption. This was due in no small measure to China's financial strength.

Inflation

After China's experience with hyperinflation under the Kuomintang (KMT), the government is quite serious about the control of inflation and has taken strong measures to ensure this policy. In contrast with the Russian hyperinflation (1992–1995) following the collapse of the Soviet Union and the Brazilian high inflation of the 1980s that exploded into hyperinflation in 1988–1994, the Chinese government took immediate steps to tame its nascent inflationary episodes and thereby avoided extreme consequences. During the years 2000 through 2005, China posted an average annual inflation rate of 1.4 percent, even less than Germany's rate of 1.6 percent per year for the same period. This remarkable result in an economy with a supercharged growth rate of over 9 percent represents a powerful argument in favor of long-term price stability in China. The Chinese government understands that price stability is of critical importance and may at times require short-term economic sacrifice. In keeping with their determination to control inflation, the government deficit was about 2.6 percent GDP in 2006.

Banking System

All Chinese banks are established as joint stock companies where the government is still the primary shareholder. However, the banking system was reformed in parallel with the economic reforms beginning in 1994. For example, the Bank of Communications, a nationwide bank with no requirement to make loans at the direction of the government, no restrictions on the scope of its lending activities, and with authorization to conduct foreign exchange transactions, has established a loan portfolio of relatively high quality with a relatively small share of nonperforming loans combined with a relatively high rate of capital adequacy.

How well the People's Bank has functioned as a central bank in controlling inflation is clear. Still, some have alleged that a major weakness of the Chinese banking system is its large volume of nonperforming loans. In 1995, the World Bank listed China's banking system as suffering from systemic banking crises. Indeed, it has been argued that China's four largest banks, accounting for 70 percent of outstanding loans, are technically insolvent. However, this issue has been addressed when China established four asset management corporations (AMCs) to help restructure the nonperforming assets of the four large state banks. As a result, the nonperforming loans ratio for the Chinese banking system was 29.8 in 2001, and was dramatically reduced to only 10.5 in 2005, according to the World Bank.

SAVINGS At no time in the reform era did the Chinese public lose confidence in their banks. By 1995, according to the International Monetary Fund (IMF), cumulative household savings were nearly 50 percent of GDP, and the addition to household savings in 1995 was 14 percent of that year's GDP. Today, cumulative household savings are more than 100 percent of GDP, while households are depositing 19 percent of GDP into savings and time deposits. According to the World Bank, total financial system deposits in 2005 had reached 147 percent of GDP, compared to only 67 percent of GDP in the United States. Overall, the banking sector capacity index—measuring the capacity of the banking system to finance economic growth—reported by the World Bank is 8.197 for China, compared to 8.395 for the United States.

Since household savings are the principal source of bank deposits in market economies, China's extraordinary growth would have been severely curtailed for lack of financing if the public had lost confidence in its banks and placed its savings in shoeboxes, as was the case in Soviet-era Russia. Clearly, China should get high marks both for the capacity and stability of its financial system

But the Chinese government recognized that in a globally integrated capital market, banking and financing misallocations are a serious issue that could derail their plans of future growth. There is now a plan that the big four banks that together make up 57 percent of all corporate loans will link up with one or more foreign banks and open to private investors. The idea is to bring openness, competition, and innovation to banking.

Bank of America bought 9 percent of China Construction Bank (CCB) for $38 billion in June 2005 and is planning on sending SWAT teams to help CCB implement sound banking. If things go well, Bank of America could exercise an option to raise its stake to 19.9 percent. Switzerland's UBS announced it was negotiating. Citigroup owns a 5 percent stake in Shanghai's Pudong Development Bank. Others, such as Goldman Sachs, HSBC and American Express, have invested over $20 billion in Chinese financial institutions.

Although these stakes are small and offer no real control by foreign investors, the door is opening and the giant nation is letting the sun shine into one of its more closed and secretive institutions. This could have a long-term result for China, as well as for foreign financial institutions seeking greater access to the money centers in order to reach Chinese consumers to offer lending, including credit cards and mortgages by the billions. There is hardly any other such place on the planet.

IPO of Chinese Bank

In October 2005, China's third largest bank, China Construction Bank (CCB), made a global offering to raise $8 billion. The offering was hugely oversubscribed. The bank, which in 2005 had $522 billion in assets, is the first bank out of four to publicly trade. CCB manager Guo Shuqing declared, "We are well positioned to capitalize on the growth in China." This continues to be a story of foreign investors' eagerness to grab a piece of China's super growth. A total of 117 Chinese companies have raised over $45 billion in global equity markets in the past decade. In August 2005, Baidu.com, a Beijing search engine company, had the best opening-day performance on Nasdaq when its shares went up fivefold to $154 per share at the end of the first day of trading. Such is the appetite for China and Chinese stocks that are deemed worthwhile.

FOREIGN EXCHANGE RATES A foreign exchange rate is simply the price of one currency in terms of another. Yet because it affects all transactions of one country with the rest of the world, it is often said that it is that country's most important price. Some governments try to keep their currency undervalued to make exports cheaper in world markets as a way to boost economic growth. This is the strategy that China has followed since 1994.

Purchasing Power Parity

Fundamentally, the Chinese currency (yuan) has been a strong currency primarily because the Chinese government has maintained an undervalued exchange rate when compared to purchasing power parity. Purchasing power parity measures the dollar cost of a typical bundle of goods purchased in the United States with the yuan cost of a similar bundle purchased in China. Based on this evaluation, the PPP exchange rate for the Chinese currency has averaged about 2 yuan per dollar, in contrast to a 10-year average market exchange rate of 8.28 yuan per dollar, or roughly four times the PPP rate. This means, for example, that a DVD player made in China and selling for, say, $40 in the United States, would carry a U.S. dollar price of four times that, or $160, if the Chinese currency traded at its PPP level. In contrast, India's exchange rate is about 5.5 times its PPP rate and Russia is 4.9 times its PPP rate, while Korea and Mexico have exchange rates only slightly above their PPP rates. Economists have found no evidence to suggest that market exchange rates will adjust to equal PPP in the long run.

A close model for Chinese leadership may be the one adopted by the Taiwanese government two decades earlier. When faced with a significant overvaluation of its currency relative to the American dollar, the Taiwan government gradually increased the value of its currency until it was close to the free market level. China, however, preferred to build its exports, particularly to the largest market in the world, the United States, by holding the value of its currency constant.

One consequence of this strategy is a significant trade surplus, especially with the United States. A corollary of this surplus is the increase in spending power of Chinese exporters that, if converted into domestic consumption, would generate inflation. The People's Bank of China has successfully neutralized such pressures when the surplus was averaging about $30 to $40 billion per year. According to the IMF, China's trade surplus surged to $125 billion in 2005 and further to $209 billion in 2006, straining the ability of the

TABLE 13.2 Foreign Debt

Country	Debt service ration (% of exports)	Debt (% of GDP)	Debt (% of exports)
Brazil	58	44	239
China	5	15	48
India	16	21	106
Korea	6	21	47
Mexico	25	22	69
Russia	13	45	117

People's Bank to stem the tide of inflation, and forcing a policy of increasing the value of the Chinese yuan relative to the U.S. dollar. If the trade surplus should continue at this unsustainable level, China will be forced to accelerate the increase in the value of its currency. Either way, long-term investors in Chinese assets can expect an additional return due to currency revaluation.

EXTERNAL DEBT Another way to understand a country's financial strength is the amount of debt owed to the rest of the world and repayable in foreign currency. China's foreign debt of about $250 billion in 2004 is among the highest in the world, but accounts for only about 15 percent of GDP and 48 percent of exports (see Table 13.2).

With debt service at only 5 percent of exports, China and Korea are in the strongest position to deal with the potential adverse impacts of financial crisis at home or abroad.

Unlike its openness to trade, the micromanaging of the CCP over economic policy has greatly enhanced China's ability to regulate fiscal policy in accordance with their objectives. Investors have continually been attracted to the Chinese government's ability to control inflation and maintain trust in the banking system, and these qualities are likely to persist in the coming years.

Growth Industries in China

Investing in China to capitalize on its growth is unfortunately neither simple nor easy. China is one of the most difficult markets for foreigner investors to access, even though progress is being made every day.

Despite this dilemma, there is a wide range of industrial sectors open to foreign investment. Such sectors are classified according to the Global Industry Classification System (GICS) and have been developed jointly by

TABLE 13.3 MSCI China Index Sector Weights (as of September 12, 2007)

Economic sector (Global Industry Classification System)	Float-adjusted shares (% of investbale index market capitalization)
Financials	40
Telecommunications	17
Oil and gas	15
Basic materials	13
Industrials	11

Standard & Poor's and Morgan Stanley Capital International (MSCI) (see Table 13.3). The GICs consists of 10 specific economic sectors covering 24 industry groups, and are further segmented into industries and sub industries. The MSCI country indexes sector weights represent 85 percent of the investable market capitalization of each economic sector of the country's economy. The index is rebalanced several times a year to ensure the index sector weights continue to reflect the underlying economy, and is thus subject to change.

Seventy percent of Chinese stocks (by market cap) continue to be locked in nontradable shares, legal pension shares, and state-owned shares. The various stock exchanges open to foreigners, however, represent almost every thriving sector of Chinese industry and offer more than enough opportunities for investors (see Table 13.4).

TABLE 13.4 Opportunities for Capitalization

Share class	Exchange	% of total market capitalization	Investment features (including availability to U.S. investors)
A	Shanghai Shenzhen	50	Denominations in Yuan. Qualified Foreign Institutional Investors (QFII)
Red chips	Hong Kong	28	Denomination in Hong Kong dollars. Hong Kong incorporation companies; majority of the business in China is available to U.S. investors
H	Hong Kong	21	Denomination in Hong Kong dollars
B	Shanghai Shenzhen	1	Chinese incorporation, available for investment

Source: Barclay Bank

TABLE 13.5 Top Holdings

Top Holdings of FTSE/Xinhua China 25 Index	% of holdings
PetroChina	9.68
China Mobile	9.60
China Life Insurance	7.76
Industrial & Commerce Bank of China	5.80
China Construction Bank	5.59
China Shenhau Energy	4.56
PNGAN Ins. Group	4.42
CNOOC Ltd.	4.36
China Merchants Bank	4.07

The I-shares FTSE/Xinhua China 25 is designed to replicate the Chinese stock index by the FTSE (Financial Times Stock Exchange) and is a constituent of the FTSE World Index. The Index represents the performance of 25 of the largest and most liquid Chinese companies that are traded on the Hong Kong Stock Exchange and are market capitalization weighted—thereby the largest companies represent the largest proportion of the index.

As is evidenced by this narrow choice of stocks represented by the index, this is only likely to represent a small slice of the Chinese market excluding many of the companies that are locally traded on Shanghai and Shenzhen exchanges (A shares).

An investor purchasing shares of an exchange-traded fund would come close to duplicating all of China's investable commodities. Another option is to buy shares of mutual funds (see Table 13.5). The weighting of certain sectors will largely depend on the opinion of the portfolio manager in regards to valuation standards and judgments, price-to-earnings (PE) ratios and profitability, projected growth rates, and other factors.

For investors wishing to get an exposure to the Chinese market, there are a large number of actively managed funds. These mutual funds, unlike passively managed index or I share, engage in active trading and overweight or underweight sectors based on their information and expertise.

In recent years, another option for an investor eager to profit from the growth of China is to invest in American Depositary Receipts (ADRs), which trade on U.S. stock exchanges or GDRs (Global Depositary Receipts), which trade on exchanges outside the United States. Lately, more Chinese companies are choosing to list on exchanges outside China, although the most popular destination continues to be Hong Kong. As these companies become global, they are expanding their reach and access to capital from global markets, which results in better transparency and corporate governance. It is, however, important for an individual investor to do thorough research on the company's prospects before investing in its stock.

In the remainder of this chapter, we will discuss these and other investment opportunities available to a foreign investor.

Financials

China's rising per-capita income is likely to result in a sharp increase in the nation's financial services sector. As incomes rise, consumers are likely to initiate mortgages and are expected to increase their use of credit cards and personal loans. The Chinese consumers' need for financial services such as insurance, mutual funds, and other banking services is also likely to increase.

Chinese consumers are quite fond of globally recognized brands, and being located primarily in urban areas, such consumers are easy to target.

This process of urbanization will continue, as millions leave rural areas and climb the economic ladder to create a new massive middle class. Early movers such as Coca-Cola and Procter & Gamble have begun to target this segment of the population. But 77 percent of urban Chinese households live on less than 25,000 RMB ($3,000); that figure will drop to 10 percent by 2025, creating the largest consumer market in the world, spending some 20 trillion RMB (according to the National Bureau of Statistics of China). These and other factors serve to illustrate the continued expansion of China's financial services sector (see Table 13.6).

We project a common measure of income inequality will remain relatively stable in urban China over the next two decades, as incomes rise at all levels. By 2011, the lower middle class will number over 290 million people, representing the largest segment in urban China and about 44 percent of the population, and by 2025, this segment will comprise a staggering 500 million people.

The other important fact is that China's population will be relatively young and, according to estimates, the majority of the population will remain

TABLE 13.6 Share of Wealth

	Global affluent > 200,000 RMB	Mass affluent 100,000–200,000 RMB	Mass affluent 25,000–40,000 RMB	Poor <25,000 RMB
2005		9.4%	12.6%	77.3%
2015	5.6%	21.2%	49.7%	23.2%
2025	7.7%	59.4%	19.8%	9.7%

Source: McKinsey Global Institute Analysis, "From 'Made in China' to 'Sold in China': The Rise of the Chinese Consumer," November 2006

between 25 and 44 years old. These Chinese households are likely to buy relatively expensive items such as automobiles and durable goods. Here is a quick snapshot of China's consumption climate:

- China's economy has grown by 9 percent since 1980.
- China's manufactures 75 percent of the world's toys.
- China produces 58 percent of the world's clothes.
- China produces 29 percent of the world's mobile phones.
- More than $1 billion in foreign direct investment (FDI) arrives each week.
- By 2008, China will be the world's largest exporter.
- By the end of the decade, China's economy will be larger than France's and the United Kingdom's.

Banks

Banks continue to be the major beneficiaries of the increase in Chinese savings rates. Chinese banks have gone through several reforms since the 1980s, yet the population's confidence in the banking system has never wavered. Large state-owned banks have, in turn, used these savings to finance major construction projects and infrastructure development. Therefore, banks such as China Construction Bank and China Merchants Bank continue to be favorites among investors, both foreign and domestic.

Prominent Financial Service Companies

- China Life Insurance
- Industrial & Commerce Bank of China
- China Construction Bank
- China Merchants Bank

Telecommunications

Though accounting for only half the sector weighting as financial services, telecommunications continues to be one of China's fastest-growing industries. As with financial services, China's telecommunications sector has risen in accordance with the nation's GDP per capita, and benefited greatly from the increasing purchasing power of the middle class. The purchase of products such as color televisions, computers, and cell phones has grown significantly every year since 1999. Similarly, Internet use has also taken off in recent years, as has the development of infrastructure to accommodate such technology.

Adding to the attractiveness of China's telecommunications industry is the fact that this sector is relatively unimpeded by the government. A 2003 study by McKinsey determined that telecommunications had the lowest rating of government interference of any economic sector. Whereas state-run enterprises had once dominated the telecom market, China's induction into the World Trade Organization forced the government to allow foreign access, and the results have been extraordinary.

Less than 10 years ago, about 1 in 12 Chinese citizens owned a landline telephone. Today, that figure has more than quadrupled, and it has been estimated that millions of new users subscribe to telephone services every month. According to China's Ministry of Information Industry, there are currently over 500 million mobile phone customers, with nearly as many fixed-line subscribers.

No discussion of Chinese telecommunications can be complete without mentioning China Mobile Communications Corporation. The largest mobile phone operation in the world, with over 300 million subscribers, the former state-owned enterprise is also the largest market capital stock on the Hong Kong Stock Exchange, as public investors account for almost 25 percent of total ownership. With an estimated market share of almost 70 percent, China Mobile and its various subsidiaries employ over 100,000 people and are likely to continue their dominance of the telecommunications sector in China for years to come.

Prominent Telecommunications Companies

- China Telecom
- China Netcom
- China Mobile
- China Unicom
- China Satcom

Oil and Gas

The Chinese economy is widely recognized for ranking among the world's top consumers of energy, yet few people realize the nation's enormous potential for producing fuel. Since the economic transformation commenced in the late 1970s, few industries in China have undergone as much of a transformation as that of oil and natural gas.

Coal has long been China's main source of energy, and this trend continues to the present day, with energy from coal accounting for almost three quarters of total energy production. This reliance on coal, however, has several drawbacks, the most obvious of which is extreme pollution. A World Health Organization study in 2000 concluded that seven of the world's most polluted cities were located in China, and it has been declared that China is also the world's leading emitter of greenhouse gases. Hoping to ease its reliance on coal-burning facilities while simultaneously developing newer, more cost-efficient methods of energy production, the Chinese government set about its tenth Five-Year Plan. Designed to restructure how the energy industry operated, the Five-Year Plan included a stated goal of developing alternative sources of energy, such as nuclear, solar, and wind, but predominantly oil and natural gas.

China National Petroleum Corporation

China's largest integrated oil company is the China National Petroleum Corporation (CNPC), which was established in 1988, yet the corporate structure has its roots in the early stages of the CCP's rule. Traded on both the New York and Hong Kong stock exchanges, CNPC holds almost 4 billion in oil barrel reserves and employs over a million people, making it the second largest corporation in the world. Even with a net income of over $13 billion per year, CNPC continues to search for new sources of both energy and profit. In addition to buying foreign companies, the oil giant is active in constructing pipelines that will connect it to more reserves, and has contracts with more than 30 nations spanning the globe.

The Chinese government quickly put these abstractions into practice, closing hundreds of coal mining operations throughout the country as it focused on developing its oil and natural gas resources. In 2004, China exported over 300,000 barrels of oil per day, while producing over 3.5 million barrels per year. Its own consumption figures, however, equated to about two times the export amounts, or roughly 7 million barrels per day. The ratio of production to consumption is significantly less with respect to natural gas. Recent data has shown that China produces slightly less natural gas than it consumes, at about 3.4 million cubic meters. With over 2.5 trillion cubic meters in proven reserves, China does not currently import any natural gas, and this trend is expected to continue for decades to come. In short, if China is to continue its upward economic climb, as most economists are predicting, it will need to become more reliant on its own resources for energy, and that commitment has been made.

Prominent Oil and Natural Gas Companies

- China National Offshore Oil Corporation (CNOOC)
- Sinopec

Basic Materials

While exports may garner most of the attention, the often overlooked basic materials sector remains a vital part of China's economy. Companies involved in construction materials, glass, paper, wood products, metals, and steel manufacturing, as well as coal mining, have proven extremely profitable for investors. China possesses vast amounts of natural resources, ranging from tin, antimony, rare earth, and titanium to zinc, iron, gold, and silver. Other mineral resources, such as talc, asbestos, cement, and limestone are also exported in mass quantities. China's growing construction industry is responsible for the major infrastructure building over the last decades. In doing so, China has relied heavily on its own natural resources.

Recent plans by the Chinese government have focused on the construction of roads, railways, airports, and bridges and the continued development of its infrastructure. Enthusiasm for such projects has attracted significant foreign investment, and made the basic materials sectors in China among its most profitable. Over the past 10 years, in fact, the construction industry has accounted for almost 7 percent of the country's GDP growth. In 2004, the government removed several barriers to the financing of construction projects by outside investors. Aside from improved infrastructure for residents, the lifting of restrictions resulted in a surge in both profits and efficiency. As the construction industry skyrocketed, so too did the demand for basic materials.

China is showing few signs of slowing down its ambitious plans for the improvement of infrastructure, and thus the basic materials sector is likely to remain one of the China's most profitable industries.

Prominent Basic Materials Companies

- Baoshan Iron & Steel
- Minmetals Development
- China Resources Enterprises
- Aluminum Corporation of China
- Maanshan Iron & Steel

Industrials

China's industrial sector includes a large number of companies involved in trades ranging from equipment and machinery manufacturing to shipping and armaments. Much like China's basic materials sectors, industrials have an exceptional potential for growth as the nation's infrastructure gradually improves. The success of a nation's industrials sector is often a leading indicator of forthcoming economic prosperity, and for China, this axiom appears to hold true.

China's energy sector has fueled, both literally and figuratively, the nation's historic period of economic growth. China's heavy industries, such as chemical, metals, and construction, currently account for almost 80 percent of the entire nation's industrial energy use. Other figures illustrate this point even further, as almost 75 percent of the nation's total energy use is derived from the industrial sector—a rate that has been growing for the last several decades. China alone presently accounts for roughly 25 percent of the world's industrial energy consumption.

Such statistics highlight China's booming industrial sector. Despite costly programs to reduce industrial pollution, profits from this sector should remain high, as construction and infrastructure projects are not likely to slow down anytime soon.

Prominent Industrials Companies

- China Communications Construction Group Ltd.
- Shanghai Construction Group General Co.
- Beijing Urban Construction Group Co., Ltd.

China has been at the forefront of globalization since its dramatic economic surge of the late 1970s. Witnessing improvements in almost every economic category, a nation that had been plagued by inflation and political instability has transformed to become the fastest growing economy in the world today. Though it will encounter more dilemmas during this progression, China, through its pivotal role in global finance, will continue to attract investments across a wide range of industries.

CHAPTER 14

A Peninsula of Perseverance

The History of Korea

History always brings glory to the people who are courageous and willing to overcome hardships.

—Park Chung-hee, former president of South Korea

Korea has one of the world's longest histories with a homogeneous people, language, and culture. Koreans trace their origins back to the Chosun, a tribal kingdom that emerged near the Chinese border around the fourth century BC. The Silla kingdom, 668 to 935 AD, marked the beginning of Korean cultural development. From the time of the Silla kingdom time until 1945, when it was forcibly divided at the 38th parallel, Korea existed as a unified country with a distinctive language and strong tradition.

Korea's physical location places it in a geopolitically strategic but precarious position. Surrounded by greater powers such as China, Russia, and Japan, the Korean Peninsula has all too often been a battleground for the clashing interests of larger nations. As such, Korea has suffered 900 invasions over the course of its 2,000-year history. The country experienced foreign occupation by China, the Mongols, Japan, the Soviet Union, and the United States. In modern history, three major wars among these neighbors have taken place on Korean soil—the Sino-Japanese war in 1894, the Russo-Japanese war in 1904, and the Korean War in 1950.

Colonial Period

The Chosun dynasty, which ruled the peninsula from 1392 to 1910, established a governmental and social system based on Confucianism, with a strictly regulated hierarchy between ruler and subject. Following the

Japanese invasion in 1592 and a subsequent invasion by the Manchus in 1636, the rulers pursued a more rigid policy of excluding foreigners, except for the Chinese and small numbers of Japanese merchants.

The isolation came to an end in the late nineteenth century, when Korea was forced to open its borders by the United States, Japan, and several European countries. Korea established diplomatic relations with Japan in 1876 by signing an unequal treaty proposed by Japan. The treaty was a legal pretext for Japanese commercial and political penetration into Korea. This was immediately followed by similar treaties with the United States and several European countries. Japan's military and commercial power came to dominate the region, gradually incorporating Korea into its sphere of influence. Korea became a protectorate of Japan in 1905, and was finally annexed in 1910.

The Japanese occupation was characterized by economic exploitation, discrimination against Koreans, and brutal suppression of Korean nationalism. From the late 1930s until 1945, an unsuccessful attempt was made to forcibly assimilate Koreans by outlawing the use of the Korean language and denying the existence of Korean culture. Most Koreans were forced to adopt Japanese names, Korean laborers were sent to Japan to work in nonstrategic industries, and Koreans were subject to conscription into the Japanese army. The objective of Korean economic development was to provide the Japanese empire with food, raw materials, and a consumer market for Japanese goods.

Brutal as the colonial experience was, there were unexpected advantages in the long run. Efficient transportation and communications systems were established, which laid the foundation for Korea's remarkable economic growth decades later. Basic industries were built, mostly in the north where the bulk of raw materials and hydroelectric power were located. The southern region was the peninsula's agricultural and commercial center, complementing the industrial north. Another legacy of the colonial period was the emergence of skilled laborers and a small but well-trained white-collar managerial class.

The Republic of Korea

Liberation from colonial rule came on August 15, 1945, when the Japanese surrendered to the Allied Forces and ended World War II. The U.S. government's decision to divide Korea at the 38th parallel had been proposed to the Soviet Union as a means of joint acceptance of the Japanese surrender. This temporary division became permanent as the Cold War power struggle between the United States and the Soviet Union dominated the region.

Economically, the postwar years in the southern region of Korea were harsh. Southern Korea's economy, long dependent on Japan and dismembered by the division of the country, was in shambles. Liberation had resulted in an influx of millions of Koreans from China, Japan, and the Soviet Union, who had been dislocated during the 36 years of colonial rule.

The economic depression was exacerbated by the failure of nationwide land reform, extremely high inflation, and the stagnation of agricultural and industrial production. The United States Army Military Government in Korea (USAMGIK)[1] failed to settle disputes over formerly Japanese-owned commercial, industrial, and agricultural assets, and thus much of the preexisting economic base was underutilized.

Politically, too, there were problems. Most Korean leaders at that time seriously lacked credibility. Many had collaborated with the Japanese colonial government, even prospering under it. Of those who did have good nationalist records, a number were considered to be left wing. The USAMGIK favored more conservative Korean leaders. Syngman Rhee was one such politician. He was brought back to Korea from the United States, where he had been living in exile during Japanese rule. The USAMGIK saw Rhee as a potential leader, one who could provide stability to an area rife with political unrest. The United States was particularly concerned with halting Soviet expansion in Asia and thought that this could be best accomplished through the establishment of a viable noncommunist state in southern Korean.

By the mandate of the UN resolution, general elections for a National Assembly were held on May 10, 1948, in southern Korea, while the government of the northern part of Korea refused to participate in the UN-supervised elections. In July, Syngman Rhee was elected first president of the Republic of Korea (hereafter referred to as Korea) by a vote of the National Assembly. The Republic of Korea was officially established on August 15, 1948, the anniversary of Korea's liberation from Japanese colonial rule.

In October 1948, the Democratic People's Republic of Korea (North Korea) was established under Kim Il-sung. Kim, a former anti-Japanese guerrilla fighter and officer in the Soviet army, had accompanied the Soviet troops into Korea in 1945. (Kim's son, Kim Jong-il, assumed office upon his father's death in 1994.)

Both the South and North Korean governments maintained that they were the only legitimate rulers of the Korean Peninsula, resulting in intense competition between the two for international recognition. By 1949, most American and Soviet troops had been withdrawn from the peninsula.

---

[1]The USAMGIK was a provisional government that ruled southern Korea from September 8, 1945, to August 15, 1948.

A Violent Divide

In a speech to the National Press Club on January 12, 1950, then-U.S. Secretary of State Dean Acheson stated that the U.S. defensive perimeter essential to military security in the Pacific runs along the Aleutians to Japan and then goes from the Ryukyus to the Philippine Islands, thus excluding the Korean peninsula from the U.S. defense line. It is believed that the North Korean government interpreted this description of the defense perimeter to mean that the United States would not intervene in a war on the Korean Peninsula.

When the Korean War began on June 25, 1950, there was no security treaty in effect ensuring an American military intervention on behalf of Korea. The U.S. government perceived the North Korean invasion to be part of a worldwide pattern of expansion by communist forces and took the issue to the UN Security Council. In the absence of the Soviet delegate, the United States obtained sanctions for and assistance in providing military aid and troops to Korea. A UN command was established at the recommendation of the Security Council and assumed operational control over all military activity on the peninsula.

The Korean War was brutally devastating for both north and south. Opposing forces destroyed large areas of both regions, including the capitals of Pyongyang and Seoul, resulting in heavy damage to infrastructure. Approximately 4 million lives were lost, and another 5 million Koreans were dislocated.

Hostilities officially ended on July 27, 1953, with the signing of an armistice by representatives of the United States, North Korea, and China. President Rhee was persuaded to accept the truce only after the United States agreed to a U.S.-Korea mutual defense treaty. South Korea did not sign the armistice, however.

Over the course of the war, the Rhee government had become increasingly dictatorial and corrupt. Afraid of the aggressive North Korean regime and of the endless social unrest within South Korea, Rhee grew more and more obsessed with staying in power. He ruthlessly oppressed political opponents, while taking whatever measures necessary to extend his presidency.

When Rhee's ruling party was found to have blatantly rigged votes in the 1960 presidential election, public discontent erupted in a massive protest on April 19, 1960. The antigovernment movement, which started as street demonstrations led by university students, evolved into a popular revolt and finally forced Rhee to step down from office.

The interim government revised the constitution to adopt a parliamentary cabinet and establish Lower and Upper Houses of the National Assembly. General elections held under the new legal institutions formed a cabinet headed by Chang Myon. Despite efforts to establish a healthy democracy, however, the new government of the Second Republic was unable to quell incessant political infighting and social instability.

Out of Poverty, Into Prosperity

The sound of sporadic gunfire at daybreak on May 16, 1961, announced the emergence of the most dominant figure in Korea's recent history. On that day, General Park Chung-hee staged a military coup, claiming that he would restore order to the nation. Park assured the Koreans that he had no designs on political office, and promised that he would restore power to the civilians (i.e., nonmilitary). Shortly thereafter, he reneged on this promise, formed a political party, and won the presidential election held under the revised constitution.

Park Chung-hee was born on September 30, 1917. At the age of 23, after he taught in an elementary school near his hometown for three years, he volunteered for the Japanese Army and was sent to Manchuria. In 1945, Park joined the newly established Korean Army and made his way up to the highest echelon.

There is no doubt that Park's greatest achievement was Korea's spectacular economic development. Throughout his presidency, Park took full charge of the economy and carefully monitored the implementation of his policies. He told one of his closest aides, "To me, eradicating poverty from my country is a mandate from heaven." Fully committed to this belief, he embarked on the first Five-Year Economic Development Plan (1962–1966) as soon as he came into power. He set up an economics situation room next to his office and frequently met with economists, officials, and businessmen. He tirelessly visited development-related government offices and construction sites all over the country to provide guidance.

Under his leadership, nominal gross domestic product (GDP) increased from $2.3 billion in 1962 to $63.8 billion in 1980, and per-capita GDP rose from about $92 in 1962 to $1,704 in 1980.

The Beginning of the Miracle

Park was not the first political leader who tried to develop Korea's economy, but he was the first to be successful because of a major policy shift from import substitution to export promotion. The plan was to promote exports of manufactured goods for which Korea possessed comparative advantage with its low labor cost. Park continuously emphasized the importance of exports in the national economy and supported any business firm involved in exports. He started "export promotion meetings" in January 1965, at which high-level government officials and business leaders gathered once a month to discuss the current issues of trade, and Park never missed a single meeting until his death in 1979. He once said, "Awake or asleep, I only think about boosting exports."

The government mobilized almost every macroeconomic mechanism at its disposal in the implementation of the export promotion plan, such as maintaining high interest rates to expand domestic savings and enacting the Foreign Capital Promotion Act to encourage the inflow of foreign investment. In order to promote exports, the government devalued the currency by nearly 100 percent and replaced the previous multiple-exchange-rate system with a single exchange rate. The government also provided short-term export financing, allowed tariff rebates on materials imported for reexport use, and simplified customs procedures.

The government's export promotion plan was not warmly welcomed in the beginning. Conservative economists and government officials argued that such a strategy would endanger the nation's economic independence because of its excessive reliance on foreign capital. Indeed, foreign capital made up 83 percent of total investment in 1962, and it was not until late in the decade that Korea boosted exports enough to attain credibility that justified the considerable amount of foreign debts. The government argued that the export plan was more palatable than the alternatives—during the 1950s, Korea had depended on grant-in-aid and concessionary loans, mainly from the United States, to finance both imports and exports.

Growing Up, Massively

In the midst of the rapid expansion in exports and consequent economic growth, President Park moved forward with another ambitious project. To a former military general, wealth and strength were inseparable. Park wanted to build industries that could support both economic growth and military buildup. Declaring that "steel is national power," he decided to invest in heavy industry.

As a priority in the third Five-Year Economic Development Plan (1972–1976), the government announced the Heavy and Chemical Industry Development Plan in 1973, which set forth an ambitious schedule for the development of technology-driven industries such as electronics and shipbuilding. To help build the new industries, another set of capital-intensive businesses, such as manufacturers of power generating equipments and heavy machinery, also began to flourish.

Park did not always rely on professional advice in pursuing economic development plans. No one believed that Korea could succeed in this endeavor. The case of POSCO (Pohang Steel Company) was a perfect example. The World Bank issued a skeptical report about Korea's plan to build a steel manufacturing plant, and the United States refused to approve financing.

Despite political opposition and many economists' warnings that his plan to establish heavy industries was impractical, he remained determined to build. As a result, he eagerly obtained Japanese loans and ambitiously pushed through the construction of a massive steel plant in Pohang on the southeast coast, which became the world's largest steel-production site and the foundation of Korea's remarkable economic growth, thus laying the foundation for another remarkable achievement in the growth of Korea's economy.

Korea's choice proved to be a wise one. In the early 1970s, the change in the international atmosphere had a significant impact on Korea. In 1971, the Nixon administration reduced the number of U.S. armed forces in Korea by around one-third, forcing the Korean government to develop its own defense industry to support its military forces. In the same year, the Bretton Woods system that had ensured stability in the international financial system collapsed. In the case of Korea, the subsequent fluctuation in exchange rates had a damaging effect on the balance of payments. The worldwide commodity shortage of 1972–1973 and the oil shock of 1973–1974 further complicated the problems. Korea had to respond to the deteriorating trade balance by modifying its export strategy. The government rebalanced the composition of exported goods in favor of more sophisticated, higher-value-added products contributed, which helped sustain the nation's economic growth.

Turmoil behind the Growth

Park's focus on economic development led to several breakthroughs in the diplomatic arena, too. Despite fierce domestic opposition, Park normalized relations with Japan in 1965, guaranteeing $800 million of immediate assistance and many more millions in foreign direct investment (FDI). Park also sent two divisions of troops to fight alongside the U.S. forces in Vietnam, in exchange for which Korean firms received a major share of war production and construction contracts.

The political situation in the early 1970s, both domestic and abroad, proved grim for Park. He barely won the 1971 presidential election against Kim Dae-jung, a formidable opponent. After the Nixon administration's decision to reduce the number of American forces in Korea and subsequent rapprochement with China, Park began to lose his confidence in the United States' military commitment. Despite the South-North Joint Communiqué in 1972, in which both Koreas agreed to work together for peaceful reunification, Park never stopped seeing North Korea as a threat, especially as the country increased its military to pursue further independence from the

Soviet Union and China. Park decided to consolidate his authority under the *Yushin* ("revitalizing reform") system in 1972 by abolishing almost all existing institutions that might have reduced his own power. He silenced the voices of dissent and tried to remain in power indefinitely. Park's authoritarian rule came to an abrupt end on October 26, 1979, when he was assassinated by Kim Jae-kyu, chief of the Korean Central Intelligence Agency.

On the evening of October 26, 1979, President Park was dining with three of his closest aides in a safe house inside the presidential residence. Among them was the Korean CIA (KCIA) director, Kim Jae-kyu, a lifelong friend of Park's; chief of security Cha Ji-Chul; and chief of staff Kim Kye Won.

At the dinner table, Park kept criticizing KCIA Director Kim for failing to put down the continuing domestic disorders. After a few minutes of this, Kim left the dining room to retrieve his .38 pistol from his office. Shots of gunfire rang out, killing Park, who is still remembered by most Koreans as the greatest leader in their history. (A subsequent government investigation showed that the assassination had been planned beforehand. During the trial, Kim testified that he killed the president in order to put an end to the tyranny and restore democracy. Kim was hanged on May 24, 1980.)

Nevertheless, the drive to boost heavy industries also created a number of negative effects. Firms were likely to accumulate excessive debt. The high demand for low-interest loans swelled the domestic money supply. The low-interest policy reduced savings significantly, while the wage gap between skilled and unskilled workers continued to widen. Moreover, government intervention became routine. At first, the dominant role of the government was crucial to the planning for and implementation of large-scale business projects. However, government involvement persisted when it should have diminished, as the economy expanded and advanced. The result was a waste of resources, inflation, and increasing social inequality. During the 1980s and 1990s, the Korean government made several attempts to liberalize and privatize the economy, but the process was not complete.

Building a "Great Korea"

The political vacuum created in the aftermath of Park's assassination was quickly filled by another military coup on December 12, 1980. A group of soldiers, led by Major General Chun Doo Hwan, soon took control of the government. They revised the constitution to introduce a single seven-year term for the indirectly elected president. Chun was elected president under the new constitution in 1980, declaring that he would build a "Great Korea" in a new era.

Not unlike Park, Chun came into power and governed the country in a violent and heavy-handed manner. The worst of all the bloody incidents was the Gwangju Democratization Movement, in which hundreds of civilians were brutally killed by military troops while protesting against Chun's coup in 1980. This event seriously damaged Chun's legitimacy.

Chun's presidency was not without some major achievements, however. The surplus in the balance of payments continued through his term, and he brought world attention to South Korea with the successful 1988 Seoul Olympics.

Toward the end of his term, public outcry for democracy led Chun to decide on a peaceful transfer of power. Under the Chun government, popular movements against the authoritarian rule spread nationwide, culminating in a massive protest rally in June 1987. The government finally accepted the people's demands. The constitution was revised again, reintroducing the direct popular election of a five-year term president. In the ensuing presidential election, Roh Tae-woo, Chun's military colleague, was elected. Roh promised to end authoritarian rule. Subsequently, the government released a number of prisoners detained on political charges while embarking on official investigations and hearings over the wrongdoings committed under Chun's leadership, such as the brutal oppression of the Gwangju Democratization Movement.

The Roh government is also credited with foreign policy achievements with the Communist bloc, including establishing diplomatic ties with eastern European countries, the Soviet Union, and China. Also notable was Roh's positive diplomatic initiatives that enabled both South and North Korea to join the United Nations simultaneously.

However, the Roh administration's pursuit of further liberalization caused significant social unrest. Strikes and demonstrations continued. Roh also failed to sever the collusive ties between politics and the conglomerates; Roh himself accepted huge private contributions from the big business firms. The mission to build a more transparent society was left to Roh's successor to be fulfilled.

Enduring all the hardships such as foreign occupation, war, and poverty during the twentieth century, Korea has become one of the most successful cases of modernization. Nearing the twenty-first century, however, Korea had to face another turning point. This time, Korea was required to restructure itself to become a responsible actor on the world stage.

CHAPTER 15

A Blessing in Disguise

Korea from 1993 to Today

At times, we were forced to go through a history of dependence, unable to determine our own destiny. But today, we are at the threshold of a new turning point.

—Roh Moo-hyun, former president of South Korea

Korea has been one of the fastest-growing economies that the world has ever witnessed. According to the Bank of Korea, in less than four decades, the country has transformed from a poor agrarian society into the tenth largest economy in the world—with an incredible increase of per-capita gross domestic product (GDP) from $92 in 1962 to over $18,200 in 2006. The remarkable achievements of the Korean economy are often called the "miracle on the Han River," named after the river that runs through Seoul, the capital.

As mentioned in Chapter 14, the miracle began in the early 1960s, when Korea undertook government-led development plans. From that point on, Korea has made unprecedented progress in building a strong economy. As such, it is often regarded by other developing countries as a role model of economic success.

Down a Thorny Path

In the presidential election held in 1993, Kim Young-sam was elected. Kim, the first civilian president since the 1961 coup, pledged to build a "New Korea" during his presidency. His government sought to eradicate corruption through legislation aimed at promoting transparency. All high-level government officials were obliged to register their property and financial transactions were to be practiced under real names (it had previously not been necessary to show identification when opening bank accounts, leading to high levels of corruption and bribery).

Despite the far-reaching reforms to fight against corruption, President Kim Young-sam and his government were unprepared for one of the most devastating economic crises in recent years.

When the Asian financial crisis swept across Asia in 1997–1998, the Korean government failed to safeguard the nation's financial institutions, eventually leading to an International Monetary Fund (IMF) bailout. Nearing the end of his term, Kim handed over the formidable task of overcoming the crisis and restructuring the country's outdated economic systems to Kim Dae-jung.

Marking the first democratic transition of power from the ruling party, President Kim Dae-jung's administration was inaugurated in February 1998. The Kim government implemented a set of reforms in the government and private sector to restructure the economy.

President Kim Dae-jung, under his "Sunshine Policy," is credited with laying the foundation for a peaceful reunification of Korea by holding the first ever inter-Korean summit meeting with North Korea. A spirit of North and South Korean economic cooperation prevailed, and families separated for years along the 38th parallel were reunited. Kim Dae-jung won the Nobel Peace Prize in October 2000 for his reunification work. However, North Korea's nuclear weapons program was revealed at the end of the Kim administration, eroding much of the progress made between the two Koreas.

Not Out of the Woods Yet

The financial crisis in 1997–1998, which started in Southeast Asia and rapidly spread to other Asian countries, including Korea, was a proving ground for the viability of Korean economy. Like a patient who had neglected a chronic illness, Korea quickly fell victim to the crisis, undergoing a severe economic contraction.

By the late 1990s, the structure of the Korean economy had become increasingly vulnerable. This was partly caused by an excessive amount of short-term foreign debt combined with insufficient foreign exchange reserves. By the end of 1996, the share of short-term debt out of total foreign debt peaked at 58 percent, while the foreign exchange reserve remained low.

The second and more important factor behind the crisis was an unstable corporate financial structure. The corporate debt was increasing substantially due to the overinvestments by *chaebol*, which is a family-owned and government-assisted big business conglomerate (i.e., Samsung, LG, Hyundai.) The *chaebol*'s overinvestment, coupled with poor governance and weak financial institutions, made Korea's economic structure increasingly vulnerable to shocks from the outside world.

Such deficiencies were the consequences of Korea's past development process. The 30 years of government-led economic growth created a collusive relationship between the government and *chaebol*. Frequently relying on *chaebol*'s full-scale engagements in big business projects, the government in turn provided them with insurance against failures. The Korean society, therefore, was accustomed to the so-called "too-big-to-fail" expectation. Under such beliefs, the business firms' main concerns were expansion rather than increasing profitability. Consequently, business firms preferred debt-financed growth to equity-financed growth. According to the Fair Trade Commission, the debt-to-equity ratio exceeded 400 percent by the end of 1997, and the average ratio for the 30 largest *chaebol* reached 512.8 percent. These figures are approximately twice the rate of Mexican firms and four times the rate of Thai firms at the time of the crisis.

Unfavorable terms of trade in 1996 severely damaged profits of Korean corporations in 1997. A series of corporate bankruptcies, especially among the major *chaebol*, including Hanbo, one of the major steel-producing companies, and Kia, the eighth-biggest *chaebol*, drastically increased the volume of nonperforming bank loans, which immediately translated into the weakening of the financial sector. The financial institutions' attempt to minimize the loss by stringent lending policies resulted in the shortage of capital, which further increased the number of bankruptcies.

In addition, President Kim Young-sam, nearing the end of his term in office, was not able to provide the necessary leadership for an extensive reform. The government's heavy-handed actions and inadequate handling largely disappointed foreign investors, who eventually pulled their investment from the fragile economy.

As a result, in October 1997, the Korean Stock Exchange plunged, followed by the sharp fall of the Korean won against the U.S. dollar. By November, Korea's foreign reserves were nearly depleted, and to prevent the total collapse of the economy, the government announced that it would seek an emergency loan from the IMF. Although this crisis was in part due to the regional instability in Southeast Asia, it was also a consequence of deep-rooted problems in the Korean economy.

The End of an Old Era

The Korean economy proved its durability after undergoing the sharpest contraction in the wake of the financial crisis. The remarkable rebound was the combined results of rigorous restructuring efforts, the elimination of bad loans through massive public money injection, and more or less favorable economic conditions during 1999–2000. The depreciation of the exchange rate and expansive macroeconomic policies also created a favorable environment for the rapid restoration.

The most notable change can be observed in the corporate and banking sectors. The creditor banks have established practices that require corporations to bear restructuring costs. The corporations are resolving their overcapacity problems and selling their noncore assets and affiliates. Consolidated financial statements, in compliance with international accounting standards, have been in effect since 2000. To enhance transparency in corporate management, the owner-management system has been checked both internally and externally. In addition, class-action lawsuits are gradually being introduced. Finally, white-collar criminals, who used to be able to evade proper punishment, now have to face the strict enforcement of laws. With these developments, one can reasonably come to the conclusion that the restructuring efforts are coming to fruition. For example, the average debt-to-equity ratio of the top 30 *chaebol* dropped from 512.8 percent in 1997 to 171.2 percent in 2000, a result that was accomplished through asset dispositions, rights offerings, and foreign direct investments (according to the Fair Trade Commission).

In the December 2002 presidential election, Roh Moo-hyun from the ruling Millennium Democratic party won by only a narrow margin. The former human rights lawyer initiated reforms, pursuing full realization of democracy in social practices as well as government operations. He also tried to promote a fair distribution of wealth. The new administration avowedly followed the engagement policy toward North Korea from the previous Kim administration, seeking a peaceful solution of the North Korean nuclear crisis. During the Roh government, generational and ideological divisions became clearer as the liberals supported the government while the conservatives favored the opposition party. The opposition party's unsuccessful attempt to impeach the president in April 2002 symbolized the divide in the Korean society. Soaring anti-American sentiment signified a shifting viewpoint among the younger generation.

Being Cured

Despite the significant progress in economic restructuring, operational efficiency remains unresolved, and passive attitudes in the corporate and financial sectors may result in sagging performance. However, the unexpected economic crisis completely shifted the mind-set of both decision makers and business leaders. Now Korea is firmly committed to the restructuring of its economy and will continue to play a crucial role in the global economy.

As the 10th biggest economy in the world, with more stable political institutions, Korea is expected to provide a good opportunity for foreign investors. Thus, some people called the crisis a blessing in disguise, as it provided an opportunity to readjust Korea's economy. Indeed, the crisis resulted in a thorough restructuring of the country's economic system. It might still be too early to judge the results of the restructuring efforts, but there is no doubt that Korea continues to play an important role in the global economy.

CHAPTER 16

High Profits in a Tricky Neighborhood

Investing in Korea

As mentioned in Chapters 14 and 15, the Korean economy has undergone a remarkable transformation since the end of the Korean War in 1953. One of the poorest countries in the world at that time, Korea today is Asia's 3rd largest economy and the 10th largest in the world, with a per-capita gross domestic product (GDP) of $24,500 (according to the *World Factbook*).

With a significant amount of foreign aid received from the United States after the war, the Syngman Rhee administration laid the foundation for a modern economic system, building roads and communications facilities, as well as schools and government buildings. By the late 1960s, Korea, which had been able to bypass spending revenues on infrastructure, was industrializing at rates unimaginable just a decade prior, relying on exports and manufacturing. A steady flow of foreign capital and a progressive government directing a massive private sector combined to make Korea the textbook model of rapid modernization.

It has been estimated that during the 1970s, Korea was the world's most productive economy. The growth would continue well into the 1980s and 1990s, as Korea had wisely anticipated the information technology (IT) age and was at the forefront in exporting these innovations. Although the Asian financial crisis in 1997 would stall this development, it would do so only temporarily, as Korea fared better than its neighbors in maintaining positive growth figures. Today, with reforms and other precautionary steps adopted, Korea, still at the forefront of technology exports, will likely continue its upward climb.

What percentage of your portfolio should you consider investing in Korea? Here is a look at present-day Korea and its prospects for the future in relation to the eight tenets of our investment model.

Demographics: *Favorable*

Korea, bordering the Sea of Japan and the Yellow Sea on southern peninsula, is home to almost 49 million people, making it the 23rd most populous nation on earth. With almost 40,000 square miles, the nation is roughly the same size as the state of Indiana, making Korea one of the most densely populated countries on the globe. With a population growth of 0.4 percent, the number of inhabitants in the country is expected to increase by 3.4 percent by the year 2020. Of the six sizzling BRIC+2 nations, Korea ranks fifth in terms of expected population growth, exceeding only that of Russia (−6.9 percent) and trailing the next lowest, China, by almost 5 percent. At present, Korea's population is overwhelmingly middle aged, with almost three quarters of its citizens in the 15-to-65 age bracket. Youths, ages 0 to 14, account for roughly 18 percent of the total number, with those over the age of 65 (9 percent) accounting for the remaining population. The population trends in Korea have not deviated much from previous decades. In 1975, for instance, Korea's population totaled 35 million, and by 1998, that figure had risen to 46 million—a rate of growth around 1 percent.

Ethnically homogeneous, Korea is also a predominantly urban society, as almost 85 percent of its citizens reside in cities such as Seoul (10.4 million), Pusan (3.9 million), Taegu (2.5 million), Inchon (2.5 million), Kwangju (1.3 million), and Taejon (1.3 million). In 1975, by contrast, that figure stood at 48 percent, illustrating how encompassing the industrialization process has been for the nation. By 2015, the urban population is expected to account for almost 92 percent of its total.

Though its population is not soaring, as in, say, Mexico or India, Korea's demographics bode well for future success. Korea's population is largely working age, resulting in an exceptionally low dependency ratio—the percentage of a nation's income to fund youths and the elderly. This figure is expected to continue to decline through 2015 due to lower birth rates. The declining birth rate translates to fewer young dependents per worker, a track Korea has been on for some time.

In 1955, a few years after the Korean War, the percentage of the population under the age of 15 was 41 percent. In 1966, that figure had fallen to 38.3 percent. As its population growth slowed, the average income rose, and the nation came to more closely resemble the industrialized economies of more developed nations. The obvious halt in population growth corresponded to a number of government initiatives designed solely for this purpose. Population controls programs, however, were not the only reason for the decline, as urbanization, higher education, and improved health care all contributed to stem the rising populace.

Birth rate statistics, for which Korea has one of the world's lowest figures, led the country's Economic Planning Board to conclude that the

Korean population will stabilize by the year 2023, at just over 52.6 million people. Between 2015 and 2020, the country's dependency ratio will begin to rise again as the percentage of those over age 65 increases.

Economic Performance: *Favorable*

As with other six sizzling BRIC+2 markets, Korea's favorable economic performance was determined by an analysis of its GDP growth, its middle-class composition, and the pattern of urbanization transpiring throughout its borders. Combined, these factors are indicative of a national economy reliant on an urban middle class with exceptional purchasing power.

THE GROWTH OF THE MIDDLE CLASS The dramatic rise of the Korean economy over the past several decades brought on the emergence of a middle class, a sector that continues to expand even in a country with the lowest birth rate among developed nations. With increasing purchase power and disposable income of its citizens, Korea, by selling its technology products domestically, had greatly curtailed its reliance on exports. A study by the World Bank in 2005, for instance, found that Internet use—a key indicator of a nation's middle class—had increased from 405 per 1,000 people in 2000, to 683 per 1,000 by 2005 (according to the International Telecommunication Union, World Telecommunication Development Report and database, and World Bank estimates).

Similarly, mobile phone subscriber rates are among the highest in the world, with about 80 percent of the population owning cell phones. Korea also has the world's highest percentage of high-speed Internet connections per household, another indicator of a thriving middle class. As the national household income rises, Koreans benefit from low housing costs, which account for only 8 percent of household income. The remaining 47 percent of household expenditures, therefore, can be used to purchase, among other things, a variety of consumer goods. According to the Korea National Statistics Office, the average household income for Korea, as of 2007, stands at just over $42,000 per year. Poverty rates are low, with the ratio of the poorest 20 percent of the population to the richest 20 percent at just 4.7, compared with 8.4 in the United States and 5.5 percent in Canada.

SHIFT FROM AGRICULTURE Another pleasant consequence of rapid modernization has been the shift from agriculture toward service industries. Aside from restaurants, hotels, and entertainment venues that emerged as industrialization spread in the 1980s, Korea has of late benefited from growing insurance and financial institutions, which now stand as the nation's leaders in the field. Health care and other social services are expected to continue their recent growth as well, as the Korean population ages—marking a stark contrast to a sector that had previously been dominated by retail.

GDP GROWTH Korea's GDP growth in recent decades has been nothing short of astonishing. From 1963 to 2005, Korea's GDP had an annual average growth rate of 7.3 percent, a considerable accomplishment when one factors in the Asian financial crisis of 1998, when Korea's GDP dropped by that same margin. From 2000 until 2005, the Korean economy grew at a rate of 4.5 percent. Nonetheless, Goldman Sachs rates Korea as well placed for strong growth potential because of its growth supportive fundamentals. This is reflected in their Growth Environment index (GES), where Korea is ranked 17th out of 170 countries, with an index of 6.9 compared with 7.0 for Germany, 7.4 for the United States, and 6.2 for Japan.

We use the growth accounting framework to divide Korea's growth potential into its fundamental components:

- Growth in labor force.
- Growth in capital stock (investment).
- Growth in productive efficiency or total factor productivity (TFP).

Demographic projections suggest labor force growth of only 0.4 percent per year going forward since Korea, with an urban population already at 81 percent, can expect little dividend from shifting labor out of agriculture. However, with investment at about 29 percent of GDP, we can expect strong growth in capital stock. But the key component for Korea is productive efficiency, which has grown at a compound rate of 2.9 percent per year from 1980 to 2005—exactly the same as China for that period. By comparison, India's TFP growth for that period is 2.4 percent, but if we measure from India's turning point, India has increased TFP at 3.4 percent per year from 1992 to 2005.

TFP is not simply gains from new technology, but it includes a more efficient use of resources and investment capital, management effectiveness, and the political and institutional environment as well. As we can see in Figure 16.1, Korea's productive efficiency more than doubled in the past 25 years, in keeping with its strong position in technology innovations such as robotics.

Following the Asian financial crisis in 1997–1998, capital stock growth slowed, as Korea instituted much needed reforms in its banks and other financial institutions, but TFP growth continued at the same rate (see Table 16.1). If these trends continue, we can project Korea's growth rate of GDP at about 5 percent per year to 2025.

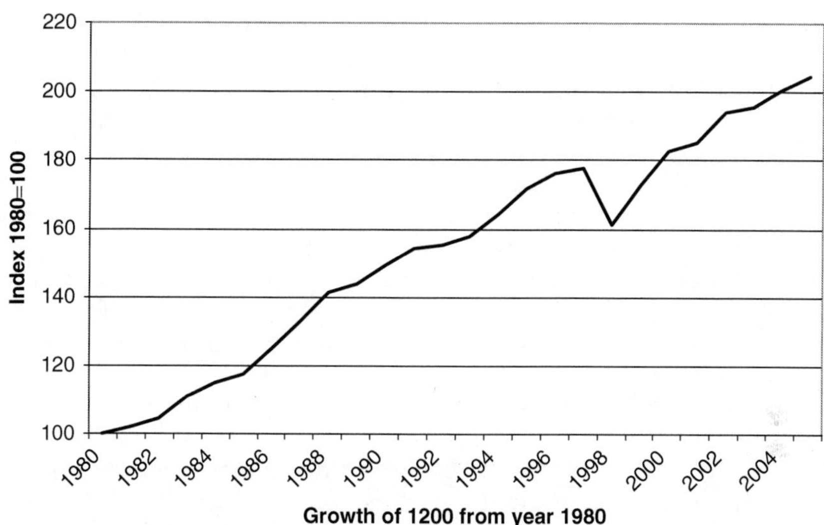

FIGURE 16.1 Korea: Productivity growth trend.
Sources: IMF International Financial Statistics, Fey (2001); Nehru and Dhareshwar (1992)

URBANIZATION Korea underwent a prolonged period of urbanization following the Korean War—a favorable economic trend that continues today. As the population moved in from the countryside, Korea saw its urban population rise from 14.5 percent of its total population in 1945, to almost 66 percent by 1985. This influx has been primarily attributed to the number of refugees coming in from the north as a result of the conflict. Yet this trend continued well into the postwar years, as Koreans migrated into the cities, not for refuge but for economic opportunities. This mass migration into Korea's cities, however, highlighted several major consequences. One, the movement drained the agricultural sector of its most capable workers. In 1963, as the economic pull began, Koreans were predominantly working on farms. As the industrial sector grew, the percentage of the Korean

TABLE 16.1 Growth Rates

	Compound growth rate	Contribution (% points)
Labor force (weight = 0.6)	0.4%	0.24
Capital stock (weight = 0.4)	4.7%	1.88
TFP	2.9%	2.90
GDP growth rate		5.02

population involved in agriculture dropped from over 60 percent in 1963 to less than 18 percent as of 2007.

Just as the farming sector lost its labor force, so too did it begin to lose land. As industrialization spread, the amount of farmable land decreased significantly and has since contributed to its stagnation in comparison with the rest of the Korean economy. Furthermore, the construction of residential and commercial buildings forced a great number of families, unable to afford the increased real estate prices, to move elsewhere. Pollution, resulting from the increased demand for fuel, proved to be a significant dilemma for a country unequipped to deal with its ramifications. Inadequate infrastructure had been tagged as a major concern, as traffic jams clogged the streets.

The effects of urbanization today, however, are far less severe than in years past, as evidenced by the emergence of Korea's tourism industry. A phenomenon known as the "Korean Wave" has put Korea at the forefront of popular culture, with thousands of young tourists, primarily from the neighboring nations, now visiting the country each year.

The Korean economy figures to remain an attractive option for foreign investors, in part due to the composition of its population and the remarkable gains in the nation's GDP over the past 40 years. With a middle class quite fond of high-end consumer products, Korea will continue to develop markets for its products inside its own borders, in addition to being a major exporter of technology.

Technology Expansion: *Favorable*

Technology and the Korean economy are virtually inseparable. Since the start of the IT age, few countries have been as progressive and forward thinking as Korea, a nation that continues to dominate the high-end consumer electronics market. As such, the technology expansion of Korea is ranked as favorable for investors.

Working with the specific industries, the Korean government has encouraged technological expansion, not only in terms of exports, but for Korea's growing middle class as well. This dedication was recognized by the investment bank of Goldman Sachs, which has designated Korea as one of the "Next 11"—a term for countries with high prospects for future growth.

Samsung

Samsung Group is Korea's largest *chaebol* and the fifth largest company in the world. Founded by Lee Byung-chul in the southeastern province of Korea, it is composed of a number of businesses, ranging from sugar production to shipbuilding. Samsung, which means "three stars" in Korean, has three major components: Samsung Electronics, the world's largest electronics company; Samsung Heavy Industries, one of the major shipbuilders; and Samsung Engineering & Construction.

A major breakthrough in Samsung Group's history came in 1993. A few years after he took over the control of the group, the new chairman, Lee Kun-hee, the youngest son of the late founder, launched a dramatic revolution from the top to make his 28 companies internationally competitive. Declaring that Samsung was second rate by global standards, he called on each employee "to change everything but your wife." Lee Kun-hee stressed quality of products over quantity and discouraged outdated managerial practices. Lee Kun-hee's rigorous efforts finally paid off: Unlike other *chaebols*, Samsung not only survived the 1997–1998 financial crisis largely unharmed, but also became a global leader in the marketplace.

Among the many companies in the group, the most notable is Samsung Electronics, which is the leader in the worldwide semiconductor business. It is the world's largest manufacturer of DRAM chips, flash memory, and optical storage drives. Along with another Korean *chaebol* company, LG Electronics, it is the world's leading manufacturer of liquid crystal displays (LCDs) and the next generation of mobile phones. In 2005, it surpassed Intel in investments and overtook Sony as the world's biggest consumer electronics company, with a net worth of $77.6 billion. According to Interbrand and *BusinessWeek,* Samsung's brand value ranked 20th (US$14.9 billion) among top global companies in 2005.

Samsung plays a huge role in the Korean economy, accounting for 20.7 percent of all exports.

Source: www.samsung.com/AboutSAMSUNG/SAMSUNGGroup/Timeline History/index.htm

Korea's success in technology has been so widely recognized that when the country announced that "every household will have a robot by 2020," hardly anyone laughed. The robotics industry, if even a quarter as successful as its technology sector, figures to be a major source of potential growth over the next few decades. Previously relying on the adaptation or "reverse engineering" of existing technology into new products, and therefore bypassing much of the research and development (R&D) costs, Korea's technology sector now invests considerable time and energy into research and analysis, making it among the world's most efficient technological economies.

Robots

Korea possesses one of the most innovative, forward-thinking electronics sectors in the world. In 2006, Baeg Moon-hong, a senior researcher with the Division for Applied Robot Technology at the Korea Institute of Industrial Technology in Ansan, unveiled plans to place a lifelike robot in every home by the year 2020.

The robot prototype, named EveR-1, has the appearance of a mid-20s Korean woman, and can speak, make eye contact, and express emotions. The Korean government, much like the robot's creator, envisions the android as a functioning member of society: able to guide tours or serve as a teacher's aide in the classroom, even perhaps as home security guards. The service-mindedness of the robots coincides with the country's aging population, and it has been expressed that such products would be tailored to the elderly.

The Korean government is already conducting a test run, having placed nearly 650 of the robots in private homes in 2006, with another 20 dispersed throughout the public sector.

Source: Stefan Lovgren, "A Robot in Every Home by 2020," *South Korea Says*, September 6, 2006

Open Trade: *Neutral*

The Korean government has intensified its efforts to attract foreign capital in the years following the Asian financial crisis. However, the open trade tenet receives a ranking of only neutral due to the government's reluctance to eliminate restrictive trade barriers, particularly with Western nations.

The government is also providing foreign companies with access to land designated for industrial purposes, and has provided funds for such companies that employ Koreans. Currently ranked seventh in terms of largest export market to the United States, Korea exported almost $44 billion in goods to the United States market as of 2005. The United States, which has invested mostly in finance, manufacturing, and banking sectors, put forth nearly $17.3 billion in foreign direct investment to Korea—a figure that has gradually risen since 2003.

Though Korea is a valued trading partner with the United States and other nations with strong economies and demand for technology products, it is not without its drawbacks. Barriers to foreign trade, although considerably less than in years past, continues to be a major sticking point for several nations. For instance, as of 2005, Korea placed strict tariffs on the imports of agriculture, at around 52 percent. This figure has been particularly troublesome for the United States, which hoped to expand its agriculture exports to the nation. Products such as fruits, vegetables, peanuts, beef, and dairy—items that the United States exports in great bulk—have a 30 percent tariff rate, sometimes as high as 40 percent. Much of Korea's tariff policy stems from precaution, as the government strives to protect its own domestic sectors.

Though these tariffs have eased up in recent years—technological equipment tariffs were reduced substantially after the Uruguay Round talks—they still trouble several governments, most notably the United States, which has maintained that even where tariffs are absent, the amount of government approval needed to import such products remains relatively high. This concern can be seen in the marketing of products entering Korea. As the world's 10th largest economy, one might expect that advertising would equally reflect that success, yet this is not the case. All advertising must first be approved through the government's Korea Broadcasting Advertising Corporation—a procedure that has frustrated many U.S. industries. Television shows from outside Korea, furthermore, are restricted to 20 percent of total airtime in yet another example of how the Korean market is sometimes difficult to penetrate.

KORUS FTA In 2006, Korea and the United States began negotiating a detailed free trade agreement called the KORUS FTA, which would further solidify an already mutually beneficial relationship. The treaty, which was finalized in April 2007, stands as the United States' second most encompassing free trade agreement, second only to the North American Free Trade Agreement (NAFTA) and entails the lifting of many import restrictions on both sides over the course of three years. As trade between the two nations reached $75 billion in 2006, the agreement figures to greatly enhance several key sectors, notably for Korea's automotive industry.

INVESTMENT OBSTACLES The Korean government has continually said that it hopes to enhance its prospects for foreign investment, yet its rhetoric has yet to be fully realized, as very few corporations have been privatized since 2005. In fact, as the government spoke of lifting restrictions and thus increasing foreign investment, it was simultaneously implementing tighter control over its public companies. In addition to the Woori Bank, which has yet to become privatized, the Korean government has also been reluctant to yield its control of the Korea Gas Corporation and the Incheon International Airport Service—two of the nation's largest corporations. On the positive side, in addition to the KORUS FTA, Korea has made great strides in promoting the sale of land to foreign buyers. The proliferation of free economic zones (FEZs), where the effects of tax breaks and tariffs are substantially lessened, have portrayed the image of Korea as a nation eager to attract foreign investment. In such zones, labor rules and standards, considered too burdensome by some investors, are relaxed, making the business environment in Korea more hospitable to foreigners than in years past.

Investors should take note of the fact that Korea continues to adhere to trade policies that frustrate foreign governments. Though this problem persists, it is also important to remember that the Korean government has stable diplomatic relations with many of these nations and, as such, is open to negotiations.

Infrastructure Development: *Favorable*

Korea's advanced infrastructure, compared to other emerging economies, has been a significant factor in its industrialization and later economic success. After the Korean War, the government, with aid from the United States, embarked on its intensive Five-Year Plan program of building roads, schools, and hospitals, in addition to improving its access to ports and methods of public transportation. The nation's first major highway project—connecting Seoul and Pusan— was completed in the mid-1970s. By 1988, the Korean infrastructure had made impressive strides, as Seoul would host the Olympic Games.

Korea's infrastructure will only enhance its capability for further economic growth, a key point for investors to consider.

Transparency and Rule of Law: *Unfavorable*

The Korean economy is still widely considered to be lacking in transparency in several areas of trade, and, as such, it has received an unfavorable ranking. The recent trade agreement between Korea and the United States greatly alleviated some of these concerns, particularly in the automobile, pharmaceutical, and agricultural sectors, yet issues of regulatory reform and the inconsistent application of domestic laws, still dominate discussions between the two nations. Uncertain of compliance laws and product standards, businesses in the United States aim to encourage the Korean government to establish clear and concise procedures, so they may compete on an equal playing field. For years, business groups, along with government officials, had been calling on Korea to remove barriers of trade, first and foremost, within the automotive sectors. Though the recent agreement figures to enhance trading between the two nations, several automotive companies, such as Chrysler and Ford, opposed the agreement, contending that Korea has not gone far enough in its attempts to remove barriers of trade and apply consistent regulatory practices, and this objection has not been taken lightly by either party.

Automotive trade between the two nations stood at $11.6 billion in 2006, and still accounts for a hefty percentage of the United States' trade deficit with Korea at the present time. As of 2006, the net value of cars entering the United States from Korea totaled $10.9 billion, whereas those entering from the United States totaled a meager $730 million by comparison. That year, automobiles accounted for almost 25 percent of all U.S. exports to Korea, an indication that transparency, notably with regards to the automotive industry, remains an issue not likely to subside anytime soon.

Corruption in the Korean economy has been perceived as a major obstacle in the eyes of foreign investors, most notably in the healthcare sector. A complex distribution system, in addition to the transparency issue of the Korean government, have long worried U.S. pharmaceutical companies, who have urged Korea to adopt a more fair policy in terms of pricing and other regulatory procedures.

Overall corruption in Korea can be described as moderate. Transparency International, a corporate watchdog organization, found that as of 2007 Korea ranked 43rd out of 180 nations surveyed in corruption. Based on surveys with business leaders and officials with agencies like Asian Development, Transparency International ranked Korea as 5.1 on its corruption scale of 1 to 10, with ten being the least corrupt. Among Asian countries, Korea was sixth in terms of corruption—a designation that continues to damage its image to the outside world. The problem of bribery, as in many developing nations, also plagues Korea's reputation, and it legal system has been either reluctant or incapable of enforcing laws prohibiting such behavior.

LEGAL SYSTEM Korea's legal system, though far more advanced than other developing nations, is still in transition. Combining elements of European civil law systems and Anglo-American law—Korea's constitution was drafted with the help of American diplomats—its legal system differs in several areas. It does not incorporate the use of a jury, as appointed judges are left to interpret all the facts and testimony of a given case. The competence of Korea's judges has also come under fire in recent years. With many fleeing to the more lucrative private sector, the pool of qualified judges is greatly deteriorating. This problem, long known to foreign investors, is also a growing concern of officials inside Korea. In recent years, the Korean government has intensified its efforts to improve its legal system, mainly by encouraging its brightest students to study law. There are currently over 150 law schools in Korea, and competition for admissions is steadily increasing. As uncertain as the legal system presently appears, there is substantial hope for improvement, as a generation eager for further democratization will eventually take the reigns in government and other leadership positions.

Though Korea's legal apparatus is poor by Western standards, it ranks above most of the BRIC+2 nations. Investors that have anxiety over the lack of transparency should consider the fact that the Korean government, with intense lobbying from the United States and various international organizations, is dedicated to improving these conditions to attract further foreign investment.

Education and Training: *Favorable*

Korea has one of the world's most educated workforces. The Korean education system has a deep cultural foundation, and as such, it is regarded as one of the most advanced systems in the world. Education is free and mandatory to all children ages 6 to 15, and the number of students pursuing secondary studies now stands at 75 percent. Curriculum is notoriously exhaustive, and entrance into Korea's 10 major universities is extremely competitive. Korea was the first nation to provide its entire student body with Internet access, an expected accomplishment given the nation's propensity for technology. This commitment to education can also be seen in the amount of funds allocated for education each year. Korea presently devotes 4.2 percent of its gross national product (GNP) to education, with only four nations providing a higher percentage. Korea ranks number one for all Asian countries in terms of student–teacher ratio, at 36 to 1, and as mentioned, has one of the highest literacy rates of any country on the globe. Korea is also the world leader in scientific literacy, slightly edging out Japan in that category.

This commitment to education will likely keep Korea in a position of great strength, as the global market increases its demand for skilled labor. As the nation continues to improve its technological capability, its students will likely remain the driving force. Innovations, therefore, will likely continue to come from within Korea's own borders. This self-reliance on research and development, for a nation already leading in technology exports, should be viewed as a positive sign for investors.

Sound Financial Systems and Policies: *Neutral*

The aftermath of the Asian financial crisis in 1997 saw Korea implement a number of economic reforms to restore stability to its markets. Though many, including the privatization of its larger banks and the restructuring of *chaebols*, are as of yet incomplete, Korea is indeed moving away from a centrally planned economy to a more free-market approach, as evidenced by the KORUS FTA. Trade with China figures to rise, and some experts believe that trade with Japan will steadily evolve in the coming years.

BANKING Though most of Korea's banks have been privatized, the ones remaining public account for an overwhelming percentage of holdings in the country. The Deposit Insurance Corporation (DIC), a government-controlled bank, owns almost 70 percent of the Industrial Bank of Korea, the nation's fourth largest bank. The DIC also owns nearly 79 percent of Woori Financial Holdings of the Woori Bank, the second largest in Korea. Though foreign banks are permitted to establish branches and subsidiaries, they are subject to a number of restrictions, including provisions on individual loans and foreign currency transactions. Also, foreign banks are required to allocate a certain percentage of their portfolio to Korean companies, and these companies do not normally include the more established organizations, such as a Samsung or Hyundai. Yet, in spite of these and other restrictions, foreign investors, as of 2005, held almost 40 percent of stocks on the Korean stock exchange (KOSDAQ).

According to the Joint IMF–World Bank Financial Sector Assessment program, Korea's financial sector was vulnerable prior to the financial crisis in 1997–1998 for a variety of reasons. Foreign borrowing by domestic banks outstripped net foreign currency assets by a significant margin. Reforms instituted after the crisis dramatically improved Korea's ability to withstand financial crises that might arise elsewhere around the world (see Figure 16.2).

In recent years, Korea has engaged in sizable exchange rate interventions in an apparent effort to maintain an undervalued won, the Korean currency unit. The resulting current-account surpluses have enabled Korea

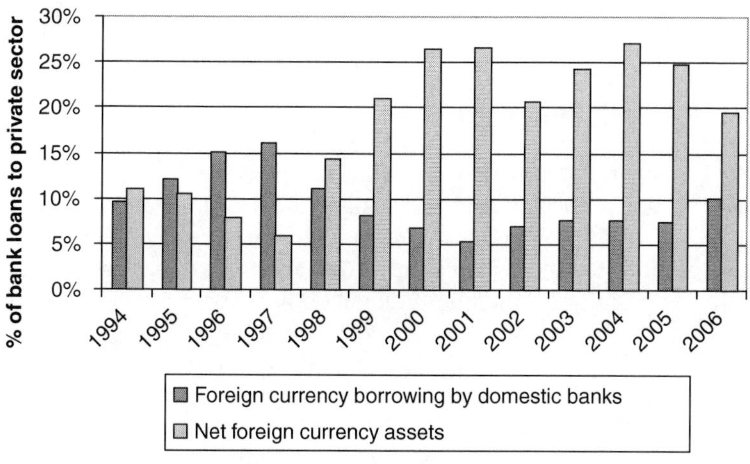

FIGURE 16.2 Foreign borrowing by domestic banks and net foreign currency assets.

TABLE 16.2 Debt Service Ratios

Country	Debt service ratio (% of exports)	Debt (% of GDP)	Debt (% of exports)
Brazil	58	44	239
China	5	15	48
India	16	21	106
Korea	6	21	47
Mexico	25	22	69
Russia	13	45	117

to acquire $239 billion in official reserves, in addition to stimulating export growth.

However, the market exchange rate of 1,145 won to the dollar is only slightly above the purchasing power parity value of the won at 840 to the dollar. The World Bank–IMF assessment gives Korea strong marks for macroeconomic performance following the Asian crisis, highlighting strong real economic growth, low inflation, and a rapidly growing official foreign reserve accompanied by improvement in financial-sector soundness. In this atmosphere, there is little reason to expect any long-term trend change in the Korean exchange rate; that is, aside from near-term volatility, the exchange rate of the Korean currency is unlikely to play a role in return on investments in Korea.

Similarly, Korea's external debt service reflects the benefits of financial reforms as seen in Table 16.2. Korea and China have the most favorable debt service ratios of the six sizzling countries, as evidenced in Table 16.2.

Korea's Growth Industries

South Korea may claim the title of "most developed" of the six countries discussed in this book, making it perhaps the safest, most attractive option for BRIC+2 investors. About 86 percent of the investable universe in Korea is in telecommunications services, materials, and consumer sectors, based on the Morgan Stanley Capital International (MSCI) Korea Index sector weights (see Table 16.3).

Because South Korea's vibrant economy has long been recognized as a potential investment destination, there are a variety of mutual funds and exchange-traded funds (ETFs) available to foreign investors. Many Korean companies have also listed American Depositary Receipts (ADRs), which are available to U.S. investors.

TABLE 16.3 MSCI South Korea Index Sector Weights (as of August 31, 2007)

Economic sector (Global Industry Classification System)	Float-adjusted shares (% of investable index market capitalization)
Telecommunication Services	37.92
Materials	19.92
Consumer Staples	17.72
Consumer Discretionary	10.98
Industrials	9.27
Financials	3.96

In the remainder of the chapter, we will discuss these and other investment opportunities available to a foreign investor.

Telecommunication Services

The telecommunications sector includes landline telephone operators, mobile phones, and broadband communications and Internet access. Korea's mobile phone industry is very well developed and operates at the cutting edge of new service capabilities. Thus, the typical Korean cell phone owner has access to products and applications long before they are available in the United States.

Beginning in 2007, for example, government regulators allowed Korea's largest telecom operators to begin providing services that combine both voice and Internet at discounted prices. This approach is expected to change the way telecommunication services are delivered across the country, and is similar to packages currently being rolled out in the United States by companies such as AT&T. Other new offerings in Korea include mobile TV and fast wireless Internet, a capability that allows mobile users to stay connected to the Internet as they motor about town from one hot spot to another.

The two main telecommunication services providers are KT Corporation and SK Telecom. Both are traded in the United States as ADRs. A third company, Hanaro Telecom, provides broadband Internet services, with about a 25 percent share of the market.

Materials

The basic materials sector of Korea includes industries in building materials and construction materials, chemicals, packaging materials, and metals and mining industries. However, chemicals are the best choice for the savvy financial investor.

South Korea is one of the world's top 10 producers of chemicals and the sixth largest market for U.S. chemical exports ($4.3 billion in 2006). The United States and South Korea negotiated a free trade agreement in 2007 that will, if approved, substantially reduce Korea's protective tariffs on chemical imports from the United States. This could potentially mean more price competition for domestic chemical manufacturers, which could in turn hurt profitability. Conversely, it could also translate to higher exports of electronic equipments, circuit boards, and other manufactured products that in turn rely on specialty chemicals in their manufacturing. KCC Corporation and LG Chem Ltd. are Korean chemical manufacturers traded on U.S. exchanges. Tong Yang Major, a cement and building materials manufacturer traded in the United States, also produces some chemical products.

Consumer Products

Consumer product companies include manufacturers of discretionary consumer products such as automobiles, retailers, apparel, and services such as travel and leisure. Consumer staples include food, housewares, and personal care products. Incremental growth for these products may come chiefly from global markets. Korea's domestic consumer market is rather small, however, compared to more populous countries such as Brazil, China, and India.

Korea's rising per-capita income is generally a positive indicator for consumer product industries. Moreover, the dependency ratio in Korea is expected to continue to decline slightly through 2015, leaving individual workers with more of their income free to spend on discretionary goods.

AUTOMOBILES Korea's auto manufacturers enjoy the active support of the Korean government, which hopes to see Korea rank among the top four auto industries by 2010. To this end, the government has supported the formation of industrial parks for companies that manufacture automotive components, and tax holidays for participating companies. Auto exports have steadily increased as Korean manufacturers win acceptance in overseas markets. Hyundai, together with its affiliate Kia Motors, is now the sixth largest auto company. Sales growth rates have slowed, however, as a stronger currency narrows the price differential that Korean manufacturers have previously enjoyed versus Japan.

A Tale of Hyundai

In 1946, one year after liberation from the Japanese, a new company called Hyundai Motor Industrial Company was founded by Chung Ju-young, the self-educated son of a North Korean farmer. His first business was making parts and repairing automobiles.

In 1947, Chung launched a second company, Hyundai Civil Industries, which greatly contributed to the reconstruction of the country after the Korean War by building most of the dams, expressways, shipyards, and nuclear power plants. By the 1970s, Hyundai's reputation as a major construction company began to reach beyond Korea, and the company won contracts to build an expressway in Thailand and a major port in Saudi Arabia.

Hyundai's first venture outside of the construction industry came in 1967 when Hyundai began building cars. In 2006, Hyundai was the tenth largest automobile manufacturer in the world. In addition to the construction and automotive industry, at the urging of President Park, Hyundai participated in the Heavy and Chemical Industry Development Plan and began to build chemical plants and vessels. The company was soon the world's largest shipbuilder. In the 1990s, Hyundai also added specialties in high-tech products such as semiconductors. Today, Hyundai's exports range from heavy industrial equipment to consumer products, and include cement, pianos, military uniforms, and consumer electronics products.

Hyundai has been involved in the political arena as well. Chung Mong-jun, the current owner of Hyundai Heavy Industries, successfully ran for National Assembly in 1988 (he would unsuccessfully run for president in 2002). In the late 1990s, Chung Ju-young dedicated himself to the reconciliation of the two Koreas. He donated cattle and corn to the north, and launched a tourism project in the Kumgang Mountains on the northern side.

On its founder's death in 2001, Hyundai was divided into three separate companies: Hyundai Heavy Industries, the Hyundai Motor Group, and Hyundai Engineering and Construction. Despite many hardships, including labor problems and charges of embezzlement, Hyundai companies continue to play a major role in the global market and may be a good investment opportunity for you.

Source: www.hyundai-motor.com/

Industrials

Korea's steel mills, shipbuilders, petrochemical operations, and other smokestack industries may be attractive candidates for investors seeking to capitalize on China's strong growth prospects. Fidelity's Emerging Market Fund chose Korean shipbuilders as a proxy for direct investments in China's growing imports, according to fund manager Robert Von Rekowsky. As China's imports of materials from Brazil and other far-flung destinations have surged, so has demand for shipping.

Financials

South Korean government officials are removing some regulations designed to limit Korea's banks from entering foreign markets. The new regulations make it easier for banks to choose to expand to other markets such as China and India. The government is also lifting restrictions on private-equity funds to further develop its financial markets. Historically, Korean banks have generated only about 3 percent of revenues from outside of domestic markets. One of the first banks to take advantage of the new laws will be Woori Bank, which will set up a wholly owned unit in China and open 53 branches in China by 2012.

Other banks are following Woori's lead, including Shinhan Bank and Hana Bank. Similarly, Korea's financial services firms are anticipating rapid growth in overseas deployments.

Korea's unprecedented growth over the past 40 years has astounded economists worldwide. As it continues its emergence onto the world market, Korea stands to remain the leading exporter of technology and a great source of domestic consumerism. Though the government is hampered by several problems, such as transparency, restrictive tariffs, and an insufficient legal system, the benefits of an economy that has diversified greatly over the past 10 years invariably outweigh the cons. As such, investors will continue to find Korea an extremely profitable and advanced market.

CHAPTER 17

Revolution and Exclusion

A History of Mexico

Wherever we are found, we always express and honor our love for Mexico, with all our hearts and our head held high.

—Ernesto Zedillo, former president

As the southernmost nation of North America and the northernmost nation of Latin America, modern Mexico forms a bridge between its close ally, the United States, and the rest of Latin America. With a population of approximately 108 million, Mexico is the world's most populous Spanish-speaking nation. Officially named the United Mexican States, Mexico is a federal constitutional republic made up of 31 states and the federal district of Mexico City, its capital. According to some estimates, the population in Mexico City is about 18 million, making it the most densely populated area in the Western hemisphere.

Since entering into the North American Free Trade Agreement (NAFTA) with the United States and Canada in 1994, Mexico's economy has diversified and grown dramatically. According to the World Bank, Mexico's economy was ranked 14th in the world in 2006 (gross domestic product [GDP]). But its growing success in the global economy stands alongside Mexico's rich and complex history, starting with the ancient peoples who first occupied the area.

Early History

A number of succeeding civilizations thrived in the area that is now Mexico for more than 1,000 years before the arrival of the Spanish in 1519. These groups had very different social and economic systems. The tribes of the arid north, for example, were relatively small groups of hunters and gatherers who were nomadic. Other native peoples practiced intensive agriculture—such as the cultivation of corn, beans, and squash—which supported more densely populated settlements. Among these tribes were the Mayas, Toltecs, Mixtecs, and Zapotecs. After the unexplained collapse of the great city of Teotihuacan in central Mexico around 650 AD, the Mayan city-states of the Yucatan peninsula became dominant.

The Maya were perhaps the greatest of these early peoples. Their empire extended from central Mexico all the way south to modern-day Honduras. The Mayas developed the most complex writing systems of all the Mesoamerican people. Among their other achievements were the development of advanced math (including the concept of zero), astronomy, complex calendars, and medical knowledge. The ruins of some of their greatest cities lie in Mexico, such as Chichen Itzá on the Yucatan Peninsula and Palenque in the state of Oaxaca.

This great empire began to falter around 900 AD. The reasons for the collapse of Mayan civilization have long been a subject of speculation among scholars. Some believe that increased warfare, plague, and overpopulation may have been contributing factors. By the time the Spanish arrived in the sixteenth century, the Mayas were greatly diminished and divided into small, competing centers.

To the north, another great civilization began to flower: the Aztecs, who called themselves the Mexica, hence the name Mexico. Late arrivals to the Valley of Mexico, the Aztecs are of obscure origin, although some evidence suggests that they may have come from northwest Mexico. They, too, developed advanced knowledge in the sciences and medicine, built great cities and public works projects, and had written language. But Aztec culture was also hierarchical, militaristic, and authoritarian. By the 1300s, the Aztecs controlled most of central Mexico through a state tribute system that extracted taxes (in the form of goods and labor) and political servility from conquered tribal groups. Their practice of human sacrifice, on a large scale, was a central part of their religious ritual, but was also used to keep subject peoples in line. The Aztecs believed that their sun and war god, Huitzilopochtli, required human blood to nourish him as he fought the moon and stars at night so he could rise every morning.

The Aztec empire had reached its zenith by the end of the fifteenth century, and Tenochtitlan was as beautiful as any city in Europe. In 1503, Moctezuma II (anglicized to Montezuma) ascended the throne.

The Spanish Conquest

In the early sixteenth century, Spanish military explorers used Cuba as a base as they organized expeditions to North America. On the first expedition to Mexico, Hernan (sometimes referred to as Hernando or Fernando)

Cortes assembled a fleet of 11 ships and an army of approximately 700 men equipped with horses and guns. In February 1519, Cortes and his army landed near present-day Veracruz on the Gulf Coast and marched to Tenochtitlan, where Moctezuma greeted him almost as a deity. According to Aztec legend, the ancient god Quetzalcoatl had fled to the lands beyond the eastern sea but promised to return one day to reclaim his dominions. To Moctezuma, the arrival of Cortes from across the sea signaled the return of the long-awaited Quetzalcoatl.

Cortes took full advantage of this unexpected opportunity. He and his soldiers seized Moctezuma and issued orders to the Aztecs through him. Their manipulation of Moctezuma, however, broke down when the Aztec chieftains revolted against these uninvited "gods"; it seems that not everyone was convinced that Cortes was the embodiment of Quetzalcoatl. In the ensuing battle, Moctezuma was killed. His nephew, Cuauhtémoc, became the last king of the Aztecs. By 1521, Spanish forces led by Cortes, along with rebellious Indian tribes, had defeated the Aztecs and executed Cuauhtémoc. The rest of Mexico was quickly subdued, and the Spanish ruled the colony of New Spain for the next 300 years. As a symbol of political continuity, the capital was built on the ruins of Tenochtitlan and renamed Mexico City.

The Colonial Period

The viceroyalty of New Spain encompassed a vast territory extending from Central America north to modern-day California, Texas, and Colorado. Similar to Spain's other colonies in the New World, the colonial experience in New Spain was markedly different from the English colonies in North America. While the wealth of both the English and Spanish colonies lay in rich agricultural lands, the method of distributing the land produced very different results. In the English colonies, a class of independent small-scale farmers and large-scale planters emerged. In their quest for more land, they drove the Native Americans from the land—sometimes by barter or purchase, other times by force—and brought in African slaves to perform heavy labor.

In Mexico, the Spanish took Indian lands and redistributed them among themselves, first as *encomiendas*, a system of tribute grants, and later as *haciendas*, or land grants. For the conquistadors, granting *encomiendas* was a way to ensure the subordination of the indigenous peoples and to reward Spanish subjects for their loyalty to the crown. Similar to the system of tributes established by the Aztecs, the Indians were required to provide goods and labor to the *encomendero*, who was responsible for their welfare, assimilation to Spanish culture, and conversion to Christianity. The Spanish crown had a powerful ally in the Roman Catholic church. The first priests arrived in Mexico with Cortes and immediately began converting the native people.

Spain viewed the colony's land and people solely as a source of wealth for the crown. This accumulation of wealth was accomplished by a form of tax known as the "royal fifth" or *quinto*. In addition to agricultural products, Mexico was also discovered to have gold and silver mines. By the late sixteenth century, silver represented 80 percent of all exports from New Spain.

While the English colonies were heavily influenced by the ideas of the Protestant Revolution, the Enlightenment, and the work of intellectuals such as Locke, Rousseau, and Voltaire, the Spanish colonies were influenced by the fear and tyranny of the Inquisition. In Mexico, there was no large middle class of well-educated planters, intellectuals, merchants, and craftsmen. Mexico had a stratified society that mirrored Spanish society, yet Mexico's population underwent significant demographic shifts over three centuries of Spanish rule.

As exposure to European diseases diminished the native population, increasing numbers of Spanish arrived in Mexico seeking fortune and opportunity. When the two populations combined, a new group was created: the *mestizos*, who were both European and Native American. Today, Mexico is predominantly *mestizo*, accounting for about 60 percent of the population. At the same time, the Spanish made a distinction between native-born Spaniards (*peninsulares*) and those born in the New World. The latter were called *criollos,* or creoles. At the very top of the social hierarchy were the white European-born Spanish, then the creoles, then the mestizos—and, at the bottom, the indigenous peoples.

In this fractured society, the Roman Catholic church was a unifying factor, as priests ministered to the rich and poor alike. But the church's growing wealth and power would prove its undoing as Mexico developed its own national identity.

Independence from Spain

Economic expansion and political reform in Mexico during the reign of the third Bourbon king of Spain, Charles III (1759–1788), combined with the successful revolutions in the United States (1776) and France (1789), resulted in a greater expectation of autonomy by colonists. The lack of cohesion in society, however, worked against a revolutionary undertaking, even though tensions continued to build. Eventually, it was a breakdown of authority in Spain—on the heels of Napoleon Bonaparte's invasion of Spain in 1808, the forced abdication of Charles IV, and the naming of Joseph Bonaparte as the new king—that initiated turmoil in New Spain over who was the legitimate ruler of the colony. Some in Spain declared Charles's son, Ferdinand VII, to be the new king. The ensuing crisis of Spanish royal authority over Mexico opened the door for independence.

The 11-year period of civil war in Mexico (1810–1821) began on September 16, 1810, in the town of Dolores, when the priest Miguel Hidalgo y Costilla rang his church's bells and exhorted Mexicans to join him against the Spanish government and the *peninsulares* (also derisively called *gachupines*) in the famous "*Grito de Dolores*" (Cry of Dolores): "Long live Our Lady of Guadalupe! Death to bad government! Death to the *gachupines*!" Less than a year later, Hidalgo was captured by royalist forces and executed for his role in the revolution. But September 16 is still celebrated as Mexican Independence Day, and the town of Dolores has been renamed Dolores Hidalgo.

After Hidalgo's death, José Maria Morelos y Pavon took control of the revolutionary movement. Morelos planned a strategic move to encircle Mexico City and cut off communication with the outside. In 1813, Morelos called a national congress of representatives from all the provinces to discuss plans for an independent Mexican state. Plans included popular sovereignty, universal male suffrage, the abolition of slavery and forced labor, an end to government monopolies, and the adoption of Roman Catholicism as the national religion. Despite initial success by Morelos's forces, the colonial authorities broke the siege of Mexico City after six months. In 1815, Morelos was captured and met the same fate as Hidalgo.

For the next six years, isolated guerrilla forces fought most of the war. Two leaders emerged: Guadalupe Victoria in Puebla and Vicente Guerrero in Oaxaca. Augustin de Iturbide, a royalist officer, joined forces with Guerrero and in February 1821 drafted the Plan of Iguala, which provided for "three guarantees": national independence under a constitutional monarchy, equal rights and privileges for *criollos* and *peninsulares*, and the adoption of Roman Catholicism as the national religion. On September 27, 1821, representatives of the Spanish crown and Iturbide signed the Treaty of Cordoba, which recognized Mexican independence under the terms of the Plan of Iguala.

While a provisional government contemplated the future of the country, Iturbide took matters into his own hands. He commanded his armies to march through Mexico City, proclaiming, "Long Live Augustin I, Emperor of Mexico!" Not surprisingly, the congress named Iturbide as the constitutional emperor, and he was crowned in July 1822. In the face of dire economic problems and growing discontent, Iturbide dissolved the congress in August and imprisoned opposition delegates. On December 1, 1822, the commander of the garrison in Veracruz, Antonio Lopez de Santa Anna, rose against Iturbide and declared a republic. He was quickly joined by other revolutionaries, including Vicente Guerrero, Nicholas Bravo, and Guadalupe Victoria.

By mid-month, Iturbide realized he was defeated and abdicated the throne. The newly formed empire had lasted less than a year.

Post-Independence

For the next 99 years, between independence in 1821 and the end of the Mexican Revolution in 1920, Mexico and its people struggled. Once the Spanish left, the alliance that had formed between the *criollos*, the *mestizos*, and the Indians quickly crumbled. The departing Spanish took what was left in the treasury, leaving the new nation bankrupt. Worse than that, the Spanish had not left a strong legacy for the Mexicans to build on. Mexico's first century after independence was a political tug-of-war between conservatives—the landed gentry and the church—and liberals who wanted to pattern the new country on Jeffersonian democracy. Unfortunately, conditions did not exist to make the liberals' vision a reality. The majority of Mexican citizens were illiterate, there was no democratic tradition, and the military generals held most of the power. The nineteenth century was marked by dictatorships, war, and chaos.

Santa Anna

With the fall of Iturbide, Mexico at last became a republic, and in 1824, a new constitution was promulgated. Several military presidents followed, each failing until General Santa Anna emerged as the dominant political force. The popular Santa Anna was elected president in 1833 as a liberal, but he retired to his hacienda and let his vice president, Valentin Gomez Farias, rule in his place. When Gomez Farias went too far in his reforms, Santa Anna promptly deposed him, dismissed congress, and assumed dictatorial powers in 1834.

Over the next 20 years, Santa Anna served as president 11 times, never completing his terms and often leaving the government in the hands of others. During this period, Mexico went to war three times and lost half of its territory through sale (because the Mexican government was constantly on the verge of bankruptcy) or military defeat. He was alternately viewed as a national savior and a corrupt, failed despot.

Santa Anna's attempt to bring Texas under the control of Mexico City pushed the Texans to the limit. On November 7, 1835, Texas seceded from Mexico, and in March 1836, declared its independence. Santa Anna marched into Texas with an army of 3,000 men and defeated a group of 150 Texans at the Alamo. This was a call to arms for the United States, and thousands of soldiers volunteered to fight. On April 21, 1836, Santa Anna and his men were soundly defeated near the San Jacinto River by a force led by Sam Houston. U.S. forces captured Santa Anna, who then signed two treaties with Texas: One pledged to end hostilities and withdraw Mexican troops; the other, a secret treaty, recognized Texas independence.

The Mexican-American War

In 1845, the U.S. Congress passed a resolution in favor of annexing Texas, an idea that had gained popularity in both Texas and the United States. This congressional act prompted Mexico to sever diplomatic relations with the United States. After Texas was admitted to the Union as the 28th state, President James K. Polk sent a special envoy, John Slidell, to Mexico City, but Mexican President José Joaquin Herrera refused to meet with him.

Military hostilities began in April 1846, and shortly after the two sides declared war, Santa Anna was called back from exile in Cuba to lead the Mexican troops. The U.S. Army attacked on three fronts and was led by three great military generals: General Stephen Kearney and his troops occupied California and New Mexico, which fell to the Americans with little bloodshed; General Zachary Taylor and his troops entered northern Mexico, where they fought a number of battles against Santa Anna; and General Winfield Scott, who landed at Veracruz and marched to Mexico City, which they occupied. The city surrendered to the Americans in September 1847.

At the end of the war, according to the terms of the Treaty of Guadalupe Hidalgo, Mexico had to relinquish territories made up of the present-day states of California, Nevada, and Utah, as well as parts of Arizona, New Mexico, Colorado, and Wyoming, and to accept the incorporation of Texas into the United States. As compensation, the United States agreed to pay $15 million for the territories and to assume $3 million worth of land claims against the Mexican government by citizens in these territories.

The loss of more than half of its territory to the United States, as well as the occupation of Mexico City by the U.S. military, engendered a deep-seated distrust of the United States that continues to resonate in Mexican popular culture today.

Santa Anna's last political act resulted in the sale of more territory. He sold additional areas of New Mexico and Arizona to the United States for $10 million in what is known as the Gadsden Purchase. The Mexican people felt betrayed. In August 1855, in response to growing opposition, Santa Anna resigned for the last time.

The Reform and Civil War

After a half century of independence, Mexico had made relatively little economic or political progress. In the late 1850s, Benito Juarez, a Zapotec lawyer and politician from Oaxaca, led a group of liberal intellectuals who initiated a series of reforms known as the Reform Laws. Among other things, these laws attempted to eliminate the dominant role of the Roman Catholic church in Mexico by appropriating its land and revoking its privileges.

At the same time that Mexican society was being divided along pro- and anti-clerical lines, preparations were being made for a new constitution. While it was derived from the constitution of 1824, the constitution of 1857 contained a bill of rights that included habeas corpus protection, religious freedom, the right to secular education, and the confiscation of Catholic church lands. It reflected a liberal vision for Mexico that brought strong objections from conservatives and the Catholic church.

Conservatives and liberals were at an impasse, and civil war erupted in 1858. Commonly known as the War of Reform, the conflict highlighted the deep divisions in Mexican society that had been present since independence. Conservatives favored the clergy, the landholders, and the military. Liberals were anti-clerical, egalitarian, and reformist. The two sides clashed for three years, with the final battle taking place just before Christmas in 1860. The victorious liberal army entered Mexico City on January 1, 1861, and Benito Juarez was elected president in March. Juarez is remembered as one of Mexico's greatest leaders, and his birthday, March 21, is celebrated as a national holiday.

After years of war and chaos, Mexico's treasury was empty. Juarez declared a moratorium on all foreign debt repayments. In December 1861, the British, Spanish, and French occupied Veracruz in order to collect Mexican debts. The British and Spanish quickly withdrew, but the French stayed and went to war with Mexico. Despite being severely outnumbered, the Mexican army won a major battle against the French on May 5, 1862. This victory is celebrated annually as *Cinco de Mayo*.

The French eventually occupied Mexico City. In 1864, with the support of both Mexican conservatives and French Emperor Napoleon III, the French army declared Mexico an empire, with Maximilian I of Austria on the throne. Maximilian had been led to believe that the Mexican people wanted him as a ruler and, once in Mexico, proved to be surprisingly liberal. He shocked Mexican conservatives by implementing some of the reforms the liberals advocated.

Because of its own Civil War, the United States was unable to enforce the Monroe Doctrine, which prohibited European involvement in the Americas. At the close of the Civil War, however, the United States threatened to send troops to Mexico, and the French army withdrew from the country. Maximilian was executed in 1867 by the Mexican military.

Juarez was soon elected for a third term, and he returned to his reform agenda, which included the implementation of the Constitution of 1857. He stressed social reform and economic development, completing the railway between Mexico City and Veracruz and making education mandatory for all citizens. After being elected to a fourth term in 1871, Juarez died of a sudden heart attack on July 18, 1872. His dreams of a modern, democratic Mexico were unfulfilled.

Porfirio Diaz: *"Porfiriato"*

Porfirio Diaz was elected president in 1876, and ruled Mexico directly or indirectly for the next 34 years. Diaz sought to modernize the perpetually bankrupt Mexican economy, and this was a period of explosive economic growth. Diaz's modernization plan included the exploitation of natural resources, the encouragement of foreign capital investment, and the expansion of export production. New railroads contributed to the revival of mining as well as promoting export agriculture and manufacturing. The results were impressive: Between 1887 and 1910, Mexico doubled its cotton production and its volume of manufactured goods.

Despite all of this forward motion, however, Diaz's policies actually had negative social consequences. Although the economy grew at an average annual rate of 2.6 percent, real income per capita had recovered only to pre-1821 levels by 1911. Part of the reason for rising unemployment was mechanization that led to a loss of jobs for artisans and skilled workers. Increasingly, assets were concentrated in the hands of a few local and foreign investors.

Diaz also promoted land policies that hurt the rural poor. Government seizure of private and communal land increased the number of landless families and led to a concentration of land ownership. It is estimated that a few wealthy families controlled close to 55 million hectares of Mexico's most productive farmland. Taking advantage of an 1883 law intended to increase foreign investment, Diaz oversaw the sale of huge tracts of land to foreign companies—which controlled one-fifth of Mexico's land by 1894.

The modernization plan promoted by Diaz also diminished personal and political freedom. Diaz made sure that order was maintained for the sake of progress, which meant using force when necessary. The press was censored, the army and the Rural Guard (*rurales*) enforced repression, and mock elections were held at all levels of government. Diaz and his friends got rich while the poor stayed poor or became poorer. In spite of the beginning of modernization, Mexico remained a predominantly poor, rural country with an entrenched class system.

Mexican Revolution, 1910 to 1921

By the turn of the century, opposition to Diaz was widespread, with liberals calling for a return to the constitution of 1857. After the fraudulent reelection of Diaz in 1910, rural revolts turned into a nationwide revolution. Diaz was forced to resign the presidency in May 1911 and fled to France. Liberal reformer Francisco Madero, who was from a wealthy mining and ranching family in northern Mexico, led a provisional government. Unfortunately, Madero's idealism didn't translate into political skill, and his presidency was short lived.

Felix Diaz, Porfirio's nephew, and General Victoriano Huerta joined together in a rebellion that ousted Madero. Huerta became president in 1913, but counterrevolutions broke out in the north, led by General Venustiano Carranza, Pancho Villa, and General Alvaro Obregon. Peasants in the south rallied behind the charismatic Indian revolutionary Emiliano Zapata. While the northern revolutionaries were largely interested in political power, Zapata and his followers, the *zapatistas*, demanded land and liberty for the peasantry. Under his Plan of Ayala, Zapata set forth a program of large-scale peasant confiscation of land. For the next 10 years, most of the struggle was between those who supported or opposed radical agrarian reform.

In 1915, Carranza overthrew Huerta to become president, but in the process he alienated Villa, among others. American support for Carranza prompted Villa to return to Chihuahua and raid towns along the U.S.–Mexican border, including Columbus, New Mexico, where a number of Americans were killed. American General John J. Pershing was sent into Mexico to capture Villa, but was unsuccessful.

Carranza used his considerable political skills to build a broad base of support and eventually emerged as the leader of the revolution. He negotiated a cease-fire among several warring factions in 1916, and restored order to most of the country by setting forth a new constitution in 1917. The Constitution of 1917 gave extensive powers to the president as well as guaranteeing civil liberties, setting forth a program for ongoing revolution, and promising extensive social reform. Despite all of the rhetoric about agrarian reform and radical changes, however, Carranza and his followers were not committed to pursuing these policies. Carranza was more conservative than either Villa or Zapata, and he was primarily interested in modernization and economic development.

Violence continued in the south until Carranza's forces assassinated Zapata in November 1920. Zapata's cause died with him but was revived, in spirit, more than 70 years later when a radical group called the Zapatista Liberation Front (EZLN) arose in the southern state of Chiapas in 1994. They staged a violent protest against the government's treatment of the country's large but impoverished Indian community and the terms of the North American Free Trade Agreement. The 1994 uprising left at least 140 people dead, and it sparked an ongoing struggle in Chiapas.

More than a million people died in the Mexican Revolution, which exacted an enormous human and economic toll on the country.

Post-Revolutionary Years

From the 1920s through the 1940s, former revolutionary generals led the Mexican government, and they provided critical stability for the country. Most presidents adhered to the constitutional mandate allowing a single, six-year term of office, known as the *sexenio*. In the late 1920s, President Plutarco Elias Calles established many of the institutions on which the Mexican political system was based for the rest of the century: an authoritarian state controlled by a single party; a powerful president; economic nationalism; anti-clericalism; and limited land reform. Calles founded the National Revolutionary Party—later renamed the Institutional Revolutionary Party or PRI—which ruled Mexico without opposition until the late 1990s.

For 70 years, the PRI dominated Mexican politics. Presidents chose their successors, a practice known as *el dedazo*, or "the tap of the finger." While this has been criticized as undemocratic, it also made Mexico the most politically stable country in twentieth-century Latin America.

The presidency of Lazaro Cardenas (1934–1940) shifted Mexican politics to the left. Cardenas redistributed more land—45 million acres—than all of his predecessors combined, built schools in rural areas, and strengthened the labor unions. But the act for which he is most remembered is the nationalization of foreign oil companies in 1938. Despite the privatization trend sweeping developing countries, the Mexican government still controls *Petroleos Mexicanos*, known as Pemex.

President Miguel Avila Camacho (1940–1946) was more conservative than Cardenas. During World War II, Mexico joined the Allies and declared war on Germany and Japan. Relations between Mexico and the United States, which had been strained since the beginning of the revolution, began to improve. President Camacho hosted U.S. President Franklin Roosevelt in Monterrey in 1943, which marked the first time a sitting U.S. president had ventured south of the border. The war also caused an economic boom in Mexico, where factories made war supplies for export to the United States.

El Milagro Mexicano: "The Mexican Miracle"

Economists have hailed the period from 1940 to 1970 as "The Mexican Miracle," and it was a time of great optimism in Mexico. During the 1940s, the pro-business wing of the PRI became dominant, and the leftist stance of the Cardenas years was toned down. Mexico underwent a dramatic transformation from a predominantly rural society to a predominantly urban one. National industries greatly expanded, and the economy developed due to government investment in infrastructure and large public works projects.

President Miguel Aleman Valdes (1946–1952) was responsible for a massive program of infrastructure improvements, including the building of major flood control and irrigation projects in northern Mexico, the expansion of paved roads, and the completion of a new campus for the National Autonomous University of Mexico (UNAM).

While the government invested heavily in the economy, it also put high tariffs into place to protect the domestic economy, and implemented the economic strategy of import substitution and fiscal and monetary restraint to promote growth while keeping inflation low.

The result of these economic policies was impressive growth. Between 1950 and 1962, GDP grew at the average annual rate of 5.9 percent. At the peak of economic expansion, between 1963 and 1971, the GDP growth rate was 7.1 percent, and Mexico appeared to have the same rates of growth as countries like West Germany and Japan. But unlike West Germany and Japan, which were able to rebuild their economies on the stable foundations of the prewar years, Mexico was trying to transform its economy from a semideveloped or "Third World" economy into a modern, technologically advanced economy.

Economic Crisis and Recovery

In the end, Mexico couldn't sustain the miracle. During the presidencies of Luis Echeverria (1970–1976) and José Lopez Portillo (1976–1982), the economy fluctuated wildly, and the public sector continued to expand. Four months before Echeverria left office, he devalued the peso, from 12.5 to 20 to the dollar, leaving his successor to deal with the consequences. After the crisis of 1976, Portillo mended fences with the International Monetary Fund (IMF) and foreign banks to convince them that Mexico was again a good credit risk. He was helped in part by the discovery of substantial offshore oil reserves. Worldwide oil prices were very high, and soon oil sales were bringing in massive revenues. Portillo continued spending, and when the money ran out, he borrowed more from abroad on the assumption that Mexico would be able to pay it back with oil revenues.

Alas, oil prices began to fall in 1981, and this, along with rising inflation, an overvalued peso, and unsustainable government spending, spelled disaster. In August 1982, the government defaulted on scheduled debt repayments, triggering a regional debt crisis and exposing Mexico as the world's second largest debtor nation after Brazil.

As a result, Portillo was forced to implement a drastic austerity program and also to devalue the peso again. In February 1982, the exchange rate was 47 pesos per U.S. dollar; by the end of the year, it was 144 pesos to the dollar. In perhaps his most controversial move, Portillo nationalized the banks, further eroding public confidence. He left the mess to his successor, Miguel de la Madrid Hurtado (1982–1988).

The crisis of 1982 was widely viewed as the result of the post-1940 economic model and the political practices that put it in place. De la Madrid's charge was twofold: to stabilize the economy and survive the crisis, and to find an alternative model of economic development. The administration began to liberalize the economy, but per-capita income, estimated at $2,405 in 1982, fell to $1,320 by the end of 1987. Inflation rose as high as 100 percent, unemployment was skyrocketing, and people became desperate. The shantytowns around Mexico City got larger, and many Mexicans illegally entered the United States looking for work. The 1980s were known as "the lost decade" because of the country's economic stagnation.

Between 1982 and 1985, the de la Madrid administration initiated a series of long-awaited economic reforms. The era of large state subsidies and a bloated public sector was over—they simply could no longer be maintained. De la Madrid sold off some state-owned enterprises and allowed the price of Mexican crude oil to float instead of pegging it at an artificial price. Paying off the foreign debt was partly resolved by obtaining a $3.5 billion "bridge loan" from the Reagan administration.

In addition to the economic crisis, de la Madrid faced a political crisis: a scandal over corruption charges against officials in the Portillo administration. The combination of a terrible economy and political corruption dealt a severe blow to the PRI. In the 1988 election, the PRI candidate, Carlos Salinas de Gortari, faced serious opposition from the left. Cuauhtémoc Cardenas, son of the former president, left the PRI to form the Party of the Democratic Revolution (PRD). The Party of National Action (PAN) also entered a candidate—Manuel Clouthier. In a contentious election, Salinas prevailed, but barely; he received 50.36 percent of the vote. He was sworn in on December 1, 1988, with many questions still unanswered about the legitimacy of the election.

Salinas began a series of reforms that moved Mexico closer to a free-market economy. Reforms included the privatization of state-owned enterprises, the encouragement of foreign direct investment (FDI), and the negotiation of a bailout loan from U.S. President George H. W. Bush. The two leaders talked about a way to benefit both economies: NAFTA, made up of the United States, Mexico, and Canada. After being approved by all three countries, NAFTA went into effect on January 1, 1994, resulting in Mexico's rise to economic and political prosperity.

CHAPTER 18

Democracy and a Free Economy

Mexico from 1994 to Today

Our number one priority is to spend every peso possible to include those who are currently excluded.

—Vicente Fox

By the mid-1990s, more than 80 years after the revolution, Mexico was poised to become a free, democratic, and prosperous nation. Starting in 1994, Mexico has had a series of bold presidents who have been willing to take the political and economic risks necessary to create a new place for Mexico in the global economy. Although the path to prosperity has not been smooth, the results are clear: Mexico is now a true democracy, grounded in the sound principles of free elections and political participation. Moreover, its economy has finally been released from government control and has adopted free-market reforms. While the economy has grown and developed, the country has also begun to address deep-seated issues of social inequality and poverty, thus establishing it as a key political and economic player.

On the Road to Economic Prosperity

After decades of a state-run economy, Mexico was ready to join the global economy and enter the ranks of the free-market nations. Although this goal was in sight, the country had some serious challenges ahead. When President Ernesto Zedillo took office in 1994, he built on the reforms initiated by the Salinas government, but he also had to face the consequences of participating in an open economy.

Specifically, President Zedillo faced intense pressure from foreign exchange markets to let the peso float freely—with the result of rapid devaluation. The peso fell to about 5 pesos to the dollar in late December 1994. As the currency continued to lose value, fears of a Mexican default escalated. Crisis loomed.

The underlying reason for the Mexican crisis was the country's tendency to borrow heavily when the economy was strong, which left it vulnerable when conditions changed. In early 1995, the newly sworn-in U.S. Treasury Secretary Robert Rubin sat in the Oval Office with President Bill Clinton and other top advisers and delivered a startling recommendation: The United States would loan $25 billion to Mexico to prevent a government default.

This wasn't a case of trying to help out a neighbor in need. If Mexico defaulted and its economy collapsed, it would have an immediate impact on the U.S. economy. At that time, Mexico was the third largest trading partner of the United States, so thousands of U.S. companies and jobs would be at risk if Mexico went into a deep recession. In addition, it would likely mean a huge increase in illegal immigration and the flow of illegal drugs.

There were also serious concerns about the effects of this crisis on other emerging markets around the world, most of which had only recently embraced market-based economic reforms. The North American Free Trade Agreement (NAFTA) had gone into effect only one year earlier. If Mexico defaulted, it would send a terrible message to other developing economies and possibly discourage necessary reforms.

While the International Monetary Fund (IMF) had pledged $7 billion, which was later increased to $17 billion, it could not solve this problem without the help of the United States. President Clinton agreed to the plan despite all of its inherent risks. The goal of the plan was give Mexico the opportunity to restructure its debt, reestablish financial stability, and be able to access private capital. Congress was understandably wary and opposed the plan. Regardless of the politics involved, however, the plan was a success.

By the beginning of 1996, the Mexican economy was growing and macroecnomic indicators were excellent. Moreover, the gross domestic product (GDP) growth rate rose to 5.1 percent in 1996 and continued to rise to 6.8 percent in 1997. In August 2006, Mexico repaid $7 billion of the loan. By January 1997, the Zedillo government completed the repayment—more than three years ahead of schedule.

A New Day in Mexico

In addition to revitalizing the Mexican economy, Ernesto initiated democratic political reforms. In July 1996, Ernesto Zedillo signed a historic agreement with the country's main opposition parties. Among other things, the agreement eliminated the Institutional Revolutionary Party's (PRI's) control of election procedures and placed limits on campaign spending.

In the midterm elections in 1997, the PRI's exclusive one-party rule came to an end. The PRI ended up with a minority in the lower house of Congress, the Chamber of Deputies, for the first time—the National Action Party (PAN) received 27 percent of the vote, and the Party of the Democratic Revolution (PRD) won nearly 26 percent. Finally, the Mexican political system had begun to move away from thinly veiled one-party rule and toward genuine multiparty democracy.

Yet 1997 was just a prelude to the 2000 presidential election, when Vicente Fox Quesada became the first non-PRI president in over 70 years.

The election in 2000 was the first presidential election since the end of the Mexican Revolution that was considered to be competitive and fair. The election had many features of an American-style presidential campaign, including televised debates, attack ads, and name-calling. The candidates were PRI favorite Francisco Labastida, who was interior secretary under Zedillo and former governor of Sinaloa; Vicente Fox, former governor of the state of Guanajuato and a member of the PAN; and Cuauhtémoc Cardenas, son of beloved president Cardenas and a member of the PRD. Fox carried 21 of the 31 states and won the election on July 2, 2000—his 58th birthday. Mexico had accomplished what had seemed impossible only six years before—that is, a free and fair election that was not controlled by the PRI.

President Fox's *Sexenio*

Born in 1942 in Mexico City, Fox was the second of nine children born to José Luis Fox Pont, a Mexican of American extraction (José's father was a German Catholic who settled in Mexico after growing up in Cincinnati, Ohio), and Mercedes Quesada Etxaide. In 1964, Fox began working for the Coca-Cola Company, eventually becoming head of Coca-Cola Mexico. After leaving to run his family's farming businesses, Fox became involved in politics, and in 1988, he joined a center-right opposition party, PAN. Fox was elected to the Chamber of Deputies and later became governor of his home state of Guanajuato.

The inauguration of Vicente Fox on December 1, 2000, marked a new era in Mexico, and expectations were very high that Fox would be able to lead the country into an era of transparent government and economic prosperity. In October, Fox had proposed a conservative economic agenda for 2001 that would keep the economy stable: 4.5 percent expected GDP growth, (foreign direct investment (FDI) of $14 billion, 7 percent inflation, and an account deficit of 3.6 percent of GDP. In his inaugural speech, Fox enumerated a broad range of issues that he planned to address during his time in office. These ambitious plans included the creation of jobs in the poor regions of the South, improving education, eradicating corruption in the police force, privatizing the electricity sector, increasing the efficiency of Pemex, and eliminating poverty.

Inspiring citizens with a reform agenda was one thing, but getting that agenda passed in Congress was quite another. Although the PRI lost the presidency, it retained a majority in the Senate, with 47 seats to PAN's 40. In the Chamber of Deputies, the PRI held 211 seats out of 500, while Fox's supporters (not all of them members of PAN) held 225 and the PRD had 60. With this new multiparty system, Fox faced an enormous political challenge.

Fox's proposed tax legislation, for example, included a value-added tax (VAT) of 15 percent on food and medicine to create revenue and lessen dependency on oil income. He faced vigorous opposition in Congress, and when the bill was finally passed in January 2002, the VAT proposal had been dropped entirely. But he did succeed in passing tax increases on corporations and capital gains. Like many of Fox's reforms, the results were mixed.

Fox was one of the few Mexican presidents to avoid a major economic upheaval or crisis during his administration. Because Mexico's economy responds to the business cycles in the United States, the Mexican economy slowed down in 2000–2001. GDP growth dropped from an annual average of 5.5 percent during Zedillo's term, to an annual average of 2.2 percent during Fox's term.

Since 2002, the U.S. economic recovery, low inflation, and high oil prices have helped fuel economic growth in Mexico. However, there continue to be systemic problems that may prevent future growth and job creation. For example, workers are often unskilled, with low levels of education, leading to an inability to compete with more developed nations. There is also a large "informal" sector of the economy—estimated to be close to 30 percent. Income distribution is highly unequal, and about half of the population lives in poverty.

Despite robust public support early in his term, Fox's position weakened when PAN lost congressional seats in the 2003 midterm elections. He and his administration had failed to create a legislative coalition that would support his reform agenda. By the end of his *sexenio*, much of Fox's agenda would remain unfulfilled.

Calderon and the Tortilla Crisis

The PAN candidate for president, Felipe Calderon Hinojosa, who had served as energy minister under Fox, ran against the popular mayor of Mexico City, Andres Manuel Lopez Obrador, the PRD candidate. (The PRI candidate was former Tabasco governor Roberto Madrazo Pintado, but he trailed in the polls. The electorate was unenthusiastic about returning the PRI to the presidency.)

Obrador opposed the neoliberal market reforms of the previous administrations and promised voters that he would create millions of jobs by funding huge public works projects. Calderon, however, announced that he would continue to work on the reform agenda, promote FDI, and increase the competitiveness of the economy. He would stay the course of free-market trade and democratic reform.

In perhaps the most controversial presidential election in Mexico's history, Calderon was declared the winner in July 2006 with 35.89 percent of the vote, compared to Obrador's 35.31 percent—a very slim plurality. Obrador contested the results, and he and his supporters took to the streets in protest. This raised concern that the protest would turn violent and undermine the country's hard-won stability. In September, the election results were validated by the Federal Electoral Tribunal. But the drama wasn't over yet. The PRD threatened to prevent Calderon from taking the oath of office at his scheduled inauguration. According to the Mexican constitution, the new president must be sworn in before the Chamber of Deputies.

In a precautionary move, the PAN took control of Congress's main floor three days before the inauguration. After days of fighting, Calderon was finally sworn in at 9:50 AM on December 1, 2006, while representatives from PAN and PRD screamed and blew whistles. Ten minutes later, Calderon left the building as the new president.

After just two months in office, Calderon faced a crisis—corn prices had risen 400 percent. Suddenly, tortillas—a dietary staple in Mexico—were unaffordable for many people. This problem was a result of American corn production. In an attempt to cut its dependency on foreign oil, the United States started to produce biofuels, such as ethanol, from industrial-grade corn. This reduced the amount of edible corn being produced and available for export to Mexico. As corn supplies dropped, some wholesalers in Mexico began to hoard corn and drive up prices.

During this time, corn tortilla prices rose as high as 15 pesos ($1.36) for a kilogram (2.2 pounds), or roughly 35 tortillas. Calderon came up with a successful compromise by persuading producers and retailers, including Grupo Maseca and Grupo Bimbo, to cap their prices at 8.5 pesos (78 cents) per kilogram. Tortilla prices rapidly stabilized, and the average price of corn fell.

CHAPTER 19

The Second Mexican Independence

Investing in Mexico

There was a saying in Mexico: rich businessmen, poor companies.
—Melissa Johns and Jean Michel Lobet

Mexico is the fifth largest of the sizzling six BRIC+2 nations, both in population and gross domestic product (GDP). Its economy is a mixture of modern and antiquated, urban and rural, and free-market industries that are dominated by monopolies. Mexico's close proximity to the massive U.S. economy affords it with ready markets for goods and labor, and trade with the United States and Canada has tripled since the implantation of the North American Free Trade Agreement (NAFTA) in 1994. But the much higher incomes available in the United States also lure many of the country's most ambitious young workers to migrate, draining the country of its most productive talent. Why, then, is Mexico considered a "sizzling" prosperous nation for investors?

Recent changes in Mexico's investor protection laws and enforcement capability are strongly positive for growth. A new law took effect in June 2006 that significantly increases investor protections and transparency. As a result, Mexico's rankings in the World Economic Forum's governance indicators have soared. Moreover, successive government administrations have sought to expand competition in key infrastructure industries, including transportation, telecommunications, and utilities. Upgrading infrastructure, modernizing labor laws, and allowing more private investment in key sectors could dramatically lower costs of doing business, attract new foreign investment, and spur economic growth.

Here is a look at Mexico today and its prospects for tomorrow in relation to the eight tenets of our investment model.

Demographics: *Favorable*

Mexico's demographics have played an important role in the nation's economic growth and have received a favorable ranking. According to the *World Factbook,* Mexico is the world's 11th largest country in terms of population. From 2006 to 2020, its population is expected to grow by 16 percent, making it one of the fastest-growing countries in the Western hemisphere (second only to Germany, forecast to grow by 18 percent over the same period). By 2020, Mexico will have moved to tenth place, pushing ahead of Japan (www.cia.gov/library/publications/the-world-factbook/geos/mx.html).

Like India, Mexico has a very high dependency ratio, which is defined as the ratio of dependents (persons under age 15 or above age 64) to the working-age population (persons ages 15 to 64). A lower ratio represents a workforce with fewer dependents; thus, more of their income is available for savings that could ultimate help finance business expansion. Table 19.1 shows that Mexico had the highest dependency ratio of the six sizzling BRIC+2 nations in 2000, but its ratio fell by 11 percent from 2000 to 2005, while India's declined by only 7 percent. As a result, Mexico ranked slightly below India in 2005. Moreover, the World Bank forecasts that Mexico's dependency ratio will fall by another 17 percent from 2005 to 2020, setting the stage for a "demographic dividend" for the Mexican economy.

Mexico's population is still fairly young, with a median age of 25. About one-third of Mexicans are below the age of 15, and about 5 percent are older than 65. Based on estimates by Deutsche Bank, the median age will still be younger than 31 years, and only 8 percent of the population will be older than 65 by 2020. Based on these estimations, Deutsche Bank also forecasts that Mexico will add around 17 million people to its labor pool by 2020, and that per-capita incomes will rise at a faster rate until at least 2030 (Deutsche Bank Research, "Mexico 2020: Tequila Sunrise," February 16, 2006).

TABLE 19.1 World Bank Dependency Ratios (%)

	2000	2005	2010	2015	2020	2025
Mexico	64.26	57.22	50.81	48.13	47.38	48.18
India	62.49	58.26	54.06	50.18	47.35	46.21
Brazil	51.38	47.52	45.85	45.64	46.19	47.06
China	47.97	42.78	40.31	40.2	43.87	46.57
South Korea	39.36	39.44	38.56	37.06	39.39	46.3
Russia	43.6	40.88	37.09	38.95	42.48	47.91

Source: World Bank data
(http://devdata.worldbank.org/hnpstats/HNPDemographic/dependency.pdf)

The recent improvements in transparency and rule of law in Mexico could help leverage these demographic trends, resulting in potentially significant increases in Mexican per-capita GDP.

Economic Performance: *Favorable*

Unlike the other BRIC+2 countries, an expanding middle class and shift from agriculture have played a minor role in Mexico's recent economic performance. In contrast, the major indicators of Mexico's economy have been its exports to the United States and Canada, particularly after the passage of NAFTA. Therefore, GDP growth and GDP per capita are more indicative of Mexico's economic performance.

GDP Growth and the Middle Class

The World Economic Forum (WEF) ranks Mexico as a stage 2 economy, along with Russia and Brazil. Mexico's macroeconomy is ranked number 54 in the WEF Global Competitive Index, compared with 114 for Brazil and 33 for Russia.

Mexico's economic growth rate over the last decade was tepid compared to the blazing economies of China and India. In 2006, real (after inflation) GDP growth reached 4.8 percent, a huge improvement over 2005's 2.8 percent, and then fell to about 3.4 percent in 2007, for a total national GDP of about $840 billion. Services currently make up about 70 percent of Mexico's economy, industry 26 percent, and agriculture 4 percent.

Selling prices of major Mexican commodity exports such as oil and metals and the strength or weakness of the U.S. economy significantly affect GDP trends. Over the past 15 years, Mexico's annual GDP growth has averaged about 3 percent, or 1.5 percent per capita. This low rate is attributed to low levels of labor productivity in services and manufacturing sectors, compared to faster-growing emerging markets in Asia. Like Brazil, Mexico has a large informal economy (about 30 percent of GDP and 50 percent to 60 percent of the working population) that can lead to slow growth in employee incomes. These informal workers do not have typical job benefits and tend to work in smaller, less efficient companies.

Yet, longer-term, forecasters project Mexico's GDP will grow in the range of 3 percent to 5 percent annually from 2005 to 2050, just fast enough to put Mexico ahead of slower-growing South Korea. For example, Deutsche Bank forecasts Mexico's GDP will reach $1.5 trillion by 2020 assuming annual growth averages 3 percent to 3.5 percent. A more optimistic forecast by PriceWaterhouse Coopers calls for annual growth to average 4 percent to 5 percent through 2050.

TABLE 19.2 Inequality Measures—Ratio of Richest 20 Percent to Poorest 20 Percent

Paraguay	27.8
Colombia	25.3
Panama	23.9
Brazil	23.7
El Salvador	20.9
Guatemala	20.3
Chile	18.7
Peru	18.6
Argentina	17.6
Ecuador	17.3
Honduras	17.2

Source: United Nations

According to World Bank data, an estimated 20 percent of Mexicans live below the international poverty line of $2 per day. As in other developing economies, this high proportion of poverty is linked to a large, rural agricultural sector. While agriculture accounts for only about 4 percent of Mexico's GDP, it represents 18 percent of the labor force. According to the *World Factbook,* 24 percent of the labor force is employed in the industrial sector, while the remaining 58 percent work in the services industry.

Per capita income in Mexico is about one-fourth that of the United States and three times that of India. On a current purchasing power parity basis, Mexico's per-capita GDP is estimated at about $11,760, and per-capita income is expected to rise by 30 percent to 40 percent from 2005 to 2020 (Deutsche Bank Research, February 16, 2006). The relatively high level of per-capita income, however, does not tell the entire story. The ratio of richest 20 percent of the population to poorest 20 percent is quite high by global standards, at 12.4. Still, as Table 19.2 shows, Mexico's income inequality measure is among the most favorable among Latin and South American countries.

Obstacles to Mexican economic growth include restrictive labor practices and bureaucracies that make it expensive and time consuming to start or expand businesses. Employers may be obligated to maintain a permanent working relationship with employees or pay stiff severance settlements. The value of employee benefits approaches 50 percent of wages compared with 25 percent to 30 percent in the United States. By one measure, the labor-market environment in Mexico is about four times as restrictive as in the United States, United Kingdom, and Australia. Side effects of these restrictive practices may include suboptimal hiring during growth spurts, widespread underemployment as workers cling to less challenging jobs because of their accumulated benefits, and greater demand for informal workers as employers try to avoid the higher costs of hiring formal workers. While the nation's unemployment rate is low, at 3.2 percent, nearly a quarter of the population is believed to be underemployed.

Labor practices are only one hurdle to Mexico's growth prospects. Another is the lack of competitive markets. A survey in 2005 found the existence of public and private monopolies (one seller) or oligopolies (a small number of sellers) topped the list of obstacles to business development in Mexico. Anticompetitive laws and practices that have hampered Mexico's economy in the past, however, have been substantially eliminated by legislation passed in 2006. The new law provides a modern framework for antitrust regulations and enforcement in order to ensure that competitive market forces can operate to keep prices from escalating arbitrarily. Observers point to Mexico's telephone industry as a classic example: When Telmex, a private phone company, operated 9 out of 10 telephone lines in Mexico, the average long distance call rate was above $0.50 per minute, among the highest in the world (*The Guardian,* July 7, 2007).

Mexico's status as a low-cost supplier of goods and services to American companies has faltered, as incomes have gradually risen and as even lower-cost companies have developed in Asia. Since 2000, some 270,000 Mexican assembly jobs (known as *maquiladora* jobs) have been lost to Chinese firms.[1] Other Latin American countries also compete with Mexican firms, with wage levels that are 50 percent to 75 percent lower. Mexico, Brazil, and Korea are now considered middle-income countries, and their economic fortune may hinge on their ability to develop strength in value-added production that requires skilled labor and better process management. However, a study by McKinsey notes that the most successful efforts at expanding into these types of jobs may come in existing industries rather than by shifting into new industries. Therefore, investors may want to look for companies that have well-established trade relationships and that are making investments in increasing their capabilities to deliver higher-level services and to tap into the unused potential of Mexico's labor force.

Technology: *Neutral*

Based on the WEF's technological readiness rankings, Mexico's technological readiness is on par with Brazil's and India's. However, Mexico ranks

[1]The *maquiladora* category refers to Mexican assembly plants that imported component parts from source countries for assembly and then shipped the completed goods back, subject to certain tariff advantages and requirements. The category was eliminated from NAFTA in January 2004.

TABLE 19.3 Technology WEF Rankings 2006 (rank, score)

	Overall index	Basic requirements	Efficiency enhancers	Innovation factors
Mexico	58, 4.18	53, 4.61	59, 3.91	52, 3.80
India	43, 4.44	60, 4.51	41, 4.32	26, 4.60
Brazil	66, 4.03	87, 4.14	57, 3.94	38, 4.09
China	54, 4.24	44, 4.80	71, 3.66	57, 3.75

significantly lower on innovation factors, achieving a WEF rank of 52 compared with 26 for India and 38 for Brazil. Thus, Mexico's investor ranking based on technology is only neutral.

While Mexico's exports of high-technology products in aerospace, computers, pharmaceuticals, scientific instruments, and electrical machinery account for about 21 percent of total exports (compared to just 5 percent for India), Mexico lacks the technology services outsourcing business that has propelled India's growth. Many of Mexico's exports in these areas relate to assembly capabilities rather than complex design or innovation capabilities (see Table 19.3).

Open Trade: *Neutral*

Mexico's openness to trade is neither a detriment nor a positive aspect of the nation's economic performance, and, as such, it has been ranked as neutral.

With exports representing about 38 percent of Mexico's economy, success in managing trade relations is a critical component of the country's future. Mexico is considered an open economy and enjoys trade with the United States under the terms of NAFTA signed in 1994. In the first decade of this historic agreement, trade between the United States and Mexico grew twice as fast as U.S. trade outside of NAFTA. (Gary Clyde Hufbauer, Jeffrey J. Schott, Paul L. E. Grieco, and Yee Wong, "NAFTA Revisited: Achievements and Challenges." Institute for International Economics, 2005.) Today, Mexico has free trade agreements with over 40 countries including the European Free Trade Area and Japan, and more than 90 percent of its trade is conducted under 12 free trade agreements. Some experts suggest that the potential value of Mexico's trade with the United States has yet to be fully realized, however. Only a relatively small number of Mexican firms currently export to U.S. markets, and these are primarily commodity and low value-added manufacturing products.

In order to diversify its export markets, however, Mexico may need to lower its most-favored-nation (MFN) tariffs and industrial tariffs, currently higher than those of its emerging-market competitors. International Monetary Fund (IMF) data shows that Mexico reduced about three-fourths of its tariffs by 3 to 10 percentage points in 2004. Mexico's industrial tariffs remain high despite these reductions, averaging 9.7 percent, compared with 6.0 percent for South Korea and 9.1 percent for China. Thus, Mexico's average tariff stood at 15 percent in 2006, about twice that of the United States and one-third higher than China's.

Tariffs are not the only barrier to free trade. Other potentially discriminative practices include import licensing requirements and exclusive quality standards. Calculations by the World Bank show the cost of Mexico's restrictive practices amounts to more than $4 billion, or 0.6 percent of GDP. Protecting local industries from foreign competitors has also led to restrictions on foreign direct investments that are among the highest of the 30 Organization for Economic Cooperation and Development (OECD) countries (only Poland, Turkey, Italy, and Canada have tighter restrictions than Mexico). These practices may have reduced inflows of new capital into the Mexican economy compared with other developing markets.

Investors should be encouraged by most aspects of Mexico's openness to trade—a common barrier for the other BRIC+2 markets. As the nation works to improve its trade relations, one can expect foreign investment to increase.

Infrastructure Development: *Unfavorable*

Mexico ranked slightly below India and China in the WEF's 2006 infrastructure sub-index, coming in at 64. While India and China have begun to see improvements as a result of aggressive investments and greater private investment, Mexico is lagging behind. As such, it is no surprise that their infrastructure development industry is an unfavorable area for foreign investments.

There are various reasons for Mexico's unfavorable infrastructure development ranking. For instance, only about one-third of roads are paved, and seaports are inadequate to support export growth. Meanwhile utility costs, including telecommunications and electricity, are well above the averages for the 30 OECD countries. Electricity costs average more than 40 percent more than in China and 10 percent more than in the United States. Needed reforms have been slow to develop. Government spending on infrastructure remains low compared to other developing countries, at about 12 percent of GDP, while state monopolies on oil, gas, and electric generation prohibit private investment.

Lack of adequate transportation infrastructure can be a significant deterrent to business and economic growth. A recent study by the World Bank and International Finance Corporation found that a day's delay in transportation translates to about a 1 percent loss in export volumes. These factors should be considered when investing in Mexico, as the inadequate infrastructure can have a major impact on the nation's ability to sustain growth.

Transparency and Rule of Law: *Favorable*

Mexico's transparency and rule-of-law scores have significantly improved since new laws governing shareholder protections took effect in mid-2006—trends that have made Mexico favorable in this regard. The new law is expected to dramatically strengthen investors' confidence in Mexico's securities markets, making it easier for domestic companies to attract equity capital and foreign direct investment (FDI). Among other things, the law imposes fiduciary responsibilities on company directors and prohibits self-dealing. It also makes it easier for shareholders to sue company directors for improper actions. As a result of these reforms, Mexico's scores on the World Bank's "Doing Business 2007" ease-of-doing-business index rose sharply, and its rank improved by 41 percent, jumping from 75 to 44.

Confidence in a nation's legal system is a crucial element for investors, and Mexico proves to be no exception. All indications point to continued advancements in this category, making investing in Mexico far more attractive than in years past.

Education and Training: *Unfavorable*

The low level of educational attainment and migration are two reasons why the educational and training tenets of Mexico are considered unfavorable. Mexico ranks at the bottom of the list of OECD countries in measures of educational attainment for working-age adults (ages 25 through 54). Educational prospects are slowly improving for today's youth, however. The typical child in Mexico spends eight years in schools today, up from 2.6 years in 1960, but well below the average of 13 years for all of Latin America.

Migration is another factor that likely influences the development of Mexico's talent pool, although the exact effects are not clear. By some estimates, migration to the United States may be 400,000 to 500,000 individuals a year. According to one study, ". . . migration may be most likely amongst the most entrepreneurial and risk-taking individuals within a community, who would have the greatest capacity to spur change and innovation. On the other hand, migration has significantly improved family incomes through remittances and it may involve additional positive spillovers—for instance increasing technological transfers from the U.S. . . ."

The lack of a functioning education system will continue to have a negative impact on Mexico's economic growth. Investors who value an educated workforce should monitor the developments implemented by the Mexican government. Though the conditions are expected to improve, they remain a major source of uncertainty.

Sound Financial Systems and Policies: *Favorable*

Mexico's efforts during the last decade to strengthen its financial stability and improve the accountability of government have resulted in a financial situation that compares favorably to most other countries in Latin America. Thus, it is a favorable area for investors for various reasons.

First, public debt is declining along with government budget deficits. The new Budget and Fiscal Responsibility Law requires that future administrations aim for a balanced budget. If adhered to, the new law promises a more stable future for Mexico's financial stability.

Second, Mexico's banking system has strengthened considerably since the peso crisis of 1994 brought the financial sector to near collapse. By 2006, the nonperforming loan ratio of Mexico's commercial banks had declined to 2 percent, down from 5.1 percent in 2001, and bank profitability had increased dramatically (according to the Economist Intelligence Unit).

Third, bank reforms have led to better financial policies and economic growth. Of the country's five largest banking groups, four are owned by foreign companies: BBVA-Bancomer (Spain), Banamex (owned by U.S.-based Citigroup), HSBC (United Kingdom) and Banco Santander Mexicano (HSBCSpain). Mercantil del Norte (Banorte) is the sole remaining large domestic bank. The infusion of capital from foreign-owned banks may help fuel faster loan growth, as will recent reforms in bankruptcy legislation that provide lenders with tighter loan guarantees and processes for recovering bad loans. These reforms could lead to lower lending rates, helping to stimulate growth.

These sound financial systems and policies have had positive impacts on Mexico's economy, especially the resulting lower inflation rates. Inflation has been cause for concern in Mexico's past, with inflation reaching about 100 percent per year just 20 years ago. Today, monetary authorities have set an inflation target of about 3 percent per year, a little lower than the 3.5 percent to 4 percent rate achieved in recent years. Inflation has trended steadily downward since 2000, when the annual consumer price index hit 9.5 percent. A 3 percent to 4 percent annual rate is only slightly higher than typical U.S. inflation rates.

Nevertheless, Mexico's capital markets are still underdeveloped, with business loans the exception rather than the rule. Lending to personal borrowers is increasing, now about $35 billion or 4.2 percent of GDP, while mortgage lending is also rising and reached 9.1 percent of GDP in 2006. Commercial lending is still lagging, at about 5.4 percent of GDP, in part due to a culture of weak enforcement of loan contracts. As a result, corporate loans for the largest companies are typically comprised of short-term bank credit lines of less than a year. Smaller companies may have access to financing through government-guaranteed loans, but this total is still minuscule, at less than 1 percent of GDP.

Mexico's securities markets have grown more slowly than comparable economies in terms of companies listed on domestic exchanges. In 2004, for example, the Republic of Korea's gross national income was similar to Mexico's ($600 to $700 billion), but it had 10 times the number of exchange-listed firms. The recent improvements in shareholder protections are expected to encourage more companies to issue new shares on Mexico's stock exchange.

Mexico's Growth Industries

Individuals who live in the United States may be limited in their ability to purchase shares in Mexican companies directly. Some convenient ways to invest include mutual funds, exchange-traded funds (ETFs), and American Depositary Receipts (ADRs).

The sectors of Mexico's economy most available to investors include telecommunications, materials, and consumer products. Table 19.4 shows a closer look at some promising industries within these sectors.

TABLE 19.4 MSCI Mexico Index Sector Weights (as of August 31, 2007)

Economic sector (Global Industry Classification System)	Float-adjusted shares (% of investiable index market capitalization)
Telecommunication Services	37.92
Materials	19.92
Consumer Staples	17.72
Consumer Discretionary	10.98
Industrials	9.27
Financials	3.96

In the remainder of the chapter, we will discuss these and other investment opportunities available to a foreign investor.

Telecommunication Services

The telecommunications sector includes providers of land phones, mobile phones, and broadband communications. Mexico's telecommunications services industry is dominated by a few large firms battling for supremacy throughout Latin America. América Móvil is headquartered in Mexico and is the region's largest multinational cellular provider, with more than 140 million mobile subscribers. Its Mexican subsidiary, Telcel, is the largest mobile operator in Mexico, with market share of more than 80 percent. The other major company in Mexico is Telmex, which provides landline phone services and broadband. América Móvil and Telmex are controlled by Mexican billionaire Carlos Slim. According to Company Financial Reports, the major competitor in the region is Telefónica S.A., which significantly expanded its hold on the South and Central American market in 2004 when it purchased BellSouth's properties for $5.85 billion.

Moderate penetration rates in Mexico and in much of Latin America continue to offer near-term growth prospects for mobile operators and Internet services.

Materials

The basic materials sector includes industries in building materials such as sand, stone and cement, chemicals, packaging materials, and metals and mining. Mexico's chemicals industry is composed almost entirely of private companies that collectively represent more than 90 percent of the Mexican market (http://goliath.ecnext.com/coms2/gi_0199-3915591/Grassroot-expansions-planned-in-Mexico.html). In the metals and mining segment, privately owned Grupo México (Grupo México S.A. de C.V.) dominates the domestic market and is the third largest copper producer in the world. Peñoles, another mining company with operations in silver and other metals, is a subsidiary company owned by the private firm Grupo Bal. Since these firms are privately owned, they are not accessible to individual investors.

More realistic opportunities for U.S. investors may lie in Mexico's building materials industry. This industry is likely to benefit from additional investments in domestic infrastructure, such as a proposed $37 billion upgrade in Mexico's transportation system. The plan includes $26 billion for improving highways and constructing three new airports and an additional $11 billion in ports and railways.

Companies within this sector include Cemex SAB, one of the world's largest cement companies. In 2007, Cemex acquired Australia's leading building materials company in a deal worth $14 billion, giving it a market share of nearly 100 percent in Mexico and around 50 percent in the United States. While the U.S. demand for building materials may cool somewhat depending on credit conditions and the housing market, many emerging markets will likely continue to see demand to support new infrastructure and housing.

Consumer Products (Staples and Discretionary)

Consumer product companies include manufacturers of durable consumer products such as automobiles, services such as travel and leisure, retail chains, and staples such as food, apparel, housewares, and personal care products.

Among these segments, some possible investments in Mexico are companies in the retail, hospitality, and media industries. Consumer industries generally fare well when populations and incomes are expanding. Mexico's population is expanding and experiencing a declining dependency ratio. This combination, coupled with stronger economic growth, could give rise to an increase in per-capita income that could fuel greater consumer spending on consumer discretionary and consumer staples.

AUTO PARTS AND COMPONENTS Consulting firm PriceWaterhouse Coopers forecasts that Mexico will jump from 11th in the world in automotive production today to fifth place by 2011. Automotive accessories and component parts are also big business. As per-capita incomes rise, car ownership is expected to increase, along with purchases of component parts that enhance the appearance of the vehicle and luxury items that customers buy to personalize their vehicles.

TRAVEL AND TOURISM Mexico's vital culture and sunny, warm weather make it a popular destination for tourists. The WEF's Travel and Tourism Index 2007 ranked Mexico 47th out of 124 countries on its overall attractiveness as a tourist destination. Several factors could drive increases in tourism in coming years. According to Mexico's tourism secretariat, approximately 70 percent of tourists in Mexico come from the United States, and as the U.S. population ages, a large number of Baby Boomers are entering retirement and may choose to travel. Continued weakness in the dollar against the euro could also result in an above-normal influx of visitors from the United States if Mexico is perceived as a more affordable destination. Mexico is home to the world's seventh largest hotel industry, according to Mexico's tourism secretariat.

PHARMACEUTICALS According to *Business Monitor*, spending on pharmaceuticals in Mexico is already the highest in Latin America and is rising at about 6 percent per year. Branded prescriptions account for more than 80 percent of sales. As the government looks for ways to stretch health care funds, new programs are being introduced that focus on generic drugs. Mexico is also beginning to emerge as an alternative for clinical trials.

Industrials

The industrials sector includes companies involved in engineering, heavy construction, and electrical equipment. Similar to the basic materials sector, firms in these industries are often multinational regional firms positioned to benefit from increased investment in infrastructure projects in Mexico and throughout Central and South America. The Mexican engineering firm ICA, for example, provides services on projects in the United States, France, and across Latin America.

The changes incorporated into Mexico's investment laws have made the nation an even more attractive option for foreign investors. As transparency increases, it is the hope of all involved that Mexico will be able to deal with the many problems it now faces, such as its poor infrastructure and relatively uneducated, urban workforce. Further economic growth will be largely dependent on how the government responds to such conditions. Yet, if the recent past provides any indication, it appears that Mexico is poised to continue its path of rapid economic growth.

CHAPTER 20

Tips for Investing in the Six Sizzling Markets

There are no shortcuts to becoming a successful investor. This is especially true of investments in developing markets including the BRIC+2 countries. Investing in these markets will take knowledge, understanding, careful judgment, and above all, patience.

In addition to using the valuable information that we have laid out in this book, there are some tips that wise investors must follow in order to profit from investing in Brazil, Russia, India, China, South Korea, or Mexico.

Tip 1: Country Selection Is Critical

When it comes to developing markets, country risks trump all other risks. Therefore, country selection is critical. Pick the countries first, as well as their relative weights in the portfolio. The reason we have spent a great deal of time discussing each of the six countries is to emphasize the importance of country selection in the portfolio. This top-down approach is especially important when it comes to markets such as the six sizzling markets, where each country has specific opportunities combined with unique challenges.

If you are picking a broad-based emerging market or a BRIC fund, then you are leaving the country selection and weighting to the portfolio managers. However, if your approach is to use specific mutual funds or an exchange-traded fund (ETF) devoted to a single country, then you will need to decide on the proportional weight of each country in your portfolio.

The task becomes somewhat more complex if you are using individual foreign stocks such as American Depositary Receipts (ADRs) for your portfolio. You will have to choose not only the country weights but also the sector and industry weights.

Tip 2: Diversify, Diversify, Diversify

Regardless of how attractive a sector or an industry in each country looks, it is prudent to spread your wealth into various sectors or industries within a country. For most investors, buying a mutual fund such as a country's ETF could provide the appropriate diversification. If, however, you are interested in using ADRs and investing in individual stocks, it is important to have an appropriate distribution of industry sectors within the country. As an example, if financial companies account for 28 percent of a country's economy, an individual investor's portfolio should optimally reflect this percentage.

Tip 3: Avoid Fads and Focus on the Long Term

As these markets continue to prosper, they tend to get very popular with investors. This "hot money" tends in many cases to have adverse results. Sometimes these investments turn into fads and capture the attention of many novice investors as well as the press, whether investments in one of the countries such as Brazil or Mexico one year, or high-tech Indian stocks another year. Pay attention to fundamentals such as valuation of companies or political or economic risks. Many times, fundamentals are hidden or understated.

Tip 4: Forget the Timing—Emerging Markets Are Volatile

The six sizzling markets strategy, as explained throughout the book, is based on our belief that for the next half century or longer, these six countries are poised for extraordinary growth and thus will be profitable investments in the long term. Therefore, for most investors, it will prove extremely difficult to pick the best time to buy or sell. However, by their nature, most emerging markets, including the BRIC+2 nations, are volatile (see Table 20.1). Yet

TABLE 20.1 Average Monthly Volatility at Five-Year Intervals

	S&P	EAFE	MSCI, emerging-market index
1986–1990	19%	23%	25%
1991–1995	10%	15%	10%
1996–2000	16%	14%	26%
2001–2005	15%	15%	21%

Sources: Agtmael (*Emerging Markets Century*), MSCIEAFE (Europe, Australia, and Far East), S&P (Standard & Poor 500 Industrials), MSCI Emerging Market Index

TABLE 20.2 Correlation Comparisons, Emerging Markets vs. U.S. Markets

	Correlation with U.S. market
Dec. 1987–Sept. 1994	.18
Sept. 1994–Aug. 1998	.51
Aug. 1998–Sept. 2001	.52
Sept. 2001–Dec. 2005	.82

Note: These are monthly correlations of MSCIF (Emerging Market Index) to Standard & Poor's 500. Although correlations have increased recently, these are not perfect.

these markets also are not perfectly correlated with U.S. markets, and therefore provide an added benefit of diversification (see Table 20.2).

Tip 5: Emerging Markets Outperform and Underperform with Regularity—Do Your Homework and Be Cautious

For an investor in developed markets such as the United States, it is important to understand that these six emerging markets have moved through different stages in the course of their existence resulting in varying performance during these cycles (see Table 20.3).

In the early stage, 1988 to 1994, developing economies were newly discovered and outperformed developed markets. Then came the shock phase, when one market or an entire region went through political or economic rises. Places such as Russia, Korea, and Latin America were hit especially hard. Anxious investors dumped their shares in many of these countries.

TABLE 20.3 Performance of Emerging Market and U.S. Market

Time	Emerging markets	U.S. market	Remarks
April 1988–Sept. 1994	+543%	+118%	Discovery years
Sept. 1994–Aug. 1998	−55%	+125%	Political and economic issues: Russian crises and Asian contagion
Aug. 1998–Sept. 2001	+12%	+13%	Technology boom and blight
Sept. 2001–July 2006	+243%	+34%	Global growth: rise of China, India, and Russia

These markets are likely to reward only long-term investors because emerging countries' volatility will make short-term profits difficult to capture. Their strength is that they are likely to grow over time and be uncorrelated with the developed markets. Investors would be wise to use the gains in these markets to rebalance their portfolios so as not to be overweighted in either a country or a sector. Rebalancing simply means selling or pruning your winners and reinvesting the proceeds into funds or stocks that have not participated so as to retain the original balance.

Tip 6: Allocate Only a Small Portion of Your Stock Portfolio to the Six Sizzling Nations

Based on the overall capitalization of world stock markets, it is considered prudent for investors to allocate only a portion of their portfolio to international investments, and only a portion of that to developing markets. How much is appropriate? To answer that question, it may be useful to start at the Morgan Stanley (MSCI) Emerging Market Index, the most widely used index. This index shows only 6.5 percent allocation to emerging markets. In addition, it only takes into account the actual float (tradable shares), which removes the shares held by family and the government and therefore comprises only 800 of the larger listed stocks. The other index is compiled by IFC and is called S&P Emerging Markets Index. By their calculations, the emerging markets portion is about 12 percent, which is more realistic based on the fact that emerging-markets account for about 12 percent of total earnings.

In his excellent book *Emerging Markets Century*, Antoine van Agtmael points out that the MSCI Emerging Index has had no major additions since 2000 and it only counts 830, or just 5 percent, of the 15,000 stocks actually listed on emerging-markets exchanges. This fails to take into account the majority of either small or less liquid stocks—the very group that may be most likely to take off.

Many U.S. institutional managers as well as pension funds have been raising their stake in foreign markets and may dedicate as much as 30 percent to 50 percent of a stock portfolio to international investments. Many of these same professional managers believe that 20 percent to 30 percent of the international allocation should be dedicated to emerging markets. We believe BRIC+2 is a select group of emerging markets that stand to gain disproportionately from the overall gain of the emerging markets.

Therefore, an allocation of 7 percent to 15 percent could be considered reasonable in BRIC+2 markets, depending on considerations such as time horizon and risk tolerance. Our discussions with emerging-markets portfolio managers and managers of BRIC funds conforms to this view. Institutional money managers continue to believe that U.S. investors are generally underinvested outside the United States.

Tip 7: If Investing in Mutual Funds, Look under the Hood!

If your investments are mostly through mutual funds, it is important to learn the details. If, for example, you are choosing a fund that is a broadly diversified emerging market fund, you leave both the country allocation as well as the stock picking to the portfolio manager. However, if you choose country funds, then the country allocation decisions are left to you as an investor. If you use funds such as ETFs they are likely to pursue a passive policy of picking stocks that replicate an index. By contrast, if you choose an actively managed fund then the portfolio composition is left to the manager who may diverge from a given benchmark such as an index.

Knowing and understanding different investment styles is important to avoid any surprises.

Methodology executed by BRIC fund managers varies from fund to fund. Since most of these funds are new it is likely that they may continue to experiment with different methodologies. For example, at the end of June 2007, Goldman Sachs BRIC Fund had underweighted China and Brazil and slightly overweighted Russia and India in relation to its own benchmark. By contrast, S&P BRIC 40 ETF had a different set of benchmarks, and was overweight in Russia and underweight in India. The different weighting resulted not only in different country allocations but also different sector allocations. For example, S&P BRIC 40 had an allocation into energy of about 35 percent versus 25 percent for Goldman Sachs BRIC fund (*Sources:* Standard & Poor's; Goldman Sachs).

This is merely to serve as an example because such allocations will vary from fund to fund depending on what benchmark is used or on the preference of the portfolio manager. As an investor it is important to be aware of these differences and to accommodate them in the portfolio management.

Tip 8: Markets Are Prone to Shocks, Both External and Internal—Use Caution

In many of the developing countries, a long history of financial and political crises, along with lack of proper institutional safeguards, make investors nervous at the first sign of trouble. The Asian financial crisis caused a contagion in 1998, along with the near collapse of the Russian stock market. A domestic or external shock dramatically affects a market or an entire region. Political events such as changes of government, which tend to be commonplace in Latin America, can decimate their stock markets from which it can take years to recover. In some cases, these have been great opportunities to enter such markets; however sometimes it takes nerves of steel to do so. An extreme example of this was a near collapse of the financial system in Argentina, causing a run on the banks and riots in the street in 2001–2002.

Tip 9: Investing in Foreign Stocks Using ADRs—Stick to High Quality

Foreign companies traded on the U.S. exchanges are available but the trading activity will depend on the size of the company and its float, as well as institutional ownership. It is therefore important for individual investors to stick to high-quality liquid issues with close bid and ask prices. Companies such as Samsung, Infosys, Tata Motors, and China Mobil are examples of high-quality companies with strong balance sheets and dynamic business models.

Building a portfolio with ADRs is possible but may create difficulties with appropriate country and sector allocation. For the purpose of diversification, select companies that are either global, have a broad diversified product, or are extremely profitable in their niche market and are financially sound. Such companies, regardless of the location, will survive and even thrive despite short-term setbacks.

Tip 10: Look at the Modern History of the Six Sizzling Markets

As we described in Tip 5, the emerging six sizzling markets have gone through different stages throughout their short histories. In the past, emerging markets were seen as risk prone by most investors. In many cases, these countries had closed economies, protected trade, poor governance, and stock markets with few companies that could be considered global.

Today, the story is dramatically different, particularly for these BRIC+2 nations. As evidenced throughout the history chapters, these countries have reasonably stable political and economic systems, governance has improved, trade is more open, and their economies are growing substantially. In addition, there are now companies located in these markets that have truly become global. Looking to future opportunities in these markets is likely to be more profitable than looking at their past performance.

APPENDIX A

Country Profiles

Country profiles are provided to inform readers of the political, economic and geographic background for each of the six countries, as well as the trends from 2000 to 2006.

TABLE A.1 Brazil Data Profile

	2000	2005	2006
People			
Population, total	173.9 million	186.4 million	188.7 million
Population growth (annual %)	1.5	1.3	1.2
Poverty head count ratio at national poverty line (% of population)	..	..	..
Life expectancy at birth, total (years)	69.7	71.2	..
Fertility rate, total (births per woman)	2.4	2.3	..
Mortality rate, infant (per 1,000 live births)	35.0	31.0	..
Mortality rate, under 5 (per 1,000)	39.0	33.0	..
Births attended by skilled health staff (% of total)	..	..	..
Malnutrition prevalence, weight for age (% of children under 5)	..	..	..
Immunization, measles (% of children ages 12–23 months)	99.0	99.0	..
Prevalence of HIV, total (% of population ages 15–49)	..	0.5	..
Primary completion rate, total (% of relevant age group)	107.8	..	..
School enrollment, primary (% gross)	150.7	..	..
School enrollment, secondary (% gross)	104.2	..	..
School enrollment, tertiary (% gross)	16.1	..	..
Ratio of girls to boys in primary and secondary education (%)	102.9	..	..
Literacy rate, adult total (% of people ages 15 and above)	86.4	..	..

(*Continued*)

TABLE A.1 Brazil Data Profile (*Continued*)

	2000	2005	2006
Environment			
Surface area (sq. km)	8.5 million	8.5 million	8.5 million
Forest area (sq. km)	4.9 million	4.8 million	..
Agricultural land (% of land area)	30.9	..	..
CO_2 emissions (metric tons per capita)	1.8	..	..
Improved water source (% of population with access)	89.0	..	..
Improved sanitation facilities, urban (% of urban population with access)	83.0	..	..
Energy use (kg of oil equivalent per capita)	1,068.1	..	..
Energy imports, net (% of energy use)	22.6	..	..
Electric power consumption (kWh per capita)	1,897.1	..	..
Economy			
GNI, Atlas method (current US$)	673.7 billion	725.7 billion	892.8 billion
GNI per capita, Atlas method (current US$)	3,870.0	3,890.0	4,730.0
GDP (current US$)	644.5 billion	882.5 billion	1.1 trillion
GDP growth (annual %)	4.3	2.9	3.7
Inflation, GDP deflator (annual %)	6.2	7.5	4.3
Agriculture, value added (% of GDP)	5.6	5.6	5.1
Industry, value added (% of GDP)	27.7	30.3	30.9
Services, etc., value added (% of GDP)	66.7	64.0	64.0
Exports of goods and services (% of GDP)	10.0	15.1	14.7
Imports of goods and services (% of GDP)	11.7	11.5	11.7
Gross capital formation (% of GDP)	18.3	16.0	16.8
Revenue, excluding grants (% of GDP)	..	..	..
Cash surplus/deficit (% of GDP)	..	..	..
States and markets			
Time required to start a business (days)	..	152.0	152.0
Market capitalization of listed companies (% of GDP)	35.1	53.8	66.6
Military expenditure (% of GDP)	1.6	1.4	..
Fixed line and mobile phone subscribers (per 1,000 people)	311.3	..	..
Internet users (per 1,000 people)	28.8	195.0	..
Roads, paved (% of total roads)	5.5	..	..
High-technology exports (% of manufactured exports)	18.6	12.8	..

TABLE A.1 *(Continued)*

	2000	2005	2006
Global links			
Merchandise trade (% of GDP)	17.7	22.2	21.2
Net barter terms of trade (2000 = 100)	100.0	101.4	97.1
Foreign direct investment, net inflows (BoP, current US$)	32.8 billion	15.2 billion	..
Long-term debt (DOD, current US$)	210.9 billion	164.0 billion	..
Present value of debt (% of GNI)	..	34.1	..
Total debt service (% of exports of goods, services and income)	93.7	44.8	..
Official development assistance and official aid (current US$)	232.3 million	191.9 million	..
Workers' remittances and compensation of employees, received (US$)	1.6 billion	3.5 billion	3.5 billion

Source: World Development Indicators database, April 2007

TABLE A.2 Russian Federation Data Profile

	2000	2005	2006
People			
Population, total	146.3 million	143.1 million	142.4 million
Population growth (annual %)	–0.0	–0.5	–0.5
Poverty head count ratio at national poverty line (% of population)	..	..	..
Life expectancy at birth, total (years)	65.3	65.5	..
Fertility rate, total (births per woman)	1.2	1.3	..
Mortality rate, infant (per 1,000 live births)	18.8	14.3	..
Mortality rate, under 5 (per 1,000)	23.6	17.5	..
Births attended by skilled health staff (% of total)	..	..	..
Malnutrition prevalence, weight for age (% of children under 5)	5.5	..	..
Immunization, measles (% of children ages 12–23 months)	97.0	99.0	..
Prevalence of HIV, total (% of population ages 15–49)	..	1.1	..
Primary completion rate, total (% of relevant age group)	..	..	..
School enrollment, primary (% gross)	..	128.7	..
School enrollment, secondary (% gross)	..	91.9	..
School enrollment, tertiary (% gross)	..	71.0	..

(*Continued*)

TABLE A.2 Russian Federation Data Profile (*Continued*)

	2000	2005	2006
Ratio of girls to boys in primary and secondary education (%)	..	98.9	..
Literacy rate, adult total (% of people ages 15 and above)	..	..	..
Environment			
Surface area (sq. km)	17.1 million	17.1 million	17.1 million
Forest area (sq. km)	8.1 million	8.1 million	..
Agricultural land (% of land area)	13.3	13.2	..
CO_2 emissions (metric tons per capita)	9.9	..	..
Improved water source (% of population with access)	96.0	..	..
Improved sanitation facilities, urban (% of urban population with access)	93.0	..	..
Energy use (kg of oil equivalent per capita)	4,196.4	..	..
Energy imports, net (% of energy use)	–57.4	..	..
Electric power consumption (kWh per capita)	5,208.8	..	..
Economy			
GNI, Atlas method (current US$)	250.3 billion	639.3 billion	822.4 billion
GNI per capita, Atlas method (current US$)	1,710.0	4,470.0	5,780.0
GDP (current US$)	259.7 billion	764.5 billion	986.9 billion
GDP growth (annual %)	10.0	6.4	6.7
Inflation, GDP deflator (annual %)	37.7	19.2	16.1
Agriculture, value added (% of GDP)	6.4	5.6	..
Industry, value added (% of GDP)	37.9	38.0	..
Services, etc., value added (% of GDP)	55.6	56.4	..
Exports of goods and services (% of GDP)	44.1	35.1	33.3
Imports of goods and services (% of GDP)	24.0	21.5	20.2
Gross capital formation (% of GDP)	18.7	20.9	20.9
Revenue, excluding grants (% of GDP)	..	30.6	..
Cash surplus/deficit (% of GDP)	..	9.9	..
States and markets			
Time required to start a business (days)	..	33.0	28.0
Market capitalization of listed companies (% of GDP)	15.0	71.8	133.9
Military expenditure (% of GDP)	3.7	3.7	..
Fixed line and mobile phone subscribers (per 1,000 people)	241.5	1,118.7	..
Internet users (per 1,000 people)	19.8	152.3	..

TABLE A.2 (*Continued*)

	2000	2005	2006
Roads, paved (% of total roads)	..	..	..
High-technology exports (% of manufactured exports)	13.5	8.1	..
Global links			
Merchandise trade (% of GDP)	57.8	48.3	47.5
Net barter terms of trade (2000 = 100)	100.0	154.6	..
Foreign direct investment, net inflows (BoP, current US$)	2.7 billion	15.2 billion	..
Long-term debt (DOD, current US$)	132.8 billion	204.9 billion	..
Present value of debt (% of GNI)	..	39.7	..
Total debt service (% of exports of goods, services and income)	9.9	14.6	..
Official development assistance and official aid (current US$)	1.6 billion	..	..
Workers' remittances and compensation of employees, received (US$)	1.3 billion	3.1 billion	3.3 billion

Source: World Development Indicators database, April 2007

TABLE A.3 India Data Profile

	2000	2005	2006
People			
Population, total	1.0 billion	1.1 billion	1.1 billion
Population growth (annual %)	1.7	1.4	1.4
Poverty head count ratio at national poverty line (% of population)	28.6	..	..
Life expectancy at birth, total (years)	62.9	63.5	..
Fertility rate, total (births per woman)	3.1	2.8	..
Mortality rate, infant (per 1,000 live births)	68.0	56.0	..
Mortality rate, under 5 (per 1,000)	94.0	74.0	..
Births attended by skilled health staff (% of total)	42.5	..	..
Malnutrition prevalence, weight for age (% of children under 5)	..	..	..
Immunization, measles (% of children ages 12–23 months)	56.0	58.0	..
Prevalence of HIV, total (% of population ages 15–49)	..	0.9	..
Primary completion rate, total (% of relevant age group)	75.4	89.8	..

(*Continued*)

TABLE A.3 India Data Profile (*Continued*)

	2000	2005	2006
School enrollment, primary (% gross)	98.8	119.2	..
School enrollment, secondary (% gross)	47.9	56.6	..
School enrollment, tertiary (% gross)	10.2	11.4	..
Ratio of girls to boys in primary and secondary education (%)	77.5	88.7	..
Literacy rate, adult total (% of people ages 15 and above)	..	..	..
Environment			
Surface area (sq. km)	3.3 million	3.3 million	3.3 million
Forest area (sq. km)	675.5 thousand	677.0 thousand	..
Agricultural land (% of land area)	60.8	60.6	..
CO_2 emissions (metric tons per capita)	1.1	..	..
Improved water source (% of population with access)	82.0	..	..
Improved sanitation facilities, urban (% of urban population with access)	55.0	..	..
Energy use (kg of oil equivalent per capita)	504.0	..	..
Energy imports, net (% of energy use)	18.6	..	..
Electric power consumption (kWh per capita)	402.0	..	..
Economy			
GNI, Atlas method (current US$)	456.8 billion	804.1 billion	906.5 billion
GNI per capita, Atlas method (current US$)	450.0	730.0	820.0
GDP (current US$)	460.2 billion	805.7 billion	906.3 billion
GDP growth (annual %)	4.0	9.2	9.2
Inflation, GDP deflator (annual %)	3.5	4.4	5.3
Agriculture, value added (% of GDP)	23.4	18.3	17.5
Industry, value added (% of GDP)	26.2	27.3	27.7
Services, etc., value added (% of GDP)	50.5	54.4	54.7
Exports of goods and services (% of GDP)	13.2	20.3	..
Imports of goods and services (% of GDP)	14.2	23.3	..
Gross capital formation (% of GDP)	24.8	33.4	..
Revenue, excluding grants (% of GDP)	11.9	..	..
Cash surplus/deficit (% of GDP)	–3.9	..	..
States and markets			
Time required to start a business (days)	..	71.0	35.0
Market capitalization of listed companies (% of GDP)	32.2	68.6	90.4
Military expenditure (% of GDP)	3.1	2.9	..

TABLE A.3 *(Continued)*

	2000	2005	2006
Fixed line and mobile phone subscribers (per 1,000 people)	35.4	127.7	..
Internet users (per 1,000 people)	5.4	54.8	..
Roads, paved (% of total roads)	47.5	..	..
High-technology exports (% of manufactured exports)	5.0	..	..
Global links			
Merchandise trade (% of GDP)	20.4	29.6	32.5
Net barter terms of trade (2000 = 100)	100.0	87.5	..
Foreign direct investment, net inflows (BoP, current US$)	3.6 billion	6.6 billion	..
Long-term debt (DOD, current US$)	95.6 billion	114.3 billion	..
Present value of debt (% of GNI)	..	15.9	..
Total debt service (% of exports of goods, services and income)	14.5	..	..
Official development assistance and official aid (current US$)	1.5 billion	1.7 billion	..
Workers' remittances and compensation of employees, received (US$)	12.9 billion	21.3 billion	25.7 billion

Source: World Development Indicators database, April 2007

TABLE A.4 China Data Profile

	2000	2005	2006
People			
Population, total	1.3 billion	1.3 billion	1.3 billion
Population growth (annual %)	0.7	0.6	0.6
Poverty head count ratio at national poverty line (% of population)	..	..	..
Life expectancy at birth, total (years)	70.3	71.8	..
Fertility rate, total (births per woman)	1.9	1.8	..
Mortality rate, infant (per 1,000 live births)	33.0	23.0	..
Mortality rate, under 5 (per 1,000)	41.0	27.0	..
Births attended by skilled health staff (% of total)	..	..	..
Malnutrition prevalence, weight for age (% of children under 5)	10.0	..	..
Immunization, measles (% of children ages 12–23 months)	85.0	86.0	..
Prevalence of HIV, total (% of population ages 15–49)	..	0.1	..

(Continued)

TABLE A.4 China Data Profile (*Continued*)

	2000	2005	2006
Primary completion rate, total (% of relevant age group)	..	..	..
School enrollment, primary (% gross)	..	112.8	..
School enrollment, secondary (% gross)	62.9	74.3	..
School enrollment, tertiary (% gross)	7.6	20.3	..
Ratio of girls to boys in primary and secondary education (%)	..	99.4	..
Literacy rate, adult total (% of people ages 15 and above)	90.9	..	..
Environment			
Surface area (sq. km)	9.6 million	9.6 million	9.6 million
Forest area (sq. km)	1.8 million	2.0 million	..
Agricultural land (% of land area)	58.8	..	..
CO_2 emissions (metric tons per capita)	2.2	..	..
Improved water source (% of population with access)	76.0	..	..
Improved sanitation facilities, urban (% of urban population with access)	68.0	..	..
Energy use (kg of oil equivalent per capita)	889.1	..	..
Energy imports, net (% of energy use)	2.9	..	..
Electric power consumption (kWh per capita)	992.7	..	..
Economy			
GNI, Atlas method (current US$)	1.2 trillion	2.3 trillion	2.6 trillion
GNI per capita, Atlas method (current US$)	930.0	1,740.0	2,010.0
GDP (current US$)	1.2 trillion	2.2 trillion	2.7 trillion
GDP growth (annual %)	8.4	10.2	10.7
Inflation, GDP deflator (annual %)	2.1	4.4	2.9
Agriculture, value added (% of GDP)	14.8	12.5	11.9
Industry, value added (% of GDP)	45.9	47.3	47.0
Services, etc., value added (% of GDP)	39.3	40.1	41.1
Exports of goods and services (% of GDP)	23.3	37.3	36.8
Imports of goods and services (% of GDP)	20.9	31.7	32.9
Gross capital formation (% of GDP)	35.1	43.3	40.7
Revenue, excluding grants (% of GDP)	7.1	..	..
Cash surplus/deficit (% of GDP)	..	..	..
States and markets			
Time required to start a business (days)	..	48.0	35.0
Market capitalization of listed companies (% of GDP)	48.5	34.8	90.9

TABLE A.4 (*Continued*)

	2000	2005	2006
Military expenditure (% of GDP)	1.8	2.0	..
Fixed line and mobile phone subscribers (per 1,000 people)	182.2	570.2	..
Internet users (per 1,000 people)	17.8	85.1	..
Roads, paved (% of total roads)	..	82.5	..
High-technology exports (% of manufactured exports)	18.6	30.6	..
Global links			
Merchandise trade (% of GDP)	39.6	63.4	66.0
Net barter terms of trade (2000 = 100)	100.0	86.8	..
Foreign direct investment, net inflows (BoP, current US$)	38.4 billion	79.1 billion	..
Long-term debt (DOD, current US$)	132.6 billion	133.3 billion	..
Present value of debt (% of GNI)	..	14.2	..
Total debt service (% of exports of goods, services and income)	9.3	3.1	..
Official development assistance and official aid (current US$)	1.7 billion	1.8 billion	..
Workers' remittances and compensation of employees, received (US$)	6.2 billion	22.5 billion	22.5 billion

Source: World Development Indicators database, April 2007

TABLE A.5 Korea Republic Date Profile

	2000	2005	2006
People			
Population, total	47.0 million	48.3 million	48.4 million
Population growth (annual %)	0.8	0.4	0.3
Life expectancy at birth, total (years)	75.9	77.6	..
Fertility rate, total (births per woman)	1.5	1.1	..
Mortality rate, infant (per 1,000 live births)	5.0	5.0	..
Mortality rate, under-5 (per 1,000)	5.4	5.0	..
Births attended by skilled health staff (% of total)	100.0	..	..
Immunization, measles (% of children ages 12–23 months)	95.0	99.0	..
Prevalence of HIV, total (% of population ages 15–49)	..	0.1	..
Primary completion rate, total (% of relevant age group)	95.3	104.1	101.0

(*Continued*)

TABLE A.5 Korea Republic Date Profile (*Continued*)

	2000	2005	2006
School enrollment, primary (% gross)	98.0	104.8	104.5
School enrollment, secondary (% gross)	97.6	92.9	95.7
School enrollment, tertiary (% gross)	72.6	89.9	91.0
Ratio of girls to boys in primary and secondary education (%)	100.1	99.9	99.9
Environment			
Surface area (sq. km)	99,260.0	99,260.0	99,260.0
Forest area (sq. km)	63,000.0	62,650.0	..
Agricultural land (% of land area)	20.0	19.2	..
CO_2 emissions (metric tons per capita)	9.1	..	..
Improved water source (% of population with access)	92.0	..	..
Energy use (kg of oil equivalent per capita)	4,060.9	..	..
Energy imports, net (% of energy use)	82.5	..	..
Electric power consumption (kWh per capita)	5,270.2	..	..
Economy			
GNI, Atlas method (current US$)	460.6 billion	766.9 billion	856.6 billion
GNI per capita, Atlas method (current US$)	9,800.0	15,880.0	17,690.0
GDP (current US$)	511.7 billion	791.4 billion	888.0 billion
GDP growth (annual %)	8.5	4.2	5.0
Inflation, GDP deflator (annual %)	0.7	–0.2	–0.4
Agriculture, value added (% of GDP)	4.9	3.4	3.2
Industry, value added (% of GDP)	40.7	40.3	39.6
Services, etc., value added (% of GDP)	54.4	56.3	57.2
Exports of goods and services (% of GDP)	40.8	42.3	43.2
Imports of goods and services (% of GDP)	37.7	39.9	42.1
Gross capital formation (% of GDP)	31.0	30.1	29.8
Revenue, excluding grants (% of GDP)	23.3	23.3	..
Cash surplus/deficit (% of GDP)	4.6	0.7	..
States and markets			
Time required to start a business (days)	..	22.0	22.0
Market capitalization of listed companies (% of GDP)	33.5	90.7	94.1
Military expenditure (% of GDP)	2.5	2.6	..
Fixed line and mobile phone subscribers (per 1,000 people)	1,120.6	1,285.6	..
Internet users (per 1,000 people)	405.0	683.5	..
Roads, paved (% of total roads)	..	..	..
High-technology exports (% of manufactured exports)	34.8	32.3	..

TABLE A.5 *(Continued)*

	2000	2005	2006
Global links			
Merchandise trade (% of GDP)	65.0	68.9	71.5
Net barter terms of trade (2000 = 100)	100.0	79.0	73.2
Foreign direct investment, net inflows (BoP, current US$)	9.3 billion	4.3 billion	..
Official development assistance and official aid (current US$)	−198,140,000.0	..	..
Workers' remittances and compensation of employees, received (US$)	735.0 million	847.0 million	918.0 million

Source: World Development Indicators database, April 2007

TABLE A.6 Mexico Data Profile

	2000	2005	2006
People			
Population, total	98.0 million	103.1 million	104.2 million
Population growth (annual %)	1.4	1.0	1.1
Poverty head count ratio at national poverty line (% of population)	24.2	..	..
Life expectancy at birth, total (years)	74.0	75.4	..
Fertility rate, total (births per woman)	2.4	2.1	..
Mortality rate, infant (per 1,000 live births)	25.0	22.0	..
Mortality rate, under 5 (per 1,000)	30.0	27.0	..
Births attended by skilled health staff (% of total)	..	..	..
Malnutrition prevalence, weight for age (% of children under 5)	..	..	..
Immunization, measles (% of children ages 12–23 months)	96.0	96.0	..
Prevalence of HIV, total (% of population ages 15–49)	..	0.3	..
Primary completion rate, total (% of relevant age group)	97.0	99.7	..
School enrollment, primary (% gross)	108.7	109.2	..
School enrollment, secondary (% gross)	71.8	80.2	..
School enrollment, tertiary (% gross)	19.4	24.0	..
Ratio of girls to boys in primary and secondary education (%)	99.6	101.5	..
Literacy rate, adult total (% of people ages 15 and above)	90.5	91.6	..

(Continued)

TABLE A.6 Mexico Data Profile (*Continued*)

	2000	2005	2006
Environment			
Surface area (sq. km)	2.0 million	2.0 million	2.0 million
Forest area (sq. km)	655.4 thousand	642.4 thousand	..
Agricultural land (% of land area)	56.2	..	..
CO_2 emissions (metric tons per capita)	4.0	..	..
Improved water source (% of population with access)	93.0	..	..
Improved sanitation facilities, urban (% of urban population with access)	88.0	..	..
Energy use (kg of oil equivalent per capita)	1,534.9	..	..
Energy imports, net (% of energy use)	−50.4	..	..
Electric power consumption (kWh per capita)	1,794.6	..	..
Economy			
GNI, Atlas method (current US$)	500.9 billion	752.8 billion	820.3 billion
GNI per capita, Atlas method (current US$)	5,110.0	7,300.0	7,870.0
GDP (current US$)	581.4 billion	767.7 billion	839.2 billion
GDP growth (annual %)	6.6	2.8	4.8
Inflation, GDP deflator (annual %)	12.1	5.5	4.5
Agriculture, value added (% of GDP)	4.2	3.8	3.9
Industry, value added (% of GDP)	28.0	26.0	26.7
Services, etc., value added (% of GDP)	67.8	70.2	69.4
Exports of goods and services (% of GDP)	30.9	30.0	31.9
Imports of goods and services (% of GDP)	32.9	31.5	33.2
Gross capital formation (% of GDP)	23.9	21.8	22.0
Revenue, excluding grants (% of GDP)	14.7	..	..
Cash surplus/deficit (% of GDP)	−1.2	..	..
States and markets			
Time required to start a business (days)	..	58.0	27.0
Market capitalization of listed companies (% of GDP)	21.5	31.1	41.5
Military expenditure (% of GDP)	0.5	0.4	..
Fixed line and mobile phone subscribers (per 1,000 people)	269.6	649.7	..
Internet users (per 1,000 people)	51.6	180.6	..
Roads, paved (% of total roads)	..	..	..
High-technology exports (% of manufactured exports)	22.4	19.6	..

TABLE A.6 *(Continued)*

	2000	2005	2006
Global links			
Merchandise trade (% of GDP)	60.0	58.1	61.8
Net barter terms of trade (2000 = 100)	100.0	103.2	..
Foreign direct investment, net inflows (BoP, current US$)	17.8 billion	18.8 billion	..
Long-term debt (DOD, current US$)	131.4 billion	160.6 billion	..
Present value of debt (% of GNI)	..	26.1	..
Total debt service (% of exports of goods, services and income)	30.4	17.2	..
Official development assistance and official aid (current US$)	−55,500,000.0	189.4 million	..
Workers' remittances and compensation of employees, received (US$)	7.5 billion	21.9 billion	24.7 billion

Source: World Development Indicators database, April 2007

APPENDIX B

World Economic Forum's Global Competitiveness Index for the Six Sizzling Markets

Raising productivity—meaning better use of available factors and resources—is the driving force behind the rates of return on investment, which in turn determine the aggregate growth rates of an economy. Thus, a more competitive economy will be one that will likely grow faster in the medium to long term.

The Global Competitive Index (GCI), ranking countries for their competitiveness, was originally developed in 2001 by Jeffrey Sachs and John McArthur. The GCI was designed using a set of factors to rate individual countries on key areas of competitiveness—the strength of their institutions and the soundness of their policies, as well as the efficient use of their resources. These factors are the result of combining hard data and survey results according to the World Economic Forum (WEF). Over the years, this index has been modified and according to the WEF in the 2004–2005 Global Competitiveness Report (Sala, Martin, and Artadi, 2004): "The GCI extends and deepens the concepts and ideas underpinning the earlier Growth Competitive Index." The GCI provides a report on the following factors, called "Economic Pillars," which, according to these researchers, are critical to driving productivity.

Nine Economic Pillars

1. Institutions
2. Infrastructure
3. Macroeconomics
4. Health and Primary Education

TABLE B.1 Six Countries and Different Phase Emphasis*

	Stage 1	Stage 2	Stage 3
China	*		
India	*		
Brazil		*	
Russia		*	
Mexico		*	
Korea			*
U.S.			*

*Countries' stages were based on per capita GDP (< $2,000, Stage 1; $3,000–$9,000, Stage 2; > $17,000, Stage 3). The scores were slightly modified based on the stage of the country.

TABLE B.2 Global Competitive Index 2006-2007

	Ranking against 125 countries	
Min 0-Max 7	GSI score	Country rank
Switzerland	5.81	1
United States	5.61	6
Korea	5.13	24
India	4.44	43
China	4.24	54
Mexico	4.18	58
Russia	4.08	62
Brazil	4.03	66

5. Higher Education
6. Market Efficiency
7. Technology Readiness
8. Business Sophistication
9. Innovation

These pillars are further classified:

Basic Requirements—Key for Economies in Early Phases of Development

1. Institutions
2. Infrastructure
3. Macroeconomy
4. Health and Primary Education

TABLE B.3 Scores and Ranking of the Six Countries on Some Significant Factors

Country	Basic*			Efficiency**			Innovation***		
	Score	Country rank	6-Country rank	Score	Country rank	6-Country rank	Score	Country rank	6-Country rank
Switzerland	6.02	5	1	5.59	2		5.99	2	
United States	5.41	27		5.66	7		5.75	4	
Korea	5.47	22	1	5	25	1	4.96	29	4
India	4.51	60	4	4.32	41	2	4.6	26	2
China	4.8	44	2	3.66	71	6	3.75	57	5
Mexico	4.61	53	3	3.91	59	4	3.8	52	4
Russia	4.43	66	5	3.9	60	5	3.55	71	6
Brazil	4.14	87	6	3.94	57	3	4.81	38	3

*Basic is measured by a composite score of country's Institution, Infrastructure, Macroeconomics, Health Care, and Primary Education ranking.

** Efficiency is measured by a composite score of country's Higher Education, Technology Readiness, and Market Efficiency ranking.

*** Innovation is measured by a composite score of country's Business Sophistication and Innovation ranking.

TABLE B.4 Business Competitiveness Ranking (BCI) of Selected Countries World Economic Forum 2007 Report

Country	2005 rank per capita PPP adjusted US$	Overall BCI rank*	BCI rank	Quality of national business environment*		Company operations and strategy ranking	
		2006	2001	2006	2001	2006	2001
United States	41,399	1	1	1	2	1	1
Korea	20,590	25	27	29	27	22	27
India	3,344	27	38	27	36	25	41
China	7,204	64	49	65	49	69	46
Mexico	10,186	57	51	56	51	42	45
Russia	11,041	79	58	77	57	78	62
Brazil	8,584	55	34	58	37	38	28

*Based on a total of 121 countries.

Efficiency Enhancers—Key for Economies in the Middle Phase

5. Higher Education
6. Market Efficiency
7. Technological Readiness

Innovation—Key for Economies in Advanced Phase

8. Business Sophistication
9. Innovation

Although all nine pillars are important for most economies, there is a need for the basic requirements to be substantially complete to move the economy forward. Accordingly, the WEF thinks it reasonable to divide the countries and weight these factors according to their stage of development.

APPENDIX C

Governance Indicators

Appendix C provides the reader with information regarding each country's status regarding political stability, government effectiveness, rule of law, and control of corruption. They are intended to assist readers in researching the legal and political framework of each country.

TABLE C.1 Brazil Governance Indicators

Governance indicator	Sources	Year	Percentile rank (0-100)	Governance score (−2.5 to +2.5)	Standard error
Voice and Accountability	14	2006	58.7	0.37	0.15
	10	2002	56.3	0.27	0.17
	7	1998	56.7	0.26	0.23
Political Stability	10	2006	43.3	−0.09	0.22
	9	2002	39.4	−0.18	0.22
	6	1998	28.8	−0.46	0.24
Government Effectiveness	14	2006	52.1	−0.11	0.16
	12	2002	56.4	−0.1	0.16
	8	1998	55	−0.1	0.15
Regulatory Quality	11	2006	54.1	0	0.18
	10	2002	60	0.22	0.19
	8	1998	62	0.37	0.26
Rule of Law	18	2006	41.4	−0.48	0.13
	15	2002	45.7	−0.34	0.13
	12	1998	47.6	−0.26	0.16
Control of Corruption	14	2006	47.1	−0.33	0.15
	11	2002	54.4	−0.09	0.15
	10	1998	57.8	0	0.17

TABLE C.2 Russia Governance Indicators

Governance indicator	Sources	Year	Percentile rank (0–100)	Governance score (−2.5 to +2.5)	Standard error
Voice and Accountability	14	2006	24	−0.87	0.13
	10	2002	39.9	−0.35	0.16
	6	1998	32.2	−0.57	0.23
Political Stability	10	2006	23.6	0.74	0.22
	9	2002	27.9	0.6	0.22
	6	1998	20.7	−0.84	0.24
Government Effectiveness	13	2006	37.9	−0.43	0.16
	12	2002	46.4	−0.3	0.16
	8	1998	38.4	−0.45	0.15
Regulatory Quality	12	2006	33.7	−0.45	0.17
	12	2002	36.1	−0.44	0.18
	9	1998	29.3	−0.46	0.25
Rule of Law	19	2006	19	−0.91	0.12
	16	2002	21.4	−0.88	0.13
	12	1998	21.4	−0.85	15
Control of Corruption	16	2006	24.3	−0.76	0.12
	12	2002	20.4	−0.92	0.13
	10	1998	16.5	0.92	0.15

TABLE C.3 India Governance Indicators

Governance indicator	Sources	Year	Percentile rank (0–100)	Governance score (−2.5 to +2.5)	Standard error
Voice and Accountability	13	2006	58.2	0.35	0.15
	9	2002	59.1	+0.40	0.17
	6	1998	58.2	0.34	0.23
Political Stability	10	2006	22.1	−0.84	0.22
	9	2002	17.8	−1.01	0.22
	6	1998	21.2	−0.83	0.24
Government Effectiveness	13	2006	54	−0.04	0.16
	11	2002	55.5	−0.11	0.16
	8	1998	53.1	−0.16	0.15
Regulatory Quality	11	2006	48.3	−0.15	0.18
	10	2002	41.5	−0.35	0.19
	8	1998	34.6	−0.28	0.26
Rule of Law	17	2006	57.1	0.17	0.13
	14	2002	53.3	−0.02	0.13
	11	1998	58.1	0.15	0.16
Control of Corruption	15	2006	52.9	−0.21	0.13
	11	2002	42.2	−0.41	0.14
	10	1998	47.6	−0.27	0.15

TABLE C.4 China Governance Indicators

Governance indicator	Sources	Year	Percentile rank (0–100)	Governance score (−2.5 to +2.5)	Standard error
Voice and Accountability	11	2006	4.8	−1.66	0.15
	9	2002	9.1	−1.4	0.17
	6	1998	10.1	−1.39	0.23
Political Stability	10	2006	33.2	−0.37	0.22
	9	2002	38.5	−0.21	0.22
	6	1998	41.8	−0.09	0.24
Government Effectiveness	12	2006	55.5	−0.01	0.16
	11	2002	60.2	0.01	0.16
	8	1998	48.3	−0.22	0.15
Regulatory Quality	11	2006	46.3	−0.19	0.18
	10	2002	31.7	−0.56	0.19
	8	1998	48.8	0.09	0.26
Rule of Law	16	2006	45.2	−0.4	0.13
	14	2002	43.8	−0.36	0.13
	11	1998	41	−0.4	0.16
Control of Corruption	13	2006	37.9	−0.53	0.14
	11	2002	42.7	−0.4	0.14
	10	1998	52.4	−0.22	0.15

TABLE C.5 Korea Governance Indicators

Governance indicator	Sources	Year	Percentile rank (0–100)	Governance score (−2.5 to +2.5)	Standard error
Voice and Accountability	11	2006	70.7	0.71	0.17
	9	2002	71.2	0.77	0.17
	6	1998	66.8	0.63	0.23
Political Stability	10	2006	60.1	42	0.22
	9	2002	55.8	0.31	0.22
	6	1998	47.6	0.07	0.24
Government Effectiveness	12	2006	82.9	1.05	0.16
	11	2002	81	0.95	0.16
	8	1998	66.8	0.41	0.15
Regulatory Quality	10	2006	70.7	0.7	0.18
	10	2002	74.6	0.76	0.19
	8	1998	63.4	0.4	0.26
Rule of Law	15	2006	72.9	0.72	0.13
	14	2002	75.2	0.79	0.13
	11	1998	71.4	0.69	0.16
Control of Corruption	13	2006	64.6	0.31	0.14
	11	2002	66.5	0.33	0.14
	10	1998	59.2	0.07	0.15

TABLE C.6 Mexico Governance Indicators

Governance indicator	Sources	Year	Percentile rank (0–100)	Governance score (−2.5 to +2.5)	Standard error
Voice and Accountability	14	2006	52.4	0.06	0.15
	10	2002	55.3	0.25	0.17
	7	1998	49	−0.05	0.23
Political Stability	10	2006	32.7	−0.4	0.22
	9	2002	46.2	0.02	0.22
	6	1998	26.4	−0.50	0.24
Government Effectiveness	14	2006	60.7	0.16	0.16
	12	2002	65.9	0.31	0.16
	8	1998	64.9	0.34	0.15
Regulatory Quality	11	2006	63.4	0.43	0.18
	10	2002	65.9	+0.48	0.19
	8	1998	71.2	0.67	0.26
Rule of Law	18	2006	40.5	−0.49	0.13
	15	2002	42.9	0	0.13
	12	1998	35.7	−0.51	0.16
Control of Corruption	15	2006	46.6	−0.35	0.14
	11	2002	47.1	−0.31	0.15
	10	1998	39.9	−0.47	0.17

APPENDIX D

American Depositary Receipts (ADRs)

The listing of American Depositary Receipts are provided for each of the six countries for those readers who may be interested in learning about these foreign companies that are traded on U.S. stock exchanges. In order to better understand these tables, please refer to the abbreviations listed below.

Key to Abbreviations

NYSE	New York Stock Exchange
NASDAQ	National Association of Securities Dealers Automated Quotation (system)
PORT	Private Offerings, Resales and Trading through Automated Linkages
OTC	Over the Counter
LUSE	Luxembourg Stock Exchange
American	American Stock Exchange
BSE	Bombay Stock Exchange
Dubai	Dubai International Financial Exchange
London	London Stock Exchange
Singapore	Singapore Stock Exchange

TABLE D.1 Brazil ADRs

Company name	Symbol	CUSIP #	Exchange	Industry	Depository bank
AES Eletropaulo - 144A	EPUMI	286203104	PORT	Electricity	MGT
AES Eletropaulo - Reg. S	—	286203203	—	Electricity	MGT
AES Tiete - Com	AESAY	00808P207	OTC	Electricity	BNY
AES Tiete - Pref	AESYY	00808P108	OTC	Electricity	BNY
Agra Empreendimentos Imobiliarios - 144A	AGRAL	00849G109	PORT	Real Estate	BNY
Agra Empreendimentos Imobiliarios - Reg. S	—	00849G208	—	Real Estate	BNY
All-Am. Lat Log - Pref - 144A	AALQY	01643R101	PORT	Industrial Transport.	BNY
All-Am. Lat Log - Pref - Reg. S	—	01643R309	—	Industrial Transport.	BNY
All-Am. Lat Log - Units - 144A	AALQL	01643R408	PORT	Industrial Transport.	BNY
All-Am. Lat Log - Units - Reg. S	—	01643R507	—	Industrial Transport.	BNY
AmBev - Com	ABV.C	20441W104	NYSE	Beverages	BNY
AmBev - Pref	ABV	20441W203	NYSE	Beverages	BNY
Anhanguera Educacional Participacoes - 144A	ANEDL	35220102	PORT	General Retailers	BNY
Anhanguera Educacional Participacoes - Reg. S	—	35220201	—	General Retailers	BNY
Aracruz Celulose	ARA	38496204	NYSE	Forestry & Paper	CIT
B2W - 144A	BCGVY	11777V109	PORT	General Retailers	BNY
B2W - Reg. S	—	11777V208	—	General Retailers	BNY
Banco Bradesco	BBD	59460303	NYSE	Banks	CIT
Banco Itau	ITU	59602201	NYSE	Banks	BNY
Bombril-Cirio	BMBBY	97929103	OTC	Household Goods	BNY
BR Malls Participacoes - 144A	BRMLL	05569B107	PORT	Real Estate	MGT

BR Malls Participacoes - Reg. S	—	05569B206	—	Real Estate	MGT
Brasil Ecodiesel - 144A	BRASXP	10552P105	PORT	Oil & Gas Producers	BNY
Brasil Ecodiesel - Reg. S	—	10552P204	—	Oil & Gas Producers	BNY
Brasil Telecom	BRP	105530109	NYSE	Fixed Line Telecom.	CIT
Brasil Telecom	BTM	10553M101	NYSE	Fixed Line Telecom.	CIT
Braskem	BAK	105532105	NYSE	Chemicals	BNY
Camargo Correa Desenvolvimento Imobiliario - 144A	CGCDY	13177M101	PORT	Real Estate	BNY
Camargo Correa Desenvolvimento Imobiliario - Reg. S	—	13177M200	—	Real Estate	BNY
Centrais Elet. de Santa Catarina-Celesc	CEDWY	15234U604	OTC	Electricity	BNY
Comp. de Transmissao-Paulista - Com	CTPTY	20441Q107	OTC	Electricity	BNY
Comp. de Transmissao-Paulista - Pref	CTPZY	20441Q206	OTC	Electricity	BNY
Comp. Energetica de Sao Paulo-CESP - Com	CSQSY	20440P308	OTC	Electricity	BNY
Comp. Energetica de Sao Paulo-CESP - Pref	CESQY	20440P407	OTC	Electricity	BNY
Comp. Paranaense de Energia-COPEL - Com	ELPVY	20441B308	OTC	Electricity	BNY
Comp. Paranaense de Energia-COPEL - Pref	ELP	20441B407	NYSE	Electricity	BNY
Companhia Brasileira de Distribuicao-CBD	CBD	20440T201	NYSE	Food & Drug Retailers	BNY
Companhia de Tecidos Norte de Minas	CDDMY	20440K309	OTC	Personal Goods	MGT
Companhia Energetica de Minas Gerais - CEMIG	CIG	204409882	NYSE	Electricity	CIT
Companhia Energetica de Minas Gerais-CEMIG	CIG	204409601	NYSE	Electricity	CIT
Companhia Siderurgica Nacional-CSN	SID	20440W105	NYSE	Industrial Metals	MGT
Companhia Vale do Rio Doce-CVRD - Com	RIO	204412209	NYSE	Mining	MGT
Companhia Vale do Rio Doce-CVRD - Pref	RIO-P	204412100	NYSE	Mining	MGT
Contax Participacoes - Pref	CTXNY	21076X102	OTC	Support Services	BNY

(Continued)

TABLE D.1 Brazil ADRs (*Continued*)

Company name	Symbol	CUSIP #	Exchange	Industry	Depository bank
Copasa - 144A	CDSDYPS	20441H107	PORT	Gas, H_2O & Multiutility	BNY
Copasa - Reg. S	—	20441H206	—	Gas, H_2O & Multiutility	BNY
CPFL Energia	CPL	126153105	NYSE	Electricity	BNY
Cremer - 144A	CERAL	225566108	PORT	HealthCare Equip. & Ser.	BNY
Cremer - Reg. S	—	225566207	—	HealthCare Equip. & Ser.	BNY
CSU Cardsystem - 144A	CSURY	126403104	PORT	General Finance	BNY
CSU Cardsystem - Reg. S	—	126403203	—	General Finance	BNY
Cyrela Brazil Realty - 144A	CYRAY	23282C104	PORT	Real Estate	BNY
Cyrela Brazil Realty - Com	CYRBY	23282C401	OTC	Real Estate	BNY
Cyrela Brazil Realty - Reg. S	—	23282C203	—	Real Estate	BNY
Cyrela Commercial Properties	CYRLY	23283A305	OTC	Real Estate	BNY
Cyrela Commercial Prprts - 144A	N/A	23283A107	PORT	Real Estate	BNY
Cyrela Commercial Prpts - Reg. S	—	23283A206	—	Real Estate	BNY
Diagnosticos da America - 144A	DAMRY	25246T107	PORT	HealthCare Equip. & Ser.	MGT
Diagnosticos da America - Reg. S	—	25246T206	—	HealthCare Equip. & Ser.	MGT
Duke Energy - Com	DEIWY	264398108	OTC	Electricity	BNY
Duke Energy - Pref	DEIPY	264398207	OTC	Electricity	BNY
Eletrobras-Centrais Eletricas Brasileiras	CAIGY	15234Q108	OTC	Electricity	MGT
Eletrobras-Centrais Eletricas Brasileiras - Ord	CAIFY	15234Q207	OTC	Electricity	MGT
Embraer	ERJ	29081M102	NYSE	Aerospace & Defense	MGT
Eucatex SA Industria e Comercio	ECTXY	297892101	OTC	Food & Drug Retailers	CIT
Fabrica de Produtos Alimenticios Vigor	SFPVY	78386Q102	OTC	Food Producers	BNY

Gafisa	GFA	362607301	NYSE	Household Goods	CIT
Gerdau	GGB	373737105	NYSE	Industrial Metals	BNY
Globex Utilidades-Pref	GBXPY	37957U207	OTC	General Retailers	BNY
Gol Linhas Aereas Inteligentes	GOL	38045R107	NYSE	Travel & Leisure	BNY
Inpar - 144A	INAAL	45776B201	PORT	Real Estate	BNY
Inpar - Reg. S	—	45776B300	—	Real Estate	BNY
Iochpe-Maxion	IOCJY	461865107	OTC	Automobiles & Parts	BNY
JHSF Participacoes - 144A	JHSFY	46619F102	PORT	Real Estate	BNY
JHSF Participacoes - Reg. S	—	46619F201	—	Real Estate	BNY
Klabin	KLBAY	49834M100	OTC	General Industrials	BNY
Medial Saude - 144A	MEDVY	58447H101	PORT	HealthCare Equip. & Ser.	BNY
Medial Saude - Reg. S	—	58447H200	—	HealthCare Equip. & Ser.	BNY
MMX Mineracao e Metalicos	MMXMY	6.07E+106	OTC	Mining	BNY
Net Servicos de Comunicacao	NETC	64109T201	NASDAQ	Media	MGT
Obrascon Huarte Lain Brasil - 144A	OHLBFPYP	674444104	PORT	Construct. & Materials	BNY
Obrascon Huarte Lain Brasil - Reg. S	—	674444203	—	Construct. & Materials	BNY
Paranapanema - Pref	PNPPY	40050K100	OTC	Industrial Metals	BNY
Perdigao	PDA	71361V303	NYSE	Food Producers	BNY
Petroleo Brasileiro - Com	PBR	71654V408	NYSE	Oil & Gas Producers	MGT
Petroleo Brasileiro - Pref	PBR/A	71654V101	NYSE	Oil & Gas Producers	MGT
Redecard	—	75734J202	—	Electron. & Electric Eq.	CIT
Redecard	REDRP	75734J103	PORT	Electron. & Electric Eq.	CIT

(Continued)

TABLE D.1 Brazil ADRs (*Continued*)

Company name	Symbol	CUSIP #	Exchange	Industry	Depository bank
Rossi Residencial	RSRZY	778434209	OTC	Household Goods	BNY
SABESP	SBS	20441A102	NYSE	Gas, H_2O & Multiutility	BNY
Sadia	SDA	786326108	NYSE	Food Producers	BNY
Santos Brasil - 144A	SBRFI	803013101	PORT	Industrial Transport.	BNY
Santos Brasil - Reg. S	—	803013200	—	Industrial Transport.	BNY
Sao Carlos Empreendimentos e Participacoes - 144A	SAOCEPYP	80304R105	PORT	Real Estate	BNY
Sao Carlos Empreendimentos e Participacoes - Reg. S	—	80304R204	—	Real Estate	BNY
Saraiva - 144A	SVLOL	803122308	PORT	Media	BNY
Saraiva - Com	SVLOY	803122100	OTC	Media	BNY
Saraiva - Pref	SVLSY	803122209	OTC	Media	BNY
Saraiva - Reg. S	—	803122407	—	Media	BNY
Suzano Papel e Celulose	SUZBY	86959K105	OTC	Forestry & Paper	BNY
Suzano Petroquimica	SUZPY	86959M101	OTC	Chemicals	BNY
TAM	TAM	87484D103	NYSE	Travel & Leisure	MGT
Tecnisa - 144A	TNSZY	87875P103	PORT	Real Estate	BNY
Tecnisa - Reg. S	—	87875P202	—	Real Estate	BNY
Tele Norte Celular	TCN	87924Y105	NYSE	Mobile Telecom.	BNY
Tele Norte Leste	TNE	879246106	NYSE	Fixed Line Telecom.	BNY
Telecomunicacoes de Sao Paulo	TSP	87929A102	NYSE	Fixed Line Telecom.	BNY
Telemig Celular	TMB	8.79E+109	NYSE	Mobile Telecom.	BNY
TIM Participacoes	TSU	88706P106	NYSE	Mobile Telecom.	MGT

Tractebel - Com	TBLEY	892360108	OTC	Electricity	BNY
Tractebel - Pref	TBLGY	892360306	OTC	Electricity	BNY
Triunfo Participacoes e Investimentos - 144A	TPISA	87262A107	PORT	General Finance	BNY
Triunfo Participacoes e Investimentos - Reg. S	—	87262A206	—	General Finance	BNY
Ultrapar	UGP	90400P101	NYSE	Chemicals	BNY
Unibanco-Uniao de Bancos Brasileiros	UBB	9.05E+111	NYSE	Banks	BNY
Usiminas - 144A	USDMY	917302101	PORT	Industrial Metals	BNY
Usiminas - Com - 144A	USDML	917302309	PORT	Industrial Metals	BNY
Usiminas - Com - Reg. S	—	917302408	—	Industrial Metals	BNY
Usiminas-Usinas Sid. de Minas Gerais	USNZY	917302200	OTC	Industrial Metals	BNY
Vivo	VIV	92855S101	NYSE	Mobile Telecom.	BNY
Votorantim Celulose e Papel	VCP	92906P106	NYSE	Forestry & Paper	BNY

Source for data: Bank of New York and JP Morgan database of ADRs

TABLE D.2 Russia ADRs

Company name	Symbol	CUSIP #	Exchange	Industry	Depository bank
Aeroflot - 144A	AETG	7771108	PORT	Industrial Transport.	DB
Aeroflot - Reg. S	—	7771207	—	Industrial Transport.	DB
AFI Development - 144A	P00106J101	00106J101	PORT	Real Estate	BNY
AFI Development - Reg. S	AFID	00106J200	London Exchange	Real Estate	BNY
Akrikhin - Ord - 144A	AKRPYP	00972R104	PORT	Pharma. & Biotech.	BNY
Akrikhin - Ord - Reg. S	—	00972R401	—	Pharma. & Biotech.	BNY
Akrikhin - Pref - 144A	AKRPPP	00972R203	PORT	Pharma. & Biotech.	BNY
Akrikhin - Pref - Reg. S	—	00972R500	—	Pharma. & Biotech.	BNY
Akrikhin - Units - 144A	AKRPUP	00972R302	PORT	Pharma. & Biotech.	BNY
Akrikhin - Units - Reg. S	—	00972R609	—	Pharma. & Biotech.	BNY
Amtel-Vredestein	AMV	03235R101	London	Automobiles & Parts	BNY
Avtovaz - Reg. S	—	05453R101	—	Automobiles & Parts	BNY
Bank Vozrozhdeniye	BKVZY	65453102	OTC	Banks	BNY
Bashinformsvyaz	BHFZY	06983P102	OTC	Fixed Line Telecom.	BNY
Buryatzoloto	BYZJY	12315Q107	OTC	Mining	BNY
Central Telecommunication	CRMUY	15548M108	OTC	Fixed Line Telecom.	MGT
Chelyabinsk Zinc Plant - 144A	CZZPGNP16	163523103	PORT	Mining	BNY
Chelyabinsk Zinc Plant - Reg. S	CHZN	163523202	London	Mining	BNY
Cherkizovo - 144A	OJSZY	68371H100	PORT	Food Producers	MGT
Cherkizovo - Reg. S	CHE.GB	68371H209	London	Food Producers	MGT

Comstar United TeleSystem - 144A	JSTKY	47972P109	PORT	Mobile Telecom.	DB
Comstar United TeleSystem - Reg. S	CMST	47972P208	London	Mobile Telecom.	DB
Concern Kalina	CCKLY	678128109	OTC	Personal Goods	DB
Energosbyt Rostovenergo - Com	—	29267W106	—	Electricity	BNY
Energosbyt Rostovenergo - Pref	—	29267W205	—	Electricity	BNY
Evraz Group - 144A	EVRASAYP	30050A103	PORT	Industrial Metals	BNY
Evraz Group - Reg. S	EVR	30050A202	London	Industrial Metals	BNY
Far East Shipping - Reg. S	—	30732K107	—	IndustrialTransport.	BNY
Far East Telecommunications	FEEOY	30732Q104	OTC	Fixed Line Telecom.	MGT
Gazprom	OGZPY	368287207	OTC	Oil & Gas Producers	BNY
Gazprom - 144A	RADGYP	368287108	PORT	Oil & Gas Producers	BNY
Gazprom - Reg. S	—	368287306	—	Oil & Gas Producers	BNY
Gazprom Neft	GZPFY	36829G107	OTC	Oil & Gas Producers	BNY
GUM (Torgovy Dom)	GUMRY	37379104	OTC	General Retailers	BNY
IBS Group Holding - Reg. S	—	450939103	—	Tech.Hardware & Equip.	BNY
Integra Group - 144A	N/A	45822B106	PORT	Oil & Gas Producers	MGT
Integra Group - Reg. S	INTE.GB	45822B205	London	Oil & Gas Producers	MGT
IRKUT	IRKTY	46271W104	OTC	Aerospace & Defense	BNY
Irkutskenergo	IKSGY	462714106	OTC	Electricity	BNY

(Continued)

TABLE D.2 Russia ADRs (*Continued*)

Company name	Symbol	CUSIP #	Exchange	Industry	Depository bank
Joint Stock Company Open Investments	—	47972M106	—	General Finance	BNY
JSC POLYMETAL - 144A	POYMY	731789103	PORT	Mining	DB
JSC POLYMETAL - Reg. S	PMTL	731789202	London	Mining	DB
JSC Sitronics - 144A	JSCSL	46630F107	PORT	Tech. Hardware & Equip.	DB
JSC Sitronics - Reg. S	SITR	46630F206	London	Tech. Hardware & Equip.	DB
JSC TGK-5 - Reg. S	—	881459101	—	Electricity	BNY
Kamchatskenergo - Reg. S	—	483556106	—	Electricity	DB
Kazanorgsintez	AKZGY	48666H106	OTC	Chemicals	BNY
Kostromskaya Gres - Reg. S	—	67418R204	—	Electricity	DB
Kuzbassenergo	KZBGY	501500102	OTC	Electricity	BNY
Lenenergo - Reg. S	—	526028105	—	Electricity	BNY
LOMO - Reg. S	—	541681102	—	Health Care Equip. & Ser.	BNY
LUKOIL	LUKOY	677862104	OTC	Oil & Gas Producers	BNY
LUKOIL - 144A	JSCLYP	677862203	PORT	Oil & Gas Producers	BNY
LUKOIL - 144A	LUKEYP	549874105	PORT	Oil & Gas Producers	BNY
LUKOIL - 144A	OAOLYP	677862807	PORT	Oil & Gas Producers	BNY
LUKOIL - Reg. S	LKOB	549874204	London	Oil & Gas Producers	BNY
LUKOIL - Reg. S	LKOR	677862872	London	Oil & Gas Producers	BNY
LUKOIL - Reg. S Interim	—	677862864	—	Oil & Gas Producers	BNY
Magnitogorsk Iron & Steel Works - 144A	P559189105	559189105	PORT	Industrial Metals	BNY
Magnitogorsk Iron & Steel Works - Reg. S	MMK	559189204	London	Industrial Metals	BNY

Mechel Steel	MTL	583840103	NYSE	Industrial Metals	DB
MINFIN-5/14/2008 - 144A	MFINY08	783064AD0	PORT	General Finance	BNY
MINFIN-5/14/2008 - Reg. S	—	783064AH1	—	General Finance	BNY
MINFIN-5/14/2011 - 144A	MFINY11	783064AL2	PORT	General Finance	BNY
MINFIN-5/14/2011 - Reg. S	—	783064AM0	—	General Finance	BNY
Mobile TeleSystems	MBT	607409109	NYSE	Mobile Telecom.	MGT
Mobile TeleSystems - 144A	MT144A	607409208	PORT	Mobile Telecom.	BNY
Mobile TeleSystems - Reg. S	—	607409307	—	Mobile Telecom.	BNY
Moscow Candy Factory Red October - Reg. S	—	619460108	—	Food Producers	BNY
Moscow City Telephone Network	MWCTY	61946A106	OTC	Fixed Line Telecom.	BNY
Mosenergo	AOMOY	37376308	OTC	Electricity	BNY
Neftynaya Companiya-Rosneft - 144A	OCRNL	67812M108	PORT	Oil & Gas Producers	MGT
Neftynaya Companiya-Rosneft - Reg. S	ROSN.GB	67812M207	London	Oil & Gas Producers	MGT
Nizhnekamskneftekhim	ONKMY	654918101	OTC	Chemicals	BNY
Nizhnekamskshina	NZKMY	65486P100	OTC	Automobiles & Parts	BNY
Norilsk Nickel	NILSY	46626D108	OTC	Industrial Metals	BNY
North-West Telecom	NWTEY	663316107	OTC	Fixed Line Telecom.	MGT
Novatek - 144A	NVATY	669888208	PORT	Oil & Gas Producers	DB
Novatek - Reg. S	NVTK	669888109	London	Oil & Gas Producers	DB
Novolipetsk Steel-NLMK - 144A	NLMK	6.70E+208	London	Industrial Metals	DB
Novolipetsk Steel-NLMK - 144A	NISQY	6.70E+109	PORT	Industrial Metals	DB
NTV - 144A	NTVBYP	67019G102	PORT	Media	BNY

(Continued)

TABLE D.2 Russia ADRs (*Continued*)

Company name	Symbol	CUSIP #	Exchange	Industry	Depository bank
OGK-3 - Reg. S	—	46627Y101	—	Electricity	DB
OGK-5 - Reg. S	—	316733104	—	Electricity	BNY
Pharmacy Chain 36.6 - Reg. S	—	7171EM108	—	Food & Drug Retailers	BNY
Pharmstandard - 144A	P717140107	717140107	PORT	Pharma. & Biotech.	BNY
Pharmstandard - Reg. S	PHST LI	717140206	London	Pharma. & Biotech.	BNY
PIK Group - 144A	N/A	69338N107	PORT	Real Estate	DB
PIK Group - Reg. S	PIK	69338N206	London	Real Estate	DB
Polyus Gold	OPYGY	678129107	OTC	Industrial Metals	BNY
Primorsk Shipping Corporation	APKSY	741625107	OTC	IndustrialTransport.	BNY
RBC Information Systems	RINFY	75523Q102	OTC	Media	BNY
Rosneftegazstroy	RNGZY	778200204	OTC	Oil & Gas Producers	BNY
Rostelecom	ROS	778529107	NYSE	Fixed Line Telecom.	MGT
Rostovelectrosvyaz	RVESY	778530105	OTC	Electricity	MGT
Rostovenergo	RTVGY	77853Q108	OTC	Electricity	BNY
Rostovenergo - Pref	RTVPY	77853Q207	OTC	Electricity	BNY
RTM - Reg. S	—	74975X103	—	Real Estate	CIT
Samaraenergo	SMRGY	79586P100	OTC	Electricity	BNY
Samaraenergo - Pref	SMRJY	79586P209	OTC	Electricity	BNY
Sberbank Rossii - Reg. S	—	80529Q205	—	Banks	DB
Seversky Tube Works	STBWY	818146102	OTC	Industrial Metals	BNY

Severstal - 144A	SVJTL	818150104	PORT	Industrial Metals	DB
Severstal - Reg. S	—	818150203	—	Industrial Metals	DB
Severstal - Reg. S	SVST	818150302	London	Industrial Metals	DB
Severstal Auto - Reg. S	—	818148108	—	Automobiles & Parts	DB
Sibirtelecom	SBTLY	825735103	OTC	Fixed Line Telecom.	MGT
Sistema - 144A	JSFCY	48122U105	PORT	Support Services	DB
Sistema - Reg. S	SSA	48122U204	London	Support Services	DB
Sistema-Hals - 144A	SHNP98277	82977M108	PORT	Real Estate	BNY
Sistema-Hals - Reg. S	HALS	82977M207	London	Real Estate	BNY
Slavneft-Megionneftegaz - Ord - Reg. S	—	831209101	—	Oil & Gas Producers	BNY
Slavneft-Megionneftegaz - Pref - Reg. S	—	831209200	—	Oil & Gas Producers	BNY
Southern Telecommunications	STJSY	843899105	OTC	Mobile Telecom.	MGT
Sun Interbrew - Class A - 144A	SIBWYPA	86677C104	PORT	Beverages	BNY
Sun Interbrew - Class A - Euro Reg. S	—	86677C401	LUSE	Beverages	BNY
Sun Interbrew - Class A - Reg. S	—	86677C302	LUSE	Beverages	BNY
Sun Interbrew - Class B - 144A	SUNBYP	86677C203	PORT	Beverages	BNY
Sun Interbrew - Class B - Reg. S	—	86677C708	LUSE	Beverages	BNY
Surgutneftegaz	SGTZY	868861204	OTC	Oil & Gas Producers	BNY
Surgutneftegaz - Pref	SGTPY	868861105	OTC	Oil & Gas Producers	BNY
Tatneft - 144A	NONE	670831106	PORT	Oil & Gas Producers	BNY
Tatneft - Reg. S	ATAD	670831205	London	Oil & Gas Producers	BNY
TMK - 144A	OATGPD298	87260R102	PORT	Industrial Metals	BNY

(Continued)

TABLE D.2 Russia ADRs (*Continued*)

Company name	Symbol	CUSIP #	Exchange	Industry	Depository bank
TMK - Reg. S	TMKS	87260R201	London	Industrial Metals	BNY
TNT-Teleset - 144A	TNTEYP	88874M109	PORT	Leisure Goods	BNY
Trading House TsUM	TDHSY	892681107	OTC	General Retailers	BNY
UHM	UHMVY	910921303	OTC	Industrial Engineer.	BNY
UHM - 144A	UHMUY	910921105	PORT	Industrial Engineer.	BNY
UHM - Reg. S	—	910921204	—	Industrial Engineer.	BNY
Unified Energy Systems of Russia	USERY	904688108	OTC	Electricity	DB
Unified Energy Systems of Russia - Pref	USEPY	904688405	OTC	Electricity	DB
Unified Energy Systems of Russia - Reg. S	—	904688603	—	Electricity	DB
Unified Energy Systems of Russia - Reg. S	—	904688207	—	Electricity	BNY
Uralsvyazinform	UVYPY	916887201	OTC	Fixed Line Telecom.	MGT
Uralsvyazinform	UVYZY	916887102	OTC	Fixed Line Telecom.	MGT
Utair	UTARY	917577108	OTC	IndustrialTransport.	BNY
Vimpel Communications	VIP	68370R109	NYSE	Mobile Telecom.	BNY
Vimpelcom - Reg. S	—	68370R307	—	Mobile Telecom.	BNY
VolgaTelecom	VLGAY	928660109	OTC	Fixed Line Telecom.	MGT
Volzhskoye Oil Tanker Ship.-Volgotanker - Reg. S	—	928863109	—	IndustrialTransport.	BNY
VTB Bank - 144A	JSCVL	46630Q103	PORT	Banks	BNY
VTB Bank - Reg. S	VTBR	46630Q202	London	Banks	BNY
Wimm-Bill-Dann Foods	WBD	97263M109	NYSE	Food Producers	DB
Wimm-Bill-Dann Foods - Reg. S	—	97263M208	—	Food Producers	DB
X5 Retail Group - 144A	XFRGY	9.84E+110	PORT	General Retailers	BNY
X5 Retail Group - Reg. S	XFRGY	9.84E+209	London	General Retailers	BNY
Yukos	YUKOY	98849W108	OTC	Oil & Gas Producers	DB
Yukos - Reg. S	—	98849W207	—	Oil & Gas Producers	DB

Source for data: Bank of New York and JP Morgan database of ADRs

TABLE D.3 India ADRs

Company name	Symbol	CUSIP #	Exchange	Industry	Depository bank
ACC LTD	AMCD LI	00429N102	PORT	Construct. & Materials	CIT
Aditya Birla Nuvo LTD	ABNPP	7027105	PORT	Personal Goods	CIT
Aftek Infosys - Reg. S	—	00831M106	—	Software & Computer Ser.	DB
Alps Industries - Reg. S	—	02109V107	LUSE	Personal Goods	BNY
Amtek Auto - Reg. S	AMKD	03233Q105	London	Automobiles & Parts	BNY
Apollo Hospitals Enterprise - 144A	AHELYP05	37608106	PORT	HealthCare Equip. & Ser.	BNY
Apollo Hospitals Enterprise - Reg. S	—	37608205	LUSE	HealthCare Equip. & Ser.	BNY
Aptech (Lux Listed) - Reg. S	—	03833M306	LUSE	Software & Computer Ser.	DB
Aptech (Unlisted) - Reg. S	—	03833M207	—	Software & Computer Ser.	DB
Arvind Mills - 144A	ARVMY	43348101	PORT	Personal Goods	MGT
Arvind Mills - Reg. S	—	Y02047200	—	Personal Goods	MGT
Axis Bank - 144A	UTIBFP44	05462W307	PORT	Banks	BNY
Axis Bank - Reg. S	—	05462W109	—	Banks	BNY
Bajaj Auto - 144A	BAJHYP	57100109	PORT	Automobiles & Parts	DB
Bajaj Auto - Reg. S	BAUD	57100208	London	Automobiles & Parts	DB
Bajaj Hindustan - Reg. S	—	05710P104	LUSE	Food Producers	CIT
Ballarpur Industries - 144A	BLPRCY	58588203	PORT	Forestry & Paper	DB
Ballarpur Indust. - Reg. S	—	58588302	—	Forestry & Paper	DB
Balrampur Chini Mills - 144A	N/A	58788100	PORT	Food Producers	BNY
Balrampur Chini Mills - Reg. S	—	58788209	LUSE	Food Producers	BNY
Bharat Forge - 144A	BFLGP	999BHA199	PORT	Industrial Metals	CIT
Bharat Hotels - Reg. S	—	88803105	—	Travel & Leisure	DB

(Continued)

TABLE D.3 India ADRs (*Continued*)

Company name	Symbol	CUSIP #	Exchange	Industry	Depository bank
BSE Dyeing & Manufact - Reg. S	—	4707559	—	Personal Goods	CIT
BSEL Infrascture Realty - Reg. S	—	11776M100	LUSE	Real Estate	BNY
Carol Info Services LTD - Reg. S	WKHTF	143708105	BSE	Pharma. & Biotech.	DB
Cat Technologies	—	148750102	LUSE	Software & Computer Ser.	DB
Centurion Bank - Reg. S	—	15642N101	LUSE	Banks	DB
Century Textiles and Indutries - 144A	CTRPP	156690109	PORT	Personal Goods	CIT
CESC - 144A	CESCYP	157128109	PORT	Electricity	BNY
CESC - Reg. S	—	Y12652148	—	Electricity	BNY
Cipla - 144A	CLYP7100	172977100	PORT	Pharma. & Biotech.	BNY
Cipla - Reg. S	—	172977209	LUSE	Pharma. & Biotech.	BNY
Core Health Care Products - 144A	CRPINAGD	21868J105	PORT	Pharma. & Biotech.	DB
Cranes Software International - Reg. S	—	224455105	LUSE	Software & Computer Ser.	BNY
Crest Communication - Reg. S	—	226064103	—	Software & Computer Ser.	DB
Crew B.O.S. Products - Reg. S	—	22652P109	LUSE	Personal Goods	BNY
Crompton Greaves - 144A	CGRVYP	227120102	PORT	Electron. & Electric Eq.	BNY
Crompton Greaves - Reg. S	CGVD	227120201	London	Electron & Electric Eq.	BNY
Cybermate Infotek - Reg. S	—	232481101	LUSE	Software & Computer Ser.	BNY
DCW - 144A	DCWFY	233160100	PORT	Chemicals	BNY
DCW - Reg. S	—	Y20245117	—	Chemicals	BNY
Dhampur Sugar Mills - 144A	DHSGY	25239R100	PORT	Food Producers	DB
Dhampur Sugar Mills - Reg. S	—	25239R209	LUSE	Food Producers	DB

Dishnet DSL - 144A	DISHN	25469Q103	PORT	Fixed Line Telecom.	CIT
Dr. Reddy's Laboratories	RDY	256135203	NYSE	Pharma. & Biotech.	MGT
Dwarikesh Sugar Industries - Reg. S	—	26740P104	—	Food Producers	BNY
E.I.D. Parry (India) - 144A	EIDPYP	268523107	PORT	Chemicals	BNY
E.I.D. Parry (India) - Reg. S	—	Y67828114	—	Chemicals	BNY
EIH - 144A	EIHMY	268525102	PORT	Travel & Leisure	BNY
EIH - Reg. S	EIHD	268525201	London	Travel & Leisure	BNY
Elder Pharmaceuticals - Reg. S	—	284502200	—	Pharma. & Biotech.	BNY
Electrosteel Castings - Reg. S	—	28616M108	—	Industrial Engineer.	CIT
Emco - Reg. S	—	290840107	LUSE	Electron. & Electric Eq.	BNY
Era Constructions (India) - Reg. S	—	29477A100	—	Real Estate	BNY
Essar Oil - Reg. S	—	29667P107	—	Oil & Gas Producers	BNY
Essar Projects - Reg. S	—	29667A100	—	Construct. & Materials	BNY
Essar Shipping - Reg. S	—	29667C106	—	Industrial Transport.	BNY
Eveready Industries India - Reg. S	—	29976W108	—	Electron. & Electric Eq.	BNY
Federal Bank - 144A	FDBAY	313162109	PORT	Banks	DB
Federal Bank - Reg. S	N/A	313162208	London	Banks	DB
Finolex Cables - 144A	FINO	317906105	PORT	Electron. & Electric Eq.	CIT
GAIL India - 144A	GAILY	36268T107	PORT	Gas, H_2O & Multiutility	DB
GAIL India - Reg. S	GAID	36268T206	London	Gas, H_2O & Multiutility	DB
Gammon India - Reg. S	—	36467M200	—	Construct. & Materials	BNY
Garden Silk Mills - Reg. S	—	Y2681N112	—	Personal Goods	BNY
Gateway Distriparks - 144A	GWDRP	36759K102	PORT	Industrial Transport.	CIT
Gateway Distriparks - Reg. S	—	36759K201	—	Industrial Transport.	CIT
Granules India - Reg. S	—	388483208	—	Pharma. & Biotech.	BNY

(Continued)

TABLE D.3 India ADRs (*Continued*)

Company name	Symbol	CUSIP #	Exchange	Industry	Depository bank
Grasim Industries	GRASM	388706400	OTC	Construct. & Materials	CIT
Grasim Industries - Reg. S	—	388706103	—	Construct. & Materials	CIT
Great Eastern Energy Corp - Reg. S	N/A	39032T106	BSE	Oil & Gas Producers	DB
Great Eastern Shipping - 144A	GESOPY	39032J405	PORT	Industrial Transport.	BNY
Great Eastern Shipping - Reg. S	—	39032J504	—	Industrial Transport.	BNY
Great Offshore - Reg. S	—	39114R101	—	Oil & Gas Producers	BNY
Gujarat Narmada Valley - 144A	GNVFYP	402044101	PORT	Chemicals	BNY
Gujarat Narmada Valley - Reg. S	—	Y29446112	—	Chemicals	BNY
GV Films - Reg. S	—	36244H102	LUSE	Media	BNY
HDFC Bank	HDB	40415F101	NYSE	Banks	MGT
Hexaware Technologies - 144A	N/A	428282107	PORT	Software & Computer Ser.	DB
Hexaware Technologies - Reg. S	HEXD	428282206	London	Software & Computer Ser.	DB
Himachal Futuristic - 144A	HFCLYP	432894103	PORT	Tech. Hardware & Equip.	BNY
Himachal Futuristic - Reg. S	—	432894202	—	Tech .Hardware & Equip.	DB
Himachal Futuristic - Reg. S	HFCD	Y3196Q111	London	Tech. Hardware & Equip.	BNY
Himatsingka Seide - 144A	HIMSYPLTD	43289Q104	PORT	Personal Goods	BNY
Himatsingka Seide - Reg. S	—	43289Q203	—	Personal Goods	BNY
Hindalco Industries - 144A	HNDCF	433064102	PORT	Industrial Metals	MGT
Hindustan Construction - Reg. S	—	433219102	LUSE	Construct. & Materials	CIT
I.T.C. - Reg. S	—	450318100	—	Tobacco	CIT
ICICI Bank	IBN	45104G104	NYSE	Banks	DB
IKF Technologies - Reg. S	—	4.50E+106	LUSE	Software & Computer Ser.	BNY
IL&FS Investsmart - 144A	ILFSYPFP	45172R107	PORT	General Finance	BNY
IL&FS Investsmart - Reg. S	—	45172R206	—	General Finance	BNY

India Cements - 144A	IAMUY	45408P503	PORT	Construct. & Materials	DB
India Cements - 144A	ICRPP	45408P107	PORT	Construct. & Materials	CIT
India Cements - Reg. S	—	Y39167112	—	Construct. & Materials	CIT
India Cements - Reg. S	—	45408P602	LUSE	Construct. & Materials	DB
Indiabulls Financial Services - 144A	IBLFY	45409R201	PORT	General Finance	DB
Indiabulls Financial Services - Reg. S	—	45409R102	LUSE	General Finance	DB
Indiabulls Financial Services - Reg. S	—	45409R300	LUSE	General Finance	DB
Indiabulls Real Estate - 144A	N/A	4.54E+105	PORT	Real Estate	DB
Indiabulls Real Estate - Reg. S	—	4.54E+204	LUSE	Real Estate	DB
Indian Hotels - 144A	IHRPP	454288101	PORT	Travel & Leisure	CIT
Indian Hotels - Reg. S	IHTD	Y3925F113	London	Travel & Leisure	CIT
Indian Petrochemicals - 144A	IPCGP	454347105	PORT	Chemicals	CIT
Indian Petrochemicals - Reg. S	—	Y39337111	—	Chemicals	CIT
Indo Rama Synthetics (India) - 144A	IRAMYP	45577Q100	PORT	Personal Goods	BNY
Indo Rama Synthetics (India) - Reg. S	—	45577Q118	—	Personal Goods	BNY
Ind-Swift Laboratories - Reg. S	—	449783109	—	Pharma. & Biotech.	DB
IndusInd Bank - Reg. S	—	455786103	LUSE	Banks	BNY
Infosys Technologies	INFY	456788108	Nasdaq	Software & Computer Ser.	DB
Ispat Industries - Reg. S	—	654554104	—	Industrial Metals	DB
Jagatjit Industries - Reg. S	—	470081100	—	Beverages	BNY
Jain Irrigation - Reg. S - EDR	—	Y42531114	—	Electron. & Electric Eq.	DB
JCT - 144A	JCCTF	466125101	PORT	Personal Goods	BNY

(Continued)

TABLE D.3 India ADRs (*Continued*)

Company name	Symbol	CUSIP #	Exchange	Industry	Depository bank
JCT - Reg. S	—	Y4435E117	—	Personal Goods	BNY
Jindal Saw - 144A	JSAWR	4.78E+206	PORT	Oil Equip., Serv. & Dist.	CIT
Jindal Saw - Reg. S	—	4.78E+305	—	Oil Equip., Serv. & Dist.	CIT
Jindal Stainless - Reg. S	—	477586200	—	Industrial Metals	CIT
JK - 144A	JKCLYP	466188109	PORT	Construct. & Materials	CIT
JK Paper - Reg. S	—	466208105	LUSE	Forestry & Paper	BNY
Jubilant Organosys - 144A	JUBEGP09	481242105	PORT	Banks	BNY
Jubilant Organosys - Reg. S	—	481242204	—	Banks	BNY
K.S. Oils	—	48269C108	—	Food Producers	CIT
Kaashyap Technologies - Reg. S	—	48282X105	LUSE	Software & Computer Ser.	BNY
KEI Industries - Reg. S	—	482468204	LUSE	Electron. & Electric Eq.	BNY
Kesoram Industries - 144A	KSRPP	492532106	PORT	Construct. & Materials	CIT
Kesoram Industries - Reg. S	—	492532205	—	Construct. & Materials	CIT
KLG Systel - Reg. S	—	498590108	LUSE	Software & Computer Ser.	BNY
Kohinoor Broadcasting	—	500231105	LUSE	Media	DB
Kotak Mahindra Bank - 144A	KMBLYD44A	50071Q101	PORT	Banks	BNY
Kotak Mahindra Bank - Reg. S	—	50071Q200	—	Banks	BNY
KRBL - Reg. S	—	482657103	LUSE	Food Producers	DB
Larsen & Toubro - 144A	LTRPP	51729V104	PORT	Industrial Engineer.	CIT
Larsen & Toubro - Reg. S	—	Y5217N118	—	Industrial Engineer.	CIT
LIC Housing Finance - 144A	LICHYP04	50186U104	PORT	General Finance	BNY

LIC Housing Finance - Reg. S	—	50186U203	—	General Finance	BNY
Lloyd Electric & Engineering - Reg. S	LLD	539373100	London	Electron. & Electric Eq.	BNY
Lyka Labs - Reg. S	—	550863104	LUSE	Pharma. & Biotech.	DB
Maars Software International - Reg. S	—	554065102	—	Software & Computer Ser.	DB
Madhucon Projects - Reg. S	—	55647P107	LUSE	Industrial Engineer.	DB
Mahanagar Telephone Nigam	MTE	559778402	NYSE	Fixed Line Telecom.	BNY
Mahindra & Mahindra - 144A	MANFFP	559832100	PORT	Industrial Engineer.	BNY
Mahindra & Mahindra - Reg. S	—	Y54164119	—	Industrial Engineer.	BNY
Mahindra Gesco Developers - Reg. S	—	559836200	—	Real Estate	BNY
Man Industries (India) - Reg. S	MAN	56164P108	Dubai	Industrial Engineer.	BNY
MARG Constructions - Reg. S	—	56656Q101	LUSE	Construct. & Materials	BNY
Mascon Global - Reg. S	—	574644100	LUSE	General Finance	DB
Mawana Sugars - 144A	MSLYY	57773F101	PORT	Food Producers	BNY
Mawana Sugars - Reg. S	—	57773F200	—	Food Producers	BNY
McDowell - Reg. S	—	91152Q206	LUSE	Beverages	DB
Micro Technologies (India) - Reg. S	—	59501G104	LUSE	Software & Computer Ser.	BNY
Morepen Laboratories - Reg. S	—	61687P106	—	Pharma. & Biotech.	BNY
MosChip Semiconductor Technology - Reg. S	—	619458102	LUSE	Tech. Hardware & Equip.	DB
Moser Baer India Ltd - Reg. S	MBI	61954P201	BSE	Tech. Hardware & Equip.	DB
Nagarjuna Construction Company - 144A	NGRJI	629726100	PORT	Construct. & Materials	DB
Nagarjuna Construction Company - Reg. S	—	629726209	LUSE	Construct. & Materials	DB
Nepc-Micon - 144A	NEPCYP	629088105	PORT	Electron. & Electric Eq.	DB
Noida Toll Bridge - Reg. S	NTBC	65527N106	London	Industrial Engineer.	DB

(Continued)

TABLE D.3 India ADRs (*Continued*)

Company name	Symbol	CUSIP #	Exchange	Industry	Depository bank
Orchid Chemicals & Pharmaceuticals - Reg. S	—	68572Y209	—	HealthCare Equip. & Ser.	CIT
ORG Informatic - Reg. S	—	6.71E+207	LUSE	Software & Computer Ser.	BNY
Oriental Hotels - Reg. S	—	Y6525B119	—	Travel & Leisure	DB
Paramount Communications - Reg. S	—	69921M102	LUSE	Fixed Line Telecom.	BNY
Patni Computer Systems	PTI	703248203	NYSE	Software & Computer Ser.	BNY
Patni Computer Systems - Reg. S	—	703248104	—	Software & Computer Ser.	BNY
Pentamedia Graphics - Reg. S	—	70963R108	—	Software & Computer Ser.	DB
Pentasoft Technologies - 144A	PNGPP	70963A105	PORT	Software & Computer Ser.	CIT
Quintant Services Private - Reg. S	—	74875M207	—	Food & Drug Retailers	DB
Rana Sugars - Reg. S	RANA	75188Q108	Dubai	Food Producers	DB
Ranbaxy Laboratories - 144A	RANYPY	751881103	PORT	Pharma. & Biotech.	BNY
Ranbaxy Laboratories - Reg. S	—	Y7187Y116	—	Pharma. & Biotech.	BNY
Rediff.com India	REDF	757479100	Nasdaq	Software & Computer Ser.	CIT
Rei Agro - 144A	REIRP	74948P104	PORT	Food & Drug Retailers	CIT
Rei Agro - Reg. S	REA	74948P203	London	Food & Drug Retailers	CIT
Reliance Capital - 144A	N/A	75945L103	PORT	General Finance	DB
Reliance Capital - Reg. S	—	75945L202	LUSE	General Finance	DB
Reliance Communications - 144A	N/A	75945T106	PORT	Mobile Telecom.	DB
Reliance Communications - Reg. S	—	75945T205	LUSE	Mobile Telecom.	DB
Reliance Energy - 144A	BSESYP	7.59E+113	PORT	Electricity	BNY
Reliance Energy - Reg. S	REYD	Y09789119	London SE	Electricity	BNY
Reliance Industries - 144A	RILYP	759470107	PORT	Chemicals	BNY
Reliance Natural Resources - 144A	N/A	75948P101	PORT	Oil & Gas Producers	DB
Reliance Natural Resources - Reg. S	—	75948P200	LUSE	Oil & Gas Producers	DB
Reliance Ports & Terminals - Reg. S	—	75950M103	—	Industrial Transport.	BNY

Reliance Utilities and Power - Reg. S	—	75953N108	—	Electricity	BNY
Rolta India - 144A	RLTAY	775790108	PORT	Tech. Hardware & Equip.	DB
Rolta India - Reg. S	RTI	775790207	London	Tech. Hardware & Equip.	DB
Ruchi Soya Industries - 144A	RCSYY	781188107	PORT	Food Producers	DB
Ruchi Soya Industries - Reg. S	—	781188206	LUSE	Food Producers	DB
Sanghi Polyesters - 144A	SPLYYP	80100P105	PORT	Chemicals	BNY
Satyam Computer Services	SAY	804098101	NYSE	Software & Computer Ser.	CIT
Shah Alloys - Reg. S	—	819013103	LUSE	Industrial Metals	BNY
Shreyas Shipping & Logistics - Reg. S	—	825540107	—	Industrial Transport.	BNY
SIEL - 144A	SIEHY	82619Y106	PORT	General Industrials	BNY
SIEL - Reg. S	SLGD	82619Y205	London	General Industrials	BNY
SIFY	SIFY	82655M107	Nasdaq	Software & Computer Ser.	CIT
Silverline Technologies	SLTTY	828408401	OTC	Software & Computer Ser.	MGT
SIV Industries - 144A	SIVIYP	78427P105	PORT	Chemicals	BNY
SIV Industries - Reg. S	—	Y8063H110	—	Chemicals	BNY
Soma Textiles & Industries - Reg. S	—	83444W109	LUSE	Personal Goods	DB
Southern Petrochemical Industries - 144A	SXPCF	843613100	PORT	Chemicals	BNY
SREI Infrastructure Finance - 144A	SIFLY	78465V105	PORT	General Finance	DB
SREI Infrastructure Finance - Reg. S	—	78465V204	—	General Finance	DB
SSI - 144A	SSI	784663106	PORT	Software & Computer Ser.	DB
SSI - Reg. S	SSBD	784663205	London	Software & Computer Ser.	DB
State Bank of India - 144A	SBKJY	856552104	PORT	Banks	BNY
State Bank of India - Reg. S	—	856552203	—	Banks	BNY
Steel Authority of India - 144A	STRPP	858055106	PORT	Industrial Metals	CIT

(*Continued*)

TABLE D.3 India ADRs (*Continued*)

Company name	Symbol	CUSIP #	Exchange	Industry	Depository bank
Steel Authority of India - Reg. S	—	858055205	—	Industrial Metals	CIT
Sterling Biotech - Reg. S	—	85916G108	LUSE	Food Producers	BNY
Sterlite - 144A	N/A	859737108	PORT	Industrial Metals	DB
Sterlite - Reg. S	—	Y8169X118	—	Industrial Metals	DB
Sterlite Industries	N/A	859737207	NYSE	Industrial Metals	CIT
Subex Azure - 144A	N/A	86428R103	PORT	Software & Computer Ser.	BNY
Subex Azure - 144A	N/A	86428R400	PORT	Software & Computer Ser.	BNY
Subex Azure - Reg. S	SUBX	86428R202	London	Software & Computer Ser.	BNY
Sujana Universal Industries - Reg. S	—	86507M108	LUSE	Industrial Metals	BNY
Taneja Aerospace & Aviation - Reg. S	—	875389108	LUSE	Aerospace & Defense	BNY
Tata Electric Companies - 144A	TERPP	876566100	PORT	Electricity	CIT
Tata Electric Companies - Reg. S	—	Y85479106	—	Electricity	CIT
Tata Motors	TTM	876568502	NYSE	Industrial Engineer.	CIT
Tata Motors - 144A	TLRPP	876568106	PORT	Industrial Engineer.	CIT
Tata Steel Limited - Reg. S	—	87656Y109	—	Industrial Metals	CIT
Tata Tea - 144A	TTAEYRP	876569104	PORT	Beverages	DB
Tata Tea - Reg. S	—	876569203	LUSE	Beverages	DB
Teamasia Semiconductors - 144A	TMSDF	87816A207	PORT	Tech. Hardware & Equip.	BNY
Teamasia Semiconductors - Reg. S	—	87816A108	—	Tech. Hardware & Equip.	BNY

Teledata Informatics - Reg. S	—	87931P105	LUSE	Software & Computer Ser.	BNY
Tricom India - Reg. S	—	896120102	LUSE	Software & Computer Ser.	BNY
Tube Investments of India - 144A	TUBEYP	898555107	PORT	Industrial Engineer.	BNY
Tube Investments of India - Reg. S	—	Y90018105	—	Industrial Engineer.	BNY
Ultratech Cemco - 144A	ULCRP	9.04E+107	PORT	Construct. & Materials	CIT
Ultratech Cemco - Reg. S	—	9.04E+206	—	Construct. & Materials	CIT
Uniphos Enterprises - Reg. S	—	Y91425101	—	Chemicals	BNY
United Phosphorus - Reg. S	—	911330108	—	Chemicals	BNY
Usha Martin - 144A	UHBTY	917300105	PORT	Fixed Line Telecom.	DB
Usha Martin - Reg. S	—	917300204	—	Fixed Line Telecom.	DB
Usha Martin Infotech - Reg. S	USHAF	91730W105	BSE	Software & Computer Ser.	DB
Uttam Galva Steels LTD - 144A	UTTM	918080102	PORT	Industrial Metals	MGT
Vaibhav Gems - Reg. S	—	918766106	LUSE	Household Goods	BNY
Valecha Engineering - Reg. S	—	91911Q109	LUSE	Construct. & Materials	DB
Vedanta Resources - Reg. S	—	92241T102	LUSE	Mining	BNY
Videocon Industries - Reg. S	—	92659X108	LUSE	Oil & Gas Producers	DB
Videocon International - 144A	VDC	92657P107	PORT	Household Goods	DB
Videocon International - Reg. S	—	Y9369D118	LUSE	Household Goods	DB
Videsh Sanchar Nigam	VSL	92659G600	NYSE	Fixed Line Telecom.	BNY
Visu International - Reg. S	—	928404102	LUSE	Support Services	DB
Wanbury - Reg. S	—	93368L104	LUSE	Pharma. & Biotech.	BNY
Webel-SL Energy Systems	N/A	94762L104	Singapore	Electricity	MGT
Welspun Gujarat Stahl Rohren Ltd. - 144A	WGS	950448100	PORT	Industrial Metals	MGT
Wipro	WIT	97651M109	NYSE	Software & Computer Ser.	MGT
WNS Holdings	WNS	92932M101	NYSE	Support Services	DB
Wockhardt - Reg. S	—	Y9675D114	—	Pharma. & Biotech.	DB

Source for data: Bank of New York and JP Morgan database of ADRs

TABLE D.4 China ADRs

Company name	Symbol	CUSIP #	Exchange	Industry	Depository bank
3SBIO	SSRX	88575Y105	Nasdaq	Pharma. & Biotech.	MGT
51job	JOBS	316827104	Nasdaq	Support Services	MGT
Acorn	ATV	4854105	NYSE	General Retailers	CIT
Actions Semiconductor	ACTS	5.07E+109	Nasdaq	Tech .Hardware & Equip.	MGT
Air China	AIRYY	00910M100	OTC	Travel & Leisure	MGT
Aluminum Corporation of China	ACH	22276109	NYSE	Industrial Metals	BNY
Angang Steel	ANGGY	03462W104	OTC	Industrial Metals	BNY
Baidu.com	BIDU	56752108	Nasdaq	Software & Computer Ser.	BNY
Beijing Beida Jade Bird Universal SciTech	BJBJY	77251106	OTC	Software & Computer Ser.	BNY
Brilliance China Automotive	BCAHY	10949Q105	OTC	Automobiles & Parts	BNY
China Eastern Airlines	CEA	16937R104	NYSE	Travel & Leisure	BNY
China Finance Online	JRJC	169379104	Nasdaq	Software & Computer Ser.	MGT
China GrenTech	GRRF	16938P107	Nasdaq	Tech. Hardware & Equip.	CIT
China Life Insurance	LFC	16939P106	NYSE	Life Insurance	MGT
China Medical Technologies	CMED	169483104	Nasdaq	HealthCare Equip. & Ser.	CIT
China Mobile	CHL	16941M109	NYSE	Mobile Telecom.	BNY
China National Offshore Oil-CNOOC	CEO	126132109	NYSE	Oil & Gas Producers	MGT
China Oilfield Services	CHOLY	168909109	OTC	Oil Equip., Serv. & Dist.	BNY
China Petroleum & Chemical	SNP	16941R108	NYSE	Oil & Gas Producers	CIT
China Shipping Development	CSDXY	169408200	OTC	Industrial Transport.	BNY
China Shipping Development - 144A	CSDWY	169408101	PORT	Industrial Transport.	BNY
China Southern Airlines	ZNH	169409109	NYSE	Travel & Leisure	BNY
China Sunergy	CSUN	16942X104	Nasdaq	Electricity	MGT
China Techfaith Wireless Communication	CNTF	169424108	Nasdaq	Tech. Hardware & Equip.	BNY
China Telecom	CHA	169426103	NYSE	Fixed Line Telecom.	BNY

China Unicom	CHU	16945R104	NYSE	Mobile Telecom.	BNY
China Wireless Technologies	CHWTY	169459104	OTC	Tech. Hardware & Equip.	BNY
ChinaCast Communication	CCHYY	16946B108	OTC	Software & Computer Ser.	BNY
CTrip.com International	CTRP	22943F100	Nasdaq	Travel & Leisure	BNY
Datang International Power Generation	DIPGY	23808Q207	OTC	Electricity	BNY
Double Coin Holdings Ltd	DCHLY	25856X109	OTC	Automobiles & Parts	BNY
E-House (China) Holdings	EJ	26852W103	NYSE	Real Estate	MGT
eLong	LONG	290138205	Nasdaq	Travel & Leisure	MGT
Far East Pharmaceutical Technology	FEPTY	30732M103	OTC	Pharma. & Biotech.	DB
Focus Media	FMCN	34415V109	Nasdaq	Media	CIT
Guangshen Railway	GSH	40065W107	NYSE	Travel & Leisure	MGT
Guangzhou Pharmaceutical	GZPHY	40066D108	OTC	Pharma. & Biotech.	BNY
Guangzhou Shipyard International	GSHIY	400656104	OTC	Industrial Engineer.	BNY
Harbin Power Equipment - 144A	HPECYP	411459100	PORT	Industrial Engineer.	BNY
Home Inns & Hotels Management	HMIN	43713W107	Nasdaq	Travel & Leisure	BNY
Hopewell Highway Infrastructure	HHILY	439554106	OTC	Construct. & Materials	CIT
Huaneng Power International	HNP	443304100	NYSE	Electricity	BNY
Hurray!	HRAY	447773102	Nasdaq	Mobile Telecom.	CIT
JA Solar	JASO	466090107	Nasdaq	Electron. & Electric Eq.	BNY
Jiangling Motors - Reg. S	—	477372106	—	Industrial Engineer.	CIT
Jiangsu Expressway	JEXYY	477373104	OTC	Industrial Transport.	BNY
Jiangxi Copper	JIXAY	47737M102	OTC	Mining	BNY
KongZhong	KONG	50047P104	Nasdaq	Mobile Telecom.	CIT

(*Continued*)

TABLE D.4 China ADRs (*Continued*)

Company name	Symbol	CUSIP #	Exchange	Industry	Depository bank
LDK Solar	LDK	50183L107	NYSE	Electron. & Electric Eq.	MGT
Linktone	LTON	535925101	Nasdaq	Mobile Telecom.	MGT
Maansham Iron & Steel - 144A	MAAPP	554059105	PORT	Industrial Metals	CIT
Mindray Medical International	MR	602675100	NYSE	HealthCare Equip. & Ser.	BNY
Netease.com	NTES	64110W102	Nasdaq	Software & Computer Ser.	BNY
New Oriental Education & Technology	EDU	647581107	NYSE	General Retailers	DB
Ninetowns Internet Technology	NINE	654407105	Nasdaq	Software & Computer Ser.	MGT
Perfect World	PWRD	71372U104	Nasdaq	Software & Computer Ser.	DB
PetroChina	PTR	7.16E+104	NYSE	Oil & Gas Producers	BNY
Ping An Insurance Co. of China	PNGAY	72341E304	OTC	Life Insurance	BNY
Ping An Insurance Co. of China - 144A	PINGYP	7.23E+110	PORT	Life Insurance	BNY
Qingling Motor - 144A	QIGPP	747273100	PORT	Industrial Engineer.	CIT
Qingling Motor - Reg. S	—	Y71713112	—	Industrial Engineer.	CIT
Shanda Interactive Entertainment	SNDA	81941Q203	Nasdaq	Leisure Goods	BNY
Shanghai Chlor-Alkali Chemical	SLLBY	819422106	OTC	Chemicals	BNY
Shanghai Erfangji	SHFGY	819423104	OTC	Industrial Engineer.	BNY
Shanghai Jinqiao Processing Dev	SJQIY	81942J109	OTC	Real Estate	BNY
Shanghai Lujiazui Finance & Trade Zone Development	SLUJY	81942W100	OTC	Real Estate	BNY
Shanghai Waigaoqiao Free Trade Zone	SGOTY	818902108	OTC	Real Estate	BNY
Shenzhen S.E.Z. Real Estate nd Properties	SZPRY	823220108	OTC	Real Estate	BNY
Simcere Pharmaceutical	SCR	82859P104	NYSE	Pharma. & Biotech.	BNY
Sinopec Shanghai Petrochemical	SHI	82935M109	NYSE	Chemicals	BNY
Sinopec Yizheng Chemical Fibre	YIRPP	985841105	PORT	Chemicals	CIT

Solarfun Power	SOLF	83415U108	Nasdaq	Electron. & Electric Eq.	BNY
Spreadtrum Communications	SPRD	849415203	Nasdaq	Fixed Line Telecom.	CIT
Suntech Power	STP	86800C104	NYSE	Electron. & Electric Eq.	BNY
Suntech Power - 144A	N/A	86800C203	PORT	Electron. & Electric Eq.	BNY
The9	NCTY	88337K104	Nasdaq	Leisure Goods	BNY
Tianjin Capital Environmental Protection	TCEPY	886303106	OTC	Gas, H_2O & Multiutility	BNY
Tingyi (Cayman Islands)	TCYMY	887495307	OTC	Food Producers	BNY
Tingyi (Cayman Islands) - 144A	TINGYP	887495109	PORT	Food Producers	BNY
Tongjitang Chinese Medicines	TCM	8.90E+107	NYSE	Pharma. & Biotech.	BNY
TravelSky Technology	TSYHY	89420Y209	OTC	Software & Computer Ser.	BNY
Trina Solar	TSL	8.96E+108	NYSE	Electron. & Electric Eq.	BNY
Tsingtao Brewery	TSGTY	898529102	OTC	Beverages	BNY
Vimicro International	VIMC	92718N109	Nasdaq	Tech. Hardware & Equip.	MGT
WuXi Pharmatech	WX	929352102	NYSE	Pharma. & Biotech.	MGT
Xinhua Finance Media	XFML	983982109	Nasdaq	Media	BNY
Yanzhou Coal Mining	YZC	984846105	NYSE	Mining	BNY
Yingli Green Energy	YGE	98584B103	NYSE	Electron. & Electric Eq.	MGT
Zhejiang Expressway	ZHEXY	98951A100	OTC	Industrial Transport.	BNY
Zhejiang Southeast Electric Power - 144A	ZHJGYP	98949U101	PORT	Electricity	BNY
Zhejiang Southeast Electric Power - Reg. S	ZSED	98949U200	London	Electricity	BNY

Source for data: Bank of New York and JP Morgan database of ADRs

TABLE D.5 Korea ADRs

Company name	Symbol	CUSIP #	Exchange	Industry	Depository bank
Daewoo Shipbuilding & Marine Engineering	DEWOYP	23373A207	PORT	Industrial Engineer.	CIT
Dongbu Steel - Reg. S	—	701638200	—	Industrial Metals	DB
Gmarket	GMKT	38012G100	Nasdaq	General Retailers	CIT
Gravity	GRVY	38911N107	Nasdaq	Leisure Goods	BNY
Hana Bank - 144A	HANAP	409636206	PORT	Banks	CIT
Hanaro Telecom	HANA	409649308	OTC	Fixed Line Telecom.	DB
Hanatour Service - 144A	N/A	409650108	PORT	Travel & Leisure	DB
Hanatour Service - Reg. S	HNTOF	409650207	London	Travel & Leisure	DB
Hansol Paper - 144A	HSPCY	411334105	PORT	Forestry & Paper	MGT
Hynix Semiconductor - 144A	HXSCL	449130400	PORT	Tech. Hardware & Equip.	CIT
Hynix Semiconductor - 144A	HXSCY	449130202	PORT	Tech. Hardware & Equip.	CIT
Hyundai Motor - 144A	HYMLY	449187707	PORT	Automobiles & Parts	MGT
Hyundai Motor - 144A	HYMPY	449187103	PORT	Automobiles & Parts	MGT
Hyundai Motor - 144A	HYMZY	449187509	PORT	Automobiles & Parts	MGT
Hyundai Steel - 144A	HYNSY	44919Q100	PORT	Industrial Metals	BNY
Industrial Bank of Korea - Reg. S	—	456036102	LUSE	Banks	CIT
KCC - 144A	KCCPY	48242K102	PORT	Construct. & Materials	MGT
Kia Motors - 144A	KIANF	493738108	PORT	Automobiles & Parts	CIT
Kookmin Bank	KB	50049M109	NYSE	Banks	CIT
Kookmin Bank - Reg. S	—	5.01E+104	—	Banks	CIT
Korea Electric Power	KEP	500631106	NYSE	Electricity	MGT
KT	KTC	48268K101	NYSE	Fixed Line Telecom.	CIT

KT&G - 144A	KTCIY	48268G100	PORT	Tobacco	BNY
Kumho Tire - 144A	KUMBYP05	50125M106	PORT	Automobiles & Parts	BNY
Kumho Tire - Reg. S	KHTC	50125M205	London	Automobiles & Parts	BNY
LG Chem - 144A	LGCLYPC	501955108	PORT	Chemicals	DB
LG Electronics - 144A	LGEGN	50186Q103	PORT	Leisure Goods	CIT
LG Electronics - 144A	LGETN	50186Q202	PORT	Leisure Goods	CIT
LG Philips LCD	LPL	50186V102	NYSE	Tech. Hardware & Equip.	CIT
Lotte Shopping - 144A	LOTS LI	54569T106	PORT	Household Goods	CIT
Macquarie Korea Infrastructure Fund - Reg. S	—	556082204	LUSE	General Finance	CIT
Mirae	MRAE	60461U109	Nasdaq	Tech. Hardware & Equip.	BNY
Naraewin Co., Ltd.	NRMWY	63080N100	OTC	Tech. Hardware & Equip.	BNY
Pixelplus	PXPL	72582A102	Nasdaq	Tech. Hardware & Equip.	MGT
POSCO	PKX	693483109	NYSE	Industrial Metals	BNY
Samsung - 144A	SACPP	796053205	PORT	Support Services	CIT
Samsung - 144A	SAMPP	796053106	PORT	Support Services	CIT
Samsung Electronics - 144A	SAEPP	796050201	PORT	Tech. Hardware & Equip.	CIT
Samsung Electronics - 144A	SAMEG	796050AB8	PORT	Tech. Hardware & Equip.	CIT
Samsung Electronics - 144A	SEEPP	796050888	PORT	Tech. Hardware & Equip.	CIT
Samsung Electronics - 144A	SEFPP	796050870	PORT	Tech. Hardware & Equip.	CIT
Samsung Electronics - Conv. Bond - 144A	SAMPEZ	796050AC6	PORT	Tech. Hardware & Equip.	CIT

(*Continued*)

TABLE D.5 Korea ADRs (*Continued*)

Company name	Symbol	CUSIP #	Exchange	Industry	Depository bank
Samsung SDI - 144A	SASDI	796054203	PORT	Electron. & Electric Eq.	CIT
Shinhan Financial	SHG	824596100	NYSE	Banks	CIT
Shinhan Financial - 144A	SFGRP	824596209	PORT	Banks	CIT
Shinsegae - Com - Reg. S	—	824630107	—	General Retailers	BNY
Shinsegae - Pref - Reg. S	—	824630206	—	General Retailers	BNY
SK Corporation - Com - 144A	SKKOP	784328205	PORT L	Oil & Gas Producers	CIT
SK Corporation - Pref - 144A	SKRPP	784328106	PORT	Oil & Gas Producers	CIT
SK Networks Co Ltd - 144A	N/A	333334334	PORT	General Retailers	CIT
SK Telecom	SKM	78440P108	NYSE	Mobile Telecom.	CIT
S-Oil - Com	SOOCY	78462W106	OTC	Oil & Gas Producers	BNY
S-Oil - Pref	SOLCY	78462W205	OTC	Oil & Gas Producers	BNY
Tong Yang Major - Reg. S	—	89023M107	—	Construct. & Materials	BNY
Webzen	WZEN	94846M102	Nasdaq	Leisure Goods	MGT
WiderThan	WTHN	967593104	Nasdaq	Software & Computer Ser.	MGT
Woongjin Coway - 144A	WCCLY	980894109	PORT	Household Goods	MGT
Woori Finance	WF	981063100	NYSE	Banks	CIT

Source for data: Bank of New York and JP Morgan database of ADRs

TABLE D.6 Mexico ADRs

Company name	Symbol	CUSIP #	Exchange	Industry	Depository bank
Acer Computec Latino America - 144A	ACEFY	4431102	PORT	Software & Computer Ser.	CIT
Acer Computec Latino America - Reg. S	—	4431201	—	Software & Computer Ser.	CIT
Alfa - 144A	ALFPP	15398100	PORT	General Industrials	CIT
Alfa - Reg. S	—	15398209	—	General Industrials	CIT
America Movil - Series A	AMOV	02364W204	Nasdaq	Mobile Telecom.	BNY
America Movil - Series L	AMX	02364W105	NYSE	Mobile Telecom.	BNY
Axtel - 144A	AXTLRCC44	05461Y106	PORT	Fixed Line Telecom.	BNY
Axtel - Reg. S	—	05461Y205	—	Fixed Line Telecom.	BNY
Bufete Industrial	BUFEY	11942H100	OTC	Construct. & Materials	BNY
Carso Global Telecom	CGTVY	14574P101	OTC	Fixed Line Telecom.	BNY
Cemex S.A.B. de C.V.	CX	151290889	NYSE	Construct. & Materials	CIT
Coca-Cola Femsa – L Shares	KOF	191241108	NYSE	Beverages	BNY
Consorcio ARA - 144A	CSRAYP	21030R100	PORT	Household Goods	BNY
Consorcio ARA - Reg. S	—	21030R209	—	Household Goods	BNY
Consorcio Hogar	CSHHY	21030U202	OTC	Construct. & Materials	BNY
Consorcio Hogar - 144A	HGARYP	21030U103	PORT	Construct. & Materials	BNY
Corp. Internamercana de Entretenimiento - 144A	CIE	21988J100	PORT	Travel & Leisure	DB
Corp. Internamercna de Entretenmento - Reg. S	—	21988J209	—	Travel & Leisure	DB
Corporacion Durango	CDURQ	21986M105	OTC	Forestry & Paper	BNY
Corporacion GEO	CVGFY	21986V204	OTC	Real Estate	BNY
Corporacion GEO - 144A	CVGEY	21986V105	PORT	Real Estate	BNY
Desarrolladora Homex	HXM	25030W100	NYSE	Household Goods	MGT

(*Continued*)

TABLE D.6 Mexico ADRs (*Continued*)

Company name	Symbol	CUSIP #	Exchange	Industry	Depository bank
El Puerto de Liverpool - Reg. S	—	3823962	—	General Retailers	CIT
Empresas ICA	ICA	292448206	NYSE	Construct. & Materials	BNY
Fomento Economico Mexicano	FMX	344419106	NYSE	Beverages	BNY
G Collado	GCLOY	36156R106	OTC	Industrial Metals	BNY
GRUMA - B Shares	GMK	400131306	NYSE	Food Producers	CIT
Grupe (El Cid)	GECDY	40051A101	OTC	Travel & Leisure	BNY
Grupo Aeroportuario del Centro Norte	OMAB	400501102	Nasdaq	Industrial Transport.	BNY
Grupo Aeroportuario del Pacifico	PAC	400506101	NYSE	Industrial Transport.	BNY
Grupo Aeroportuario del Sureste	ASR	4.01E+206	NYSE	Industrial Transport.	BNY
Grupo Carso	GPOVY	400485207	OTC	General Industrials	BNY
Grupo Carso - 144A	GCSY	400485108	PORT	General Industrials	BNY
Grupo Casa Saba	SAB	40048P104	NYSE	Food & Drug Retailers	BNY
Grupo Comercial Gomo	GOMMY	40049D100	OTC	Electron. & Electric Eq.	BNY
Grupo Continental - Com	GPOCY	40050H107	OTC	Beverages	BNY
Grupo Dataflux	GDFXY	40050X102	OTC	General Retailers	BNY
Grupo Financiero Inbursa	GPFOY	40048D101	OTC	Banks	BNY
Grupo Gigante	GPGJY	400487500	OTC	Food Producers	BNY
Grupo Gigante - 144A	GPGNY	400487401	PORT	Food Producers	BNY
Grupo Herdez - B Shares	GUZBY	40050P109	OTC	Food Producers	BNY
Grupo Industrial Saltillo - Series B	GISXY	40051B109	OTC	General Industrials	MGT
Grupo Modelo	GPMCY	40051F100	OTC	Beverages	BNY

Grupo Posadas – A Shares - 144A	GRPALP	400489209	PORT	Travel & Leisure	BNY
Grupo Posadas – L Shares - 144A	GRPYP	400489100	PORT	Travel & Leisure	BNY
Grupo PYPSA – B Shares	GPPSY	40050F101	OTC	Construct. & Materials	BNY
Grupo Qumma	GPQMY	4.01E+108	OTC	Media	BNY
Grupo Radio Centro	RC	40049C102	NYSE	Media	CIT
Grupo Simec - B Shares	SIM	400491106	American	Industrial Metals	BNY
Grupo Televisa, S.A.B.	TV	40049J206	NYSE	Media	BNY
Grupo TMM	TMM	40051D105	NYSE	Industrial Transport.	CIT
Hilasal Mexicana	HLMXY	431293109	OTC	Household Goods	BNY
Industrias Bachoco	IBA	456463108	NYSE	Food Producers	BNY
Kimberly Clark de Mexico	KCDMY	494386204	OTC	Personal Goods	MGT
Promotora y Operadora de Infraestructura	PUODY	74343W100	OTC	Construct. & Materials	BNY
Sanluis - 144A	SLRPP	219870870	PORT	Automobiles & Parts	BNY
Sanluis - Reg. S	—	219870862	—	Automobiles & Parts	BNY
Sare Holding	SARHY	803606102	OTC	Household Goods	BNY
Telefonos de Mexico – Series A	TFONY	879403707	Nasdaq	Fixed Line Telecom.	MGT
Telefonos de Mexico – Series L	TMX	879403780	NYSE	Fixed Line Telecom.	MGT
Urbi Desarrollos Urbanos - 144A	URBQY	91724R104	PORT	Household Goods	BNY
Urbi Desarrollos Urbanos - Reg. S	—	91724R203	—	Household Goods	BNY
US Commercial	USMLY	90335M108	OTC	General Finance	MGT
Vitro	VTO	928502301	NYSE	Construct. & Materials	BNY
Wal-Mart de Mexico	WMMVY	93114W107	OTC	General Retailers	BNY

Source for data: Bank of New York and JP Morgan database of ADRs

APPENDIX E

Mutual Fund Profiles by Country

Brazil

Name: iShares Morgan Stanley Capital International Brazil Index Fund (data as of 10/2/07)
Symbol: EWZ
Sales Charge: 0%
Gross Expense Charge: 0.70%
Inception Date: 7/10/2000

Top 5 Stock Holdings		Top 5 Sectors	
Petrobas	12%	Materials	31%
Cravaledo	12%	Energy	22%
Rio Doce	10%	Financials	16%
Pref. A. Petrobras Cia Valedo Rio	10%	Consumer Staples	7%
Doce—ADR: Banco Italian Holding Performance	5%	Utilities	7%

For more information: www.ishares.com; 800-474-2737

China

Name: Alliance Bernstein Greater China 97 A
Symbol: GCHAX
Sales Charge: 0%
Gross Expense Charge: 2.14%
Inception Date: 9/97

Top 5 Stock Holdings		Top 5 Sectors	
China Mobile	9%	Financial Services	22%
Sinopec	7%	Energy	16%
Petro China	6%	Telecom	12%
Dairy Farm	4%	Utilities	6%
CNOOC	4%	Information Tech. Hardware	6%

For more information: www.alliancecapital.com

Name: Columbia Greater China A
Symbol: NGCAX
Sales Charge: 5.75%
Gross Expense Charge: 1.75%
Inception Date: 5/97

Top 5 Stock Holdings		Top 5 Sectors	
China Mobile Ltd.	15%	Financial Services	34%
PetroChina	8%	Telecom	18%
China Life Ins.	7%	Energy	17%
China Merchants Bank	6%	Business Services	11%
Sinopec	4%	Industrial Goods	8%

For more information: www.columbiafunds.com; 800-423-3737

Name: Dreyfus Premier Greater China A
Symbol: DPCAX
Sales Charge: 5.75%
Gross Expense Charge: 1.92%
Inception Date: 5/98

Top 5 Stock Holdings		Top 5 Sectors	
Bengang Steel Plates	4%	Industrial Goods	266%
China Travel Int'l Inv.	3%	Financial Services	24%
China Telecom	3%	Business Services	12%
Inner Mongolia Yitai Coal	3%	Consumer Services	11%
Hunan Nonferrous Metals	3%	Telecom	64%

For more information: www.dreyfus.com; 800-554-4611

Name: Eaton Vance Greater China A
Symbol: EVCGX
Sales Charge: 5.75%
Gross Expense Charge: 2.39%
Inception Date: 10/92

Top 5 Stock Holdings		Top 5 Sectors	
China Mobile Ltd.	5%	Financial Services	11%
Ports Design Ltd	3%	Industrial Goods	16%
China Life Ins.	3%	Consumer Services	14%
China National Bldg Materials	3%	Telecom	11%
Guangzhou R&F Prop.	3%	Business Services	11%

For more information: www.eatonvance.com; 800-202-1122

Name: Guinness Atkinson China and Hong Kong
Symbol: ICHKX
Sales Charge: NA
Gross Expense Charge: 1.59%
Inception Date: 6/94

Top 5 Stock Holdings		Top 5 Sectors	
China Mobile	8%	Industrial Goods	21%
PetroChina	7%	Energy	20%
CNOOC Ltd	7%	Financial Services	19%
Angang New Steel	6%	Telecom	8%
China Shipping Dev.	5%	Consumer Services	9%

For more information: www.gafunds.com; 800-915-6566

Name: J.P. Morgan China Fund
Symbol: JPMF JF
Sales Charge: 5%
Gross Expense Charge: 1.90%
Inception Date: 2/02

Top 5 Stock Holdings as of 8/07		Top 5 Sectors as of 8/07	
China Life Insurance	10%	Financials	38%
China Mobile	10%	Energy	13%
China Construction	6%	Telecom	11%
China Petroleum	6%	Industrials	9%
China Merchants Bank	4%	Consumer Discre.	7%

For more information: www.jpmorgan.com

Name: Templeton China World
Symbol: TCWAX
Sales Charge: 5.75%
Gross Expense Charge: 2.16%
Inception Date: 8/03

Top 5 Stock Holdings		Top 5 Sectors	
China Mobile	9%	Financial Services	22%
Sinopec	7%	Energy	16%
PetroChina	6%	Telecom	12%
Dairy Farm	4%	Utilities	6%
CNOOC	4%	Information Tech.	6%

For additional information: www.Franklintempleton.com; 800-632-2301

Name: US Global Investors China Register
Symbol: USCOX
Sales Charge: 0%
Gross Expense Charge: 2.51%
Inception Date: 2/94

Top 5 Stock Holdings	
China Nat'l Building Materials	3%
China Life Insurance	3%
China Mobile Ltd	3%
Shandong Weigao Grp.	2%
Sinopec	2%

For more information: www.usfunds.com; 800-873-8637

India Mutual Fund Profiles

Name: Matthews India
Symbol: MNDX
Sales Charge: 0%
Gross Expense Charge: 1.41%
Inception Date: 10/31/05

Top 5 Stock Holdings		Top 5 Sectors	
Dabur India Ltd.	5%	Healthcare Services	19.3%
CESC Ltd	4%	Industrial Goods	16%
Glenmark Pharm.	4%	Software	11.2%
Bharti Airtel Ltd	4%	Consumer Goods	11%
Infosys Technologies	4%	Financial Services	11%

For more information: www.matthewsIndia.com; 800-789-742

Name: Eaton Vance Greater India A
Symbol: ETGIX
Sales Charge: 5.75%
Gross Expense Charge: 2.19%
Inception Date: 5/2/94

Top 5 Stock Holdings		Top 5 Sectors	
Reliance Industries	6%	Industrial Goods	29%
Tata Consulting Serv	5%	Consumer Goods	17%
Infosys Tech	5%	Business Services	16%
Bharat Heavy Electricals	4%	Software	11%
Jaiprakash Assoc.	4%	Healthcare Services	8%

For more information: www.eatonvance.com; 800-262-1122

Name: iPath Morgan Stanley Capital International India Index ETN[1]

Primary Exchange: NYSE
Symbol: INP
Itraday Indicative Value Ticker: INP.IV
Bloomberg: ETN
Short Sales: Yes, on an up- or downtick
Bloomberg Index Ticker: CUSIP 06739F291
Inception Date: 12/19/06
Maturity Date: 12/18/2036
Yearly Fee: 0.89%

Top 10 Stock Holdings		Top 10 Sectors	
Reliance Ind	14%	Financial	25%
Infosys Tech	11%	Energy	19%
ICICI Bank Ltd.	9%	Information Tech.	16%
Housing Dev.	5%	Industrials	11%
Reliance Commun.	4%	Materials	7%
Larsen & Toubro	3%	Consumer Disc.	5%
HDFC	3%	Consumer Staples	5%
Oil & Nat'l Gas	2.86%	Telecom	5%
Satyam Comp. Serv	3%	Healthcare	4%
Bharat Heavy Electricals	2%	Utilities	2%

[1]The iPath MSCI India ETNs are linked to the MSCI India total Return Index. The Index is a free-float-adjusted market capitalization index designed to measure the market performance, including price performance and income from dividend payments of Indian equity securities. The Index seeks to represent approximately 85% of the free-float-adjusted market capitalization of equity securities by industry group within India. As of March 31, 2007, the Index was comprised of 69 countries listed on the National Stock Exchange of India (NSE).

Index Sector Breakdowns	
Financials	23%
Information Tech.	18%
Energy	18%
Industrials	12%
Materials	7%
Consumer Disc.	6%
Consumer Staples	5%
Telecom	5%
Healthcare	4%
Utilities	2%

Performance % / year as of 6/30/07

	1-year	3-year	5-year	Standard Deviation Annualized
MSCI India Total Return Index	60.41	52.15	41.18	23.75
S&P 500 Index	20.59	11.68	10.71	11.58
Lehman US Aggregate Index	6.12	3.98	4.48	3.71
MSCI EAFE Index	27	22.24	17.73	12.91
MSCI Emerging Markets Index	44.99	38.20	30.25	17.58

Issuer Details

Barclays Bank PLC long-term unsecured obligations

S&P Rating: AA

Moody's Rating: Aa1

(*Sources:* MSCI, S&P, Lehman Brothers, BGI, based on monthly returns for period 6/30/02 to 6/30/07)

Mexico Mutual Fund Profile

Name: iShares Morgan Stanley Capital International Mexico Index Fund

Symbol: EWW

Sales Charge: 0%

Gross Expense Charge: 0.54%

Inception Date: 3/12/96

Top 5 Stock Holdings		Top 5 Sectors	
American Mobile	25%	Telecom	38%
CEMEX	14%	Materials	20%
Telefonos de Mexico	10%	Consumer Staples	18%
WalMart de Mexico	5%	Consumer Discre	11%
Grupo Televisión	5%	Industrials	10%

For more information: www.ishares.com; 800-747-2737

Russia Mutual Fund Profiles

Name: ING Russia A
Symbol: LETRX
Sales Charge: 5.75%
Gross Expense Charge: 2.11%
Inception Date: 7/96

Top 5 Stock Holdings		Top 5 Sectors	
Savings Bank of the Russian F.	15%	Energy	40%
Lukoil Co ADR	10%	Financial Services	19%
Gazprom OAO	9%	Industrial Goods	14%
MMC Norilsk Nickel	6%	Telecom	13%
United Energy System of Russia	6%	Utilities	7%

For more information: www.ingfunds.com; 800-992-0180

Name: J.P. Morgan Russia A
Symbol: JRUSX
Sales Charge: 5.25%
Gross Expense Charge: 2.42%
Inception Date: 2/28/07

Top 5 Stock Holdings		Top 5 Sectors	
Sberbank Rossii	15%	Materials	35%
Novilsk Nickel	12%	Financials	21%
Raoves of Russia	6%	Energy	8%
Mechel	6%	Telecom	7%
Severstal	4%	Utilities	6%

Name: Third Millennium Russia
Symbol: TMRFX
Sales Charge: 5.75%
Gross Expense Charge: 2.89%
Inception Date: 10/98

Top 5 Stock Holdings		Top 5 Sectors	
Savings Bk of the Russian F.	16%	Financial Services	40%
Open Investments	9%	Industrial Goods	23%
Renshares Utilities	8%	Telecom	16%
MMC Norilsk Nickel	7%	Energy	13%
Uralalii OAO	7%	Utilities	4%

For more information: www.theworldfunds.com; 800-527-9525

South Korea Mutual Fund Profiles

Name: Fidelity Advantage Korea A
Symbol: FAKAX
Sales Charge: 5.75%
Gross Expense Charge: 1.82%
Inception Date: 11/94

Top 5 Holdings		Top 5 Sectors	
Samsung Ltd	10%	Industrial Goods	31%
POSCO	6%	Consumer Goods	20%
Kookmin Bank	6%	Financial Services	18%
Doosan Infracore	5%	Business Services	17%
NHN	4%	Hardware	4%

For more information; www.fidelity.com; 800-208-0098

Name: iShares Morgan Stanley Capital International South Korea Index Fund
Symbol: EWY
Sales Charge: 0%
Gross Expense Charge: 0.89%
Inception Date: 5/9/2000

Top 5 Stock Holdings	
Samsung	14%
POSCO	10%
Kookmin Bank	6%
Shinhan Fin. Grp	4%
Hyundai	4%

For more information: www.ishares.com; 800-747-2737

Name: Matthews Korea
Symbol: MAKOX
Sales Charge: 0%
Gross Expense Charge: 1.3%
Inception Date: 1/95

Top 5 Stock Holdings		Top 5 Sectors	
Samsung Electronics	9%	Financial Services	26%
Kookman Bank	6%	Consumer Goods	20%
Hana Financial Group	6%	Healthcare Services	15%
NHN	5%	Business Services	14%
SK Telecom	4%	Telecom	9%

For more information: www.matthewsfunds.com; 800-789-2747

APPENDIX F

BRIC Fund Profiles

The following mutual funds invest in four countries (Brazil, Russia, India, China). Individual portfolio managers, except in the case of index funds determine the allocation between countries, as well as any investment decisions.

Goldman Sachs BRIC Fund

Name: Goldman Sachs BRIC Fund
Symbol: GBRAX
Sales Charge: 5.75%
Gross Expense Charge: 2.47%
Inception Date: 6/30/07

Country Allocations in %

	Brazil	Russia	India	China
GS BRIC Fund	25.0%	20.9%	17.6%	35.2%
MSCI BRIC Index	26.4%	22.7%	19.6%	28.9%

Industry Allocations in %

Industry	GS Fund	MSCI Index
Energy	25%	25.02%
Financials	24.7%	23.9%
Industrials	16%	8.6%
Telecom.	10%	11.2%
Materials	9%	13.2%
Information Tech.	6.2%	3.9%
Consumer Discretionary	3%	3.8%
Utilities	1.9%	5.2%
Consumer Staples	1.8%	4.2%
Healthcare	1.6%	0.8%

Performance %/year as of 6/30/2007

	GS BRIC	MSCI BRIC Index
3/30/07 to 6/30/07	18.95%	17.11%
1/1/07 to 6/30/07	19.05%	16.60%
6/30/06 to 6/30/07	53.86%	51.13%

SPDR Standard & Poor's BRIC 40 Exchange-Traded Fund

Name: SPDR Standard & Poor's BRIC 40 Exchange-Traded Fund (This fund's objective is to replicate S&P BRIC 40)

Symbol: BIK

Sales Charge: 0%

Gross Expense Charge: 0.72%

Inception Date: 8/31/07

Top 5 Stock Holdings		Top 5 Sectors	
China Mobile Ltd	11.5%	Energy	36%
Grazprom	6.57%	Financial	29%
Lukoil	5.48%	Telecom	16%
Companhia Vale Do RIO Doce	5.40%	Materials	10%
Petrolea Brasilorlo	5%	Information Technology	3%
China Life	5%		

Performance %/year as of 8/31/2007

1/1/07 to 6/31/07	7.32%

Templeton BRIC Fund

Name: Templeton BRIC Fund

Symbol: TABRX

Sales Charge: 5.75%

Gross Expense Charge: 2.19%

Inception Date: 6/1/06

Top 5 Stock Holdings		Top 6 Sectors	
Gazprom OAO	7%	Energy	29%
Cia Valedo Rio Doce	6%	Materials	18%
Petrolea Brasileiros (Petrobras)	6%	Bank	12%
Norilsk Nickel	4%	Capital Goods	6%
Unibanco Uniao	3%	Utilities	6%
		Transport.	5%

Geographical Breakdown as of 7/31/2007	
Brazil	32%
Russia	25%
China	21%
Indo	11%
Other	4%

APPENDIX G

Just Ask the Experts

While researching for *Six Sizzling Markets*, I conducted a series of informal interviews with prominent portfolio managers. These experts have extensive experience in the global markets and offer valuable insight on how investors can profit from investing in these six sizzling BRIC+2 markets. In the sections below, I have written a condensed and paraphrased version of my conversations with them.

The Six Sizzling Markets

The following comments reflect an interview that I had with Dan Elfson, a portfolio manager at U.S. Trust. The paraphrased comments address the questions: What are the big themes in the global economy? and What are the negative implications of these themes?

The big themes in the global economy are the shift of wealth from developed to developing markets. Specifically, several themes include:

- The rise of China and its middle class.
- India's outsourcing boom.
- Brazil's opportunities due to its being resource rich.
- Mexico's becoming more integrated with the U.S. market (NAFTA) and proving that it can manage the windfall from trade.
- All of the BRICs and Mexico are better at managing their economies. Their microeconomies have improved along with their governance.
- Domestic consumption in most of these countries (BRIC+2) is growing.
- Countries such as Russia, China, and Korea are becoming flush with cash.
- Emerging markets are decoupling from the United States and are no longer as dependent on the U.S. economy as in the past and no longer hostage to developed markets.

As a result of these developments, concerns within the economy are as follows:

- Too much aggressive investment and these markets will have been "discovered."
- This issue is particularly of concern with low-yield assets; for example, the Australian money fund went into investments such as equities in Hungary, Brazil, and so on. With the rise of interest rates, the carry trade may come to a sudden end, creating difficulties for these "emerging markets" or "newly discovered" investments.
- Infrastructure issues in India may be a concern.
- The dollar's weakening against the Indian rupee may translate into lower earnings for Indian global technologies.
- Russian political issues are likely to loom large until the election, creating uncertainty in that market.

Brazil

The following comments reflect an interview that I had with Bob von Rekowsky, a portfolio manager at Fidelity Emerging Markets Fund. The paraphrased comments address the question: What role does Brazil play among the six sizzling markets?

Brazil is likely to be the slowest grower among the six sizzling BRICs in the next five years. Valuations remain reasonable, and there are stock-picking opportunities. From a macroeconomic point of view, the government deserves good marks on macroeconomic performance, but I believe interest rates are too high. The result is a very strong currency. Overall, there is a stable budget, and the debt is being repaid and is likely to become investment grade very soon. They have huge iron ore reserves for which there is a huge demand, particularly in emerging growth economies like China. Decision making seems slow in Brazil, given state versus federal decision making.

View from the top down:

- Interest rates need to come down.
- The central bank is too cautious in thinking the market will award it permanent favors in having crushed inflationary expectations.

Overall thoughts:

- Brazil is in a position to survive turbulence in global markets given the wall of foreign exchange reserves and current account balance it has. It has repaid debt and has room to cut rates.
- "Brazil doesn't look great from the top down, but there are tons of stocks to invest in." (I don't believe I said that.)

Russia

The following comments reflect an interview that I had with Oleg Biryulyov, a portfolio manager for the JP Morgan Russian Fund. The paraphrased comments address the questions: What are the major financial themes for Russia's economy? and How do these themes impact Russia?

The major financial themes that are occurring with Russia are:

- JP Morgan is the biggest institutional investor in Russia.
- Russia is a part of the EMEA (Europe, Middle East, and Africa) region and is about 65 percent of the MSCI Emerging Europe index.
- Russia is one of the newest emerging markets, less than 20 years old. However, Russia is now a dominant market. There are four themes in play.

  1. A strong commodity cycle has been persisting for several years and, in addition to Russia, includes the Middle East and parts of Africa as well as Latin America. Russia is fully participating in this cycle, not only through oil and natural gas but coal as well as iron ore.
  2. The convergence of Poland, Hungary, and the Czech Republic (as well as other markets in Eastern Europe) by upgrading on the scale toward more developed markets. (Convergence is applicable mainly to central European countries, as it is a process of expanding the European Union by adding new member countries. Russia is unlikely to become part of the EU anytime soon.)
  3. The consumption cycle is getting stronger with the growth of these economies, including Russia.
  4. The eastern European region, including Russia, is going through a massive uplift in infrastructure; this region is as big as China, and therefore, this theme is likely to continue for a long time.

These themes impact Russia in the following areas:

- *Infrastructure*. Russia has the basic infrastructure such as railways, ports, and major roadways. However, due to growth, the country will need to upgrade all infrastructure.
- *Raw materials*. Russia is the beneficiary of large deposits of natural gas as well as oil. Oil exploration is proceeding at a high rate. Natural gas, in addition to local consumption, is exported. In addition, Russia is the second largest producer of coal and iron ore. Russia is one of the leading global steel exporters; however, increasing domestic demand is likely to reduce volumes available for export in the coming years.

- *Natural resources.* Both China and India, the other two large economies, suffer from lack of energy and are short of other natural resources.
- *Consumption and higher standard of living.* The Russian government is making a major push to diversify investments into local consumption and to raise living standards for Russians. Social spending is on the increase; pensions have increased at about 15 percent annually and by 2010 will almost double from their levels in 2006.
- *Other social spending.* Housing allowances and health care spending are also up.
- *Redistribution of income.* There is a clear effort to redistribute income and increase the quality of life for the average Russian.
- *Energy tax.* The Russian government has steadily increased the taxation of Russian energy sources. The government currently takes about 87% of any increase in oil prices above $27 price per barrel. It is estimated at current prices. The Russian government gets about $46 price per barrel of export duty for each barrel of oil sold on export (using $80 price per barrel price).
- *Consumption growth.* Currently, Russia's per-capita GDP of about $7,000 ($1 trl GDP vs. 144 m population) is 4.3 to 10 times that of China ($2.1 trl GDP vs. 1.3 trl population) and India ($800 bln GDP vs. 1.1 trl population). Therefore, Russian consumption is likely to be quite strong despite its smaller population.
- *Human capital.* The quality of human capital is quite high compared to India and China, as well as other emerging markets, because of large numbers of educated Russians as well as due to established social institutions supporting health care, education, and pension system.
- *GDP growth.* GDP has been growing at close to 7 percent for almost decade.
- *Political system.* Currently, there is some uncertainty about political changes, particularly the impact on Russia after Mr. Putin leaves office. However, the Russian political system is stable and is similar to both China and Japan. All three have a one-party system. It is expected that Mr. Putin will possibly remain involved in the background and continue to be a powerful figure. There is no major opposition. Foreign investors are visibly uncertain and therefore nervous. The risk discount of political uncertainty has been building in the equity markets. In the past, the market has gone up in the periods around elections.
- *Lack of equity culture.* Russians do not currently invest much in equities. Returns on equities have been quite strong. The Russian stock market is near its all-time high. The Russian stock market is not deep, and of the 2,000 Russian companies, only 300 are tradable in some meaningful

size. Several large sectors are not even represented in the market, such as:

- Pulp and paper
- Insurance
- Chemicals
- Banks (only two)
- Materials sector

In discussing the major holdings within specific sectors, he stated the following:

- Financial companies such as Sberbank (joint stock commercial savings bank of the Russian Federation; 14 percent of fund) comprise the largest position. Sberbank has about 30 percent of the market share, and based on that, we can estimate that the entire Russian banking sector has a market cap of about $240 billion. It has the largest penetration of any bank in Russia, with about 22,000 branches, including many in villages and rural areas. Sberbank has about 60 percent market share in mortgages and is likely to keep its position in this segment.
- It will benefit from higher consumption, more diversified products, and more lending and banking activity.
- MMC Norilsk Nickel is one of the cheapest commodity players and has about 45 percent of the global nickel market and is selling at about six times earnings.
- Mechel is an international steel producer with significant growth possibility.

India

The following comments reflect an interview that I had with Bob von Rekowsky, a portfolio manager at Fidelity Emerging Markets Fund. The paraphrased comments address the questions: What are the major financial themes within India's economy? and What are the concerning economic issues in India?

The Indian companies have better management and are much more likely to meet targets. There are huge opportunities. The valuations can appear stretched but their returns on equity are higher. The Indian currency has strengthened, thereby weakening the earnings of many of the large global technology companies that have most of their earnings coming from overseas, particularly from the United States. The concerning economic issues with India include government budget and current account deficits. Inflation was an issue last year, but the Reserve Bank of India has tightened interest rates. We see India and China as having the potential to be complementary economies. China manufactures; India services. The market tends to view them as constant either-or investments; it is not that simple.

China

The following comments reflect an interview that I had with Bob von Rekowsky, a portfolio manager at Fidelity Emerging Markets Fund. The paraphrased comments address the question: What are the most optimal stock options in China's new economy?

Fidelity Emerging Fund is focused on bottom-up stock-by-stock analysis, even though top down is a serious consideration. Stock picking in emerging markets can be critical.

China is very complex. It has extremely strong GDP growth, but valuations are stretched. Even some utilities are selling at 20 to 30 times and need to be careful. Domestic liquidity is extremely strong, and therefore A shares are extremely hot because of huge demand. H shares are better valued. Comparison is generally made between China and India, but the economics in India is much different from China, even though both countries are growing. India are more focused on domestic consumption, even though it is exporting services; China is currently mostly emphasizing exports.

■ ■ ■

The following comments reflect an interview that I had with Mark Headley, a co-portfolio manager with Matthews China Fund. The paraphrased comments address the questions: What are the major financial themes in China's economy? and What are the short-term impacts on the economy?

The major financial themes that are occurring in China are:

- China has a stunning combination of a managed economy and foreign investors.
- Valuation of Chinese companies is high but growth is strong.
- Earnings continue to be strong, and many companies continue to grow by 25 percent to 30 percent.
- It is a bifurcated market of high-growth companies with extremely high price-to-earnings ratios, and moderately growing companies not performing well.
- The Chinese are extremely confident and feel they can handle growth ("We are the new U.S.").
- There is a speculative presence in the markets—property values are rising at 30 percent to 40 percent annually.

- Chinese H shares have better valuation than A shares.
- There is a huge building boom, particularly in major centers.
- I mostly invest in defensive sectors in materials, energy, and cement companies trading in Hong Kong.
- Large numbers of new brokerage accounts (200,000) are opening every day.
- There is pent-up demand for stocks. Retail investing is a moving force.

The short-term issues, other than valuation, in China include:

- Inflation is creeping up.
- Pork prices have risen (a staple of Chinese food).
- Wages are rising.

Korea

The following comments reflect an interview that I had with Mark Headley, a co-portfolio manager with Matthews China Fund. The paraphrased comments address the question: What are the major financial themes in Korea?

The major political and economic themes that are occurring with Korea are:

- Political climate is better.
- Macroeconomics is good.
- Business-friendly government.
- Inflation is rising.
- Highly cyclical companies have gone up.
- Korean construction companies are undervalued.
- It is still a highly export-driven economy.
- If the United States enters a recession, there could be a problem for Korea.
- Valuations are very reasonable.
- Samsung is better value than Sony or Hitachi.
- LG high-quality manufacturing at better prices.
- Domestic consumption is rising.

Recommendation: Construction companies are a play on the potential turnaround in the domestic property market.

■ ■ ■

The following comments reflect an interview that I had with Nicholas Bratt, a portfolio manager of the Korea Fund. In the paraphrased comments below, he shares his general observation of Korea.

- Koreans, for most of their history, until recent times, have been ruled, exploited, and victimized by outside conquerors.
- Koreans are generally skeptical of foreigners and not generally open to foreigners owning local companies.
- Korea has an extremely skilled labor force.
- The financial crisis in 1997–1998 was painful but healthy.
- Badly managed companies as well as highly leveraged companies got wiped out.
- New guidelines were instituted, with better governance and supervision.
- There were outstanding bargains after the crisis.
- Chinese growth is a fantastic opportunity for Koreans, who are more cost-effective in delivering products and services than the Japanese.
- Korea has what it takes to be successful and has some of the best-managed companies.
- Korea is less dependent on exports to the United States and Europe because of the growing importance of exports to China. In many ways, it is a flywheel on the world economy.
- It is unique among emerging markets and is likely to be a developed market soon.
- Korea places a great deal of importance on education and one major indication of that may be that it has more PhDs per capita than any other country in the world.
- The personal savings rate is very high in Korea.
- It will likely be one of the most successful markets long term and a major power in Asia Pacific.

Recommendation: As for allocation to emerging markets by U.S. investors, most U.S. investors are underinvested. It is reasonable to allocate about 40 percent to non-U.S. stocks as a part of equity allocation, and about half of that could be into developed markets and the other half into emerging markets.

■ ■ ■

The following comments reflect an interview that I had with John Lee, a portfolio manager for the Lazard Korea Fund. Mr. Lee was previously part of a team that ran the Korea Fund, a closed fund launched in 1984 with $60 million in original capital. Since 1991, Mr. Lee has been managing the Korea Fund at Lazard and the assets have increased from about $200 million to

$1.48 billion. John Lee was born and raised in Korea, and in his capacity as portfolio manager, he travels often to Korea.

Korean strategy at Lazard is focused on discovering smaller and less well-known names, sometimes second-tier companies that are undervalued. The overall style appears to be valued at discounted prices.

According to John, Korea has several themes that are likely to drive the economy forward and benefit its corporations and propel the stocks. They are listed below:

- *Human capital.* Korean society's stress on education is a major advantage. The Korean population, particularly the younger population and their parents, are focused on education to distinguish themselves. They believe they can be the best-trained knowledge workers available. Many parents will sacrifice to finance their children's higher education, including sending them to universities in the United States.
- *Growth.* GDP growth will be strong, based on Korea's export markets, particularly high-tech and electronics. China's growth will continue to be a great source of demand for Korea's goods and services. China is Korea's number one trading partner, replacing the United States.
- Korea has learned its lesson from the economic crisis of 1998. Korea has considerably reformed its economic supervision as well as corporate governance dramatically. After the financial crisis, which provided a much needed shock, Korean society started to reform itself by modifying and strengthening banking supervision, as well as making corporate boards more responsible to individual stockholders. Reforms such as changing the law to include independent board members with strict implementation and accounting standards were tightened. For example, John cited the chairman of SK Telecom, who went to jail after being convicted of accounting fraud.
- Trade between China and Korea continues to be a significant growth driver for the Chinese economy.

On the topic of trade between China and Korea, John made the following points:

- There are now flights almost hourly between Seoul and Shanghai.
- There is export of heavy machinery, autos, technology, and electronics.
- Korea is much more global, effective, and has provided value-added opportunities.
- Trade with Europe and Asia is on the increase because of Korea's strong manufacturing and technology.
- Foreign companies are setting up operations in Korea to facilitate their trade with the growing nations of China and Korea, thereby benefiting Korea.

Korea is becoming a hub that can provide capital financial and management with technology skills. Korean stocks are reasonably priced at about ten times earnings and the growth is averaging at about 15 percent. However, the Korean market is more correlated with developed markets because the companies are more global and depend on exports. Koreans in general have not invested in equities; about 90 percent of savings are dedicated to bank deposits. However, the younger people are becoming more comfortable with the stock market and more willing to take risk. This may push the valuation of stocks higher.

An increasing number of asset managers, such as Merrill Lynch and Deutsche Bank, are entering the Korean market to capitalize on that future trend. Banks like Kookmin are also taking advantage of setting up operations to diversify their financial products.

Mexico

The following comments reflect an interview that I had with Bob von Rekowsky, a portfolio manager at Fidelity Emerging Markets Fund. The paraphrased comments address the question: What are the major financial themes for Mexico's government and economy?

The Mexican government has stabilized the political situation tremendously since the last election. The Calderon government is focusing on balancing the needs of all Mexicans and that looks very encouraging. There are not a lot of new ideas in Mexico. It is much more tied to the U.S. economy because of trade through NAFTA, and therefore may suffer from prolonged U.S. weakness. Overall, my reaction to the state of the Mexican economy is as follows:

- The top-down view looks great; government is moving ahead with reforms.
- I am very happy that the political situation has worked out.
- They used to watch what the locals were doing (about business and investments), but now Bob is trying to "see through the noise" of the local environment. Often, the locals only react to factors within the country, rather than considering the global backdrop.
- Calderon moved to the center; he shocked everyone with the pace of reform, moving ahead in a disciplined and bold way.

Bibliography

Abrams, Irwin (ed.). *Nobel Lectures in Peace 1981–1990.* River Edge, NJ: Nobel Foundation World Scientific Publishing Company, 1996.

Ahluwalia, Montek S. "Economic Reforms in India since 1991: Has Gradualism Worked?" *Journal of Economic Perspectives, American Economic Association*, 16 (3): 67–88, Summer 2002.

Andrade, Eduardo, Roberto Fantoni, and William Jones Jr. "What's Ahead for Business in Brazil." *The McKinsey Quarterly*, May 2007.

Bank of New York Mellon: *Depositary Receipt Directory*. Bank of New York Mellon. New York, 2007.

Binyan, Liu. *China's Crisis, China's Hope*. London: Harvard University Press, 1990.

Pointreau, Bertrand. "Rethinking Korea Full Speed Ahead." *Asian Wall Street Journal*, Bain & Company, November 13, 2000.

Brown, Archie. *The Gorbachev Factor*. London: Oxford University Press, 1996.

Buchanan, Mike, Sun Bae Kim, and Jim O'Neill. *Global Economics Paper No: 147*. Goldman Sachs, & Co., New York, 2006.

Buckman, Robert T. *Latin America: 2005*. West Virginia: Stryker-Post Publications, 2005.

Burgleman, Robert, and Aneesha Capur. *Infosys Consulting in 2006*. Boston: Harvard Business School, May 16, 2006.

Caprio, Gerard, and Daniela Klingebiel. "Episodes of Systemic and Borderline Financial Crises." World Bank Working Paper, p. 2, 2003.

Central Intelligence Agency. *The World Factbook*. Washington, DC: CIA Publications, 2007.

Chaze, Aaron. *India: An Investors Guide to the Next Economic Superpower*. Singapore: John Wiley & Sons, 2006.

Chow, Gregory C. *China's Economic Transformation*. Oxford: Blackwell Publishing Professional, pp. 294–295, 2002.

Chow, Gregory C. *Understanding China's Economy*. Hackensack, NJ: World Scientific Publishing Company, p. 91, 1994.

Churchill, Winston. BBC Radio Broadcast, October 1, 1939.

Craig, Albert M., William A. Graham, Donald Kagan, Steven M. Ozment, and Frank M. Turner. *The Heritage of World Civilizations*. Upper Saddle River: Prentice Hall, 1997.

Das, Gurcharan. *India Unbound: The Social and Economic Revolution from Independence to the Global Information Age*. New York: Random House, 2000.

David, Ruth. "Boeing Ups Forecast for Size of India Market." *Forbes Online*, July 31, 2007.

Deutsche Bank Research. "Mexico 2020: Tequila Sunrise." Deutsche Bank, February 16, 2006.

Deutsche Börse Group: *DAXglobal Russia Index*. Deutsche Börse Group. 2007

Djankov, Simeon, Caroline Freund, and Cong S. Pham. "Trading on Time: Reforms in Developing Countries Can Boost Exports." The World Bank, January 26, 2006.

Dunlop, John B. *The Rise of Russia and the Fall of the Soviet Empire*. Princeton, NJ: Princeton University Press, 1993.

Eakin, Marshall C. *Brazil: The Once and Future Country*. New York: St. Martin's Press, 1997.

Easterly, William, and Stanley Fischer. "The Soviet Economic Decline: Historical and Republican Data," in *World Bank Economic Review* 9 (3): 341–371.

Economic Information and Education Center, KDI. *Republic of Korea Economic Bulletin Vol. 29 No. 6*. Korea National Statistics Office, June 2007.

Economic Information and Education Center, KDI. *Republic of Korea Economic Bulletin Vol. 29 No. 7*. Korea National Statistics Office, July 2007.

Economist Intelligence Unit. *Russia: Financial Services Profile*, 2004.

Economist Intelligence Unit. *India: Financial Services Profile,* 2007.

Economist Intelligence Unit. *Mexico: Financial Services Profile,* 2007.

Engardio, Pete. *Chindia*. New York: McGraw Hill, 2006.

Epstein, Jack. "Unbundling Telebras: Latin America's Largest Privatization Turns a Stodgy Brazilian Giant into a Dozen Would-Be Dynamos." *Time*, August 10, 1998.

Euromonitor International. *Consumer Lifestyles in India Report*. Euromonitor International, June 2006.

Fausto, Boris. *A Concise History of Brazil*. Cambridge, UK: Cambridge University Press, 1999.

Fitzpatrick, Sheila. *The Russian Revolution*. Oxford, UK: Oxford University Press, 2001.

Gaddis, John Lewis. *The Cold War: A New History*. New York: Penguin Group, 2006.

Gatrell, Peter. *The Tsarist Economy, 1850–1917*. New York: St. Martins Press, 1986.

Goldman, Marshall I. *Lost Opportunity: Why Economic Reforms in Russia Have Not Worked*. New York: W. W. Norton & Company, 1994.

Goldman Sachs Asset Management. *Goldman Sachs BRIC Fund*. Goldman Sachs, & Co., New York, 2007.

Granville, Brigitte, and Peter Oppenheimer. *Russia's Post-Communist Economy*. New York: Oxford University Press, 2001.

Gregory, Paul R., and Robert C. Stuart. *Soviet and Post Soviet Economic Structure and Performance*. New York: HarperCollins College Division, 2001.

Hamnett, Brian R. *A Concise History of Mexico*. Cambridge, UK: Cambridge University Press, 2006.

Ho, Alfred K. *China's Reforms and Reformers*. London: Praeger, 2004.

Hufbauer, Gary Clyde, Jeffrey J. Schott, Paul L. E. Grieco, and Wong, Yee. "NAFTA Revisited: Achievements and Challenges." Institute for International Economics, 2005.

Hyundai Motor Company. www.hyundai-motor.com/. Historical profile, 2007.

International Monetary Fund. *Population Statistics for 2007*. World Economic Outlook Database, April 2007 www.imf.org/external/pubs/ft/weo/2007/01/data/weoselgr.aspx.

International Monetary Fund. *World Economic Outlook: The Global Demographic Transition*. International Monetary Fund, September 2004.

International Monetary Fund. *World Economic Outlook: Korea Country Profile*. International Monetary Fund, April 2007.

International Telecommunication Union. *World Telecommunication Development Report*. Geneva, 2006.

James, Lawrence. *Raj: The Making and Unmaking of British India*. New York: St. Martin's Griffin Press, 1997.

Johns, Melissa, and Jean Michael Lobet. "Case Study: Protecting Investors from Self-Dealing." World Bank Reformers Club, www.reformersclub.org/documents/reform/Mexico.pdf.

Johnson, Juliet. *A Fistful of Rubles: The Rise and Fall of the Russian Banking System*. London: Cornell University Press, 2000.

Kahn, Joseph, and Jim Yardley. "China—Pollution-Environment: As China Roars, Pollution Renders Deadly Extremes." *New York Times*, September 28, 2007.

Keay, John. *India: A History*. Washington, DC: Atlantic Monthly Press, 2000.

Klein, Lawrence R., and Marshall Pomer. *The New Russia: Transition Gone Awry*. Palo Alto, CA: Stanford University Press, 2001.

Klonsky, Joanna, and Stephanie Hanson. "Mercosur: South America's Fractious Trading Bloc." Council on Foreign Relations, accessed at www.bilaterals.org, March 1, 2007.

Kochhar, Kaplana, Utsav Kumar, Raghuran Rajan, Arvind Subramanian, and Ioannis Tokatlidis. "India's Pattern of Development: What Happened, What Follows." *Journal of Monetary Economics*, 53: 1021–1026, May 30, 2006.

Korea National Statistical Office (KNSO). *Population Statistical Survey*. Korean National Statistics Office, 2007.

Korea National Statistical Office (KNSO). *Economy Statistical Survey*. Korean National Statistics Office, 2007.

Korea National Statistical Office (KNSO). *Business Activities Statistical Survey*. Korean National Statistics Office, 2007.

Korea National Statistical Office (KNSO). *Korean Statistical Yearbook*. Korean National Statistics Office, January 2007.

Lardy, Nicholas R. *China's Unfinished Economic Revolution*. Brookings Institution Press, p. 119, September 1998.

Lardy, Nicholas R. *China: Toward a Consumption-Driven Growth Path*. Peterson Institute for International Economics, October 2006.

Leiven, Dominic. *Empire: The Russian Empire and its Rivals*. New Haven, CT: Yale University Press, 2002.

Levine, Robert M. *The History of Brazil*. Westport, CT, and London: Greenwood Press, p. 143, 1999.

Library of Congress—Federal Research Division. *Country Studies: Mexico*, July 2006 www.countrystudies.us/mexico.

Lieberthal, Kenneth. *Governing China: From Revolution through Reform*. New York: W. W Norton & Company, 2004.

Lincoln, W. Bruce. *The Great Reforms: Autocracy, Bureaucracy and the Politics of Change in Imperial Russia*. Bloomington: Indiana University Press, 1990.

Lovgren, Stefan. "A Robot in Every Home by 2020, South Korea Says." *National Geographic*, September 6, 2006.

Macedo, Robert. "Macroeconomic Volatility and Social Vulnerability in Brazil: The Cardoso Government." UN Special Studies Unit, p. 32, June 2003 www.eclac.org/publicaciones/xml/5/12645/lcl1914i.pdf.

Mackerras, C., P. Taneja, and G. Young. *China Since 1978*. New York: Longman Cheshire, 1994.

MacMillan, Margaret. *Nixon and Mao*. New York: Random House, 2007.

Marshall, Rebekkah. "Grassroot Expansion Planned in Mexico." *Chemical Engineering*, March 5, 2001.

McKinsey Global Institute. *A Tale of Two Financial Systems: A Comparison of China and India*. McKinsey & Co. Inc., September, 2006.

McKinsey Global Institute. *From "Made in China" to "Sold in China": The Rise of the Chinese Urban Consumer*. McKinsey & Co. Inc., November, 2006.

McKinsey Global Institute. *The 'Bird of Gold': The Rise of India's Consumer Market*. McKinsey & Co. Inc., May, 2007.

Meisner, Maurice. *Mao's China and After*. New York: Free Press, 1986.

Melser, Daniel. *Asia Pacific Outlook*. Moody's Economy.com. Australia, 2006.

Morgan Stanley Capital International. *MSCI Russia Index*, Table 7.3, September 12, 2007.

Musacchio, Aldo. "Brazil under Lula: Off the Yellow BRIC Road." Harvard Business School Publishing, February 15, 2007.

NASSCOM. *Indian IT Industry Factsheet (2008)*. NASSCOM, 2008.

Newsroom. "CVRD Expands Brazilian Steel Industry Partnering with ThyssenKrupp," *Brazzil Magazine*, November 24, 2006.

Nolan, Peter. *Transforming China*. London: Wimbledon Publishing Company, 2004.

Noland, Marcus. "The Strategic Importance of US-Korea Economic Relations." National Bureau of Asian Research, July 2003.

North, Robert C. *Chinese Communism*. New York: World University Library, 1966.

Nove, Alec. *An Economic History of the USSR, 1917–1991*. New York: Penguin Books, 1990.

Oberdorfer, Don. *The Two Koreas: A Contemporary History*. Massachusetts: Addison-Wesley, 1997.

Ofer, Gur. "Soviet Economic Growth, 1928–85." *Journal of Economic Literature*, 25 (4): 1767–1883.

Pipes, Richard. *Russia under the Bolshevik Regime*. New York: Knopf, 1994.

Pitsilis, Emmanuel, Jonathan Woetzel, and Jeffrey Wong. "Global Report on China: China Foreign Trade Yearbook 2003." McKinsey & Company.

Poterba, James M. "The Impact of Population Aging on Financial Markets." National Bureau of Economic Research, October 2004.

PricewaterhouseCoopers Publications. *From Bejing to Budapest: Winning brands, Winning Formats: 2005/2006—4th Edition*. Pricewaterhouse Coopers, 2006.

Purushothaman, Roopa, and Dominic Wilson. *Global Economics Paper No: 99*. Goldman Sachs, & Co., New York, 2003.

U.S. Government, Presidential News Releases. Joint Statement on the Occasion of the Visit by President Luiz Inácio Lula da Silva to Camp David. Office of the Press Secretary, March 31, 2007.

Read, Christopher. *The Making and Breaking of the Soviet System: An Interpretation*. New York: Palgrave Macmillan, 2001.

Research and Markets. Indian Retail Industry: Strategies, Trends and Opportunities 2007. www.researchandmarkets.com, June 2007.

Rosenbaum, Arthur. *State and Society in China*. Oxford: Westview Press, 1992.

Roy, Medvedev. *Post-Soviet Russia*. New York: Columbia University Press, 2000.

Rubin, Robert E. *In an Uncertain World*. New York: Random House, 2003.

Samsung. Group Timeline and History, www.samsung.com/AboutSAMSUNG/SAMSUNGGroup/TimelineHistory/index.htm.

Schott, Jeffrey J. "The Korea-US Free Trade Agreement: A Summary Assessment." Washington: Peterson Institute for International Economics, August 2007.

Seton-Watson, Hugh. *The Russian Empire 1801–1917.* Gloucestershire, UK: Clarendon Press, 1967.

Shevtsova, Lilia. *Yeltsin's Russia: Myth and Reality.* Washington, DC: Carnegie Endowment for International Peace, 1998.

Shleifer, Andrei, and Daniel Treisman, *Without a Map: Political Tactics and Economic Reform in Russia.* Boston: MIT Press, 2000.

Srinivasan, T. N., and Suresh D. Tendulkar, "Reintegrating India with the World." Economy Instiute for International Economics, 2003.

Tharoor, Shashi. *India: From Midnight to the Millenium.* New York: Harper Collins, 1997.

The Goldman Sachs Economic Group. "The World and the BRICs Dream." New York: Goldman Sachs Group Inc., 2006.

The World Bank. *China: Air, Land, and Water.* Washington, DC: The World Bank, pp. 11–13, 77, 2001.

The World Bank. *Country Profile: Russian Federation Data Profile, 2005*, http://devdata.worldbank.org/external/CPProfile.asp?PTYPE=CP&CCODE=RUS, Washington, DC.

The World Bank. *Trade Restrictiveness Index and Dead Weight Loss Based on 2006 data.* Washington, DC.

The World Bank Institute. *Governance Matters 2006.* The World Bank, Washington, DC, 2006.

The World Bank Institute. *Governance Matters 2007.* The World Bank, Washington, DC, 2007

Tyers, Rod, Jane Golley, and Ian Bain. "Projected Economic Growth in China and India: The Role of Demographic Change." Australian National University Working Papers in Economics and Econometrics, November 2007.

United Nations. *Human Development Report 2006.* New York: United Nations Development Programme, pp. 148–149, 2006.

Vietor, Richard H. K., and Rebecca Evans. "Mexico: The Unfinished Agenda." Harvard Business School Case 701-116, December 10, 2003.

Ward, Thomas. "Brazil: Forestry Fortunes." *Oxford Analytica*, April 29, 2003.

Westin, Peter. *The Wild East: Negotiating the Russian Financial Frontier.* New York: Reuters, 2001.

Wolf, Charles Jr., and Thomas Lang. "Russia's Economy: Signs of Progress and Retreat on the Transitional Road." Santa Monica: National Defense Research Institute and RAND Corporation, 2006.

Wilson, Purushothaman. "Dreaming with the BRIC's Path to 2050." *Goldman Sachs Report*, p. 10, October 2003 (www.gs.com).

Wine, Michael. "Russian Nominee Warns of Chaos If He Is Rejected." *New York Times*, September 7, 1998.

World Economic Forum. "The Global Competitiveness Report 2007." www.weforum.org.

Glossary[1]

Active management A money management approach based on informed, independent investment judgment, as opposed to passive management (indexing), which seeks to match the performance of the overall market (or some part of it) by mirroring its composition or by being broadly diversified.

Alpha A coefficient, which measures risk-adjusted performance, factoring in the risk due to the specific security, rather than the overall market. A high value for alpha implies that the stock or mutual fund has performed better than would have been expected given its beta (volatility).

American Depositary Receipt (ADR) A negotiable certificate issued by a U.S. bank representing a specific number of shares of a foreign stock traded on a U.S. stock exchange. ADRs make it easier for Americans to invest in foreign companies, due to the widespread availability of dollar-denominated price information, lower transaction costs, and timely dividend distributions.

Beta A quantitative measure of the volatility of a given stock, mutual fund, or portfolio, relative to the overall market, usually the S&P 500. Specifically, the performance the stock, fund or portfolio has experienced in the past five years as the S&P moved 1 percent up or down. A beta above 1 is more volatile than the overall market, while a beta below 1 is less volatile.

Capitalization weighted index A stock index in which each stock affects the index in proportion to its market value. Examples include the Nasdaq Composite Index, S&P 500, Wilshire 5000 Equity Index, Hang Seng Index, and EAFE Index. Also called *market-value weighted index*.

Closed-end fund A fund with a fixed number of shares outstanding, which does not redeem shares the way a typical mutual fund does.

[1]This Glossary is provided by InvestorWords.com and is being printed here with permission.

Closed-end funds behave more like stock than open-end funds: Closed-end funds issue a fixed number of shares to the public in an initial public offering, after which time shares in the fund are bought and sold on a stock exchange, and they are not obligated to issue new shares or redeem outstanding shares as open-end funds are. The price of a share in a closed-end fund is determined entirely by market demand, so shares can either trade below their net asset value ("at a discount") or above it ("at a premium"). Also called *closed-end investment company* or *publicly traded fund.*

Consumer Price Index (CPI) An inflationary indicator that measures the change in the cost of a fixed basket of products and services, including housing, electricity, food, and transportation. The CPI is published monthly. Also called *cost-of-living index.*

Currency risk The risk that a business's operations or an investment's value will be affected by changes in exchange rates. For example, if money must be converted into a different currency to make a certain investment, changes in the value of the currency relative to the American dollar will affect the total loss or gain on the investment when the money is converted back. This risk usually affects businesses, but it can also affect individual investors who make international investments. Also called *exchange rate risk.*

CUSIP number A nine-character number that uniquely identifies a particular security. CUSIP is an acronym for the Committee on Uniform Securities and Identification Procedures, the standards body that created and maintains the classification system. Foreign securities have a similar number, called the CINS number.

EAFE Index The Europe, Australia, and Far East Index from Morgan Stanley Capital International. It is an unmanaged, market-value weighted index designed to measure the overall condition of overseas markets.

European Depositary Receipt (EDR) A negotiable certificate held in the bank of one country representing a specific number of shares of a stock traded on an exchange of another country. American Depositary Receipts make it easier for individuals to invest in foreign companies, due to the widespread availability of price information, lower transaction costs, and timely dividend distributions. Also called *Global Depositary Receipt (GDR).*

European Monetary System System established to encourage monetary stability in Europe through the implementation of credit and exchange rate policies.

Exchange-traded fund (ETF) A fund that tracks an index, but can be traded like a stock. ETFs always bundle together the securities that are in an index; they never track actively managed mutual fund portfolios (because most actively managed funds only disclose their holdings a few times a year, so the ETF would not know when to adjust its holdings most of the time). Investors can do just about anything with an ETF that they can do with a normal stock, such as short selling. Because ETFs are traded on stock exchanges, they can be bought and sold at any time during the day (unlike most mutual funds). Their price will fluctuate from moment to moment, just like any other stock's price, and an investor will need a broker in order to purchase them, which means that he/she will have to pay a commission. On the plus side, ETFs are more tax efficient than normal mutual funds, and since they track indexes, they have very low operating and transaction costs associated with them. There are no sales loads or investment minimums required to purchase an ETF. The first ETF created was the Standard and Poor's Deposit Receipt (SPDR, pronounced "Spider") in 1993. SPDRs gave investors an easy way to track the S&P 500 without buying an index fund, and they soon become quite popular.

Expense ratio For a mutual fund, operating costs, including management fees, expressed as a percentage of the fund's average net assets for a given time period. The expense ratio does not include brokerage costs and various other transaction costs that may also contribute to a fund's total expenses.

Fiscal Pertaining to money, especially government taxation and spending policies.

Float (1) The number of shares of a security that are outstanding and available for trading by the public. (2) The amount of money or time represented by checks that are in transit between deposit and payment, or credit card purchases that are between the purchase and the payment. (3) To allow the value of currency to be determined solely by supply and demand without outside interference.

Foreign direct investment (FDI) Direct investments in productive assets by a company incorporated in a foreign country, as opposed to investments in shares of local companies by foreign entities. An important feature of an increasingly globalized economic system.

Foreign exchange Instruments, such as paper currency, notes, and checks, used to make payments between countries.

Front-end load A sales charge paid when an individual buys an investment, such as a mutual fund, limited partnership, annuity, or insurance policy. The load is clubbed with the first payment made by an investor, so the total initial payment is higher than the later payments. The purpose of a load is to cover administrative expenses and transaction costs and sometimes to discourage asset turnover. Opposite of back-end load.

FTSE The Financial Times Stock Exchange 100 stock index, a market cap weighted index of stocks traded on the London Stock Exchange. Similar to the S&P 500 in the United States.

Global Depositary Receipt (GDR) A negotiable certificate held in the bank of one country representing a specific number of shares of a stock traded on an exchange of another country. American Depositary Receipts make it easier for individuals to invest in foreign companies, due to the widespread availability of price information, lower transaction costs, and timely dividend distributions. Also called *European Depositary Receipt (EDR).*

Gross domestic product (GDP) The total market value of all final goods and services produced in a country in a given year, equal to total consumer, investment, and government spending, plus the value of exports, minus the value of imports. The GDP report is released at 8:30 AM EST on the last day of each quarter and reflects the previous quarter. Growth in GDP is what matters, and the U.S. GDP growth has historically averaged about 2.5 percent to 3 percent per year but with substantial deviations. Each initial GDP report will be revised twice before the final figure is settled upon: the "advance" report is followed by the "preliminary" report about a month later and a final report a month after that. Significant revisions to the advance number can cause additional ripples through the markets. The GDP numbers are reported in two forms: current dollar and constant dollar. Current dollar GDP is calculated using today's dollars and makes comparisons between time periods difficult because of the effects of inflation. Constant dollar GDP solves this problem by converting the current information into some standard era dollar, such as 1997 dollars. This process factors out the effects of inflation and allows easy comparisons between periods. It is important to differentiate gross domestic product from gross national product (GNP). GDP includes only goods and services produced within the geographic boundaries of the United States, regardless of the producer's nationality. GNP doesn't include goods and services produced by foreign producers, but does include goods and services produced by U.S. firms operating in foreign countries.

Gross national product (GNP) GDP plus the income accruing to domestic residents as a result of investments abroad, minus the income earned in domestic markets accruing to foreigners abroad.

Hang Seng Index A market-value weighted index of the stock prices of the 33 largest companies on the Hong Kong market.

Hedge fund A fund, usually used by wealthy individuals and institutions, which is allowed to use aggressive strategies that are unavailable to mutual funds, including selling short, leverage, program trading, swaps, arbitrage, and derivatives. Hedge funds are exempt from many of the rules and regulations governing other mutual funds, which allow them to accomplish aggressive investing goals. They are restricted by law to no more than 100 investors per fund, and as a result most hedge funds set extremely high minimum investment amounts, ranging anywhere from $250,000 to over $1 million. As with traditional mutual funds, investors in hedge funds pay a management fee; however, hedge funds also collect a percentage of the profits (usually 20 percent).

Index fund A passively managed mutual fund that tries to mirror the performance of a specific index, such as the S&P 500. Since portfolio decisions are automatic and transactions are infrequent, expenses tend to be lower than those of actively managed funds.

Inflation rate The percentage increase in the price of goods and services, usually annually.

International Monetary Fund (IMF) An organization set up in 1944 to lower trade barriers between countries and to stabilize currencies by monitoring the foreign exchange systems of member countries and lending money to developing nations.

International Monetary Fund (IMF) An organization set up in 1944 to lower trade barriers between countries and to stabilize currencies by monitoring the foreign exchange systems of member countries, and lending money to developing nations.

London Interbank Offered Rate (LIBOR) The interest rate that the banks charge each other for loans (usually in Eurodollars). This rate is applicable to the short-term international interbank market, and applies to very large loans borrowed for anywhere from one day to five years. This market allows banks with liquidity requirements to borrow quickly from other banks with surpluses, enabling banks to avoid holding excessively large amounts of their asset base as liquid assets. The LIBOR is officially fixed once a day by a small group of large London banks, but the rate changes throughout the day.

Monetary policy The regulation of the money supply and interest rates by a central bank, such as the Federal Reserve Board in the United States, in order to control inflation and stabilize currency. Monetary policy is one of two ways the government can impact the economy. By impacting the effective cost of money, the Federal Reserve can affect the amount of money that is spent by consumers and businesses.

Mutual fund An open-ended fund operated by an investment company, which raises money from shareholders and invests in a group of assets, in accordance with a stated set of objectives. Mutual funds raise money by selling shares of the fund to the public, much like any other type of company can sell stock in itself to the public. Mutual funds then take the money they receive from the sale of their shares (along with any money made from previous investments) and use it to purchase various investment vehicles, such as stocks, bonds and money market instruments. In return for the money they give to the fund when purchasing shares, shareholders receive an equity position in the fund and, in effect, in each of its underlying securities. For most mutual funds, shareholders are free to sell their shares at any time, although the price of a share in a mutual fund will fluctuate daily, depending upon the performance of the securities held by the fund. Benefits of mutual funds include diversification and professional money management. Mutual funds offer choice, liquidity, and convenience, but charge fees and often require a minimum investment. A closed-end fund is often incorrectly referred to as a mutual fund, but is actually an investment trust. There are many types of mutual funds, including aggressive growth fund, asset allocation fund, balanced fund, blend fund, bond fund, capital appreciation fund, clone fund, closed fund, crossover fund, equity fund, fund of funds, global fund, growth fund, growth and income fund, hedge fund, income fund, index fund, international fund, money market fund, municipal bond fund, prime rate fund, regional fund, sector fund, specialty fund, stock fund, and tax-free bond fund.

National debt The sum of all previously incurred annual federal deficits. Since the deficits are financed by government borrowing, national debt is equal to all government debt outstanding.

Net asset value (NAV) The dollar value of a single mutual fund share, based on the value of the underlying assets of the fund minus its liabilities, divided by the number of shares outstanding. Calculated at the end of each business day.

Nikkei Index Index of 225 leading stocks traded on the Tokyo Stock Exchange.

No-load fund A mutual fund that does not impose a sales or redemption charge, selling and redeeming its shares at net asset value. Opposite of load fund.

Open-end fund A fund operated by an investment company that raises money from shareholders and invests in a group of assets, in accordance with a stated set of objectives. Open-end funds raise money by selling shares of the fund to the public, much like any other type of company that can sell stock in itself to the public. Mutual funds then take the money they receive from the sale of their shares (along with any money made from previous investments) and use it to purchase various investment vehicles, such as stocks, bonds, and money market instruments. In return for the money they give to the fund when purchasing shares, shareholders receive an equity position in the fund and, in effect, in each of its underlying securities. For most open-end funds, shareholders are free to sell their shares at any time, although the price of a share in an open-end fund will fluctuate daily, depending upon the performance of the securities held by the fund. Benefits of open-end funds include diversification and professional money management. Open-end funds offer choice, liquidity, and convenience, but charge fees and often require a minimum investment. Also called mutual fund.

Organization for Economic Cooperation and Development (OECD) An organization that acts as a meeting ground for 30 countries that believe strongly in the free market system, The OECD provides a forum for discussing issues and reaching agreements, some of which are legally binding.

Political risk The risk of loss when investing in a given country caused by changes in a country's political structure or policies, such as tax laws, tariffs, expropriation of assets, or restriction in repatriation of profits. For example, a company may suffer from such loss in the case of expropriation or tightened foreign exchange repatriation rules, or from increased credit risk if the government changes policies to make it difficult for the company to pay creditors.

Privatization (1) The repurchasing of all of a company's outstanding stock by employees or a private investor. As a result of such an initiative, the company stops being publicly traded. Sometimes, the company might have to take on significant debt to finance the change in ownership structure. Companies might want to go private in order to restructure their businesses (when they feel that the process might affect their stock prices poorly in the short run). They might also want to go private to avoid the expense and regulations associated with remaining listed on a stock exchange. Also called *going private.* Opposite of going public. (2) The process of moving from a government-controlled system to a privately run, for-profit system.

Productivity The amount of output per unit of input (labor, equipment, and capital). There are many different ways of measuring productivity. For example, in a factory productivity might be measured based on the number of hours it takes to produce a good, while in the service sector productivity might be measured based on the revenue generated by an employee divided by his/her salary.

Prospectus A legal document offering securities or mutual fund shares for sale, required by the Securities Act of 1933. It must explain the offer, including the terms, issuer, objectives (if mutual fund) or planned use of the money (if securities), historical financial statements, and other information that could help an individual decide whether the investment is appropriate for him/her. Also called *offering circular* or *circular.*

Purchasing power parity The theory that, in the long run, identical products and services in different countries should cost the same in different countries. This is based on the belief that exchange rates will adjust to eliminate the arbitrage opportunity of buying a product or service in one country and selling it in another. For example, consider a laptop computer that costs 1,500 euros in Germany and an exchange rate of 2 euros to 1 U.S. dollar. If the same laptop cost $1,000 in the United States, U.S. consumers would buy the laptop in Germany. If done on a large scale, the influx of U.S. dollars would drive up the price of the euro, until it equalized at 1.5 euros to 1 U.S. dollar—the same ratio of the price of the laptop in Germany to the price of the laptop in the United States. The theory applies only to tradable goods, not to immobile goods or local services. The theory also discounts several real-world factors, such as transportation costs, tariffs, and transaction costs. It also assumes there are competitive markets for the goods and services in both countries.

Real GDP The number reached by valuing all the productive activity within the country at a specific year's prices. When economic activity of two or more time periods is valued at the same year's prices, the resulting figure allows comparison of purchasing power over time, since the effects of inflation have been removed by maintaining constant prices.

Securities and Exchange Commission (SEC) The primary federal regulatory agency for the securities industry, whose responsibility is to promote full disclosure and to protect investors against fraudulent and manipulative practices in the securities markets. The Securities and Exchange Commission enforces, among other acts, the Securities Act of 1933, the Securities Exchange Act of 1934, the Trust Indenture Act of 1939, the Investment Company Act of 1940, and the Investment Advisers Act. The supervision of dealers is delegated to the self-regulatory bodies of the exchanges. The Securities and Exchange Commission is an independent, quasi-judiciary agency. It has five commissioners, each appointed for a five-year term that is staggered so that one new commissioner is being replaced every year. No more than three members of the commission can be of a single political party. The Securities and Exchange Commission is comprised of four basic divisions. The Division of Corporate Finance is in charge of making sure all publicly traded companies disclose the required financial information to investors. The Division of Market Regulation oversees all legislation involving brokers and brokerage firms. The Division of Investment Management regulates the mutual fund and investment adviser industries. The Division of Enforcement enforces the securities legislation and investigates possible violations.

Sharpe ratio A risk-adjusted measure developed by William F. Sharpe, calculated using standard deviation and excess return to determine reward per unit of risk. The higher the Sharpe ratio, the better the fund's historical risk-adjusted performance.

Standard deviation A statistical measure of the historical volatility of a mutual fund or portfolio, usually computed using 36 monthly returns. More generally, a measure of the extent to which numbers are spread around their average.

World Bank An organization whose focus is on foreign exchange reserves and the balance of trade.

World Trade Organization (WTO) An international agency that encourages trade between member nations, administers global trade agreements, and resolves disputes when they arise.

Index

Active management, 357
ADRs. *See* American Depositary Receipts
Air India, 142
Air Sahara, 138
Alexander the Great, 97
Alpha, 357
Aluminum Corporation of China, 192
American Depositary Receipts (ADRs), 291, 357
  usage. *See* Foreign stocks
Apollo Hospitals, 147
Arvind Eye Care Center, 147–148
Arvind Mills Ltd., 143
Ashoka, 97–98
Ashok Leyland, 137
Associated Cement, 139

Bajaj Auto, 142
Baoshan Iron & Steel, 192
Bata India Ltd., 143
BCI. *See* Business Competitiveness Index
Beijing Urban Construction Group Co., Ltd., 193
Beta, 357
Bhagwan Mahaveer Viklang Sahayata Samiti (BMVSS), 148
Bharat Electronics, 138
Bharat Forge, 137
Bharat Heavy Electricals Limited (BHEL), 138
Bharat Heavy Elements, 137
Bharti Televentures, 145
Bibliography, 351
Biodiesel opportunity. *See* Brazil
Bolsheviks, power consolidation. *See* Russia

Brazil
  ADRs, 292–297
  biodiesel opportunity, 54
  colonization, 26–28
  data profile, 269–271
  demographics, 41–44
  economic challenges, 35–36
  economic crisis, 31–32
  economic miracle, 30–31
  economic performance, 44–46
  education/training, 50–51
  energy, 53–54
  examination, 342
  exports, 47–48
  financials, 54–55
  financial system/policies, 51–52
  forest products, 53
  free elections, 32
  GDP growth, expansion, 44–46
  governance indicators, 287t
  growth industries, 52–55
  history, 25
  index sector weights. *See* MSCI Brazil Index sector weights
  industrialization, beginnings, 29–30
  inflation, 31–32
    low level, 35–36
  infrastructure development, 48
  investment, 41
  metals/mining, 53
  middle class, expansion, 44–46
  modern history, 33
  mutual funds, 327, profiles
  open economy, 32
  open trade, 47–48
  opportunity, 41
  performance, 7–8

Brazil (*Continued*)
population
growth, 42f
percentage, combination, 43f
PPP per-capita GDP, growth, 45f
presidential election (1998), 36–37
real GDP, 46f
recession, 31–32
slavery, legacy, 27–28
society, change, 28
technology, 46–47
total population, children (percentage), 43f
transparency, Rule of Law (relationship), 50
Brazil Russia India China (BRIC) fund profiles, 337
Business Competitiveness Index (BCI) ranking, 286t

Calderon Hinojosa, Felipe, 246–247
Capitalization weighted index, 357
Cardoso, Fernando Henrique
first term, 33–35
Plano Real, 33–34
privatization, 34–35
second term, 37
CESC Ltd, 134
Change, tenets, 2–7
China
ADRs, 316–319
agriculture, shift, 173
ancient history, 150–152
automobile capacity, 172
banking
reform, 163–164
system, 182–185
banks, 189
basic materials, 192
capitalization, opportunities, 186t
cash crops, 161
corruption, 180
cultural revolution, 156–158
data profile, 275–277
demographics, 169–171
digital electronics, 175–176
economic experimentation, encouragement, 162–163
economic performance, 171–175
education/training, 180–181
environment, 178–179
examination, 346–347
external debt, 185
financials, 188–189
financial systems/policies, 181–185
foreign debt, 185t
foreign exchange rates, 184–185
future, 169
GDP growth, 173–174
governance indicators, 289t
Great Leap Forward, 155–156
growth industries, 185–193
history, 149
holdings, ranking, 187
India, equity markets (comparison), 132–133
industrials, 192–193
inflation, 181–182
infrastructure development, 177–179
investment, 169
land reforms, 152–153
market economy, transformation, 161–162
middle class, growth, 171–173
modern history, 159
mutual funds, profiles, 327–330
oil/gas, 190–191
open trade, 176–177
performance, 9
politics, Deng (role), 166
population, aging, 170f
population growth, 42f
post-Deng years, 166–167
purchasing power parity, 184
Russia, support, 154–155
savings, levels, 182–183
seasons, change, 150–152
socialism, change, 164–165
success, consequences, 165
technology, 175–176
telecommunications, 189–190
Tiananmen Square, 165–166
trade surplus/openness, 177f
transparency, Rule of Law (relationship), 179–180
urban economy, 153–154
urban households, share, 172t

urbanization, 174–175
victory, coping, 152–156
water supplies, 179
wealth, share, 188t
China Communications Construction Group Ltd., 193
China Construction Bank, 189
China Construction BAnk (CCB), IPO, 183
China Life Insurance, 189
China Merchants Bank, 189
China National Offshore Oil Corporation (CNOOC), 191
China National Petroleum Corporation (CNPC), 191
China Resources Enterprises, 192
Cipla, 147
Closed-end fund, 357–358
Cognizant, 136
Cold War. *See* Russia
Colgate Palmolive India, 144
Consumer markets, ranking. *See* World consumer markets
Consumer Price Index (CPI), 358
Container Corporation, 138
Countries. *See* Nations/countries
Crompton Greaves, 137
Currency risk, 358
CUSIP number, 358

DAX Russia Index sector weights, 89t
Demographics, impact, 2–3
Diaz, Porfirio *(Porfiriato),* 237
Diversification, importance, 264
Divide-and-rule policy, 101–102
Dr. Reddy's Laboratories, 147

EAFE. *See* Europe Australia and Far East
East India Company, 99–100
Economic crisis. *See* Brazil
Economic growth, 17–18
Economic performance, impact, 3–4
Economic pillars, 283–284
Economies
advanced phase, 286
development phases, 284
middle phase, 286
EDR. *See* European Depositary Receipt
Education
impact, 6
investments, 19
Efficiency enhancers, 286
Eldorado, 93
Embraer *(Empresa Brasileira de Aeronáutica SA),* company profile, 48–50
Emerging markets
caution, 265–266
correlation comparisons. *See* U.S. markets
performance, 265t
volatility, 264–265
European Depositary Receipt (EDR), 358
Europe Australia and Far East (EAFE) Index, 358
Exchange-trade fund (ETF), 358–359
Expense ratio, 359

FDI. *See* Foreign direct investment
Financial systems/policies. *See* Brazil; Russia
soundness, 7
Financial Times Stock Exchange 100 (FTSE), 359
Fiscal, term (usage), 359
Float, 359
Foreign direct investment (FDI), 359
Foreign exchange, 359
Foreign stocks (investment), ADRs (usage), 268
Fox, Vicente, 243
Sexenio, 245–246
Front-end load, 359
FTSE. *See* Financial Times Stock Exchange 100

GAIL Limited Energy Oil & Gas Operations, 134
Gandhi, Mohandas Karamchand, 101
Gazprom, 90
Gazprom Neft, 91
GCI. *See* Global Competitiveness Index
GDR. *See* Global Depositary Receipt
GKO bonds (short-term government bonds), issuance. *See* Russia
Glenmark Pharmaceuticals, 147

Global Competitiveness Index (GCI), 283
  2006–2007, 284t
Global Depositary Receipt (GDR), 360
Godrej Agrovet Ltd., 143
Goldman Sachs BRIC Fund, 337–338
Gorbachev, Mikhail, 63–64
  coup, attempt, 64–66
Governance indicators, 287
Great Korea, building. *See* Korea
Gross domestic product (GDP), 360
Gross national product (GNP), 360

Hang Seng Index, 360
HCL Technologies, 136
Hedge fund, 360–361
Hindustan Construction, 138
Hindustan Lever, 144
Hotel Leelaventure, 142
Housing Development and Infrastructure Ltd., 138
Hyundai Motor Industrial Company, 226–227

Ikea, 93
Index fund, 361
India
  ADRs, 305–315
  agriculture, shift, 115–116
  automobile market, 140–141
  basic materials, 138–139
  biotech innovation, 121
  Britain, financial impact, 99–100
  businesses, success, 109–110
  cell phones, usage, 117
  chemicals, 139
  civilization, origins, 95–96
  construction/engineering/heavy industry, 138
  consumer discretionary sector, 139
  consumer staples, 144
  currency, exchange rates, 129
  data profile, 273–275
  demographics, 111–113
  divide-and-rule policy, 101–102
  drama, 105
  economic performance, 113–116
  economic reform, 106
  economy
    awakening, 103–105
    obstacles, 107–108
  education/training, 128
  energy/utilities/power, 133–148
  entertainment (TV/movies), 143–144
  equity markets, comparison. *See* China
  examination, 345–346
  external debt, 130
  eye care, 147–148
  financials, 132
  financial systems/policies, 128–130
  fiscal control, 130
  foreign direct investment (FDI), 124
  Gandhi, appearance, 101
  GDP growth, 113–115
  governance indicators, 288t
  growth industries, 130–132
  health care, 145–146
    companies, 147
    innovations, 147–148
  history, 95
  hotel developers, 142
  IMF, impact, 108–109
  independence
    achievement, 102–103
    challenge, 100
  index sector weights. *See* MSCI India Index sector weights
  industrials, 136–137
  inflation, 129–130
  information technology, 121–123, 134–136
    performance, highlights, 136t
  infrastructure development, 124–126
    finance corporation, 137
  investment, 111
  law and order governance indicator, 127t
  leaders/invaders, 96–98
  medical tourism, 120
  middle class, growth, 113
  modern history, 107
  monetary policy, 129
  Mughals, impact, 98–99
  Muslim invasions, 98
  mutual funds, profiles, 330–332
  nation, awakening, 100–101
  open trade, 123–124
  outsourcing, 118–120
  performance, 8–9
  pharmaceutical/biotechnology market, 146–147

population growth, 42f
power, 111
privativization, 124
religion, rise, 96–97
retailing, 142–143
securities market, 130
technology
expansion, 116–117
penetration, 117–118
Toyota, involvement, 140
transparency, Rule of Law (relationship), 126–128
transportation, 137–138
travel/hospitality, 142
urbanization, 116
44-145India
telecommunication services, 1
India Airlines, 142
India Hotels Company Ltd. (IHCL), 142
Industrial & Commerce Bank of China, 189
Inequality measures, 252t
Inflation rate, 361
Infosys Technologies, 118–119, 135
Infrastructure development, impact, 5–6
International Monetary Fund (IMF), 361
impact. *See* India
Investment
capital, inflows, 18–19
long-term focus, 264
returns, relationship. *See* Success factors
timing, unimportance, 264–265
Investor opportunities, 23
ION Exchange, 139
ITC, 144

Jaiprakash Construction, 138
Jaipur foot, development, 148
Jet Airways, 138, 142
Jubilant Organosys, 139

Kingfisher Airlines, 138, 142
Korea. *See* South Korea
Korus FTA, 219

Larsen & Toubro, 138
Larsen & Turbo, 137
London Interbank Offered Rate (LIBOR), 361
LukOil, 91
Lula da Silva, Luiz Inácio, 37–39
reelection, 38–39

Maanshan Iron & Steel, 192
Mahindra & Mahindra, 142
Market, investment, 13
advice, 263
development, diversification benefits, 22
Markets
examination, 341
experts, interviews, 341
external/internal shocks, caution, 267–268
modern history, examination, 268
volatility. *See* Emerging markets
Maruti Udyog, Ltd., 142
Metro AG, 93
Mexican-American War, 235
Mexican Revolution (1910–1921), 237–238
Mexico
ADRs, 323–325
auto parts/components market, 360
civil war, 235–237
colonial period, 231–232
consumer products (staples/discretionary) market, 260–261
data profile, 279–288
democracy, 243
demographics, 250–251
early history, 229–232
economic crisis/recovery, 240–241
economic performance, 251–253
economic prosperity, 243–244
education/training, 256–257
examination, 350
financial systems/policies, 257–258
free economy, 243
GDP growth, 251–253
governance indicators, 290t
growth industries, 258–261
history, 229
independence, 232–235
industrials, 261
infrastructure development, 255–256
investment, 249
materials, 259–260

Mexico (*Continued*)
middle class, 251–253
miracle. *See* Milagro Mexicano
mutual funds, profiles, 332–333
open trade, 254–255
performance, 10
pharmaceuticals, 261
political reforms, 244–245
post-independence, 234
post-revolutionary years, 239–240
reform, 235–237
Santa Anna, 234–235
Spanish conquest, 230–231
technology, 253–254
telecommunication services, 259
Tortilla crisis, 246–247
transparency, Rule of Law (relationship), 256
travel/tourism market, 260
Milagro Mexicano, El (Mexican Miracle), 239–240
Millennium Bug phenomenon, 134–135
Minmetals Development, 192
Monetary policy, 361
MSCI Brazil Index sector weights, 52t
MSCI China Index sector weights, 186t
MSCI India Index sector weights, 131t
MSCI Mexico Index sector weights, 258t
MSCI Russia Index sector weights, 89t
MSCI South Korea Index sector weights, 225t
Mughals, impact. *See* India
Muslim invasions. *See* India
Mutual funds, 361–362
investment, examination, 267
profiles, 327

Nagarjuna Construction Co. Ltd., 138
National debt, 362
National financial systems, 18
Nations/countries
investment, 14–15
phase emphasis, 284t
profiles, 269
quality, 7–10
scores/ranking, 285t
selection, importance, 263
stock portfolio allocation, 266–267
Nehru, Jawaharlal, 103
Nestle India, 144
Net asset value (NAV), 362
Nicholas Piramal India Ltd., 147
Nikkei Index, 362
NIT, 122
No-load fund, 362
Norilsk Nickel, 94
NTPC, 134

OECD. *See* Organization for Economic Cooperation and Development
Oil & Natural Gas Corporation, 134
Open-end fund, 362–363
Open Investment (financial service company), 93
Organization for Economic Cooperation and Development (OECD), 363

Pantaloon Retail India Ltd., 143
Patni Computer Systems, 136
Plano Real. *See* Cardoso
Political risk, 363
Portfolio managers, interviews, 341
Potential return, search, 15–19
Privatization, 363
Productivity, 363
Profit-making, 10–11
Prospectus, 363–364
Purchasing power parity, 364
Putin, Vladimir, 75–77
Pyaterochka, 93

Rao, Narashimha, 108
Real GDP, 364
change, estimation, 21t
Reliance Communications, 145
Reliance Energy, 134
Reliance Industries, 137
Rosneft Oil, 91
Rule of Law. *See* Brazil
impact, 6
Russia
ADRs, 298–304
agriculture, shift, 82
Asian financial crisis, impact, 72–74
Bolsheviks, power consolidation, 59–60
cellular telecommunications, 91

Cold War, 62
collectivization, 60–61
constitutional crisis (1993), 66
consumers, impact, 93
demographics, 79–80
domestic disturbance, 70–72
economic crisis (1980–1990), 62–63
economic crisis (1998)
  initiation, 74
  intervention, 73–74
economic performance, 81–83
economic problems, 66–68
economy, change, 79–80
education/training, 87–88
election (1996), 68
environment, 85–86
examination, 343–345
financial crisis, 72–74
financials, 92
financial systems/policies, 88
GDP growth, 81–82
GKO bonds (short-term government bonds), issuance, 73
governance indicators, 288t
government
  change, 75–77
  no confidence vote, 71–72
Great Terror, 60–61
growth, problems, 69
growth industries, 88–94
history, 57
index sector weights. *See* DAX Russia Index sector weights; MSCI Russia Index sector weights
infrastructure development, 84–86
middle class, growth, 81
mining/metals, 93–94
modern history, 69
mutual funds, profiles, 333–334
natural gas, 90–91
oil, 91
open trade, 84
performance, 8–9
prerevolutionary period, 57–59
problems, 58–59
reforms, 63–64
resources, 79
revolution, 59–61
rubles, purchase, 74–75
Russian Federation, data profile, 271–273
support. *See* China
technology, 83
transparency, Rule of Law (relationship), 86–87
urbanization, 82–83
USSR
  dissolution, 64–66
  rise, 59–61
World War I, 59–61
World War II, 61–62

Samsung Group, 216–217
Santa Anna. *See* Mexico
Satyam Computer Services, 136
Sberbank, 92
Securities and Exchange Commission (SEC), 364
Sexenio. *See* Fox
Shanghai Construction Group General Co., 193
Sharpe ratio, 365
Short-term government bonds, issuance. *See* Russia
Sical Logistics Limited Air India, 138
Sinopec, 191
South Korea, 195
  ADRs, 320–322
  agriculture, shift, 213–214
  automobile market, 226
  banking, 223–224
  colonial period, 195–196
  consumer products, 226
  data profile, 277–279
  debt service ratios, 224t
  demographics, 212–213
  division, 196–197
    violence, 198–199
  economic growth, 199–200
    problems, 201–202
  economic performance, 213–216
  economic restructuring, 208–209
  economy, durability, 207–209
  education/training, 222
  examination, 347–350
  expansion, 200–201
  financial crisis (1997–1998), 206–207
  financials, 228

financial systems/policies, 222–224
foreign borrowing, 223f
GDP growth, 214
governance indicators, 289t
Great Korea, building, 202–203
growth industries, 224–228
growth rates, 215t
history, 195
industrials, 227–228
infrastructure development, 220
investment, 211
obstacles, 219–220
legal system, 221–222
materials, 225–226
middle class, 213
modern history, 205
mutual funds, profiles, 334–335
net foreign currency assets, 223f
open trade, 218–220
performance, 9–10
poverty/prosperity, 199–202
productivity growth trend, 215f
profits, 211
reforms, 205–207
republic, 196–197
robots, creation, 328
technology expansion, 216–217
telecommunication services, 225
transparency, Rule of Law (relationship), 220–221
South Korea, index sector weights. *See* MSCI South Korea Index sector weights
SPDR Standard & Poor's BRIC 40 Exchange-Traded Fund, 338
Sportmaster, 93
Stalin, Joseph, 60–61
collectivization/Great Terror, 60–61
Standard deviation, 365
Stock portfolio, allocation. *See* Nations
Success factors, investment returns (relationship), 19–22
SUN Interbrew, 93
Sun Pharmaceuticals Ltd., 147

Tata Communications, 145
Tata Consultancy Services, 135
Tata Group, 141
Tata Motors Ltd., 140–142
Tech Mahindra, 136
Technology, impact, 4–5
Templeton BRIC Fund, 338–339
Tiananmen Square. *See* China
Timing, unimportance. *See* Market
Tortilla crisis. *See* Mexico
Training, impact, 6
Transparency, impact, 6
Trent Ltd., 143

Ultratech India Limited, 139
Unified Energy Systems, 91
U.S. markets
emerging markets, correlation comparisons, 365t
performance, 265t

Vargas, Getúlio, 28–30
industrialization, beginnings, 29–30
Videocon Appliances Ltd., 143

Wimm-Bill-Dann, 93
Wipro Technologies, 120–121, 135
World Bank, 365
dependency ratios, 80t, 250t
World consumer markets, ranking, 114f 115f
World Economic Forum (WEF). *See* Global Competitiveness Index
Report (2007), 286t
World Economic Forum (WEF), technology rankings, 254t
World Trade Organization (WTO), 365
World War I. *See* Russia
World War II. *See* Russia

Xiaoping, Deng, 160–166

Yeltsin, Boris
cabinet, resignation, 70–71
constitutional crisis, 66
reforms, 65–66

ZeeTee Films, 144